Cyber Crime and the Victimization of Women:

Laws, Rights and Regulations

Debarati Halder
Centre for Cyber Victim Counselling (CCVC), India

K. Jaishankar
Manonmaniam Sundaranar University, India

A volume in the Advances in Digital
Crime, Forensics, and Cyber Terrorism
(ADCFCT) Book Series

Senior Editorial Director:	Kristin Klinger
Director of Book Publications:	Julia Mosemann
Editorial Director:	Lindsay Johnston
Acquisitions Editor:	Erika Carter
Development Editor:	Myla Harty
Production Editor:	Sean Woznicki
Typesetters:	Natalie Pronio, Milan Vracarich, Jr.
Print Coordinator:	Jamie Snavely
Cover Design:	Nick Newcomer

Published in the United States of America by
Information Science Reference (an imprint of IGI Global)
701 E. Chocolate Avenue
Hershey PA 17033
Tel: 717-533-8845
Fax: 717-533-8661
E-mail: cust@igi-global.com
Web site: http://www.igi-global.com

Library of Congress Cataloging-in-Publication Data

Halder, Debarati, 1975-
  Cyber crime and the victimization of women: laws, rights and regulations / by Debarati Halder and K. Jaishankar.
    p. cm.
  Includes bibliographical references and index.
  Summary: This book investigates cyber crime, exploring gendered dimensions of cyber crimes like adult bullying, cyber stalking, hacking, defamation, morphed pornographic images, and electronic blackmailing --Provided by publisher.
  ISBN 978-1-60960-830-9 (hardcover) -- ISBN 978-1-60960-831-6 (ebook) -- ISBN 978-1-60960-835-4 (print & perpetual access) 1. Sex crimes. 2. Computer crimes. 3. Women--Crimes against. I. Jaishankar, K. II. Title.
  K5194.H34 2011
  345 .0268--dc22
                                        2011016122

This book is published in the IGI Global book series Advances in Digital Crime, Forensics, and Cyber Terrorism (ADCF-CT) Book Series (ISSN: 2327-0381; eISSN: 2327-0373)

British Cataloguing in Publication Data
A Cataloguing in Publication record for this book is available from the British Library.

All work contributed to this book is new, previously-unpublished material. The views expressed in this book are those of the authors, but not necessarily of the publisher.

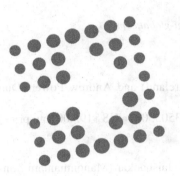

Advances in Digital Crime, Forensics, and Cyber Terrorism (ADCFCT) Book Series

ISSN: 2327-0381
EISSN: 2327-0373

MISSION

The digital revolution has allowed for greater global connectivity and has improved the way we share and present information. With this new ease of communication and access also come many new challenges and threats as cyber crime and digital perpetrators are constantly developing new ways to attack systems and gain access to private information.

The **Advances in Digital Crime, Forensics, and Cyber Terrorism (ADCFCT) Book Series** seeks to publish the latest research in diverse fields pertaining to crime, warfare, terrorism and forensics in the digital sphere. By advancing research available in these fields, the **ADCFCT** aims to present researchers, academicians, and students with the most current available knowledge and assist security and law enforcement professionals with a better understanding of the current tools, applications, and methodologies being implemented and discussed in the field.

COVERAGE

- Computer Virology
- Cryptography
- Cyber Warfare
- Database Forensics
- Digital Crime
- Encryption
- Identity Theft
- Malware
- Telecommunications Fraud
- Watermarking

IGI Global is currently accepting manuscripts for publication within this series. To submit a proposal for a volume in this series, please contact our Acquisition Editors at Acquisitions@igi-global.com or visit: http://www.igi-global.com/publish/.

Titles in this Series

For a list of additional titles in this series, please visit: www.igi-global.com

The Psychology of Cyber Crime Concepts and Principles
Gráinne Kirwan (Dun Laoghaire Institute of Art, Design and Technology, Ireland) and Andrew Power (Dun Laoghaire Institute of Art, Design and Technology, Ireland)
Information Science Reference • copyright 2012 • 372pp • H/C (ISBN: 9781613503508) • US $195.00 (our price)

Cyber Crime and the Victimization of Women Laws, Rights and Regulations
Debarati Halder (Centre for Cyber Victim Counselling (CCVC), India) and K. Jaishankar (Manonmaniam Sundaranar University, India)
Information Science Reference • copyright 2012 • 264pp • H/C (ISBN: 9781609608309) • US $195.00 (our price)

Digital Forensics for the Health Sciences Applications in Practice and Research
Andriani Daskalaki (Max Planck Institute for Molecular Genetics, Germany)
Medical Information Science Reference • copyright 2011 • 418pp • H/C (ISBN: 9781609604837) • US $245.00 (our price)

Cyber Security, Cyber Crime and Cyber Forensics Applications and Perspectives
Raghu Santanam (Arizona State University, USA) M. Sethumadhavan (Amrita University, India) and Mohit Virendra (Brocade Communications Systems, USA)
Information Science Reference • copyright 2011 • 296pp • H/C (ISBN: 9781609601232) • US $180.00 (our price)

Handbook of Research on Computational Forensics, Digital Crime, and Investigation Methods and Solutions
Chang-Tsun Li (University of Warwick, UK)
Information Science Reference • copyright 2010 • 620pp • H/C (ISBN: 9781605668369) • US $295.00 (our price)

Homeland Security Preparedness and Information Systems Strategies for Managing Public Policy
Christopher G. Reddick (University of Texas at San Antonio, USA)
Information Science Reference • copyright 2010 • 274pp • H/C (ISBN: 9781605668345) • US $180.00 (our price)

www.igi-global.com

701 E. Chocolate Ave., Hershey, PA 17033
Order online at www.igi-global.com or call 717-533-8845 x100
To place a standing order for titles released in this series, contact: cust@igi-global.com
Mon-Fri 8:00 am - 5:00 pm (est) or fax 24 hours a day 717-533-8661

Dedicated to the loving memories of

Dr. Dipak Halder (1933 - 2008) and

Mrs. Rukmani Karuppannan (1951 - 1999)

Table of Contents

Foreword

Cyber Crime and the Victimization of Women: Laws, Rights and Regulations, is a unique and a very important contribution to the literature analyzing various aspects of cyber crime. This book deals directly with an issue that is usually addressed only interstitially, i.e., as an incidental aspect of a particular cyber crime case or a particular cyber crime issue.

Cyber crime against women has all of the characteristics that define cyber crime as a general phenomenon, e.g., online, often anonymous communication, messages, and other tactics that are designed to inflict "harms" of varying types and degrees on the victims and perpetrators who, for a variety of reasons, are unlikely to be identified and / or punished for the injury they inflict. Cyber crime against women tends to involve additional characteristics that distinguish it in varying ways from generic cyber crime.

As you will see from the following chapters, women are the primary targets of cyber crimes such as online harassment, stalking, and / or bullying. The behavior at issue in these crimes can involve the use of emails and / or social networking sites to bombard the victim or the victim's co-workers and family with messages that falsely accuse the woman of engaging in offensive and / or embarrassing conduct. The behavior can also involve posting nude photographs of the victim online, photographs that were either taken while the two were involved in an intimate relationship or that have been altered to make it appear that the woman posed nude when she did not.

These hostile behaviors can have devastating consequences for the victims. Two years ago, I did a presentation on Internet defamation and invasion of privacy at a law enforcement conference. Afterward, a prosecutor approached me and told me of a particularly heinous case she had handled recently: Jane Doe and her sister Julie Doe were twins. Jane was married with two children and had a job she enjoyed, both for the work itself and for the close relationships she had with her co-workers. Julie tended to live on the "wild side." Her exploits were notorious, at least among her family and friends. For some reason, someone posted a photograph of Julie, in which she was nude and in a compromising situation with an unidentified male, on a website and included a caption that identified the woman in the photograph as Jane Doe. The person who did this then sent emails to Jane's family, friends, and co-workers that directed them to the website on which the photo of Julie-identified-as-Jane was posted.

By the time Jane learned about the photo and the emails, she had been fired from her job. Neither her employer nor her co-workers would believe her denials that the person in the photograph was her and her claims that it was, in fact, a photograph of her sister, Julie. Her employer and former co-workers had "seen the photograph for themselves" and were certain they recognized the woman in it as Jane Doe. Therefore, Jane lost her job and all of the people she once worked with told others in the small city in which Jane lived about the site and about Jane's photograph. The visual lie the anonymous perpetrator of this cyber crime created ripples through the community, seriously damaging Jane's once impeccable reputation.

And the virtual lie almost ended her marriage. We might think that Jane's husband, who knew Julie and knew about her exploits, would instantly realize that the photograph was of Julie, not his wife Jane. However, he did not. He blindly believed the photograph was, in fact, of his wife and persisted in that belief for some time, despite Jane's pleas for him to believe her and to assess the situation rationally, given what he knew of her sister. He finally relented and decided not to file for a divorce, but the relationship between the two was still strained.

Jane came to the prosecutor I spoke to, asking her to find the person who had posted the photography and prosecute him or her. The prosecutor told Jane that the U.S. State in which they lived had a sixty-year old statute that made defamation a crime. The prosecutor told Jane she believed she could use the statute to prosecute the person who posted the photograph for criminal defamation, since the statute did not limit the conduct at issue to the use of traditional print media, such as a newspaper or magazine. That was the good news. Then the prosecutor told Jane the bad news: She was not at all sure her investigators would be able to identify the person responsible for posting the photograph, and even if they were able to identify him or her, criminal defamation under that State's statute was a misdemeanor, which meant that if the person was convicted the punishment would almost certainly consist only of a small fine and perhaps a period of probation or community service. In fact, the investigators were never able to find out who posted the photograph.

The above-mentioned relatively simple case illustrates the problems and policy issues you will read about in this book. You will learn more about cases like this that are handled in the United States; you will also learn about how they are handled in several other countries. Most importantly, perhaps, you will be able to review a model charter that is designed to improve how governments respond to cyber crimes against women.

Susan W. Brenner
NCR Distinguished Professor of Law and Technology
University of Dayton School of Law, Dayton, Ohio, USA
April 2011

Susan W. Brenner *is NCR Distinguished Professor of Law and Technology at the University of Dayton School of Law, USA. She specializes in two distinct areas of law: grand jury practice and cyberconflict, i.e., cybercrime, cyberterrorism, and cyber-warfare. A renowned cyber crime scholar, Professor Brenner has spoken at numerous events, including two Interpol Cybercrime Conferences, the Middle East IT Security Conference, the American Bar Association's National Cybercrime Conference, and the Yale Law School Conference on Cybercrime. She has also spoken at a NATO Workshop on Cyberterrorism in Bulgaria and on terrorists' use of the Internet at the American Society of International Law Conference. She was a member of the European Union's CTOSE project on digital evidence and served on two Department of Justice digital evidence initiatives. Professor Brenner chaired a Working Group in an American Bar Association project that developed the ITU Toolkit for Cybercrime Legislation for the United Nation's International Telecommunications Union. She is a senior principal for Global CyberRisk, LLC. She has published a number of law review articles dealing with cybercrime. Her books, Cybercrime: Criminal Threats from Cyberspace (Praeger, 2010), and Cyberthreats: the Emerging Fault Lines of the Nation State (Oxford University Press, 2008) are significant contributions to the field of Cyber Criminology and Cyber Laws. She also writes a blog, CYB3RCRIM3.*

Preface

Telecommunications worldwide have experienced rapid change since the accessibility to emails and e-commerce facilities were made easily and readily available to the common citizens starting in the early 1990s. Such e-communication got legalized with the European conventions on Information Technology, which was followed by some developed and less developed nations. E-communication gained popularity among men and women in a short span of time. Along with the emails came the electronic ways to express and expose oneself in front of a large global audience through their personal blogs, personal and professional websites, digital albums, electronic banking, and shopping facilities, which became hugely popular with homemakers; and then electronic socialization, which literally turned human beings to e-living.

Human relations have considerably improved since the beginning of the public usage of emails, chat rooms, public forums, popular websites, and social networking websites. Seeing from the perspective of third wave feminism and usage of the electronic media to practice third wave feminism, women of post millennium era are more benefited than their predecessors belonging to the second and first wave feminism. The digital media created a huge platform for women of Web 2.0 era to expand their world to build new relationships, renew old friendships, and practice and profess own ideologies about various issues including feminism. The digital era witnessed new phase of feminism whereby women who belonged to more orthodox patriarchal societies were now enabled to practice self dependence norms through electronic shopping, "digital awareness camps" (blogs and open forums) for healthcare and baby care, higher education, modes to transform leisurely passions into profitable professions, et cetera. Ironically, this digital freedom also made women unknowingly / knowingly open Pandora's Box and explore the evil side of the Internet. Indeed, the "box" was opened long back, but it successfully hid its whiff of inside-danger for a long time. Media reports on morphed pornographic images of female movie stars, cyber stalking female celebrities, blackmailing female celebrities through email or mobile phones, et cetera, provide us some good examples of victimization of women in the cyber space. However, until recently, common Internet users, including adult men and women (especially) never realized that such mischief can happen to them.

Cyber crime against women was largely ignored and therefore, not truly addressed until the first cyber crime convention, which was adopted at Budapest in 2001. International conventions, as well as domestic laws of many countries, may have developed legislatures to protect society as a whole from the clutches of the "dark side" of cyber technology. Academics, researchers, as well as lawmakers kept themselves occupied with discussing and analyzing problems of cyber crime targeting the economic front and children. But full attention was not given to several cyber crimes like adult bullying, stalking, defamations, et cetera, from women victim's perspective even though women often outnumber men in becoming victim of interpersonal cyber crimes. There is an unequivocal need to highlight this important issue by bringing attention, as far as the role women play in cyber victimization, to scholars and laypersons. This book is one small effort in that direction.

The key inspiration to write this book came from myriad forms of victimization of women in the cyber space and lacuna of necessary laws to mitigate it. Women victims are near invisible in the eyes of universal cyber crime conventions and domestic internet and cyber communication related laws. The effect of this lawlessness is so huge that government-reporting agencies also sometimes deny any help to the woman in need. This book was also largely motivated by the personal experiences of the lead author who works as counselor for cyber crime victims and takes keen interests in the legal issues involving victimization of women in the cyber space and several painful stories retold by female friends and relatives who had gone through the trauma of being victimized in cyber space.

We have formed this book on presumption that the velocity of victimization of women in the cyber space is unmatched with the legal efforts to regulate the same. The goal of this book is to identify and explain the mostly unexplored crimes of the Internet targeting women in particular. This book is designed to define cyber victimization from women victim's perspective, analyze the trends of victimization, formulation of core rights of women internet users and examine the legal protections towards women victims of cyber crimes in five prime countries. We have concluded this book with a model charter for prevention of victimization of women in the cyber space.

We take responsibility of any errors or omissions in the book that would have crept out of our oversight. All the Urls / websites cited in this book are up to date, until this book went to print. We have taken adequate efforts to precisely cite the references / authors and quote laws / sections of laws, and sought permission from copyright holders and have reproduced them with apt acknowledgments; however, if there are any issues on citations or quotes that are overlooked, we take the accountability to rectify them in the future editions.

Debarati Halder
K. Jaishankar
Tirunelveli, Tamil Nadu, India
May 2011

Acknowledgment

Professor Susan Brenner was kind enough to accept our request to write the foreword for this book, for which we are grateful. We sincerely acknowledge the benevolent assistance and guidance of Jayne Hitchcock, President of *"Working to Halt Online Abuse"* (WHOA), USA, for permitting us to evaluate and draw conclusions from the statistical data obtained from WHOA. We are deeply indebted to Professor David S. Wall, Durham University, UK for his valuable comments on various forms of cyber victimization and to Dr. Subhajit Basu, University of Leeds, UK for effectively sharing his knowledge on various cyber crime regulations. We wish to thank Caroline Valet and Dr. Gillian Dempsey for their helpful comments pertaining to Canadian and Australian laws regarding cyber harassment, respectively. We have cited / quoted scholars like, Danielle K. Citron, David S. Wall and Susan W. Brenner more than once. These are the authors, who have most shaped our ideas and perspectives in writing this book. We are deeply grateful to them, for their own ability to persevere and to express their experience with such profound insight and clarity.

We are indebted to Ankur Raheja and CyberLawTimes.com for valuable updates on cyber laws of India, and other countries, which we have focused in this book. Sincerely, we would like to thank our beloved friend Michael Pittaro and Priti Bharadwaj for their skillful assistance in proofreading and copyediting a part of the manuscript. We also thank Prof. Dipika Halder, who was kind enough to proofread the manuscript. Elizabeth, Christine, and Myla, the assistant editors of IGI Global, are sincerely appreciated for their effective coordination. We also thank the two anonymous reviewers for their patient reading of our draft manuscript and for their constructive comments, which were greatly helpful in improving the quality of the book.

Our sincere thanks are due to a very special friend who had been a victim herself and have motivated us to take up this project. We wish to thank all our friends, especially the women from various social networking sites like Orkut and Facebook, who took a keen interest in providing us their feedback. Finally, words alone cannot express the debt we owe to our daughter, D. J. Mriganayani, who has provided us with highest level of unalloyed emotional support. Without her love and understanding this book could not have been completed.

Chapter 1
Introduction

CHAPTER OVERVIEW

This introductory chapter gives a detailed overview of the book. This chapter explores the historical aspect of victimization of women users in the internet. This includes the discussion on why mostly women are targeted in the cyberspace and what methods the offenders use to attack them in the cyber space. The time periods or the spaces in which women are attacked are also discussed. We have also provided the reasons why we chose to write a book on only women victims of internet crimes. This chapter also gives a detailed description on the research done to write this book. This chapter also gives the aims and the audience that the book is aiming to attract. In addition, the scope and the expected implications of the book are presented.

1.1 INTRODUCTION

I am feeling panicked. I am ashamed of my womanhood; I am tired of the constant pricking in the cyber space; can I ever live a normal happy life? Oh God!! Why I had to be born as a woman? Why can't I be spared even in the cyber space? - A women victim of cyber crime.

Rosy (name changed due the victim's request) was a new internet user and she immensely enjoyed cyber socializing after she and her husband moved to a remote township from a busy city hub in Florida. She started frequenting a particular online chatting site, chatted with her friends, accepted new friends irrespective of gender and even exchanged her residential address. She invited everyone to visit her town, which she described as a "serene place". One quiet afternoon, when she logged in the chat room,

DOI: 10.4018/978-1-60960-830-9.ch001

she received a request from a user to talk to him in one of the 'private rooms' that could be created by the users. She knew this user for quite sometime and she had chatted with this person in the public chat frequently. Therefore, she agreed to move into a "private room" where only two users can chat. The first question posed by the user to her was, did she ever miss her husband when he went for long business tours? When she answered affirmatively, this friend who had a gender-neutral name asked her whether she would like to stay with this friend during those "short holidays" as "she" (friend) also stays nearby. Rosy was eager to have real life friends in this new area. She readily consented and promised to visit the friend very shortly.

Strangely, on the very next week when her husband went for a week long tour, she received an email from a stranger asking her to meet him at a local pub for dating as she might be "missing her husband". She was afraid and never replied to that mail; neither went to the "meeting place". Next morning she received an angry mail from the same stranger who threatened her to mail her husband that she was having an illicit relationship with him, if she fails to show up the following evening. She replied to him that she does not meet strangers. That was the beginning. Every fortnight whenever her husband went for official tours, she received "mating call" from this stranger who used to send her emails from various email ids. She was perplexed and opined "I never knew how this man understood that my husband was out of the station". However, the "friend" in the regular chat room never gave any reason to suspect "her" as "she" used to be in Rosy's "comfort zone". "She" became her best friend during those "hard days" and used to hear her agonies with great patience and sympathy. It was only after the "friend" mentioned about the probable meeting place (the same local pub where the stranger invited her) "finally" to have a "girly" get together, that Rosy understood that she had fallen a victim of a big trap laid by the virtual "friend", who is actually the "stranger" who have stalked her.

This is not an uncommon experience for majority of women in the internet. Victimization of women continues in the internet era through myriads of such 'traps'. Indeed, few researches (Citron, 2009; Halder & Jaishankar, 2008&9; Bartow, 2009) have established the Internet as the most chosen mode of the offenders to harass and victimize women. The foremost aim of such sorts of victimization remains the same as that of pre-internet era, i.e., damaging the reputation of the woman victim and creating fear factor in the victim's mind (Citron, 2009). The behavioral factors that contribute to such victimization may include broken relationships, ex-partner harassments, professional rivalry, male dominance and chauvinism, sudden exposure to digital technologies, mischievous intentions to experiment with online adult entertainment in a digital way (Citron, 2009a, Whitty, 2005, Halder, 2009a) and even for monetary gains (Bartow, 2009). Victimization may begin by numerous methods, such as, either befriending the victim with original name but portraying as a 'good Samaritan', or winning her trust under a camouflaged identity, or shadowing her cyber activities, or encouraging others to add to the ongoing victimization process of the victim. Cyber technology has become a prime tool to carry out such victimizations in an almost successful manner due to digital ways and similarly, cyber space has provided the biggest platform to harass women in a most cruel way as the victimization can be viewed by millions of digital audiences. Emails, public and private chat rooms, search engines, social networking sites and web sites along with various digital technologies are the chosen modes of many offenders who victimize innocent women.

There could be three factors for offenders choosing these unique methods for victimizing women; viz.

1.   It successfully generates instant fear and trauma in the minds of the victims;
2.   The perpetrator is omnipresent, yet no one can find him out and prevent his atrocious activities;

3. Once the electronic devices through which these communications were accessed by shrewd perpetrator(s) are destroyed, it becomes really hard for the victim as well as the government reporting agencies like the police to nab him/them.

If we divide the cyber era in separate 'periods' depending upon the usage of cyber communications, we can see that so far three distinct periods have been formed:

i.   The email-period (could be said to have begun since the 1990s): when emails were the only ways of digital communications (Clemmit, 2006) and no strong universally accepted regulation other than the EU convention on cyber crime, 2001, ruled the cyber world;

ii. The chat-room period (could be said to have begun in late 1990s and early 2000): after the digital communication saw a boom through email period, came the public and private chat room period, where by people could exchange their personal information, see their pictures and chat instantly (Clemmit, 2006).

During these two 'periods' domestic laws on digital communication were being framed in many leading cyber savvy countries and cyber psychology and behavioral patterns were getting highlights due to new and unique reports of misuse and abuse of digital identities.

iii. The cyber social networking period (begun in early 2000): In 1997, the launching of social networking website named "six degrees.com" in the United States could be said to be the beginning of this age (Boyd & Ellison, 2007). Even though, this website failed to survive for a long time, the concept became immediately popular among other entrepreneurs, internet users and numerous social networking sites were born in the US in, and around 2000 - 2001.This period also saw booms in social interactions through blogs, adult dating sites, online bulletin boards etc.

It could be seen that with each of these 'periods', new methods of have been adopted by the perpetrators to victimize innocent women on the internet. The statistical resources of WHOA would show that in the year 2000, 87% victims were female[1] and the highest chosen mode of victimization was through emails.[2] The 2006 WHOA statistics would show that there were 70% female victims and 31% of the victimizations had been carried out through emails, 17% through instant messaging, 16.5% through message boards including forums, groups, user nets etc and nearly 7.5% of the victimizations had been done through chat etc.[3] WHOA also reported 5% victimizations through social networking sites like My Space and 1.5% victimizations through dating sites in 2006.[4] In 2010, there were 73% female victims and along with emails, Instant Messaging (IM), Social networking sites, blogs, Skype, gaming sites, Craig list, dating sites etc, were used to victimize the victims.[5] The recent statistics published by the "Centre for Cyber Victim Counselling" (CCVC) also shows that in India, 74% internet users feel that women are prone to cyber attacks[6] and such attacks are mostly carried out in emails, social networking sites, various blogs, message boards etc.[7]

There are various factors, which instigate cyber crime against women to grow. One of the main factors is the patriarchal approach of the law and justice machineries of most of the cyber savvy nations towards this grave issue. Most crimes in the internet are judged by cyber crime conventions and the domestic laws of the countries from three basic angles, i.e., economic crimes, crimes against State including hate speech through the web-forums to instigate violence, and crimes against children. On the other hand, cries of the women victims of crimes of the internet are often ignored; as such, these crimes mostly do not fall in the categories mentioned above. For instance, bullying or teasing a woman in the open web space never attracts any law enforcement intervention as the female victim is expected to be matured enough to handle the situation as an adult.[8] Using of the female models for pornographic websites cannot bring any criminal charges against the concerned website authority, especially when the site exhibits the 'consent notice' of the models. However, truth is, many women are actually depicted as 'models' in these sites without their valid consents. This is mostly done by men who contribute to these sites by misusing the private information including still pictures or video images of innocent women (Halder, 2009b).[9] Unless the victim is establishing the fact that her rights has been infringed (which in majority of cases is extremely painful and traumatizing for the victim), the law guarding the freedom of speech and expression of the individuals, will remain a silent motivator for enhancing the defamation of the victim herself.

The most contemporary form of victimization of women is "sexting" where mostly teenagers and young adults are involved. In such cases, either the victim's sexted messages may be misused or she may suddenly see her mailbox flooded with sexted images from male acquaintances accompanied with obscene or harassing text messages.[10] These sorts of harassments make the situation more complicated as the victim is expected to be mature enough to not to indulge in these sorts of activities. A sudden raise of sexting offences in the time period of 2006-09 in the US saw the huge metamorphosis of provisional as well federal criminal laws to adapt and adjust to the concept of victim turned offender (Jaishankar, 2009). However, this new trend of offence is becoming rapidly popular among young adults worldwide and still needs to be recognized as another add up in the wagon of cyber crime against women.

1.2 WHY DID WE FOCUS ONLY ON WOMEN?

During the gestational period of this book, we had met several people including cyber crime counselors, victims, cyber security experts, police personnel, professors of cyber law and cyber crime and common individuals who have never heard of non-economic, women focused cyber victimization. Almost everyone, excluding those who have their hands burnt in the cyber victimization incidences, opposed the idea of a book specifically based on women. Most of them told that cyber crimes can happen to everyone irrespective of their gender and the gravity of the victimization remains the same. We agree to the first point, but not the latter one. Many asked us what is meant by 'cyber crime against women'. How it can be generalized? Where does it happen? Why does it happen? Why these crimes happen to women alone? Finally, why does it bother us? We knew our focus was going to be challenging as these queries proved that 'cyber crime against women' is a subject, which remains undefined and unrecognized.

There are five basic factors, which motivated us to choose cyber victimization of women as the subject matter of this book. These are as follows:

1. *The high, unequal ratio of men and women victims of cyber crimes:* The first and foremost reason which inspired us to take up this work was an analysis of cyber stalking statistics of Haltabuse. org (WHOA) for the period from 2000 till 2010. We saw that in 2000, among 353 victims who approached WHOA, 87% were women and 13% were men; among the harassers, there were 68% men and 27% women.[11] In 2001, among 256 victims, 79.3% were women and 16% were men; whereas 58.6% harassers were men and 32.5% were women.[12] In 2002, among 218 victims, 71%

were women and 28% were men; whereas 52% harassers were men and 35% harassers were women.[13] In 2003, among 198 victims, 70% were women and 27% were men; whereas 52.5% harassers were men and 38% harassers were women.[14] In 2004, among 196 victims, 69% of the victims were women and 18% were men; whereas 52.5% harassers were men and 23.5% harassers were women.[15] This unequal ratio of men and women victims as well as harassers continued even until 2010, where among 349 victims, 73% are women and 27% are men; whereas, 44.5% harassers were men and 36.5% harassers were women.[16] Even though these statistics are mostly meant for cyber stalking, the consistent high ratio of the female victims and male harassers for the past ten years would indeed prove that women remained the most vulnerable targets for cyber crimes. Apart from WHOA statistics, we have also analyzed some available cyber crime statistics from the UK and used survey results from India on cyber victimization in developing several chapters of this book.[17] Besides, we have personally interacted with many women victims, feminist scholars and counselors who are dealing with cyber crime victims who helped us to understand myriad forms of victimizations, which happen to women. Almost all of these scholars and counselors opined that women are more prone to cyber attacks due to various reasons including patriarchal social outlook towards women and various legal drawbacks.

2. *The difference in the impact of victimization between men and women:* When a man's email id or private data stored in websites and also personal computers are accessed and modified in an unauthorized way, he can afford to live on by informing the police and his acquaintances. Unlike a woman victim, he may not be subjected to gross humiliation by the society as a whole; he may neither be reduced to a mere 'sex item' like his female counterpart. His victimization may be judged only from the perspective of economic losses. On the contrary, a woman victim may be ostracized by the society. Unlike her male counterpart, she may not be able to take the online humiliation so easily; it may engulf her in the feeling of shame and hatred for herself. Besides the risk of being reduced to a sex avatar (Franks, 2009), a woman victim may find it hugely difficult to gain back her social and professional reputation. We understand that even though second and third wave feminism have compelled the world to accept women's rights against discrimination based on sex, race and color (Robinson, 2007) sexuality still remains the biggest disadvantage for women in establishing equal rights. Virtually vandalized women amuse the world more than digitally robbed men or digitally threatened security of the nations.

3. *The global approach towards the issue of cyber crime against women:* We found that researches on this issue have not gained momentum. We noticed that majority of the researches on online women victimization were done from the US perspective, with an exception of few researches from European perspectives. This has limited the scope of analyzing the issue from transnational perspective, especially from the orthodox viewpoints of the oriental societies. It has considerably influenced the law and justice machinery as well. The concept of cyber crime against women has therefore become standstill within the meaning obscenity and pornography and stalking to a certain extent. The cyber savvy nations still need to develop rules and regulations to implement the promises of the CEDAW as well as the guarantees of fundamental freedoms to provide safe and dignified cyber-life to women. We do not deny the fact that new laws are being drafted and old laws are being refined in countries like US, Canada, UK, Australia and India to deal with the traditional cyber crimes that may target the safety of women and children both online and offline. However, an analysis of such laws would reveal that the drafters are not acquainted with the present cyber cultures to draft gender protective regulatory laws for online communications as well as stronger

online data privacy laws. A need has arisen now to consider broadening the scope of "unprotected speech"[18] under the US Federal constitution for the sake of women. Similarly, it has become very essential to recognize the malicious web activities that are done to harm women.

4. *New trends of victimization of women:* As could be seen from our discussions in the above paragraphs, each new period of 'cyber era' unfolded new trends of victimizations of women. We have discussed these trends elaborately in chapter two. Some of these trends are the traditional methods to victimize women in the offline world. Some methods adopted by the perpetrators are, sending derogatory letters about the character of the victim to her family members and also work place colleagues, spreading reputation damaging rumors about her in the society, threatening her with dire consequences and blackmailing her banking upon her good virtues, children and family, physical assaults, offline stalking etc. However, when these methods are utilized by the perpetrators in the cyber space, they create newer modes for victimization. The laws dealing with cyber crimes in general may have recognized some of these new modes of victimization. However, the global approach to the issues of cyber crimes against women has narrowed down the scope of these laws for combating online victimization of women. We claim that this vacuum has further instigated the growth of ongoing experiments with digital technologies to victimize women.

5. *The shifting reliance of the cyber victims on the non governmental agencies, who are involved in "private policing" (Yar, 2010) of the internet:* One of the major factors which pushed us to concentrate on the victimization of women is the rapid growth of non governmental private policing agencies to help the victims of online crimes since the mid Nineties (Yar, 2010), and women victim's growing reliance on these agencies. These agencies are expected to monitor the unwanted offensive contents with strict confidentiality (Yar, 2010, p. 548). The Internet Watch Foundation (IWF) of UK, was established in 1996 and it works towards preventing child sexual abuse, criminally obscene contents targeted towards adults, abusive racial hate speech etc. The NGO, Working to halt online abuse (WHOA) was founded by Jayne Hitchcock in the US in 1997 to help primarily online stalking victims. Cyberangels was created in 1995 in the US for promoting online safety education programmes for children (Yar, 2010, p. 548). Wired safety is another notable non-governmental US based organization who work for internet safety of men, women and children.[19] In India, an NGO, Centre for Cyber Victim Counselling (CCVC), was established in 2009, to help victims of cyber crimes.[20] Statistics available from some of these organizations may show that victims, especially women victims had preferred to rely more on such non-governmental organizations than the law enforcement agencies. Similarly, many women refuse to approach the police in India and elsewhere due to the fear of media exposure. Instead, they prefer to rely on the advises of the non governmental agencies like the CCVC, cyber safety tips discussed in various blogs and websites of various well known cyber crime experts and scholars etc. From our experiences, we have also noticed a growing tendency among women victims to approach the professional hackers to stop the online harassment (Halder, 2010b) on an emergency basis, besides contacting the non-governmental agencies.

From the above discussion, it could be deducted that women victims need faster restorative procedures to avoid further escalation of agony and trauma, but they may feel reluctant to approach the police for such restorative procedures. We consider the lack of professionalism of the police (Halder, 2010a; Walden, 2010) in dealing with crimes targeting women and failure of the laws to protect the rights of women as two major contributing factors for this shifting of reliance. At this juncture, it has become almost an undisputable fact that the method of analysis of the data privacy laws by the police and the courts from the perspective of national security issues and individuals financial and health records, and the usage of the free speech guarantees by internet users have eclipsed the issues of online victimization of women.

In this book, we have emphasized on the fact that women victims of cyber crimes need different treatment from that of the child victims, or the victims of financial frauds. A child victim could feel extremely stressful and even suicidal due to pedophilia or bullying. To save the children from vicious internet traps, the States have extended child protection laws to cover child pornography, online grooming and online bullying.[21] Victims of financial frauds are protected by numerous legislations preventing identity theft, online monetary scams and anti-phishing guidelines. Women victims on the contrary, do not get emergency help from the State (Citron, 2009a&b) as crime patterns remain unrecognized and overshadowed by general trends of cyber crimes. In this book, we propose to establish that women form a separate group of cyber victims.

1.3 THE STRUCTURE AND METHODOLOGY

This book is based on criminological, victimological as well as legal analysis of cyber victimization of women. The book opens with discussions as to why did we choose women victims only and is then followed by definition of cyber crime from women victim's perspective. The first three chapters research upon the characteristics of the crimes, reasons for growth etc. We have also developed various typologies of cyber crimes against women, categories of perpetrators and their victims and examined the reasons and motivations of perpetrators. The fourth chapter discusses on the rights and duties of women in cyberspace. Chapters 5, 6, 7, 8 and 9, examine the country wise situational analysis of cyber victimization of women, and related legal provisions in the US, Canada, UK, Australia and India, the relevant domestic laws of these countries to protect women online, etc This had been the most challenging part in writing this book, as hardly few countries have drafted specific laws for preventing cyber crime in general. Creating regulations for crimes targeting women in the internet is still a thought to be materialized by many cyber savvy nations. The book ends with a model charter in Chapter 10, to tackle the problem of cyber crime against women, globally.

These chapters are developed on the basis of various cyber behaviors and their effects on women and are supported by relevant case studies and related discussions. We have randomly selected the reported cases from the internet resources, newspapers, TV news channels and from the press releases of WHOA (Working to Halt Online Abuse, URL: www.haltbuse.org). We have also included personal experiences shared by close friends and acquaintances who preferred to remain anonymous, especially for the purpose of this book. This book also exhibits the detailed statistics of various cyber crimes against women in the US[22] and also in India.[23]

We have used various articles from journals of psychology, criminology and law, as the main resources for our chapters dealing with women victims, typology, motive etc. Every typology of cyber crime against women has been supported by cross discussions as to why we call this a "crime against women" in particular. The "motivation" and categorization of the offender – victim chapter was formed to show the relativity of sex, age and past experiences of the cyber offenders. This chapter tries to highlight the fact that majority of the offenders, who attack females in the cyber space, had been a cyber crime victim in the past. For the chapters, which deal with legal analysis of the situation, internet sources were used to scrutinize appropriate international laws as well as domestic laws of countries such as USA, UK, India, Canada etc.

1.4 AIMS AND AUDIENCE

This book aims to analyze the cyber victimization of women from a legal perspective. This book sums up three basic questions about cyber victimization of women: What is it? How does it happen and why is it growing? In addition, we aim to establish that victimization of women in the internet also involves traditional cyber crimes like hacking and infringement of privacy. We further aim to establish that women are the "forgotten species" in the global war against cyber crime. We have examined every possible crime that can happen to women in the internet and have discussed legal solutions. We also intend to showcase cyber rights and duties of women in this book. Besides, there is a discussion of the existing national and international laws which are being used or which can be stretched for preventing cyber crime against women in the respective countries. This book is written in a narrative style, but at places, we have included various experts' opinion in their own language. This book is intended for (i) students and researchers of cyber crime and laws, cyber criminology, cyber psychology, victimology and information technology; (ii) practicing lawyers, (iii) the police and (iv) the online private police agencies (NGO's). We also hope that our book will enable common internet users to be more aware of cyber crimes that can happen to women, the code of conduct, which is expected from each user of the internet and the rights of women users in the cyber space. Above all, this book hopes to send the awareness–signal to millions of internet users, irrespective of their gender.

1.5 SCOPE AND EXPECTED IMPLICATIONS

In the process of writing this book, we had found out much legislation, which were actually framed for offline offences, but could have been used well for the online offences too. However, some countries try to stretch the law, which is essentially formed to protect e-commerce, to online crimes attacking individuals. We think this is where the law fails to protect the interest of cyber citizens irrespective of their gender. The list of problems that we have researched upon in this book does not stop with victimization of women alone. We ask the readers if at all, an offender is convicted, could he be reformed by the punishments prescribed by the law. The offender is not a petty criminal but a highly intelligent hi-tech harasser. In such case, does he not become a potential Crime-Guru to teach others and make them his paid servants to commit a bigger crime. Could a juvenile offender understand the gravity of his offence when he is sentenced as per the regular law? This book tries to answer these hitherto unanswered questions.

We would like to mention that even though this book is from a feminist perspective, we do not want to ignore the basic reasons behind cyber victimization of women, and agree to put the onus on female netizens in certain cases. Those basic reasons include (i) lack of cyber-culture awareness among majority of women internet users and (ii) lack of proper universal as well domestic laws to address the problem of cyber attacks on women in general. In this book, we purposely did not include victimization of men by women or even by men. We also want to mention that we did not cover online financial crimes including phishing, economic fraud and identity fraud. Further, we have limited our discussions only to the relevant laws, which may have wider scope to prevent online atrocities against women in the chapters dealing with laws of various countries. We have not included any discussions as how the prosecution is testing these laws for the prevention of online crimes against women.

This book aims to cover mostly the non-economic, social crimes targeted towards women. In addition, we do not intend to make this book only a criminological or victimological analysis of cyber crimes, which target women alone. We aim to discuss the issues from a feministic point of view, with legal analysis of the existing laws, coupled with victimological perceptions and criminological assessments of the nature of the crimes. We tried to frame certain queries, which were never researched before, that forced women victims of cyber crime to sail across the cyber space without any navigation device. This book will also help legal researchers to find out new components for cyber legislations directed towards individual protection. We strongly believe that this book will be able to make women (and men) be aware of their cyber rights and duties towards other internet users.

REFERENCES

Bartow, A. (2009). Internet defamation as profit center: The monetization of online harassment. *Harvard Journal of Law and Gender, 32*, 384–428.

Boyd, D. M., & Ellison, N. B. (2007). Social network sites: Definition, history, and scholarship. *Journal of Computer-Mediated Communication, 13*(1), article 11. Retrieved on May 24th, 2010, from http://jcmc. indiana.edu/vol13/issue1/boyd.ellison.html

Citron, K. D. (2009). Cyber civil rights. *Boston University Law Review. Boston University. School of Law, 89*(61), 69–75.

Clemmitt, M. (2006). Cyber socializing. *CQ Researcher, 16*(27), 625–648.

Halder, D. (2009a). *Online domestic violence, the lawyer speaks.* Retrieved on May 24th, 2010, from http://debaraticyberspace.blogspot.com/2009/11/ online-domestic-violence-lawyer-speaks.html

Halder, D. (2009b). *For sale: A woman of your choice.* Retrieved on May 24th, 2010, from http://debaraticyberspace.blogspot.com/ 2009/11/for-sale-woman-of-your-choice.html

Halder, D. (2010a). *A tale of few cities: Cyber harassments and reactions of the police authorities.* Retrieved on 25th May, 2010, from http://cybervictims.blogspot.com/2010/02/ tale-of-few-cities-cyber-harassments.html

Halder, D. (2010b). *"Ethical hacking: How far safe?".* Retrieved on 25th May, 2010 from http://cybervictims.blogspot.com/2010/04/ ethical-hacking-how-far-safe.html

Halder, D., & Jaishankar, K. (2008). Cyber crimes against women in India: problems, perspective and solutions. *TMC Academic Journal, 3*(1), 48–62.

Halder, D., & Jaishankar, K. (2009). Cyber socializing and victimization of women. *Temida - Journal on Victimization, Human rights and Gender, 12*, 5-26.

Halder, D., & Jaishankar, K. (2010). *Cyber victimization in India: A baseline survey report.* Tirunelveli, India: Centre for Cyber Victim Counseling. Retrieved on 8th October, 2010, from http://www.cybervictims. org/ CCVCresearchreport2010.pdf

Halder, D., & Jaishankar, K. (in press). Cyber Gender Harassment and Secondary Victimization: A Comparative Analysis of US, UK and India. Special Issue of *Victims and Offenders* - Victim and Offender Research: A Cross-National Perspective.

Jaishankar, K. (2009). *Sexting: How do we protect the Victim Turned Offender?* Presentation in the Workshop on "Victim Protection" in the International Conference on "Protecting Children from Sexual Offenders in the Information Technology Era" organized by the International Scientific and Professional Advisory Council of the United Nations Crime Prevention and Criminal Justice Programme (ISPAC), in cooperation with United Nations Office on Drugs and Crime (UNODC) during December, 11 - 13, 2009, at Courmeyeur, Mont Blanc, Italy

Robinson, J. (2007). Feminism and the Third Wave. Retrieved on 25th May, 2010 from http://womensstudies.homestead.com/thirdwave.html.

Scott, A. (2009). *Flash flood or slow burn? Celebrities, photographers and the protection from harassment act* (June, 11 2009). (LSE Legal Studies Working Paper No. 13/2009). Retrieved on 30th June, 2010, from http://ssrn.com/abstract=1417907

Walden, I. (2010). Computer forensics and the presentation of evidence in criminal cases. In Y. Jewkes & M. Yar. (Eds.), *Handbook of internet crime* (pp. 603-631). Cullompton: Willan Publishers.

Whitty, M. T. (2005). The realness of cyber cheating: Men's and women's representations of unfaithful Internet relationships. *Social Science Computer Review, 23*, 57–67. doi:10.1177/0894439304271536

Yar, M. (2010). The private policing of internet crime. In Y. Jewkes & M. Yar. (Eds.), *Handbook of internet crime* (pp.546 - 561). Cullompton: Willan Publishers.

ENDNOTES

[1] See WHOA statistics for 2000, available @ http://www.haltabuse.org/resources/stats/2000stats.pdf

[2] ibid

[3] See WHOA statistics, 2006, available at http://www.haltabuse.org/resources/stats/2006Statistics.pdf

[4] ibid

[5] See WHOA Statistics @ http://www.haltabuse.org/resources/stats/2010Statistics.pdf

[6] See http://www.cybervictims.org/CCVCresearchreport2010.pdf

[7] ibid

[8] Cyber bullying adults still awaits any legal tag, even though most countries like the US, have developed laws to prevent cyber bullying against children. More on this is discussed in Chapter 5.

[9] It must be noted that in such cases, it is expected that the victim will make a formal police report for blackmail or threat. However, neither the police, nor the courts may take any *suomotu* action against the concerned website where the woman is exhibited, unless, it is being proved that these activities are infringing someone's rights.

[10]   Such instances are rarely reported. For more understanding, see Spinderalla (2010) *Another woman claims Tony Parker was sexting her* published on November 22, 2010. Retrieved from http://thesoulofdfw.com/national/news-gossip/spinderella/another-woman-claims-tony-parker-was-sexting-her/

[11]   See http://www.haltabuse.org/resources/stats/2000stats.pdf

[12]   See http://www.haltabuse.org/resources/stats/2001stats.pdf

[13]   see http://www.haltabuse.org/resources/stats/2002stats.pdf

[14]   See http://www.haltabuse.org/resources/stats/2003stats.pdf

[15]   See http://www.haltabuse.org/resources/stats/2004stats.pdf

[16]   See http://www.haltabuse.org/resources/stats/2010stats.pdf

[17]   These databases have been shown and analyzed in various chapters of this book.

[18]   In 1984, Catharine MacKinnon and Andrea Dworkin prepared an ordinance to address pornography as violation of civil rights under the title: "An Act to protect civil rights of women and children", which is popularly known as MacKinnon's ordinance. They stated that pornography is a discrimination of women and denies free speech for women. Therefore it should be excluded from the protection of the first amendment. The ordinance did not come into effect as the Mayor of Minneapolis vetoed it on the ground that it is too broad and vague. The US district court also ordered to strike down version of this ordinance passed by City of Indianapolis. The court held that "the interest in prohibiting sex discrimination did not outweigh the interest in free speech". This judgment was upheld by the US Court of Appeal. Url: http://www.nostatusquo.com/ACLU/dworkin/OrdinanceMassComplete.html

[19]   See http://www.wiredsafety.org/

[20]   See www.cybervictims.org

[21]   Most notable is the Megan Meier Cyber Bullying Prevention Act, 2008, passed by the US Congress.

[22]   WHOA statistics are available at http://www.haltabuse.org/resources/stats/index.shtml. Reproduced with permission from WHOA's President Jayne Hitchcock.

[23]   Statistics from the research report (2010) of our NGO "Centre for Cyber Victim Counselling" (CCVC), which is available at http://www.cybervictims.org/CCVCresearchreport2010.pdf

Chapter 2
Definition, Typology and Patterns of Victimization

CHAPTER OVERVIEW

In this chapter, an attempt is made to operationally define cyber crimes against women, as we have found that the definitions of cyber crimes have changed in the past decade and we presume that even this will change in the future decades to come. In addition, the current definitions do not specifically fit in to the nitty-gritty issues of cyber crimes against women and a succinct operational definition is provided. A new set of typology is made with regard to the cyber crimes against women as not all type of crimes fit to the category of cyber crimes against women. The patterns of victimization of women in cyberspace are dealt by qualitative case studies along with the typology.

2.1 INTRODUCTION

Post world wars, many had been victimized by different types of crimes including war crimes, terrorism, human rights violations, economic crimes etc. Later, with the advancement of telecommunication technologies in post 60's, victimization by the ugly side of technology such as cyber crime occurred. During the initial period of the occurrence, the term "Cyber Crime" was never defined by any legal provisions, Bills, draft laws or conventions. It had been more an effort by the academicians and computer specialists to define and analyze the term "cyber crime" from the perspectives of (i) attack on the "machine" and (ii) computer assisted crimes (Wall, 2005, revised in 2010; Katyal, 2001)

DOI: 10.4018/978-1-60960-830-9.ch002

The US Department of Justice (1989), defined computer crimes as "those crimes where knowledge of a computer system is essential to commit the crime" (Parker, 1989, p. 22). According to the report prepared by McConnell International (2000, p. 1), cyber crimes are, "harmful acts committed from or against a computer or network". Katyal (2001, p. 12-13) suggests that "computer crime can be explained as the crime where the computer is used to carry out or facilitate a criminal offence either (i) by electronically attacking the computer as a machine, or (ii) by using the computer to commit a traditional crime". In the first case, cyber crime can happen when computer files and computer programmes are unauthorisedly accessed (Katyal, 2001), or these files or computer programmes are unauthorisedly disrupted, or when electronic identity is stolen (Katyal, 2001). In the second case, cyber crime can happen when computer is used as a device to commit traditional crimes (Katyal, 2001) like creating or distributing child pornography, or carrying on some white collar crimes like insurance frauds or copying popular copyrighted songs and thereby violating the copyrights of the song etc. Nonetheless, these definitions show that the term "cyber crime" carries a connotation of any crime done with cyber assistance.

The definition of cyber crime got a facelift by the creation of Convention on Cyber Crime of Council of Europe, presented at a meeting held at Budapest, Hungary, in 2001. The Convention on Cyber Crime (2001) is the first of its kind which tried to look at the concept of 'cyber crime' from a global angle. This convention presented the concept of cyber offences in five dimensions. They are (i) offences against the confidentiality, integrity and availability of computer data and systems; (ii) Computer related offences; (iii) content related offences; (iv) offences related to infringements of copyright; (v) abetting or aiding such offences (Council of Europe, 2001).

The first group, i.e., offences against the confidentiality, integrity and availability of computer data and systems included the following:

(a) Intentional illegal access to the whole or any part of the computer system by infringing security measures. The motive could be either to obtain computer data, or any other dishonest intention, or illegal access in relation to a computer system that is connected to another computer;

(b) Intentional illegal interception without any proper rights whatsoever, made by technical means, of non-public transmissions of computer data to, from or within a computer system, including electromagnetic emissions from a computer system carrying such computer data;

(c) Intentionally interfering with the data without any proper rights what so ever;

(d) System interference, i.e., hindering of the functioning of a computer system by inputting, transmitting, damaging, deleting, deteriorating, altering or suppressing computer data;

(e) Misuse of devices; this includes the production, sale, procurement for use, import, distribution of a computer device or programme designed or adapted primarily for the purposes of offences mentioned above under point (a) or a computer password, access code, or similar data by which the whole or any part of a computer system is capable of being accessed, and the possession of any of these items with a criminal intent (Council of Europe, 2001).

The second group, i.e. 'Computer related offences' would mean:

(a) computer related forgery i.e., the input, alteration, deletion, or suppression of computer data resulting in inauthentic data with the intent that it may be acted upon for legal purposes as if it were authentic for fraudulent purposes; and

(b)   computer related fraud, i.e., intentionally causing of a loss of property to another person by either (1) any input, alteration, deletion or suppression of computer data, or (2) any interference with the functioning of a computer system, or both with fraudulent purpose for procuring monetary gain for one person or for another person (Council of Europe, 2001, Para 18, 19).

The third group indicates content related offences which deal with child pornography only. It includes procuring, making, offering, distributing and possessing child pornographic materials in the computer system or using the computer systems to do all these for the monetary gains. Child pornography is defined and described as materials that visually portray (i) an act by a 'minor', where he is engaged in sexually explicit conduct; or (ii) an act by a person "appearing" to be a minor, who is engaged in sexually explicit conduct; or (iii) realistic images representing a minor, who is engaged in sexually explicit conduct. The Convention shows the age limit to be termed as minor, as less than 18 years. The Convention also specifies that lower age limit could be shown as 16 years in some cases (Council of Europe, 2001).

The fourth group indicates 'Offences related to infringements of copyright', i.e., when the offence infringes the law copyrights and related rights of the member country. The last group includes aiding and abetting any or all of the cyber offences that are grouped above (Council of Europe, 2001).

These conceptualizations and definitions of cyber crimes, as has been attempted by the Convention on Cyber Crime discussed above, show two facets of approach towards cyber crime, viz., (a) crimes assisted by the knowledge of computer technology and (b) the criminal conduct motivated / assisted by computer technology. It can be noticed that these general definitions were formatted to explain cyber-assisted attacks on national security policies, economic or commercial policies etc. In other words, these definitions, which are still in use, define cyber crime broadly from the perspectives of hacking; attacks on the computer system, Trojan attacks, cyber terrorism etc. The definition and conceptualization also covered the promotion of child pornography through internet. However, it can be seen that with the Convention of Cyber Crime, 2001, the attempts to define cyber crime has turned more towards computer –assisted attack on internet users in general. To be more precise, the above definitions say, cyber crimes are crimes that are done with an ill motive in and outside "cyber space".[1]

2.2 CHANGING DEFINITIONS OF CYBER CRIME

The trend of defining cyber crime saw a metamorphosis in the new millennium. Prior to 2001, most definitions explained cyber crime as a medium of attack on commercial ventures and security breaching techniques like hacking and cracking. The Convention on Cyber Crime (2001), broadened the term by including crimes against children done through the internet and also slightly touched on attacks on human emotions, banning usage of "improper words" in the cyber space. This was originally meant to prevent usage of derogatory words which may promote terrorism, danger to national security and/or racial hatred.[2] However, this particular approach by the Convention on Cyber Crime (2001) helped a section of academicians and researchers to drift from the then prevailing perception of cyber crime, i.e., *everything is hacking or attack at e-commercial transactions*. This drift helped to include emotional attack on internet users as offence. In other words, the preference to understand cyber crime as an attack at the machine and organization, transmuted to a more advanced approach to look at it from individual victim's perspective.

Wall (2007, p. 10) describes cyber crimes as "those crimes that occur in the cyber space". He further feels that in this internet era this term (Cyber crime) symbolizes insecurity and risk online (Wall, 2007). The definition provided by Answer's.com,[3] perhaps gives the most compact answer to what is cyber crime; it says, cyber crime is "any use of a computer as an instrument to further illegal ends, such as committing fraud, trafficking in child pornography and intellectual property, stealing identities, or violating privacy".[4] According to Mason (2008, p. 1), "It is helpful to think of "cyber crime" as any crime in which a computer or other digital device plays a role, which is to say that digital evidence is involved, regardless of whether the crime fits under any statutory definition of computer crime". He further gives a functional definition of cyber crime which shows computer as itself, a target, tool and even a container of evidences (Mason, 2008). This is again, a broader definition of cyber crime which includes "attacks" assisted by computer and information technology from all perspectives. Wall (2008, p. 862) further describes cyber crime as "online insecurity and risk and it is widely used today to describe the crimes or harms that are committed using networked technologies." We may note that Wall (2008) includes the term "harm" to describe cyber crime. This particular term makes this definition more inclined to offences against human emotions like stalking, harassing bullying etc. However, the modern trends of defining cyber crime expanded the meaning of the term to include various cyber crimes such as identity theft, illegal gambling, cyber money laundering, phishing, cyber terrorism, cyber squatting, crimes targeting children, such as creating and distributing child pornography, cyber bullying, abetment of several offences where internet is used as a tool, etc.

Reviewing the literature on the definitions of cyber crime, we understand that the modern researches aim to show that the ever expanding arena of cyber crime affects all sects of society. Thus it could affect the private individuals and at the same time, organizations like the government, company constituted for financial gains or even groups or associations of individuals constituted for non-profit purposes. The offences could be either traditional cyber crimes like hacking, or morphing, spoofing, tampering the computer sources, obscene publication, Trojan attacks, phishing, cyber stalking, cyber pornography; or some evolving crimes like cyber defamation, e-mail harassment, cyber bullying, cyber blackmailing, cyber threatening, and cyber assisted murder. In all these cases the computer system and the internet are only the basic tools and the motive is to intentionally harm the reputation of the victim, no matter whether the victim is known to the perpetrator or not. Cyber murder is the new dreadful discovery of information technology era, where by the victim or groups of victims are targeted directly, allured to come out of the cyber space and then physically attacked or even murdered in the physical space. The motive may vary from personal hatred, anger, frustration to even well-groomed anti-peace settlement actions.

Hence, when defined from the perspective of general cyber crime victims, we operationally define cyber crimes as: *Offences that are committed against individuals or groups of individuals with a criminal motive to intentionally harm the reputation of the victim or cause physical or mental harm to the victim directly or indirectly, using modern telecommunication networks such as Internet (Chat rooms, emails, notice boards and groups) and mobile phones (SMS/MMS).* The types of cyber crimes that are included in the above definition are: hacking, morphing, spoofing, tampering the computer sources, obscene publication, Trojan attacks, phishing, cyber stalking, cyber pornography, cyber defamation, cyber bullying, e-mail harassment, cyber blackmailing, cyber threatening, cyber murder, cyber terrorism and abetment of such offences.

2.3 ISSUES IN DEFINING CYBER CRIMES AGAINST WOMEN

A minute analysis of the definitions mentioned earlier would show that the definitions of cyber crimes have gradually expanded to cover victimization of human beings and not the attack at the machines alone. It is also quite notable that there is a sharp inclination of researches on cyber crime from the perspective of online harassment, particularly targeting children and women in general. Researchers like Yar (2007), Hinduja and Patchin (2008, 2009), Bocij (2003), Wall (2007), Shariff (2005, 2006), Jaishankar (2008), Citron (2009b), and Halder and Jaishankar (2009) etc, have taken up studies on different aspects of on-line harassments like cyber stalking, cyber bullying, and cyber hatred etc, moving beyond attacks at the machines. These researches have shown that in maximum cases, online harassment is targeted towards the teenagers (see Hinduja & Patchin, 2007, 2008; Bocij, 2004; Ellison & Akdeniz, 1998; Jaishankar, Halder, & Ramdoss, 2008; Shariff, 2009) (inclusive of both the sexes) and adult female internet users (see Citron, 2009b; Bartow, 2009; Halder & Jaishankar, 2009).

Since our present work concentrates more on women and not on children, we would highlight on the issues of women victimization. We understand that there is no compact definition for cyber crimes against women as these crimes are not seen as distinct crimes. What does the term 'cyber crimes against women' imply and include? Does it mean only sexual crimes and bullying in the internet? Does it mean attack on privacy only? Does it mean attacking a group of individuals of a particular age or particular sex through internet? When we reviewed the literature on definitions and general characteristics of cyber crimes, we felt these questions remained unanswered. Further, can the term "cyber crime" be gender sensitive from a legal perspective? Also, we found in most cases gender sensitive "attacks" are termed as "harassment" and rarely any researcher has used the term "crime" or "offence". Further, when the characteristics of such attacks (specifically targeted towards adult female users) are discussed in legal perspective, they fail to include the term "crime" or "offence". We understand that the term "crime" or "offence", when used in a very technical implication, attracts penal sanction and "attacks" which target women in the internet (for instance, stalking, bullying, defaming etc) are still considered as behavioral fault and do not attract penal sanction.[5] But we insist to term the *attacks* as "crime" and not simple harassment. To make our argument stronger, we will refer to the definitions of cyber crime which were coined by several international conventions.

The Council of Europe Recommendation of 1995 described IT offences as "encompassing any criminal offence, in the investigation of which investigating authorities must obtain access to information being processed or transmitted in computer systems, or electronic data processing systems."[6] The Council of Europe Recommendation of 1989, described computer related crime as "offences enumerated and defined in the proposed guidelines or recommendation for national legislators".[7] Further, Sofaer and Goodman (2000, p. 26) described cyber crime as "conduct with respect to cyber systems that is classified as an offense punishable by this Convention".

A logical deduction from the above definitions would prove that the "attacks" which are generalized, do happen to adult female users of the internet as well and these attacks, which are targeted to women through internet, need to be termed as crime or offences. But at the same time, the characteristics of the attacks, the motives, the trend of victimization and the aftermath may vary and be unique from that of the regular cyber crimes. Hopelessly, the definitions and /or descriptions of cyber crimes in general have failed to define "cyber crime against women". We appreciate several researchers' attempt to analyze the characteristics of certain types of offences which are targeted to women in majority. But at the same time, we feel, instead of researching on one or two particular types of online attacks targeted towards women, there is a need to view this problem in a holistic way. We feel that the existing definitions and descriptions fail to fulfill this need. They give zero perception of cyber crime against women.

2.4 WHY DO WE NEED TO HAVE A SEPARATE DEFINITION?

Cyber victimization of women exists and it is growing in number (Citron, 2009a; Finn & Banach, 2000). Cyber crimes of general nature, such as hacking, phishing, cyber squatting, identity theft, stalking, online bullying, online defamation etc, target men and women alike. But certain offences, such as email/profile hacking, morphing, spoofing, obscene publication, cyber stalking, cyber pornography, internet voyeurism, cyber defamation, cyber bullying, e-mail harassment, cyber blackmailing/threatening, emotional cheating by impersonation (Whitty, 2005), intimate partner violence through internet (Jenson, 1996) and abetment of such offences may happen more to women than their male counterparts. As such, cyber attack on a woman leaves her more traumatized than her male counterpart. It could be seen that attacks against women are carried out to destroy their personal reputation, create fear for physical safety and also monetary losses (Citron, 2009a). On the contrary, men are targeted more for illegal economic gain. Men generally become victims of hacking and phishing and they do not get affected by cyber stalking/ bullying or cyber defamation to a greater extent as their female counterparts do. We support our statement with some common observations, such as: a. Cyber bullying and online defamation may lead to cyber sexual attack on women, which is not the case for men; b. in cases of males victimizing females, it is the female victim who suffers; but in case of females victimizing females, both the perpetrator and the victim become sufferers.

In the internet era, the concept of victimization of women is no more confined within the meaning of physical violence meted out by male intimate partners. Women victimization includes both physical and psychological abuse (Dekeseredy, 2010). With the growth of internet based society, the concept of victimization has taken a turn more towards emotional abuse. The male-meted-out physical tortures have become more hi-tech emotional tortures. The effect of victimization remains the same. The victim feels brutalized, horrified and even suicidal in some cases, not due to physical torture, but due to cyber assisted emotional torture, which is unique to women alone. Further, a woman can also be forced to join pornography sites against her will and even without her knowledge through voyeurism which makes her vulnerable and this victimization can even lead to social isolation. Men are lesser targets of voyeurs compared to women. The greatest distinguishing factor between male and female cyber victimization lies in the motive and the ways of victimization and after-effects of the offence on the victim.

Unfortunately, most of the reported incidences of cyber victimization affect the personal lives of the women victims as it may awkwardly reveal private informations, giving enough chance to be virtually stripped off by a wide global audience. The case of Model Liksula Cohen and her "anonymous blogger" critic, who called her "skank",[8] is a notable example of embarrassment and cyber harassment of women following huge undue negative attention (Citron, 2009b). The "anonymous blogger" who was later identified as a regular female blogger named Rosemary Port, had commented on model Liksula Cohen's hygiene and sexual habits, which the model took as very derogatory and defaming comment. The fact that Cohen being a woman herself had been victimized by another woman brought the model to the centre of anatomic discussions about her sexual habits. The discussion was virtually enriched by inputs of a gigantic audience who didn't spare the blogger also. Her anonymity was pierced open and right to privacy was penetrated (something which American constitution preserves so well even in the digital era). Several threads of discussions followed there after pointing at her sexuality and even comparisons as to "who is the hottest" between the blogger and the model. It should be noted that, earlier when women bloggers or writers or activists were publicly defamed by men, it was the only the victim who was more harassed and discussed and not the male perpetrator.

It is an irony that the existing international researches, discussions and conventions have encouraged many cyber savvy nations to develop cyber crime preventive laws, but only few have considered including online victimization of women in the preventive and protective laws. The lack of legal protection, lack of universal definition of "cyber victimization of women" and less research on the trends of cyber victimization targeting women have resulted in continuous ill treatment of women both in the cyber space as well as in the physical space. Goodman (1997) has pointed out that several institutional factors de-motivate the police departments to pursue cyber crime cases.

Their observations stand true for women victims of cyber crime. Zero definition and less perception of cyber crime against women push the victim as well as the police to hollowness as to how to deal with the case and proceed further. It becomes exceptionally hard for the police to further investigate when the complaint contains a conglomeration of offences targeting women which have no proper legal terminology either to suit the offline or the online crimes.

2.5 TOWARDS AN OPERATIONAL DEFINITION OF CYBER CRIME AGAINST WOMEN

Considering the above discussions, we propose an operational definition of cyber crimes against women. Cyber crimes against women are: *"Crimes targeted against women with a motive to intentionally harm the victim, using modern telecommunication networks such as the Internet (Chat rooms, emails, notice boards and groups) and mobile phones (SMS/MMS)"*. This definition is further expanded and explained. Cyber crimes against women:

a)   can be either sexual or non sexual in character;

b)   include online crimes like hacking, morphing, spoofing, obscene publication, cyber stalking, cyber pornography, internet voyeurism, forceful invasion of privacy, cyber defamation, cyber bullying, e-mail harassment, cyber blackmailing and threatening, emotional cheating by impersonation in the internet and intimate partner violence through internet and abetment of such offences;

c)   may not be contended to economic crimes like severe phishing or identity theft;

d)   are done with a criminal motive for intentionally harming the reputation of the victim;

e)   include situations where the offender and the victim may or may not have prior personal or professional interactions;

f)   includes those cyber behaviors of the perpetrators which leave the victim traumatized, shocked, even socially secluded, suicidal, and may also create threat to physical security of the victim;

g)   can be done by male or even female perpetrator; however, the targeted victim group is restricted to women only.

This definition:

- aims to cover only women victims. It is unique in itself that it does not cover children or male victims, but only adult female victims of cyber crime; it also aims to prove that the harassers can be either male or female;
- challenges the traditional concepts which may indicate that cyber crimes against women as simple "harassments". This definition establishes that they must be termed as "crimes" or "offences";
- can be used to draft gender supportive legislations for the purpose of international and domestic laws, and for regulating cyber space for the safety of women;
- clarifies that cyber crime against women can be sexual or non sexual;[9]
- opens a new vista on the reasons to understand why women tend to fall victim of these cyber crimes;
- Provides an answer to the question "What makes her more vulnerable online"?
- Establishes that cyber crime against women is mostly done with a criminal motive to cause emotional harm and damage to reputation of the victim. At the same time, this definition also emphasizes on the fact that in extreme cases, cyber crime against women can also abet to physical harm of the victim.
- This definition categorizes several cyber behaviors[10] like cyber stalking, "forcefully" befriending the victim, bullying, publicly defaming, blackmailing and threatening, emotional cheating by impersonation in the internet and intimate partner violence through internet etc, as most chosen 'offences' done in the internet.
- This definition also includes legally recognized crimes such as hacking, modification of data including personal pictures of the victims, voyeurism etc as component parts of the crimes against women in the cyber space.

The proposed definition can be used for both theoretical and practical purposes. This definition will not only help researchers and common internet users to understand the nature of cyber crime against women, but also will pave a way for further legal, criminological as well as victimological researches on nuances of cyber crimes against women.

2.6 TYPOLOGY AND PATTERNS OF VICTIMIZATION

Kim (2009) describes cyber harassments in two separate categories, viz., verbal cyber harassment and harassment through visual/auditory help. In line with the categories created by Kim (2009), we categorize cyber crime against women in to three types, non-sexual crimes, sexual crimes and cyber assisted offline crimes. Even though all cyber crimes that affect women are carried out to harass them, we have distinguished these three broad categories on the basis of the results of the harassment. It could be seen that crimes which are categorized under nonsexual crimes, do not generally accompany sexually perturbed images and it may or may not involve texted sexual bullies (without any obscene image or cartoon). In other words, the victim is not exposed by her photographs or her residing addresses and information. They can either disturb the privacy of the victim or make her an object of mass hatred, or may even assist for physical harm outside cyber space. On the other hand, sexual crimes can make her an unwanted "sex-item" to a bigger audience. Sexual crimes in the internet can also attract more dangerous outcomes from the real world, outside the virtual world.

Figure 1 will elaborate the typology.

2.6.1 Non Sexual Crimes

As we have mentioned above, non sexual crimes mostly penetrate the privacy of the victim to disturb her. We use the term "non sexual" because these crimes generally do not involve usage of her real life information like residential addresses, phone numbers etc to make her "serve the people sexually", or creation, distribution or destruction of any graphic image or photograph or picture of women depicting private parts, nudity, sexual performances or obscenity; But these crimes do happen to women because they are women and vulnerable.

Although it is very hard to say that crimes grouped under non sexual crimes do not have a flavor of sexual teasing remarks, we have tried to categorize certain offences which are done to women without the help of such "leaking of information" and images. Non sexual crimes can be grouped under three sub-categories. They are hate crimes, emotional injuries, and hacking related crimes. These crimes generally do not target the sexuality[11] of the victim. Even though these crimes are of unisexual nature, they happen more to women than men.[12] Many of these offences are not recognized as serious gender sensitive crimes done in the cyber space. Many of these crimes also await penal sanction from various domestic laws of cyber savvy nations.

2.6.1.a Hate Crimes[13]

According to the Matthew Shepard and James Byrd, Jr. Hate Crimes Prevention Act (HCPA) (2009) of US, "*hate crime means a crime in which the defendant intentionally selects a victim, or in the case of a property crime, the property that is the object of the crime, because of the actual or perceived race,*

Figure 1. Typology of cyber crimes against women

Cyber crimes against women

1. Non Sexual Crimes	2. Sexual crimes	3. Cyber assisted offline crimes
Hate crimes	Obscenity	Abetment to suicide
Emotional injuries	Forced pornography	Cyber assisted offline invasion of privacy
Hacking related crimes	Cyber sexual defamation	Cyber assisted offline physical harm
	Hacking related crimes	Cyber assisted rape
	Hacking and morphing	Cyber assisted murder

color, religion, national origin, ethnicity, gender, disability, or sexual orientation of any person" (National Defense Authorization Act for Fiscal Year 2010/Division E, OpenCongress, 2009). In the above definition, we are particular about the hate crimes against women based on their gender. Though there is nothing specific on the hate crimes in the internet committed against women in this definition, it does not preclude the internet offenders to be punished under this Act. In the internet, multiple attacks on the woman victim occur, when the perpetrator(s):

- continuously send the victim "I hate you" mails either with the sender's own name or with anonymous names;
- spread "hate her" message through emails to the victim's and the perpetrator's acquaintances;
- reach out to social networking sites by creating groups or communities to hate her, and also encouraging others to join in;[14]
- write blogs or create websites to tell the "story" about the victim, taking her name and thereby publicly defaming her.

A woman can be targeted in cyber space for various reasons, for example; she may not have any direct relationship with the perpetrator, but she may be the target of hatred due to her various political, academic or social ideologies which are not liked by the perpetrator; or she may be an actor whom the perpetrator "loves to hate". She could even be the object of hatred due to her past relationship with the perpetrator in the form of a former colleague whom the perpetrator never liked, ex-spouse or ex-girlfriend etc. In such cases, it is seen that the perpetrator uses internet as a medium to express his inner hatred in foul languages and feels this is the best possible way to make the victim as well as other onlookers know his feelings. [15] Online hate crimes can be grouped under two heads namely, (i) cyber verbal abuse expressing hatred and (ii) cyber defamation targeting the victim.

2.6.1.a.1 Cyber Verbal Abuse Expressing Hatred

This is a sort of cyber attack done by one or more perpetrator(s) to a particular female victim or a group of victims. Studies have shown that these types of attacks on women are becoming very common in the cyber space (Citron, 2009a). This attack could be started by one individual who may have been directly or in some cases indirectly affected by the victim's ideologies and offline activities. The perpetrator may eventually start bombarding the victim by emails and / or text messages. The reasons could be either clash of interests, hating her feministic ideologies, disliking the victim etc.

In case of cyber hatred not amounting to defamation, the perpetrator(s) may limit the perpetration within certain specific activities like sending hate mails to the victim, threatening with dire consequences, teaming up with fellow "aggrieved men" and attacking the victim by sending repeated annoying mails from various users, reporting her blogs to report abuse sections of the Internet Service Providers (ISPs) in mass, alluring her in the private chat rooms and then attacking her, or banning her from any forum or group where these perpetrators create a majority number of members etc. We do not aim to term this as cyber defamation, even though we agree that this is a very weak form of defamation. We argue that this sort of attack is motivated by anger and hatred and is limited to severe flaming words including hate messages targeted to the victim. The attack is limited between the perpetrator(s) and the victim, and the perpetrator(s) generally term themselves as her direct or indirect victims. In such cases, the perpetrator(s) may or may not involve the wider internet audience. These attacks tend to die down once the perpetrator is satisfied that the hate message has been successfully conveyed to the victim.

Example: The victim ran an online web page for helping aspiring job seekers. The victim, as well as the users used to chat, discuss and exchange ideas in various forums in the webpage about various course topics. The victim received a complaint from one member of the group against the perpetrator that he has created multiple ids and disturbing the said user. The victim warned the perpetrator in the open forum. The perpetrator then abused the victim in the same open forum, threatened to defame her, wrote hate mails, used nasty words against her and created a messy situation by creating long list of "I hate you" threads by pulling a majority of male members to his side for fighting back with the victim.[16]

2.6.1.a.2 Cyber Defamation Targeting the Victim

Cyber libel and defamation are some common crimes against women in the internet. There is a thin line of difference between cyber hate not amounting to defamation and cyber defamation. In case of cyber hate not amounting to defamation, the perpetrator may or may not spread the flame outside the "fighting zone" (communication space between the perpetrator and the victim). But in case of cyber defamation, the perpetrator does not remain satisfied with sending hate messages to the victim only; he tends to make his victim a "public figure" by asking everyone irrespective of known or unknown individuals, to hate her and ridicule her. In such cases, the perpetrator may open blog or webpage to belittle the victim; may mob attack her in her own webpage or blog (Citron, 2009b); may send mails containing malicious, false, cooked up stories to the victim as well as his own acquaintances; and may use the social networking sites to create "I hate you" communities taking up the name of the victim. Cyber defamation may start from personal animosity between the victim and the perpetrator, or may even start from disliking the feminist ideologies of the victim or even from simple jealousy.

Reported cases: Popular Tech-writer Kathy Sierra was attacked in early 2007 by groups of anonymous individuals for her blog "creating passionate users". They had publicly posted malicious comments about Sierra and started hate campaign against her. The attack also included death threats depicting a noose beside Sierra's picture. BBC reported that Sierra felt this attack was a result of gender oriented jealousy, because "she is a woman in the male dominated technology world" (BBC, 2007, Para 10; Bartow, 2009).

The Auto admits case (Citron, 2009b) stands as the best example of cyber defamation. In this case the victim, Jill Philipovic, a law student of the New York University, was attacked by anonymous perpetrators in the social networking site 'Auto Admit'. The perpetrator ran a thread discussing Jill's physical stature and how she could be raped. This thread attracted many like minded respondents all of whom remained anonymous. They even posted their future plan to morph Jill's picture by Photoshop effect and affixing her head to a porno-star's body. This attack not only defamed the victim online, but had a trail of defamatory incidences in the real life too. Such online defamatory remarks affected her student life; she felt uncomfortable with the inquisitive behavior of her neighbors and did not prefer to answer any thing in relation to the online harassment which she feared may appear in the online threads again harming her reputation. She felt distressed even to continue her blogs which were inspired by feministic ideologies (Citron, 2009b).

Example: The lead author being an active member of the popular social networking site Orkut notes that several users have formed groups to criticize works of several female celebrities, the most popular of these being the groups created for works of famous Indian TV serial writer and producer, Ekta Kapoor.[17] Kapoor writes and produces family dramas and soaps based on culture of elite North Indian families; on rituals, cultures followed by North Indian women; marital value systems of North Indian upper class Hindu families etc. Some of the extremely popular soaps of this female writer/producer are *"kahani ghar ghar ki"*, *"kyunki saas bhi kabhu bahu thi"*, *"kasauti jindagi ki"* etc. These groups not only criticize

Kapoor's works and her literary powers;[18] they also tend to portray her as 'villain of Indian cultures',[19] run threads depicting how bad she is as a woman herself and how much unwanted she is as a bride.[20]

2.6.1.b Emotional Injuries

Certain cyber offences target women to sabotage and threaten her. The peculiarity of these offences lies in the fact that they destroy the victim from within. Some of the offences that would be described here are getting enough highlights from the researchers and academicians, but unfortunately they fail to get legal sanctions. This is because they are not widely recognized as "crimes done to women" in the cyber space. Secondly, when the fundamental rights to speech and expression collides with such offences which we term as "emotional injuries", the lawmakers and the courts mostly uphold the fundamental rights neglecting the need to penalize offences against women in the cyber space. We understand that in most cases, the burden of proof falls on the victim and expecting an adult female to stay away from such victimizations is but natural. This is especially pressed upon when there are several safety tips available in the internet through websites, blogs and various write-ups. Unless these offences are seen from a feministic view point, emotional injuries on adult female internet users will continue to exist. A true legal term which could have described this offence in a single word could be 'harassment', or 'criminal intimidation' or 'insult'. But we have used the words "emotional injuries" to coat the pains suffered by a woman due to these offences as there is no proper legal term to describe it. Modes of emotional injuries are as follows:

2.6.1.b.1 Email Harassment

Email harassment is one of the many modes of "emotional injuries" inflicted upon the victim. Finn (2004) had stated that email harassment had been the main mode of cyber stalking. Email harassment happens in the following ways:

- Sending repeated e-mails or instant messages that may or may not directly threaten the recipient (Finn, 2004);
- Flooding a victim's e-mail box with unwanted mails, sending the victim files with a virus (Finn, 2004);
- Misusing the victim's email id and listing it for receiving continuous spam messages like sexually erotic messages, adult content advertisements and also phishing emails.
- Spreading the email id to others to disturb the privacy of the victim.
- Randomly searching email ids of women and continuously sending messages like "I like you", "talk to me", and "want to be friends".
- Referring email ids bearing female names to social networking sites, chat rooms, forums etc without prior permission of the owner of the email id.
- Continuously sending "add me" requests for online chatting.

Email harassment targeting women thus leads to not only stalking, but also conglomeration of cyber harassments like invasion of privacy, blackmailing etc. However, as we have shown above, by email harassment we do not mean to limit the harassment only in sending or receiving the messages, but it also includes using the email id for mischievous purposes; for instance, anonymous predators may push the victim to more dangerous zones by "leaking" the victim's email id in the internet. The perpetrator may or may not have any previous relationship with the victim; the harassment could also be the result of accidental exposure of the email id of the victim by third persons like the victim's friend or acquaintances, who may have shared the email id with the perpetrator or perpetrator's close acquaintances without foreseeing any consequences. Email harassments can happen due to various reasons, it could be done

- for fun, where the perpetrator tries to experiment with his newly found internet skills;
- due to jealousy or revenge taking mentality. In such cases, the perpetrator could also be a woman. The perpetrator(s) could misuse the email id for impersonating, blackmailing or could even float the email id of the victim in various websites to solicit more humiliation to the victim by strangers;
- to increase the perpetrator's female friend's list, and for that he may randomly select women's email ids from various sites.

2.6.1.b.2 Blackmailing

A very common offence that is done to women online is blackmailing. In this case,

- The perpetrator could be known to the victim either through real life meetings or through internet / telephone communications.
- The perpetrator could also be an unknown individual.
- The blackmailing could be a result of "jilted love affair", sexually biased professional jealousy, continuous rejection on the part of the victim to meet the perpetrator outside the virtual world etc;
- The blackmailing could also be done to forcefully extract money.

It could be seen that in cases where the victim and perpetrator are known to each other, the blackmailing begins by sending mails to the victim which carry ugly secrets of her private life, accompanied by threats to either publish them in front of a larger audience in the internet or reveal secrets to her family members who may be oblivion of the facts. The victimization can happen through email communications, text messages or private chat rooms. In some cases the perpetrator may also befriend the victim (committed or married women) through various internet communications after doing a thorough research on the monetary and social background of the victim. When the perpetrator succeeds to win her trust as a reliable virtual friend, the blackmailing begins for monetary gain with a threat to reveal their "immoral relationship" to her suitor or husband, or threat to kill her husband or defame the victim in front of a larger public etc.

Reported case: Famous Sitar player Anouska Shankar was blackmailed by a Mumbai based engineer in 2009 (Oneindia, 2009). As per the report lodged by her father the renowned sitar maestro Pandit Ravi Shankar, when Anouska gave her laptop to a service centre in early 2009, someone had copied some materials from the laptop, including her "private photographs" without her permission. The investigation revealed that the suspect, an engineer from Mumbai sent continuous mails to Anouska demanding one million US dollars for not publicizing her photos.

2.6.1.b.3 Cyber Stalking

According to Bocij (2003) cyber stalking means:

A group of behaviors in which an individual, group of individuals or organization, uses information and communications technology to harass another individual, group of individuals or organization. Such behaviors may include, but are not limited to, the transmission of threats and false accusations, damage to data or equipment, identity theft, data theft, computer monitoring, the solicitation of minors for sexual purposes and any form of aggression (Para 3).

According Yar (2006, p. 123), "Cyber stalking can be understood as an online variant of similar behaviors that take place in other non-virtual contexts and environments." However, most researchers believe that cyber stalking is cyber harassment which includes continued unwanted contacts (Philips & Morrissey, 2004), threatening, and defamation (Wykes, 2007) and even over powering the victim's virtual existence. Cyber stalking is often a "form of revenge" (Brenner, p. 50). Most cyber stalkers harass women due to a spilled relationship built up either online or offline; some times cyber stalking can also occur as a continuation of offline domestic violence targeted on former spouses (see Halder, 2009; Whitty, 2005).

Researches on cyber stalking have been getting prominence since the beginning of this millennium. Most of the research survey results and statistics show that women constitute majority of the victims. Bocij (2003) pointed out in his study on victims of cyber stalking that, among total 169 respondents, 56.3% were women and men constituted only 43.7%. As per the recent statistics (2010) published by the cyber safety organization, Working to Halt Online Abuse (WHOA), 73% of the victims of cyber stalking are women and 45.5% of the harassers were male, when compared to 36% harassers who were women (WHOA, 2010).[21]

Analyzing the above definitions and discussions on cyber stalking, we understand that:

- Cyber stalking involves constant following of the female victim in the cyber space with an intention to harm.
- Stalking may start through email communications, chat room communications, acquaintances through social networking sites, texting etc.
- Stalking may lead to threatening, blackmailing through cyber communications, defamation (posting the victim's information in open forums or bulletin board, portraying the victim as amoral woman in different internet postings), and introducing unknown cyber predators to the victim etc.
- Online Stalking may also lead to offline threat.
- Cyber stalking does not necessarily extend to sexual harassment.

Cyber stalking may begin due to the following reasons:

- Cyber stalking can result from a split in the emotional affair. The obsessed lover finds stalking as the best way to keep himself updated and let the world know that he has not yet given up.
- Stalking can also happen as a result of broken marriage where abusive husband or even ex-husband tries to make the victim's life miserable in the cyber space.
- Cyber stalking can also result from female celebrity hunt by obsessive fans in the internet whereby the stalker(s) attempt(s) to gain attention of the favorite screen goddess.
- Cyber stalker can also randomly choose his victim to experiment with his cyber dominance and make the victim literally his slave by creating fear factor in the mind of the victim.

Cyber stalking is a malicious cyber activity of following the victim online to commit some harm to her with the assistance of other cyber offences like email harassment, blackmailing, defamation etc.

Online stalking involves two steps in the process of victimization; however, these two steps per se do not constitute cyber stalking. The first step involves zeroing down upon the victim's identity in the cyber space; the second step includes extensive following of the victim's internet activities. this may involve monitoring her web acquaintances, the frequencies of her communications with others her activities in blogs, public forums, personal walls, bulletin boards etc and also professional updates about her in corporate websites. This stage could be called as shadowing stage. Cyber stalking qualify as an offence only when these shadowing activities result in personal harm to the victim like damage to reputation, extensive harassment etc.

Example: The victim, a divorced young woman went to live in another city to make her life. The perpetrator searched the victim's name in the internet and came to know her present residential and work place addresses. He mailed to her employer with obnoxious information about her and prepared fake profiles only to insult, humiliate and defame her.[22]

Reported case: Jayne Hitchcock, President of US based organization Working to Halt Online Abuse (WHOA) had been victim of cyber stalking which begun with "email bombing" (Palmer, 2010). Hitchcock's impersonated profiles appeared on many controversial websites including adult sex sites. Her residential address and phone number were also published in open forums to encourage others to call her at odd hours. When she changed her phone number, the stalkers identified her neighbors and tried to track her phone number by calling the neighbors. Hitchcock had to live in perpetual trauma since no federal or provincial law recognized cyber stalking as a penal 'offence' until Maryland made a law on email harassment in April 1999 and finally in 2001 the authorities arrested the stalkers.

2.6.1.b.4 Defamation
Cyber defamation remains the biggest gateway for causing emotional injury especially to women. We have already discussed this under the heading "hate crimes". Hence we will go to the next segment of emotional injury, i.e., cyber bullying.

2.6.1.b.5 Cyber Bullying
Jaishankar (2008) defines cyber bullying as *"abuse/ harassment by teasing or insulting, victims' body shape, intellect, family back ground, dress sense, mother tongue, place of origin, attitude, race, caste, class, name calling, using modern telecommunication networks such as mobile phones (SMS/MMS) and Internet (Chat rooms, emails, notice boards and groups)"* (p.13). Contrary to the popular belief, cyber bullying is not limited to children, but adults are also victimized. Nonetheless, women are top favorites of adult cyber bullies (Angela, 2009; Itson, 2009). The bully may start from small disagreements in the forums/chat rooms or even in the real life social hubs; the victim then becomes target of huge attack. It can be seen that:

- Adult bullies may pick up a trivial issue to "fight" and corner the victim.
- Both men and women can be perpetrator while bullying women.
- Bully may have been in the habit of bullying others.
- Perpetrator may target the victim with obscene/vulgar remarks.
- Adult bully targeting women may not always end in online sexual harassment of the victim like portraying her character as that of a "hot babe". However, this may involve comments on her parenting skills (if she is a mother), how she fails to satisfy her husband sexually (in case she is

married), how and why she fails to attract men (in case she is single and dating) and invite others to participate in the bullying.

- Once the victim starts responding to the harsh messages, bullying begins.
- Bullying may lead to online defamation and infringement of privacy as the bully may play lead role in leaking the personal information of the victim in the web.
- Bullying can also involve anonymous mob attack on the victim (Citron, 2009b).
- The bully may try to convince the victim that she is the bad person and not the perpetrator (Itson, 2009).

Examples:

Example 1. The perpetrator was a habitual bully. When the victim was trapped in an unwanted misunderstanding, the perpetrator started bullying by commenting on her professional skills. The victim received nearly 15 mails in ten minutes which were also forwarded to her business partner, to defame her. The perpetrator nearly convinced the victim that she was never a good manager and she lacked the professional skills because she did not go to better institutions.[23]

Example 2. The perpetrator was an old acquaintance of the victim. The problem begun when the perpetrator contacted the victim through her email chat option for some business networks. After a small disagreement over a trivial issue, the perpetrator started bullying the victim in the chat, questioning her professionalism and authenticity of works. When the victim tried to make the perpetrator understand that she does not like the language that this perpetrator is using, he shunned the victim by answering that there is no better way to communicate with a person of her stature than this.[24]

2.6.1.c Hacking and Hacking Related Crime

Wall (2007, p. 53) describes hacking as "deliberate unauthorized access to cyber spaces over which rights of ownership or access have already been established, committed with the primary aim of breaching the integrated security of the computer system." Earlier, hacking had been used to describe as cyber crimes targeting electronic commerce, and government websites. Slowly the patterns of hacking related to victimization have changed and presently hacking emails, personal non-commercial websites or web links, and personal profiles in the networking sites have become a common phenomenon.

It is noted that when hacking forms one of the constituting elements of cyber harassment or cyber crime targeting women, it is done either as a mode to take revenge for broken emotional affairs or for professional jealousy. It could also be the result of digital "experiments" by pranksters and new users of internet who fail to understand the serious consequences. In cases of nonsexual hacking, it is observed that:

- The hacker can unauthorisedly access the victim's web pages as well as data retained in the personal computer.
- The hacker can hack the email id of the victim to harass her, reach out to her friends with malicious mails and contents, defame her and debar her from further communicating with her acquaintances through her hacked email id.
- The hacker may also hack and block the victim's profile pages in various socializing sites;
- The hacker can also deactivate all her cyber activities.

- The hacker can also hack personal website or webpage of the victim especially when the webpage speaks about feministic ideologies and the hacker does not agree with these ideologies and wants to harass or tease the female web page creator.
- The perpetrator may hack and then withdraw his evidences. He may also disappear temporarily under "disguises" to save himself from the clutches of police.

Example: India based freelance writer and journalist Resmi Jaimon had shared her harrowing experiences with the lead author in this regard. She stated that her brother found 'her' online in her Gtalk chat-id when she was actually not online in reality. He was shocked when the online identity of Resmi started enquiring about him and then continued to transmit obscene chat-messages to him. Resmi's brother suspected foul play, kept the chat conversation on hold and called up Resmi to find out the truth. Resmi confirmed that she had used internet from a cyber café and had logged out from her emails and chat rooms nearly eight hours ago and she was not online with any of her cyber identities when her brother was chatting with the online 'Resmi'. Alerted, Resmi rushed to the cyber café where she had last operated her email id, and found the 'culprit' still chatting with her brother through the same computer that she had last used. He had hacked into her account and misused her email identity to send obscene messages to her brother who was online. Resmi said they caught him red-handed and handed him over to the law enforcement authorities.[25]

2.6.2 Sexual Crimes

While internet pornography or sexual grooming of children for misuse in the internet have successfully generated wide spread alarm, and inspired the lawmakers to draft laws, cyber sexual harassment of women still remains an unanswered conundrum. Cyber sexual crimes can be categorized under several heads like Obscenity, Forced pornography, Morphing etc.

Brenner (2001) has categorized cyber sexual crimes as crimes against morality. However, this hardly includes crimes against women, especially pornography and related defamation when it comes to prosecution of the case. Rather, this categorization is mostly used to emphasize crimes against children in the internet (see Smith, Grabosky & Urbas, 2004, p. 89). In cyber sexual crime cases, child victims are given more highlight by the lawmakers than the women victims. Majority of legislations preventing cyber sexual crimes approach the problem from two specific perspectives: (i) using children as models for cyber pornography and (ii) distribution of sexual contents to children through internet.[26] However, when cyber safety of women is concerned, the picture is very different. We find that in many cases, protection of "freedom of expression" is given priority when it comes to government initiatives to save women from severe humiliation in the cyber space.[27] In the following paragraphs, we will analyze the different genres of cyber sexual crimes against women.

2.6.2.a Cyber Obscenity

Creating obscene profiles and web pages with innocent women's pictures and information, sending obscene remarks and obscene images to women etc, could be identified as the most chosen trend to harass women in the cyber space. The very first legal attempt to define obscenity was made in the landmark case of Miller v. California,[28] which defined obscenity as "hard core pornography". The verdict also specified several activities which would amount to obscenity; these are: lewd caricature of sexual organs or sexual activities communicated by photography or graphic designs or even lascivious messages; comments or texts about the recipient's/sender's body, sexual acts etc. We have noticed that often obscenity in the cyber space is linked with pornography and the trend leads to discussions about child pornography. While it is true that obscenity and pornography are interlinked, it is to be noted that pornography is one of the modes to express obscenity. Pornography is largely used to explain sexual activities with the help of graphics including movies and still photos. Obscenity can be expressed even by verbal written words not which may not include such images. In the cyber space, not only children but also adult females are targeted for obscenity attacks.

The question which arises at this point is; which are the constituting elements that make obscenity a crime against women? We will analyze this question from two angles; firstly, from the behavioral aspect of the harasser and the victim, and secondly in the light of Miller's verdict.

When seen from the first aspect, i.e., the behavioral aspect, the constituting elements could be as below:

1. The concupiscent act of forcefully sending obscene, lewd messages about the victim's body or lustrous images of a female or male naked/semi nude body depicting sexual organs in an indecent way to create unnecessary hatred or fear or uncomfortable feeling for the victim to look at the message.
2. Sending to one's inbox the visual images depicting sexual activities portraying women as "sex slaves".
3. Creating stories in prurient language about sexual activities involving victim's name and/or photographs, cartoons, graphic images etc and floating on the web, which successfully portrays the victim as a perverted sex partner and generate huge despise against the victim among common people and not sympathy.

When seen from the second aspect, i.e., in the light of Miller vs. California,[29] the constituting elements would include the following logical deductions:

a) Whether "the average person, applying contemporary community standards" would find that the work, taken as a whole, appeals to the prurient interest,
b) Whether the work depicts or describes, in a patently offensive way, sexual conduct specifically defined by the applicable state law, and
c) Whether the work, taken as a whole, lacks serious literary, artistic, political, or scientific value.

In short, the Miller verdict emphasizes on the societal acceptance of the behaviors and social value systems when terming such activities as crime. Most of the countries that have developed their own internet laws, have accepted Miller's judgmental analysis concerning obscenity.[30] However, cyber obscenity targeting women is getting momentum due to ever improving digital tools.

Reported case: A woman was targeted by a man who kept on filling her message box of the mobile phone with obscene nude pictures of men including his own nude pictures. The investigations lead to reveal constant stalking by the harasser and consequently sending the lewd pictures to the victim to disturb her privacy (Webster Parish Sheriff's Department, 2009).

2.6.2.b Cyber Pornography

Unlike obscenity, pornography remains an undefined term by the laws and it is more perilous for women. When the term is used in the context of cyber space, it is mostly used to mean child pornography (see Bryce, 2010; Quayle, 2010). Ironically, pornography in the cyber space also targets women, but it is hardly recognized as a crime against women due to the clash of fundamental freedoms of speech and expression and dignity of women.[31] However, it is to be noted that pornography may not be treated as a crime when a woman who is depicted as a model therein, consents for her involvement. In this section, we stress upon *forced* pornography or non consensual pornography which constitutes a crime in itself when the woman is either made a target without her knowledge or made to give her consent under threat.

Forced pornography involves the following elements:

- Voyeurism including stealing the victim's personal pictures, or capturing her images which may or may not show the victim in compromising positions through secret camera.
- Using the visual images of the victim (either the original picture or the morphed image) without her permission to create pornographic clippings, gallery etc for fulfilling sexual gratifications of others in lieu of monetary gains.
- Threatening the victim with dire consequences and forcefully pressurizing her to consent for either sending her photographs for pornographic uses or acting as a porno star.

A woman can be victim of forced pornography when:

a) her picture, either already available in the net or digitally scanned without her consent, is morphed without her knowledge and distributed to the wider audience for evil motive;
b) her picture is used to digitally design the graphics to depict her involved in sexual activities with a man/groups of men;
c) her picture is used without her consent in adult websites to invite others to virtually striptease, rape or molest her (Sanders, 2010);
d) her profile has been hacked and her pictures in the profile have been morphed. Victimization begins when the hacked profile is used to cater the needs of sexually perverted internet users;
e) the harasser captures her private moments through voyeurism and uses these voyeur images for monetary gain.

Reported cases:

Example 1. The harasser had rented out a holiday cottage in England where he fixed up secret hidden cameras and video recorders in fake smoke alarms to watch guests taking showers, changing dresses and having sex. He used to have CCTV monitor where he used to watch these voyeur recordings. When one of the guests suspected and complained to the police, the whole foul play was unearthed. The police reported that he captured images of 10 females and 2 male guests (BBC, 2009).

Example 2. An Orthopedic Physician in Chennai, India, used his women patients as models for cyber pornography. He captured photographs of his forcefully consented women patients and used it in an "obscene" way for uploading them in the cyber space. The physician was sentenced for life imprisonment (Rediffnews, 2008).

2.6.2.c. Cyber Sexual Defamation

Cyber sexual defamation is one of the most common modes of sexual crime against women in the cyber space. Obscenity and forced pornography are the two main elements of cyber sexual defamation and such sort of defamation can take place due to broken emotional relationships. Cyber sexual defamations can thus shape in:

- Sending obscene mails to bulk recipients (which may include the victim, her friends and family members and also the friends and acquaintances of the harasser) telling cooked up stories about the victim. The mails also carry victim's photos (may be morphed or may be the original photo) as attached documents ;
- Creating fake profiles in social networking sites, adult advertisement sites etc with her picture, terming her as "hot babe" who is ready to have sex with anyone. Such profiles may carry her personal information like residential address and phone numbers.
- Distributing compromising pictures of the victim and the harasser that may have been captured during "good old times" to others.
- The harasser may act as a cyber pimp where he uploads the victim's name, address and "private photographs" for pornographic sites or advertisements indicating him as the main contact person.
- Cyber sexual defamation can be done by women harassers as well. In such cases the main motives could be to demean the victim for either professional jealousy or personal conflicts with the victim due to emotional affairs with ex / present partners etc.

Reported Cases:

Example 1. In this 2008 case, the victim Tessa Komer was defamed by her ex boy friend (Morgan, 2008). When they broke up, the ex boyfriend hacked in the victim's Myspace account and sent message from the hacked account to her new boyfriend stating that she has sexually transmitted disease and then uploaded her naked picture in his Facebook page. In 2008 he was charged with 32 misdemeanors (Morgan, 2008).

Example 2. In another 2007 case, a university student video taped sexual activities of himself with his 19 year old girlfriend (Weaver, 2008). After they broke up, the man threatened to upload the sex-video in the internet unless the girl accepts to continue having sex with him. The girl reported him to the police and he was charged with felony and blackmail.

2.6.2.d. Unauthorized Access to Personal Data and Modification

Morphing is one of the widely practiced modes of online mischief that victimizes women in the cyber space. Morphing is nothing but unauthorized modification of personal picture of the woman. This essentially includes unauthorized access to the personal data of the victim stored in either social networking websites or corporate websites or even the personal computer of the victim. While many social networking sites treat this as infringement of copyrighted materials, in general this activity is seen as hacking and modification of web-contents. In such cases the perpetrator can

- Create another web profile with the morphed picture of the victim and misuse the accessed personal data by describing her in an obscene fashion to mislead others.
- Modify the existing web contents to exhibit the victim in a 'dirty' manner.
- Use the modified contents to defame the victim in every possible manner.
- Misuse the contents for blackmailing the victim.

2.6.3. Cyber Assisted Offline Crimes

By cyber assisted offline crimes, modern researchers signify either monetary crimes or crimes against government including terrorism (Stroik & Huang, 2008, Damphousse, 2008). In this segment, we will analyze the term 'cyber assisted offline crimes' from the perspective of individual victimization. While the other instances of cyber crimes that are discussed above may not show the harasser's knowledge about preconceived consequences, the cyber assisted or cyber motivated crimes need a well reasoned, highly motivated and intelligent executor who knows the consequences of the crime. Usually these crimes are well planned and the perpetrators feel confident about their hide and seek game in the virtual as well as in the real world. The cyber assisted offline crimes can be grouped into the following categories: abetment to suicide, cyber assisted offline invasion of privacy, cyber assisted offline physical harm, cyber assisted rape, and cyber assisted murder.

2.6.3.a. Abetment to Suicide

The finest example is Megan Meir's suicide case (Ruedy, 2008; Halder & Jaishankar, 2009). Megan was an American teenager who committed suicide after severe cyber bullying by a jealous woman who pretended to be a boy of her age and told her she was ugly and not capable of attracting any boyfriend. Even though this case involved a teenager and a woman perpetrator who was the mother of another teenager, and there had been, umpteen numbers of legal debates whether Lori Drew, the perpetrator, has used cyber space to abet the suicide of Meir (see Brenner, 2010, p. 100).

2.6.3.b. Cyber Assisted Offline Invasion of Privacy

When the victim's personal information including phone number and residential address are floated on the web as a result of cyber defamation or even cyber sexual defamation, a new batch of harassers come up to disturb the victim. They are not necessarily associated directly with the revengeful activities of the harasser in the cyber space which may be the root cause for offline harassment. They are rather the 'invited and uninvited guests' who come to abuse the victim after getting the information from the web. In such cases;

- The victim may continuously receive phone calls asking her for a 'date';
- The victim may see uninvited visitors knocking at her door at odd hours who may have come thinking her as prostitute.
- The victim's family members may be targeted as 'secondary victims' (Condry, 2010) by the harasser.

2.6.3.c. Cyber Assisted Offline Physical Assault

The cyber space may be used as a trap to allure the victim to come outside the virtual world and meet the perpetrator in real life only to cause physical harm to the victim. A peculiar trend is seen in some of such cases where the actual harasser disguises as a "new friend", who is compassionate enough to understand the victim's pains related to the ongoing harassments by the harasser.[32] The victim is cajoled to meet the 'new friend' in the real world. When the victim falls in trap, the harasser uses this opportunity to attack the victim physically.

2.6.3.d. Cyber Assisted Rape

Similar to that of cyber assisted offline physical harm, the victim may be goaded to meet the perpetrator in the physical world. When they finally meet up, the perpetrator may go ahead to physically assault, molest and even rape the victim and may threaten her with dire consequences if she reports to the police or family members.[33]

2.6.3.e. Cyber Assisted Murder

In such cases, cyber relationships may contribute to the cause of the murder. This happens especially when the victim discovers the true information about the perpetrator, with whom the victim may have developed emotional relationship in the cyber space. Murder may also take place when the perpetrator and the victim are cyber acquaintances and victim's attitude makes him furious and extremely revengeful. The perpetrator carefully convinces the victim to meet him alone to resolve the issues and forces her to keep the meeting plan secret from her family. The process of convincing the victim by mails / messages could stretch over a long period and once the victim feels confident to meet the perpetrator in person, he attacks the victim to kill her as per prior plans.[34]

Reported case: Kaushambi, young software personnel had befriended Manish Thakur and got romantically involved. They used to keep contact with each other regularly through Orkut (Mathews, 2007). However, Manish never told that he was already married. His profile in the Orkut also revealed him as "single". The victim blindly believed him. But by chance she came to know that Manish is already married and he will never marry her, instead he will continue to 'flirt' with her. When she wanted to speak about this with Manish, the harasser asked her to come to Mumbai for a talk. A day later she was found dead in a pool of blood in a hotel room where they had checked in as Mr. and Mrs. Thakur (Mathews, 2007).

2.7. CONCLUSION

Victimization of women in the cyber space has increased in a rapid manner since the inception of the era of electronic socialization. But it remained unnoticed from the legal point of view for long due to the absence of proper definitions as well as proper legal attention. Ironically, law cannot take any action against a growing crime unless and until it is properly recognized and well defined by law makers. Perhaps this is the reason that the concept of cyber crime against women was eclipsed for a long time behind the shadow of online victimization of female children and sexual harassments of women. Our definition and conceptualization will defy the idea that the concept of "cyber crime against women" is restricted within the meaning of online sexual bullying or pornography. We agree with Citron (2009 a&b) that the biggest risk factor for women in the cyber space is their reputation which may or may not involve sexual reputation.

The major challenge against forming a universal definition of cyber crime against women could come from the constitutional guarantees of freedom of speech expression. However, we expect more challenges to test our definition and we hope this will further help the understanding of the gravity of the issue. The definition is the foundation of the problem and this can help to identify the crime hubs to create awareness among the general web-users. We feel '*prevention is better than cure*' stands good for cyber crime scenario, especially for victimization of women and this can be done only when there is a proper definition of the crime, the crime hubs are identified and strong laws are made accordingly. We aim to enrich it by the discussions in the following chapters, which will reveal various trends of cyber victimization on women, reasons for its growth and the legal steps that are being taken or are necessary to be taken to prevent cyber crime against women.

REFERENCES

Angela. (2009). *Adult cyber bullies: Staying safe on Shine and around the Net*. January, 18, 2009. Retrieved on 28th June, 2010, from http://shine.yahoo.com/channel/health/adult- cyber-bullies-staying-safe-on- shine-and-around-the-net-353386/

Bartow, A. (2009). Internet defamation as profit center: The monetization of online harassment. *Harvard Journal of Law and Gender, 32*, 384–428.

Bocij, P. (2003). Victims of cyberstalking: An exploratory study of harassment perpetrated via the Internet. *First Monday*. Retrieved on 28th June, 2010, from http://131.193.153.231/www/issues/ issue8_10/ bocij/index.html

Bocij, P. (2004). *Cyberstalking: Harassment in the Internet age and how to protect your family*. Westport, CT: Praeger.

Brenner, S. W. (2001). Cybercrime Investigation and Prosecution: The Role of Penal and Procedural Law. *Murdoch University Electronic Journal of Law, 8*(2), (June 2001). Retrieved on 15th March from http://www.murdoch.edu.au/elaw/ issues/v8n2/brenner82nf.html

Brenner, S. W. (2010). *Cybercrime: Criminal Threats from Cyberspace*. Santa Barbara, CA: Praeger.

British Broadcasting Corporation (BBC). (2007). *Blog death threats spark debate*. Retrieved on 28th June, 2010, from http://news.bbc.co.uk/1/hi/6499095.stm

British Broadcasting Corporation (BBC). (2009, October 15). Man guilty in cottage voyeur case. *BBC News*. Retrieved on March 3, 2010, from http://news.bbc.co.uk/1/ hi/wales/mid/8308836.stm

Bryce, J. (2010). Online sexual exploitation of children and young people. In Y. Jewkes, & M. Yar (Eds.), *Handbook of Internet crimes* (pp. 320–342). Cullompton, UK: Willan.

Citron, K. D. (2009a). Cyber civil rights. *Boston University Law Review. Boston University. School of Law, 89*(61), 69–75.

Citron, K. D. (2009b). Law's expressive value in combating cyber gender harassment. *Michigan Law Review, 108*, 373.

Condry, R. (2010). Secondary victims and secondary victimization. In S. G. Shoham, P. Knepper, & M. Kett (Eds.), *International handbook of victimology* (pp. 219–250). Boca Raton, FL: CRC Press, Taylor and Francis Group. doi:10.1201/EBK1420085471-c8

Council of Europe. (2001). *Convention on cybercrime*, Budapest, 2001. Retrieved on 3rd March, 2010, from http://conventions.coe.int/Treaty/ EN/Treaties/html/185.htm

Damphousse, K. (2008). The dark sides of the Web: Terrorist's use of the Internet. In F. Schmallager, & M. Pittaro (Eds.), *Crimes of the Internet* (pp. 573–592). Upper Saddle River, NJ: Prentice Hall.

Dekeseredy, S. W. (2010). The hidden violent victimization of women. In S. G. Shoham, P. Knepper, & M. Kett (Eds.), *International handbook of victimology* (pp. 559–584). Boca Raton, FL: CRC Press, Taylor and Francis Group. doi:10.1201/EBK1420085471-c21

Ellison, L., & Akdeniz, Y. (1998). Cyber-stalking: The regulation of harassment on the Internet. *Criminal Law Review, December Special Edition: Crime, Criminal Justice and the Internet*, 29-48.

Finn, J. (2004). A survey of online harassment at a university campus. *Journal of Interpersonal Violence, 19*(4), 468–483. doi:10.1177/0886260503262083

Finn, J., & Banach, M. (2000). Victimization online: The downside of seeking human services for women on the internet. *Cyberpsychology & Behavior, 3*(5), 785–796. doi:10.1089/10949310050191764

Goodman, M. D. (1997). Why the police don't care about computer crime. *Harvard Journal of Law & Technology, 10*(3), 466–495.

Halder, D. (2009). *Online domestic violence: Lawyer speaks*. Retrieved on 28th June, 2010, from http://debaraticyberspace.blogspot.com/ 2009/11/online-domestic-violence-lawyer-speaks.html

Halder, D., & Jaishankar, K. (2009). Cyber socializing and victimization of women. *Temida - The Journal on Victimization. Human Rights and Gender, 12*(3), 5–26.

Hinduja, S., & Patchin, J. W. (2007). Offline consequences of online victimization: School violence and delinquency. *Journal of School Violence, 6*(3), 89–112. doi:10.1300/J202v06n03_06

Hinduja, S., & Patchin, J. W. (2008). Cyberbullying: An exploratory analysis of factors related to offending and victimization. *Deviant Behavior, 29*(2), 1–29. doi:10.1080/01639620701457816

Hinduja, S., & Patchin, J. W. (2009). *Bullying beyond the schoolyard: Preventing and responding to cyberbullying*. Thousand Oaks, CA: Sage Publications, Corwin Press.

Itson, C. (2009). Adult cyberbullying: The anonymous attacks of adult cyberbullying cross the line and enter the "real world." Retrieved on 28th June, 2010, from http://www.overcomebullying.org/ cyberbullying.html

Jaishankar, K. (2008). *Cyber bullying in India: A research report on developing profile, legal reviews and policy guidelines*. Tirunelveli, India: Department of Criminology and Criminal Justice, Manonmaniam Sundaranar University.

Jaishankar, K., Halder, D., & Ramdoss, S. (2008). Pedophilia, pornography and stalking: Analyzing child victimization in the Internet. In F. Schmallager., & M. Pittaro. (Eds.), *Crimes of the Internet*. (pp. 28-42). Upper Saddle River, NJ: Prentice Hall.

Jenson, B. (1996). *Cyber stalking: Crime enforcement and personal responsibility in the online world.* Retrieved on 28th June, 2010, from http://www.sgrm.com/art-8.htm

Katyal, N. K. (2001). Criminal law in cyberspace. *University of Pennsylvania Law Review, 149.* Retrieved on 25th June, 2010, from http://ssrn.com/abstract=249030 or doi:10.2139/ssrn.249030

Kim, S. N. (2009). Website proprietorship and cyber harassment. *Utah Law Review, 3,* 993–1059.

Mason, D. (2008). *The dimensions of "cyber crime."* National Center for Justice and the Rule of Law, University of Mississippi School of Law. Retrieved on 28th June, 2010, from http://www.olemiss.edu/depts/ncjrl/pdf/The%20Dimensions%20of%20%27Cyber%20Crime%27.pdf

Mathews, D. (2007, May 19). Koushambi's ill-fated end puts others on caution. *Merinews*. Retrieved on March 3, 2010, from http://www.merinews.com/article/koushambis- ill-fated-end-puts-others-on-caution/125078.shtml

McConnell International. (2000). *Cyber crime…and punishment? Archaic laws threaten global information- A report.* Retrieved on 20th May, 2010, from http://www.witsa.org/papers/ McConnell-cybercrime.pdf

Morgan, R. (2008). *Revenge porn: Jilted lovers are posting sex tapes on the Web—And their exes want justice.* Retrieved on March 3, 2010, from http://www.details.com/sex-relationships/porn-and -perversions/200809/revenge-porn

O'Connell, R. (2009). A typology of cybersexploitation and on-line grooming practices. Preston, UK: Cyberspace Research Unit, University of Central Lancashire. Retrieved on 21st May, 2010, from http://www.jisc.ac.uk/uploaded_documents/ lis_PaperJPrice.pdf

OneIndia. (2009, September 20). Man blackmailing Anouska Shankar arrested. *Oneindia.in*. Retrieved on 28th June 2010 from http://news.oneindia.in/2009/09/20/ man-blackmailing-anoushka-shankar-arrested.html

OpenCongress. (2010). National Defense Authorization Act for Fiscal Year 2010/Division E. Retrieved on May 27, 2011, from http://www.opencongress.org/bill/111- h2647/text

Parker, D. B. (1989). *Computer crime: Criminal justice resource manual.* Washington, DC: The agency or organization that supported or funded the work or production of the document via a contract or grant. Department of Justice, National Institute of Justice. Cambridge, MA: Abt Associates, Inc. Retrieved on 20th May, 2010, from http://www.eric.ed.gov/ PDFS/ED332671.pdf

Philips, F., & Morrissey, G. (2004). Cyberstalking and cyberpredators: A threat to safe sexuality on the Internet. *Convergence: The International Journal of Research in to New Media Technologies, 10*(1), 66–79. doi:10.1177/135485650401000105

Quayle, E. (2010). Child pornography. In Y. Jewkes & M. Yar (Eds.), *Handbook of Internet crimes* (pp. 343–368). Cullompton, UK: Willan.

Rediffnews. (2008). *Doc gets life term in cyber pornography case.* February 07, 2007. Retrieved on March 3, 2010, from http://www.rediff.com/news/ 2008/feb/07doc.htm

Ruedy, C. M. (2008). MySpace Teen Suicide: Should Anti-Cyberbullying Law Be Created? *North Carolina Journal of Law and Technology,* 9(2), 323 - 346 (July 2008). Retrieved on 15th April 2010 from http://www.ncjolt.org/sites/default/ files/323-346_Ruedy_v9i2.pdf

Sanders, T. (2010). The sex industry, regulation and the internet. In Jewkes, Y., & Yar, M. (Eds.), *Handbook of Internet crimes* (pp. 302–319). Cullompton, UK: Willan.

Shariff, S. (2005). Cyber-dilemmas in the new millennium: Balancing free expression and student safety in cyber-space. Special Issue: Schools and courts: Competing rights in the new millennium. *McGill Journal of Education,* 40(3), 467–487.

Shariff, S. (2006). Balancing competing rights: A stakeholder model for democratic schools. Special issue: Democracy and Education. *Canadian Journal of Education, 29*(2), 476–496. doi:10.2307/20054173

Shariff, S. (2009). *Confronting cyber-bullying: What schools need to know to control misconduct and avoid legal consequences.* New York, NY: Cambridge University Press. doi:10.1017/CBO9780511551260

Smith, R. G., Grabosky, P., & Urbas, G. (2004). *Cyber Criminals on Trial.* Cambridge: Cambridge University Press. doi:10.1017/CBO9780511481604

Sofaer, A. D., & Goodman, S. E. (2000). *A proposal for an international convention on cyber crime and terrorism.* Center for International Security and Cooperation (CISAC): Stanford University. Retrieved on 28th June, 2010, from http://iis-db.stanford.edu/pubs/ 11912/sofaergoodman.pdf

Stroik, A., & Huang, W. (2008). Nature and distribution of phishing. In F. Schmallager., & M. Pittaro. (Eds.), *Crimes of the Internet.* (pp. 191-224) Upper Saddle River, NJ: Prentice Hall.

Wall, D. S. (2005). The Internet as a conduit for criminals. In A. Pattavina (Ed.), *Information Technology and the criminal justice system* (pp. 77–98). Thousand Oaks, CA: Sage.

Wall, D. S. (2007). *Cybercrimes: The transformation of crime in the information age.* Cambridge, MA: Polity.

Wall, D. S. (2008). Cybercrime and the culture of fear: Social science fiction(s) and the production of knowledge about cybercrime. *Information Communication and Society, 11*(6), 861–884. doi:10.1080/13691180802007788

Weaver, P. (2008). *Blackmail charge against former OSU student dropped: Refiled as misdemeanor.* Retrieved on March 3, 2010, from http://www.1600kush.com/ story.php?id=186&section=1

Webster Parish Sheriff's Department. (2009). *Webster man arrested for cyber-stalking and obscenity.* Retrieved on March 3, 2010, from http://www.webstersheriff.us/releases/ release/6955128/19343.htm

Whitty, M. T., & Carr, A. N. (2003). Cyberspace as potential space: Considering the Web as a playground to cyber-flirt. *Human Relations, 56*(7), 861–891. doi:10.1177/00187267030567005

Whitty, T. M. (2005). The realness of cyber cheating: Men's and women's representation of unfaithful Internet relationships. *Social Science Computer Review, 23,* 57–67. doi:10.1177/0894439304271536

Working to Halt Online Abuse (WHOA). (2008). Cyber stalking statistics. Retrieved on 28th April, 2010, from http://www.haltabuse.org/resources/ stats/2008Statistics.pdf

Wykes, M. (2007). Constructing crime: Culture, stalking, celebrity and cyber. *Crime, Media, Culture: An International Journal, 3*(2), 158–174.

Yar, M. (2006). *Cybercrime and society*. London, UK: Sage Publications.

ENDNOTES

[1] Cyber space actually means "electronic medium of computer networks". The word 'cyber space' was coined by science fiction writer William Gibson and was first used in his 1982 story Burning Chrome. For more information, see http://pespmc1.vub.ac.be/cybspace.html

[2] See Additional Protocol to the Convention on Cyber crime, concerning criminalization of acts of a racist and xenophobic nature committed through computer systems, adopted on 28.01.2003. Url: http://conventions.coe.int/treaty/en/treaties/html/189.htm

[3] For more information see http://www.answers.com/library/Britannica+Concise+Encyclopedia-cid-1819162

[4] See 'Cyber crime' @ http://www.answers.com/topic/cybercrime

[5] We have discussed broadly about this in later chapters.

[6] Recommendation No. R (95) 13, approved by the European Committee on Crime Problems (CDPC) at its 44th plenary session, May 29 – June 2, 1995: Concerning problems of criminal procedural law connected with information technology. See http://cm.coe.int/ta/rec/1995/95r13.htm see

[7] Recommendation No. R (89) 9, adopted by the Committee of Ministers of the Council of Europe on September 13 1989 and Report by the European Committee on Crime Problems: Computer-related crime. See http://cm.coe.int/ta/rec/1989/89r9.htm

[8] For more information see http://www.pamil-visions.net/vogue-model-liskula-cohen/24352/

[9] We have discussed about it in later chapters.

[10] We call it "cyber behavior" because these harassments often do not get legal sanction until they are coupled with other severe criminal charges like defamation, fraud etc, (unfortunately, this sort of legal treatment of these "cyber behaviors" towards adult women is very rare).

[11] By sexuality we mean to say sexually abusing women by doctoring pictures or leaking their phone numbers, emails and real life addresses for sexual enjoyment purposes.

[12] The research surveys are shown in the next chapter.

[13] Even though this terminology is presently being used to denote hate against humanity as a whole, we prefer to use this terminology to show the online crimes targeting women that can be generated by hatred or those crimes, which can generate hatred against the particular victim.

[14] Hate crime can also give rise to forcefully creating unwanted sexual images of the female victim. We have discussed this under the category of the sexual crimes.

[15] From the personal experiences of the lead author as a cyber victim counselor.

[16] This case study was obtained from a victim who kindly consented to use her case details by remaining anonymous. Source: Personal email from the victim to the lead author.

17   See Orkut communities such as "We hate Ekta Kapoor"(http://www.orkut.co.in/ Main#Community?cmm=158633), I hate Ekta Kapoor (http://www.orkut.co.in/ Main#Community?cmm=16469601) etc.

18   See supra @ 33

19   ibid

20   ibid

21   Source: WHOA statistics for 2010. URL: http://www.haltabuse.org/resources/stats/2010Statistics. pdf

22   This case detail was provided by a victim who kindly consented to use her case details by remaining anonymous to the lead author. Source: personal email conversation with the victim.

23   This case detail was provided by a close friend who prefers to remain anonymous.

24   This case detail was provided by a victim who preferred to remain anonymous. Source: personal email conversation between the victim and the lead author.

25   From a personal email from Resmi Jaimon to the lead author.

26   These laws are broadly discussed in Chapters 5,6 and 7

27   There are some legal provisions worldwide, which are being used to prevent atrocities against women in the cyber space. We have discussed these about applicability of the laws and their scopes from feministic point of view in chapters 5,6 and 7.

28   Miller v. California, 413 U.S. 15 (1973): In this case the appellant was convicted for mailing sexually unsolicited material. This action of the appellant was in violation of a California statute. Miller's case established certain landmark criteria for judging obscenity in the US. It was held that obscene material is not protected by the First Amendment. Pp. 24-25. Retrieved on 02.12.2009 from http://www.law.cornell.edu/supct/html/historics/USSC_CR_0413_0015_ZS.html

29   ibid

30   See supra @ 28

31   See Supra @ 14 Url: http://www.nostatusquo.com/ACLU/dworkin/OrdinanceMassComplete.html

32   From the experiences of the lead author as a counselor for cyber crime victims.

33   See the reported case below for further understanding.

34   Men and women can equally fall victims of such heinous preplanned crimes. We have specifically discussed such sorts of crimes to highlight the extreme risk factors for women who can fall victims of blind online relationships.

Chapter 3
Etiology, Motives, and Crime Hubs

CHAPTER OVERVIEW

This chapter describes various aspects that surround victimization of women in the cyberspace and goes in depth to analyze the reasons for such victimization. The etiology of cyber crimes against women is something novel as this has overridden the conventional causes of criminality. The motivation behind the cyber crimes against women is also analyzed. Spatial aspect of physical space crime is a well-researched subject and in this chapter the 'crime hubs' or the hotspots of cyber crimes are dealt. Apart from this, an attempt is made to develop characteristics of victims and perpetrators of cyber crimes against women.

3.1. INTRODUCTION

Victimization of women in the cyber space and the nature of cyber crimes that may happen to women may properly be understood if deeper research is done on the etiology of the crimes, the motives of the perpetrators, "crime hubs" and nature and characteristics of the victims and perpetrators. In the previous chapter we established that the concept of cyber crime against women is not limited only to sexual crimes. The next question, which needs to be addressed for understanding the nature of cyber crimes against women is, *why crimes are done against women in the cyber space.* In this chapter, we have approached this issue from four different perspectives: etiology, motives, crime hubs and the characteristics of the victims and the perpetrators.

DOI: 10.4018/978-1-60960-830-9.ch003

3.2. ETIOLOGY

We have observed that majority of studies on gender violence indicate the gender of the victim, the myth of vulnerable reputation of women, social practices of male dominance over the women, and victim precipitation as some of the main causes for victimization of women (Melton, 2000; Fisher, Cullen & Turner, 2002; Mustain & Tewsbury, 1999; Biber et.al, 2002; Bryant, 2009; Milivojevic & Copic, 2010; Condry, 2010; Machado, Dias & Coelho, 2010). In this chapter we will examine few more grounds, other than the traditionally established reasons like the gender of the victim, which could be the main cause for crimes such as stalking and sexual harassment as the raison d'être for the growth of cyber crime against women. These are as follows:

3.2.a The Hi-Tech Help

The hi-tech help had remained the largest reason for the growth of crime in the cyber space, including cyber crimes against women. Along with misusing the technology for harassing women, crooks use it for hiding behind the cyber veil. They attack like Meghnaada[1] by shielding themselves behind the cloud of pseudonymity in the cyber space in different 'avatars'.[2] This is explained well by Citron (2009a). She speaks about mob attacks as well as individual attacks on women internet users from behind the cloak of anonymity and she further shows how misuse of technology wins in a battle with 'rights' (Citron, 2009a). Jaishankar's (2008) criminological theory on the behavior of the perpetrators in the cyber space[3] can be used aptly for explaining how 'hi-tech helps' fuel the growth of cyber crime against women.

3.2.b Victim Precipitation

The victim precipitation theory introduced by Hans Von Hentig in 1940's (Tark, 2007) stands good for explaining the growth of cyber crime against women. This theory suggests that the victim may initiate his/her own victimization either actively or passively (McGrath, 2009). Analyzing the typology of the crimes that can happen to women in the cyber space and examining the trends thereof, we observe that active precipitation attracts crimes when women victims knowingly visit dating sites or adult sites and give/display their real information to the 'visitors' of their profiles. The saga continues when women wantonly befriend strangers in online public chat rooms or social networking sites and give away their real space information. This is especially true in cases when victims find their morphed pictures and fake profiles in various sites which are not created by them. Such nuisances are often created by the perpetrator for experimenting his technical knowledge. We call it *active precipitation;* because it is often seen that in such cases the victim allures the crime by exposing herself in spite of warning notes provided by the internet safety regulations in general and safety tips provided by the policy guidelines in the ISP rules and regulations. Active precipitation also works when the victim decides to 'fight' the perpetrator by verbally accusing him publicly. However, the theory of active precipitation may not stand good for certain offences like voyeurism. Further, we do not blame the victim as a female identity, but what attracts our attention is the lack of cyber awareness in many female victims which in a way encourages active precipitation.

An examination of our typology would suggest that majority of the cyber crimes targeted against women also happen due to passive precipitation. Instances of passive precipitations could be found in cases of *hate crimes* motivated by feminist outlooks of the victim, *emotional injuries* motivated by broken relationships etc, happen mostly due to passive motivations from the victim herself.

Interestingly, it can be seen that women offenders in the cyber space who attack women, are mostly motivated by active precipitation when they pick up a verbal duel with the victim as a result of disagreements over trivial issues. In certain cases the women offenders are also motivated by passive precipitations when the female victim turns out to be one in a competition for winning the man of her choice.

3.2.c Growth of Victim-Turned-Offenders

The third major reason for the growth of cyber crimes against women is the continuous rise of victim –turned offenders in the cyber space. Some researchers say that mostly this happens in cases of young victims who are abused as a subject of child pornography or even bullying (Hinduja & Patchin, 2008). We would like to emphasize that this hypothesis works even for adults who had been victims in the cyber space earlier, either by their own victimization or by others. Such turnover could be a result of suppressed anger and revenge taking attitude. Often it is seen that victims of school bullies continue to bully others because they feel it is but natural to break the ethical value system in the cyber space. In certain cases, the victims of hacking also experiment with their 'being a victim' sentiment by hacking or cloning others, especially profiles of women.[4]

3.2.d Secondary Victimization of the Victims by Police, Courts and the Media

The secondary victimization of women in the cyber space can happen in three major ways:

In the first case, when the victim reports the crime to the police, her much rejoiced success story of standing up against the victimization may turn a curse in disguise when the perpetrator takes this (the reporting to the police) as another insult to his male ego. The constant cheer up, congratulations and such positive messages by friends and well wishers may in some cases encourage the victim to tell about the 'journey' publicly. The victim takes up mails / messages / blogs / bulletin boards of social networking sites etc, to tell the world how she had won over the battle and in return, her inbox or wall gets flooded with sympathy messages, congratulations notes etc. But the underlying incidents may build up another plot for victimization. As Jaishankar's theory (2008) suggests, it may very often be seen that the perpetrator surrenders to the police in the real life like a good law abiding human being, promises never to venture in the same boat and even readily pays damages or serves his sentences in the prison. But when he sees himself out of the clutches of the police and notices how his victim is being praised for what she has done; he may again enter the cyber space to wear his old cloak with a new veneer and may become even more ferocious to teach a life time lesson to his victim.

In the second case, the secondary victimization may begin in the phase of reporting to the police, investigation and court procedures. When the crime persists and the perpetrator refuses to step down from harassing the woman, often counselors for cyber crime victims advise the victim to visit the local police station and take help of the police. Most local police stations (if situated in interior parts) may not be very familiar with the cyber harassment cases and when the issue in question is as delicate as harassing the woman, they may first try to frame it as a traditional gender harassment case.[5] The problem becomes intense when the 'evidence' is lost the moment police steps in such cases. The lead author from her personal experiences has often seen that before registering the case, the victim has to almost force the police to believe that there had been a crime and evidence has been *"erased off" "just a few hours back*". The police loose interest in the case then and there. The concerned police officer may also humiliate the victim by mocking at her 'power of imagination'. Some of the very common comments that the victim may get to hear from the police are "do you believe in evil spirits or paranormal activities"? "Have you checked your mental state of affairs recently?" or even "don't waste our time".[6] The victim does not even get the least chance to lick her wounds when she returns home to see messages sent by the harasser to her inbox, mocking at her guts to challenge him.

When the victim lives in a metropolitan city, the story may be different. The victim has to run from pillar to post to find out the correct police station having the right jurisdiction to deal with the case (Halder, 2009). Then the question arises as to whether the harassment has really amounted to any penal offence as per the laws of the land; the officer in charge, may completely refuse to understand the nature of the case and there by reject the complaint on the face of the victim. The officer may even summon the victim again and again to repeat the painful story and then bring in the perpetrator (if he is a local resident) to resolve the case without going into the formal legal procedures of registering the case even though the victim may badly need a judicial interference for fear of ultimate harassment by the perpetrator.

Even if the victim successfully crosses this particular stage, the next stage of victimization begins with the legal battles over establishing the infringement of rights of the victim. The clash of personal freedom, and right to privacy, zero domestic legislation and overall an endless search for well versed, understanding lawyer for managing the messy case for the victim pushes her further back to the depressing and frustrating stage.

The third sort of secondary victimization begins with the media when she is through the court proceedings stage. Wall (2008, p. 867) explains this situation in the following lines:

News reporting tends to simultaneously feed the public's lust for 'shocking' information, but also feeds off it – the relationship is dynamic rather than causal. This endless demand for sensationalism sustains the confusion of rhetoric with reality to create, what Baudrillard described as 'le vertige de la realite'' or 'dizzying whirl of reality' (1998, p. 34). By blurring predictions about 'what could happen' with 'what is actually happening' the message is given by various media that novel events are far more prevalent than they really are. Once a 'signal event', such as a novel form of cybercrime, captures media attention and heightens existing public anxiety then other news sources will feed off the original news story and spread virally across cyberspace. In such manner, relatively minor events can have significant impacts upon public beliefs compared with their actual consequences, especially when they result in panics and moral panics (Garland, 2008).

Wall's (2008) comments stand good for the purpose of our discussion. Whether the victim wins her battle over crime in the cyber space or not, often by this stage she is exposed by the media. Her right to privacy, which was probably her first priority, at this stage becomes completely overpowered by the enthusiastic media and millions of readers of her 'news'. Also, she becomes a subject for further 'research'. Torn between a world '*out* there' and a world '*in* there', the victim prefers to remain a victim than be a subject of constant attention. Indeed many women victim thus prefer to remain in the gloom forever after being threatened with consequences similar to those who are already exposed in this way.

3.2.e Step Motherly Attitude of the Laws

Non reporting (Wall, 2008) for the fear of unwanted publicity coupled with fear of loosing the legal battle due to poor cooperation from the law of the land further creates a ground for the increase in victimization of women in the cyber space. A brief research in the international cyber regulatory provisions could show that victimization of women in the cyber space is quite a neglected issue in all the conventions which were framed for the promotion of the legal policies and guidelines for preventing cyber crime.

It was first the Tenth United Nations Congress on the Prevention of Crime and the Treatment of Offenders, held in Vienna from 10-17 April, 2000 that spoke about transnational crimes, plight of women and also cyber crimes. It should be noted that in the year 2000, cyber crimes against women was not a big problem for the legal jurists as it had been for economic crimes which started gripping the world through electronic media. Hence this convention mentioned in its 5th paragraph that "We shall accord high priority to the completion of the negotiation of the United Nations Convention against Transnational Organized Crime and the protocols thereto, taking into account the concerns of all States". The convention then in the 12th paragraph spoke about developing action oriented policy guidelines for women basing on their special needs. The convention promised to look after women's needs from the perspective of criminal justice practitioners, victims, offenders as well as prisoners.

The declaration of the convention is pertinent to this book's objectives. It says: "We also commit ourselves to the development of action-oriented policy recommendations based on the special needs of women as criminal justice practitioners, victims, prisoners and offenders" to emphasize the need for women centric laws and policy guidelines for preventing cyber victimization. This correlates further with the declaration in the 18th paragraph which states: "We decide to develop action-oriented policy recommendations on the prevention and control of computer-related crime, and we invite the Commission on Crime Prevention and Criminal Justice to undertake work in this regard, taking into account the ongoing work in other forums. We also commit ourselves to working towards enhancing our ability to prevent, investigate and prosecute high-technology and computer-related crime". The convention has thus highlighted the "special need" of action oriented policy recommendations from four perspectives; criminal justice practitioners, victims, prisoners and offenders. It is evident that each of these categories is in need of separate policy guidelines for the betterment of their present conditions.

However, the convention saw a fruitful consequence in the next year with the EU convention on cyber crime. The European Union convention on cyber crime, held at Budapest, in 2001, categorized cyber offences into four groups, (i) Offences against the confidentiality, integrity and availability of computer data and systems, which deals with Illegal access, Illegal interception, Data interference, System interference and Misuse of devices; (ii) Computer related offences which deals with computer related forgery and fraud; (iii) Content related offences which deals with child pornography; and (iv) Offences related to infringement of copyrights and related rights. This convention could be termed as *mother* of all cyber laws and legal policy guidelines, as almost all the computer savvy nations created their own Information Technology laws on the basis of this convention. It is to be noted that, even though each and every offence that may happen in the cyber space has been included in this convention, it has failed to address the problems of women. Ironically the convention addresses pornography and labels it as crime when it is done to children only. Also, we have to remember that in 2001 the trend of cyber crime was still limited to traditional offences like the financial offences, hacking, pornography etc. However, we must accept the truth that cyber crime has growing dimensions. Each reported offence gives the lawmakers new chances to think about another sets of preventive guidelines and laws to make the cyber space a safer place to "habituate".

This was reflected again in the United Nation's Congress on crime prevention and criminal justice, held at Bangkok in 2005. In the Bangkok declaration, it was noted that "in the current period of globalization, information technology and the rapid development of new telecommunication and computer network systems have been accompanied by the abuse of those technologies for criminal purposes." The declaration welcomed "efforts to enhance and supplement existing cooperation to prevent, investigate and prosecute high-technology and computer-related crime, including by developing partnerships with the private sector". The declaration also recognized "the important contribution of the United Nations to regional and other international forums in the fight against cyber crime and invite the Commission on Crime Prevention and Criminal Justice, taking into account that experience, to examine the feasibility of providing further assistance in that area under the aegis of the United Nations in partnership with other similarly focused organizations." The Bangkok declaration was the first of its type to address the various types of crimes emanating from information technology. But this convention also failed to address the problems of women in the cyber space in particular; rather it concentrated more on cyber economic crimes and cyber terrorism.

These conventions further resulted in influencing domestic laws of several countries.[7] But, the issue of considering taunting, bullying communications or even adult nonconsensual pornography as crimes in the cyber space against women remained a perceptive issue in many countries (Citron, 2009b). Even though the concept of "cyber crime" as it is, has found place in domestic penal laws as well as information technology related laws, cyber crime against women still remains an area which is less focused by the criminal justice systems. If the penal laws can prescribe punishments for offline criminal intimidation to women, why online intimidation to women should be treated as *'part of internet life'* and would be termed as *behavioral mistakes*? As Citron (2009b) has rightly pointed out, several cyber crimes including cyber communications are indicated to women at large, and these actions against the female victim(s) make people believe that she is not a normal human being; her reputation, both online as well as offline, her professional profile, economic independence, security factors etc may all be jeopardized due to public humiliation in the internet. The law however, "trivializes" (Citron 2009B) the pains of the women victims. Such paternalistic laws also further aggravate the victimization.

3.3 MOTIVES

Every act of crime must be accompanied by a motive and cyber crimes are no exception. In cases of cyber crimes against women, there could be typical motives which contribute to the online harassment of the victim. But it must be noted that cyber space is used to execute these motives in maximum cases. These motives could be:

- *Personal enmity with the victim due to failure of marriage, broken emotional commitments, professional jealousy etc (Citron, 2009a; Halder, 2007; Whitty, 2005):* These motives could be executed through hacking, sexual as well as non-sexual defamations, emotional injuries including stalking, obscenity and pornography etc. These motives could also motivate cyber assisted offline crimes.

- *Sexual obsessions (Halder, 2007; Halder & Jaishankar, 2009; Whitty, 2005):* This could be common motives for emotional cheating, stalking, forced pornography including voyeurism, obscenity etc.
- *Desire to establish himself as a powerful cyber identity:* Desperateness to establish his point of view in any online discussions etc (Shariff, 2005) could generally motivate cyber bullying, gender harassment, cyber flames, creation of fake web portals etc.
- *Intention to test his knowledge about newly evolving digital tricks, playing pranks and amusing friends by his digital tricks:* In cases of creation of cloned profiles, hacking, morphing pictures etc, these factors could stand as one of the common motives besides personal enmity.

3.4 CRIME HUBS

Maximum cyber victimization happens to women at some chosen 'hubs' in the cyber space. According to a preliminary cyber victimization study conducted in India (Halder & Jaishankar, 2010), 85% victims received hideous harassing mails in their email inbox from strangers as well as male acquaintances; 11.7% had bad experiences in the cyber space, including social networking sites like Orkut, Facebook, etc; 40% of the victims presume that they have been victimized by their "virtual friends".[8]

As has been provided by WHOA statistics for the year 2010, among 349 cases, 73% constitute female victims and only 27% of the victims are male (WHOA, 2010); and most chosen 'hubs' for general cyber harassments are emails (34%), Instant Messaging (IM) (6%), message boards, including forums, groups, usernet, newsgroups etc (9.5%), website (4.5%), chat (2.5%), Facebook (16.5%), MySpace (4.5%), dating (1.25%), blogs (1.25%) etc (WHOA, 2010). However, it should be noted that the statistics provided by WHOA includes both men and women victims. As we have discussed in the operational definition of cyber crime against women in the earlier chapter, it is evident there are two separate 'hubs' or focal points in the cyber space for attacking women; these are (i) the emails of the victims and (ii) socializing sites including online chat rooms, blogs, public message boards and social networking sites (see Halder & Jaishankar, 2009; Citron, 2009b; Wall, 2007).

Personal emails of the victims had remained a 'first-preferred' place of attack for many predators in the pre-social networking sites era. Apparently we presume that the victims were attacked through their email ids either by their ex-intimate partners or ex-boyfriends who knew the email ids. In several cases email ids were also 'leaked' through peers and/or professional work places of the victims. In such cases the groups of perpetrators were not limited to the ex-partners alone who chose to attack women through email ids; it also included unknown *'techies'*, who took such email ids with feminine screen names to experiment their internet-perpetration. The perpetrators used these email ids to send constant messages with offensive contents, spoofing, teasing and also to make fun of the victims by linking these email ids in open web services for adult entertainment purposes.[9] Some examples of such usage of email ids of the female victims are as follows:

- In Missoula, a man continued to send emails to his former girlfriend with threatening and abusive contents for nearly 3 months from October to December in 2007. He used her email id for threatening her, abusing her and posting pictures of dead women to make her understand that she will be like those in the picture very soon. He was sentenced for 3 years and one month imprisonment after cyber stalking charges were proved against him (Billingsgazzette, 2009).

- In Mumbai, India, a complaint was lodged by a 31-year-old woman against the CEO of Cricket Club of India, Kamaljeet Rajpal to the cyber crime police station. The woman reported to the police that the accused in March, 2007, sent mails attached with obscene video clippings to her inbox. Her inbox started getting flooded with such emails almost every day till she reported the case to the police in 2009 (Indian Express, 2009).

Along with emails, chat rooms were also used and are still being used to harass women.[10] These chat rooms which were earlier exclusively available through Yahoo messenger, AOL chats etc, are used as 'grooming classes' for women where they can be seduced and emotionally overpowered and thereby personal information could be 'stolen' for future misuse. These chat rooms are also used to transmit slang, obscene languages, name calling and sexually abusive words to female chat partners. In cases where these chat rooms are public, such activities of the predator attract others to join in and mob attack the female victim (Citron, 2009b).

Apart from chat rooms, it is the 'blog-sites' which claim to be another hub for generating cyber crime against women (Citron, 2009b). Even though blog sites are created with ultimate purpose of expressing one's views, many times such views have seen to be inclusive of sexual fantasies about women, one's own revengeful thoughts about harming the reputation of ex-girlfriend, publishing past stories from private life of the female victim and thereby putting her in total embarrassment etc. The blogs also openly invite others to see and comment on the outputs of the original author, which adds more harassment to the victim. Dowd (2009) provides a perfect example of harassment via blogs:

Liskula Cohen, a 37-year-old model and Australian Vogue cover girl, was surprised to find herself winning a "Skankiest in NYC" award from an anonymous blogger. The online tormentor put up noxious commentary on Google's blogger.com, calling Cohen a "skank," a "ho" and an "old hag" who "may have been hot 10 years ago." She filed a defamation suit to force Google to give up the blogger's e-mail. And she won. "The words 'skank,' 'skanky' and 'ho' carry a negative implication of sexual promiscuity," wrote Justice Joan Madden of State Supreme Court in Manhattan, rejecting the Anonymous Blogger's assertion that blogs are a modern soapbox designed for opinions, rants and invective. The judge cited a Virginia court decision that the Internet's "virtually unlimited, inexpensive and almost immediate means of communication" with the masses means "the dangers of its misuse cannot be ignored. The protection of the right to communicate anonymously must be balanced against the need to assure that those persons who choose to abuse the opportunities presented by this medium can be made to answer for such transgressions." Cyberbullies, she wrote, cannot hide "behind an illusory shield of purported First Amendment rights." (Paras 6-11)

The open web space is also no exception in creating cyber crime against women. Open web space is often used by private individuals to create domains for exclusively harassing the victim. These are also used for advertising women in indecent manner, creating groups / forums exclusively for attacking a particular woman or women in general.

The other trend is to use popular social networking sites to harass women. These sites have become popular hubs for predators after the arrival of bunch of social networking sites like Facebook, Myspace, Orkut, etc. The predators use these sites to ridicule women in every possible way (Halder & Jaishankar, 2009). We have observed two main modus operandi for victimizing women in these social networking sites, i.e., either modifying the content of a woman's profile and republishing them in indecent manner to impersonate her, or creating offensive communication including stalking the woman. The reasons behind using social networking sites for ridiculing women vary from revenge taking to making fun.[11]

Some also use such sites to dupe women for monetary gain. By monetary gain we signify befriending and cheating by taking away money on this pretext or that. However, this must be noted that while before the era of social networking sites, emails and open forums were largely used for victimizing women. Afterwards, when the social networking sites became popular as online socializing hubs, emails became 'one of the focal points among many' for harassing women. This is because almost all social networking sites as well as web domains like dot coms etc require a primary email id of the registrant. As such, either the perpetrator(s) may create fake email ids using the victim's name and personal information to operate these sites, or they may also hack the victim's ids to operate these sites.[12]

If the trend of using cyber space for harassing women can be followed for past 5 years, it can be seen that the topography has changed as such:

Emails → Chat rooms → open web forums like dot.coms, blogs etc → social networking sites (which are inclusive of emails + profile homepage + community message board). Figure 1 may elaborate it broadly.

Some examples of how these web spaces used are presented below:

1.   The harasser selected women at random from East Devon in a website called 'Plenty of fish.com' for love and relationship. When such relationships didn't work out as per his expectations, he abused his victims with offensive communications, death threats, threats to rape etc. He was later sentenced to jail for severe bullying and using offensive words (ThisisExeter, 2010).

2.   The former husband of the victim in order to take revenge posted the victim's name and information in the Craiglist so that people can contact her for booking her for 'hot sex'. Immediately after the information was published, the victim got several harassing phone calls from strangers. The Craiglist authorities however, removed the postings after they were notified (KMBC, 2010).

Figure 1. Cyber crime hubs

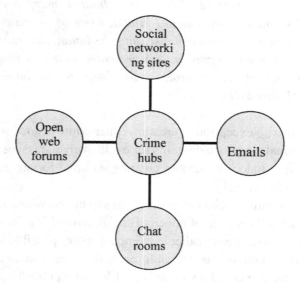

3. A British divorcee was duped by a suitor whom she met online and who forced her to believe that he was an ideal match for her. He started seeing her in real life and slowly started using her credit cards and money for his own use. It was later discovered that he has similarly duped many women whom he met through online dating services and made a little fortune for himself. He was found guilty of deception and fraud (Levin, 2010).

4. In one more British stalking case, the producer of a British TV channel was jailed for stalking and harassing his former classmate. The reports reveal that he had searched her name in Google to find out her whereabouts for 40,000 times, downloaded her information, photographs including her husband's information and disturbed her by late night phone calls. The victim reported to have gone through deep mental and physical trauma and she even had a miscarriage due to the stress that was created due to this harassment (Martin, 2010).

5. In 2009, Sneha, a South Indian actress found out her morphed photos being used in the adult entertainment sites. The perpetrator, who also took pictures of the actress without her permission from the shooting spot used them for mischievous purposes, was arrested by the police (Bollywoodactress.com, 2009).

As we have mentioned in Chapter 2, online harassment encourages offline crimes which may also result in deep emotional injuries like cheating, physical harm including bodily harm and even murder. One of the apt examples could be this: Oscar award wining composer Joseph Brooks was booked for several charges for sexual assaults after one of his female victims reported that he allured women by placing advertisements for starring role in his upcoming films in sites like Craiglist. Reports revealed that he raped 11 women who went to his apartment for appointments (Daily Mail Reporter, 2009).

3.5 CHARACTERISTICS OF VICTIMS AND PERPETRATORS

3.5.1 Characteristics of Victims

WHOA reports on cyber harassment statistics[13] could suggest two broad factors to analyze the trends of crimes against women in the cyber space as well as impact of victimization of women. These two factors are as follows:

1. *Crimes done against active and/or passive female users of the cyber space:* Victims of cyber crime against women can be divided into two broad categories: (i) those who are regular users of the cyber space and (ii) those who are not regular users of the cyber space, or those who do not use cyber space other than official communications and related purposes. While the first category of victims may get to see the offensive messages in their email inboxes, profile message boxes, chat rooms where they are active participators etc, the second category of victims may not get to see the offences directly. They could be informed of the victimization, either by the perpetrator himself or by her friends or peers who had visited these web spaces, or the regular users of web spaces where the victimization has taken place, or persons who are contacted by the harasser by emails etc to spread the harassment of the victim. In both these cases, the common forms of crimes could be publishing personal information in the websites, creation of impersonated profiles by the harasser,

creating write-ups in blogs or websites about the victim and also misusing the picture in the web space(s).

2. *The marital status of the victims:* The WHOA statistics had shown that majority of the harassments had been meted out to victims who are 'single'.[14] Even though, this statistics do not single out the marital status of the female victims, it is evident from the literatures (Citron, 2009 a&b; Halder & Jaishankar, 2009; Whitty, 2005; Bartow, 2009) that single women are the most chosen targets for cyber crimes such as stalking, defamation (both sexual and non sexual defamation), blackmailing, impersonation, emotional cheating and resultant traumatizing etc. Divorced women are mostly targeted by their ex-spouses to damage their social and professional reputation,[15] whereas married women may get to see harassments from fake profiles,[16] ex-lovers of either spouses, professional competitors etc.

3.5.2 Characteristics of Perpetrators

Cyber crime perpetrators could be of the following categories:

1. Ex-lovers;
2. Ex-spouses;
3. Jealous colleagues who could be either male or female.
4. Individuals who do not agree with feministic ideologies of the victims;
5. Obsessive fans of female celebrities;
6. Individuals who take cyber space to have short time emotional affairs and who love to play pranksters with women;
7. Victims of bully who prefer to bully 'weaker sex' to overpower them.

It should be noted that the perpetrators of cyber crimes against women include not only men, but women too. Instances like that of Model Cohen (Dowd, 2009) or Megan Meier's (Ruedy, 2008) prove that women can also be perpetrators. But reports of WHOA[17] or CCVC,[18] and feministic views of Citron (2009 a&b), Halder (2007), Bartow (2009), Halder and Jaishankar (2009), etc would prove that male harassers dominate the ratio. Whereas female perpetrators may victimize their victims due to professional jealousy or personal jealousy over men in their lives, or performances of their children in the school etc, male perpetrators may attack women victims mostly for frustration over failed relationships and ego clashes. A deep analysis of the motives of the perpetrators belonging to both the genders may however show that jealousy remains the biggest underlying factor in cyber crimes against women.

3.6 CONCLUSION

A crime is a combined result of motives and actions. In addition, the mode of usage of a particular place may also influence the nature of the crime. It must also be noted that the nature of the victimization that may happen through the cyber space can also be influenced by the characteristics of the victims and perpetrators. The etiologies that are discussed here may not only help to understand the elements of crimes targeting women in the cyber space, they may also help to build logical hypothesis in this regard.

REFERENCES

Baudrillard, J. (1998). *The consumer society: Myths and structures*. London, UK: Sage.

Biber, J. K., Doverspike, D., Baznik, D., Cober, A., & Ritter, B. (2002). Sexual harassment in online communications: Effects of gender and disclosure medium. *CyberPsychology & Behaviour, 5*, 33–42. doi:10.1089/109493102753685863

Billings Gazette. (2009). *Missourian gets 3 years for cyber stalking*. Retrieved on 28th June, 2010, from http://billingsgazette.com/news/state-and-regional/montana/ article_393926a4-bf0d-5f0f-a0fe-f181ccc5ff2b.html

Bollywoodactress.com. (2009). *Cyber crime captured actress Sneha's morphed photos*. Retrieved on 28th April, 2010, from http://thebollywoodactress.com/cyber-crime- captured-actress-snehas-morphed-photos/

Bryant, P. (2009). Predicting Internet pornography use and arousal: The role of individual difference variables. *Journal of Sex Research, 46*, 344–357. doi:10.1080/00224490902754152

Citron, K. D. (2009a). Cyber civil rights. *Boston University Law Review. Boston University. School of Law, 89*(61), 69–75.

Citron, K. D. (2009b). Law's expressive value in combating cyber gender harassment. *Michigan Law Review, 108*, 373–415.

Daily Mail Reporter. (2009). *Oscar-winning composer, 71, raped 11 women using Craigslist to lure victims with promise of film role*. Retrieved on 28th April, 2010, from http://www.mailonsunday.co.uk/news/worldnews/ article-1195157/Oscar-winning-composer- Joseph-Brooks-raped-11-women-using-Craigslist-attract-victims-promise-film-role.html #ixzz0nywMfoeL 24th June 2009

Dowd, M. (August 25, 2009). Stung by the Perfect Sting. *New York Times*. Retrieved on 13th April 2010 from http://www.nytimes.com/2009/08 /26/opinion/26dowd.html

Fisher, B. S., Cullen, F. T., & Turner, M. G. (2002). Being pursued: Stalking victimization in a national study of college women. *Criminology & Public Policy, 1*, 257–308. doi:10.1111/j.1745-9133.2002.tb00091.x

Garland, D. (2008). On the concept of moral panic. *Crime, Media, and Culture, 4*(1), 9–30. doi:10.1177/1741659007087270

Halder, D. (2007). Cyber crime against women in India. *CyberLawTimes.com Monthly Newsletter, 2*(6), June 2007.

Halder, D., & Jaishankar, K. (2009). Cyber socializing and victimization of women. *Temida - The Journal on Victimization. Human Rights and Gender, 12*(3), 5–26.

Hinduja, S., & Patchin, J. W. (2008). Cyberbullying: An exploratory analysis of factors related to offending and victimization. *Deviant Behavior, 29*(2), 1–29. doi:10.1080/01639620701457816

Indian Express. (2009). *Harassment case against CCI top official*. Retrieved on 28th April, 2010, from http://www.indianexpress.com/news/ harassment-case-against-cci-top-official/452874/

Jaishankar, K. (2008). Space transition theory of cyber crimes. In Schmallager, F., & Pittaro, M. (Eds.), *Crimes of the Internet* (pp. 283–301). Upper Saddle River, NJ: Prentice Hall.

KMBC. (2010). *Woman claims ex is getting revenge online.* Retrieved on 28th April, 2010, from http://www.kmbc.com/news/ 22743556/detail.html

Levin, A. (2010). *I was caught in the seducer's net: It began with an internet date...now attractive divorcee Sara Terry is alone, stressed and £35,000 poorer.* Retrieved on 24th May, 2010, from http://www.mailonsunday.co.uk/femail/article- 1275558/I-caught-seducer-s-net-It-began-internet- date--attractive-divorcee-Sara-Terry-stressed-35- 000-poorer.html#ixzz0nyi32O6W

Martin, A. (2010). *Sky TV producer who stalked former classmate and Googled her name 40,000 times is jailed for only 16 weeks.* 19th January 2010. Retrieved on 28th April, 2010, from http://www.mailonsunday.co.uk/news/article-1244219/ TV-producer-stalked-classmate-Googled-40-000- times-jailed.html#ixzz0nylyLkJh

McGrath, J. (2009). *Theories of victimization: Victim precipitation, lifestyle, deviant place and routine activities.* April 29, 2009. Retrieved on July 10, 2009, from http://www.associatedcontent.com/article/ 1680773/theories_of_victimization_victim_ precipitation.html?cat=51

Melton, H. C. (2000). Stalking: A review of the literature and direction for the future. *Criminal Justice Review, 25,* 246–252. doi:10.1177/073401680002500206

Mustaine, E. E., & Tewsbury, R. (1999). A routine activity theory explanation of women's stalking victimization. *Violence Against Women, 5,* 43–62. doi:10.1177/10778019922181149

Palmer, C. (2010). *Cyberstalkers: Living with fear every minute of the day.* Retrieved on 17th November, 2010, from http://www.independent.ie/lifestyle/ cyberstalkers-living-with-fear-every-minute-of- the-day-2423762.html

Ruedy, C. M. (2008). MySpace Teen Suicide: Should Anti-Cyberbullying Law Be Created? *North Carolina Journal of Law and Technology, 9*(2), 323 - 346 (July 2008). Retrieved on 15th April 2010 from http://www.ncjolt.org/sites/default/ files/323-346_Ruedy_v9i2.pdf

Tark, J. Y. (2007). *Crime victims.* Retrieved on July 10, 2009, from http://www.fsu.edu/~crimdo/TA/ JONGYEON/finalvictim.htm

ThisisExeter. (2010). *Jail for bully who told women he would rape them.* Retrieved on 28th April, 2010, from http://www.thisisexeter.co.uk/news/Jail-bully- told-women-rape/article-1910438- detail/article.html

Wall, D. S. (2007). *Cybercrimes: The transformation of crime in the information age.* Cambridge, UK: Polity.

Wall, D. S. (2008). Cybercrime and the culture of fear: Social science fiction(s) and the production of knowledge about cybercrime. *Information Communication and Society, 11*(6), 861–884. doi:10.1080/13691180802007788

Working to Halt Online Abuse (WHOA). (2010). Cyber stalking statistics. Retrieved on 28th April, 2010, from http://www.haltabuse.org/resources/ stats/2010Statistics.pdf

ENDNOTES

[1] 'Meghnaada', who is also known as Indrajit, is the epic character of Ramayana. He was born to Lankan King Ravana and his queen Mandodori. Valmiki Ramayana describes him as a unique warrior among the Lankan princes who could hide himself behind the clouds and attack enemies off-guarded.

[2] 'Avatar' is a Sanskrit term, which is meant to describe reincarnation.

[3] See *"Space Transition Theory"* by Jaishankar (2008). "The theory is an explanation the nature of the behavior of the persons who bring out their conforming and non-conforming behavior in the physical space and cyberspace (Jaishankar, 2008, pp. 283-301). Space transition involves the movement of persons from one space to another (e.g., from physical space to cyberspace and vice versa). Space transition theory argues that, people behave differently when they move from one space to another. The postulates of the theory are: 1. *Persons, with repressed criminal behavior (in the physical space) have a propensity to commit crime in cyberspace, which, otherwise they would not commit in physical space, due to their status and position. 2. Identity Flexibility, Dissociative Anonymity and lack of deterrence factor in the cyberspace provides the offenders the choice to commit cyber crime. 3. Criminal behavior of offenders in cyberspace is likely to be imported to Physical space, which, in physical space may be exported to cyberspace as well. 4. Intermittent ventures of offenders in to the cyberspace and the dynamic spatio-temporal nature of cyberspace provide the chance to escape. 5(a). Strangers are likely to unite together in cyberspace to commit crime in the physical space. (b) Associates of physical space are likely to unite to commit crime in cyberspace. 6. Persons from closed society are more likely to commit crimes in cyberspace than persons from open society. 7. The conflict of Norms and Values of Physical Space with the Norms and Values of cyberspace m*ay lead to cyber crimes" (Jaishankar, 2008 pp. 283-301).

[4] From the experiences of the lead author as a counselor for cyber crime victims and cyber rights activist.

[5] From the personal experiences of the lead author as an advocate and counselor for cyber crime victims.

[6] These were real life experiences of one victim who contacted the lead author for legal help and preferred to remain anonymous. Source: personal telephonic conversations between the victim and the lead author.

[7] We have discussed these regulations in chapters 5, 6 and 7.

[8] See Table no.5 of the Baseline Survey Report (2010) on cyber victimization in India, available at http://www.cybervictims.org/CCVCresearchreport2010.pdf

[9] We have discussed on these types of crimes in chapter 2.

[10] See WHOA Statistics from 2000 to 2010 @ http://www.haltabuse.org/resources/stats/Cumulative2000-2010.pdf

[11] We have discussed it elaborately in later chapters.

[12] The contribution of search engines like the Google or yahoo cannot be over looked when discussing about cyber spaces where the crime takes place. However, we have not included search engines under this topics because they only lead to more victimization by directing the viewer to the particular site or the 'link'; they do not "host" the actual crime as the particular website where the crime has taken place.

[13] See supra @ 10

[14]   ibid

[15]   From the personal experiences of the lead author as a counselor for cyber crime victims and cyber right activist.

[16]   Fake profiles could be created by the harasser to portray impersonated profile of the victim, or could be created by the harasser to portray himself as a 'good friend'. The harasser can even use impersonated profiles to blackmail and/or cheat the victim to extract money.

[17]   See supra @ 10

[18]   See Halder, D., & Jaishankar, K. (2010). *Cyber Victimization in India: A Baseline Survey Report.* Tirunelveli, India: Centre for Cyber Victim Counselling; Available at http://www.cybervictims. org/CCVCresearchreport2010.pdf

Chapter 4
Women's Rights in the Cyber Space and the Related Duties

CHAPTER OVERVIEW

Rights of women in cyber space are as important as rights of women in physical space. In this chapter, both rights of women in cyber space and their related duties are placed with equal emphasis. Role of conventions, which support the rights of women in cyber space, their successes, their failures in the execution in cyberspace, are discussed. The importance of CEDAW and its execution in cyber space is strongly emphasized. Laws and constitutions of countries like USA, Canada and India are also analyzed. Various duties of women in cyber space is newly created and examined in-depth with a discussion.

4.1. INTRODUCTION

Crimes are the results of violations of rights of any kind. Cyber space is no exception to this rule. It is true that cyber space has no physical boundaries and as such, no strict rule / regulation belonging to any particular geographic region can regulate cyber space as a whole (Lessig, 1999). But at the same time, the essence of basic rights which have been embedded in various Charters on Human Rights, Conventions for protection of women's rights etc and which have been universally followed by many civilized, democratic countries to formulate domestic fundamental freedoms for citizens, suggest that basic fundamental rights of human beings, such as freedom of speech and expression, right to privacy, right to live a safe life etc, prevail universally both in the physical space as well as in the virtual space. But the big difference between the rights prevailing in the physical space and those prevailing in the

DOI: 10.4018/978-1-60960-830-9.ch004

virtual space lies in the modes of legal recognition of the same and acknowledgement of the violation of these rights. The issues of women's rights in the cyber space could be contributed largely to the sluggish modes of the governments in executing the gender equality and gender justice promises made by the States in the form of fundamental rights.

4.2 ROLE OF CONVENTIONS FOR ESTABLISHING WOMEN'S RIGHTS IN THE CYBER SPACE

Even though the International Covenant on Civil and Political Rights in Article 17 (1) states that "No one shall be subjected to arbitrary or unlawful interference with his privacy, family, home or correspondence, nor to unlawful attacks on his honor and reputation;" and Council of Europe convention for cyber crimes (2001) does protect human rights to a certain extent, we observe that there are no universal codes for specifically protecting women's rights in the cyber space. Most of the cyber crimes against women happen due to lack of recognition of women's rights and zero or less laws to protect women's interest in the cyber space. In this context, a mention must be made of "Convention on the Elimination of All Forms of Discrimination against Women", 1979. The primary aim of this convention was to eradicate discriminations against women and establish equality for women in the society.[1]

Article 2 of the Convention mentions that:

States Parties condemn discrimination against women in all its forms, agree to pursue by all appropriate means and without delay a policy of eliminating discrimination against women and, to this end, undertake: (a) To embody the principle of the equality of men and women in their national constitutions or other appropriate legislation if not yet incorporated therein and to ensure, through law and other appropriate means, the practical realization of this principle; (b) To adopt appropriate legislative and other measures, including sanctions where appropriate, prohibiting all discrimination against women; (c) To establish legal protection of the rights of women on an equal basis with men and to ensure through competent national tribunals and other public institutions the effective protection of women against any act of discrimination; (d) To refrain from engaging in any act or practice of discrimination against women and to ensure that public authorities and institutions shall act in conformity with this obligation; (e) To take all appropriate measures to eliminate discrimination against women by any person, organization or enterprise; (f) To take all appropriate measures, including legislation, to modify or abolish existing laws regulations, customs and practices which constitute discrimination against women; (g) To repeal all national penal provisions which constitute discrimination against women.[2]

This particular provision could be considered as the soul of the anti discriminatory provision in Article 1 of the convention. The convention opens with firm notes on defining what 'discrimination against women' shall mean in Article 1. To quote Article 1;

For the purposes of the present Convention, the term "discrimination against women" shall mean any distinction, exclusion or restriction made on the basis of sex which has the effect or purpose of impairing or nullifying the recognition, enjoyment or exercise by women, irrespective of their marital status, on a basis of equality of men and women, of human rights and fundamental freedoms in the political, economic, social, cultural, civil or any other field.[3]

Truly, this definition of discrimination against women suggests that government as well as non-governmental efforts is needed to establish equality between men and women. It is indeed accurate to point out that non-governmental social efforts mean the cultural practices, customary rituals etc which a society adheres to for long. The social practices give reasons to create laws and regulations. These regulations must be of that nature that they can successfully distinguish the pre and post state of affairs for good. The concept of 'gender equality' needed a universal recognition for future legal recognition in various countries and the Convention on the Elimination of All Forms of Discrimination against Women (CEDAW) successfully endorsed the said need. Article 3 and 4 further confirmed the inherent meaning of Article 2;

Article 3 pressurizes that:

States Parties shall take in all fields, in particular in the political, social, economic and cultural fields, all appropriate measures, including legislation, to en sure the full development and advancement of women, for the purpose of guaranteeing them the exercise and enjoyment of human rights and fundamental freedoms on a basis of equality with men;

And Article 4 emphasizes that:

Adoption by States Parties of temporary special measures aimed at accelerating de facto equality between men and women shall not be considered discrimination as defined in the present Convention, but shall in no way entail as a consequence the maintenance of unequal or separate standards; these measures shall be discontinued when the objectives of equality of opportunity and treatment have been achieved;[4]

Article 4 further mentions that Adoption by States Parties of special measures, including those measures contained in the present Convention, aimed at protecting maternity shall not be considered discriminatory.[5] It could be seen that Article 3 especially encourages the State parties to look after women's development in all possible forms besides creating rules and regulations. This Article along with Article 5 (a) may prepare the base for ensuring equality of women even in the cyber space.

Article 5 (a) states that

States Parties shall take all appropriate measures to modify the social and cultural patterns of conduct of men and women, with a view to achieving the elimination of prejudices and customary and all other practices which are based on the idea of the inferiority or the superiority of either of the sexes or on stereotyped roles for men and women.

We note that this 'social and cultural patterns' may include abuse of women or ridiculing women both by the society as well as by the law and justice machinery. It could be seen that the tendency of male - female verbal abuse in the cyber space, (as has been explained in Chapter 2) and the trail of such humiliation by the government reporting agencies (as has been mentioned in chapter 3), are the direct effects of age old patriarchal social practices against women's efforts to voice their opinions etc. Prohibitory laws may lay restrictions on human beings to cross the 'limits'. But when considering from fundamental freedoms of speech and expressions in the light of digital age, the object of such prohibitory laws may look like simple water marks which may be washed away by strong arguments for freedom of speech. From a feministic perspective, we note that this clash of legal debates may pose as the biggest obstacle

Figure 1. Prime objectives of CEDAW

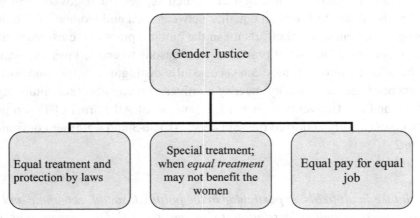

towards establishing equality of women in the cyber space. The hypothesis that is formed in this stage is: *In this era of internet, if the provisions of CEDAW are followed with a vision to ensure equality of women in the cyber space, the society could be influenced as a whole to reduce the rate victimization of women online*. The following segment tests our hypothesis.

4.3 EXPANDING THE AIMS OF THE CONVENTIONS TO THE CYBER SPACE

A brief examination of the provisions of the CEDAW would show that this convention's aim in establishing equal gender justice has three prime objectives which are elaborated in Figure 1.

It could therefore be seen that in the first case, the primary aim is to guarantee equal treatment and protection by laws for safeguarding basic needs of life, viz., education, health, exercising fundamental rights such as speech and expression, privacy and right to lead to dignified life. In the second case, the convention aims to guarantee "special treatment" in case the physical disparity or familial duties bars the women from getting equal treatment / protection of the laws, for example maternity benefits, special time-frames for working mothers of infant or under-age children, protection for physical and / emotional abuse both in the work place as well as at home etc. In the third case, the convention aims to guarantee equal right to financial security in the form of "equal pay for equal job". This convention was considered as the foundation for many democratic nations to build women's rights agendas. Constitutions of these nations, who adhered to the CEDAW principles, were strengthened with provisions for equal rights and laws were made for providing extra protection to women to fulfill the goals of the CEDAW. For example, Article 14 of the constitution of India guarantees equal protection of law for every one[6] and Article 15 of the constitution prohibits the State to discriminate between citizens on ground of religion, race, caste, sex, place of birth etc.[7] The provisions of CEDAW are further carried out through Article 15(3) of the constitution which says "Nothing in this article shall prevent the State from making any special provision for women and children."[8] Hence, it can be seen that many laws and regulations are made to safeguard Indian women's interest, the more prominent of which are Indecent representation of women (prohibition) Act, 1986; Section 509 of the Indian Penal Code which prohibits inflicting injury or harm against women's modesty etc; laws to protect interest of women in marriage;[9] equal payment to men and women for equal work,[10] etc.

Similarly, the Canadian Charter of Rights and freedoms guarantees equal protection of laws for men and women under Section 15. It says:

Every individual is equal before and under the law and has the right to the equal protection and equal benefit of the law without discrimination and, in particular, without discrimination based on race, national or ethnic origin, colour, religion, sex, age or mental or physical disability.[11]

Further, the Section also guarantees special care for those who are in need of the same in subsection 2. It thus says:

Subsection (1) does not preclude any law, program or activity that has as its object the amelioration of conditions of disadvantaged individuals or groups including those that are disadvantaged because of race, national or ethnic origin, colour, religion, sex, age or mental or physical disability.[12]

The charter further strengthens women's rights in section 28 which says: "Notwithstanding anything in this Charter, the rights and freedoms referred to in it are guaranteed equally to male and female persons."[13] Basing upon this 1982 Charter, the Canadian judiciary had taken many important steps to safeguard women's rights and interest.[14] *R. v. Butler*, [1992][15] had been a landmark case which established legalities and illegalities of pornography. It was held that prohibition against pornography violates freedom of expression. But at the same time, when pornography is of that nature that it "tends to corrupt the morals of the society", Section 163(8) of the Canadian Criminal Code which prohibits pornography of violent nature, can be justified and the offender can be booked under the same law.[16] The decision turned to be a huge booster for the ongoing feminist move against pornography and publication of unconsented sexual activities (Majury, 2002).

Australia also ratified CEDAW and had made several changes in its legislatures to respect equality of women.[17] To give a few examples, Sex Discrimination Act, 1984 was amended by The Human Rights and Equal Opportunity Legislation Amendment Act (No. 2) 1992 influenced by the CEDAW. The legislation simplified the procedure to establish victimization by sexual harassment by emphasizing on the "fear factor" of the victim over the behavior of the harasser.[18] The said law was meant to cover sexual discrimination on the basis of gender, marital status, pregnancy etc and all sorts of discriminations and harassments in the home, educational institutions, workplace, health care institutions etc. Along with these laws, portrayal of women in the print and audio-visual media was also touched upon with the introduction of Code of Practice in 1993 in accordance with Australian Broadcasting Corporation Act, 1983. This was aimed to prohibit portrayal of women in a manner which "degenerates" women's status and rights in the society etc.[19]

UK in its 6th periodic report in accordance with the ratification of CEDAW, had also implemented several new policy guidelines, created new legislations and amended the existing laws for the betterment of gender equality in workplace, education, science and information technology, health, social and monetary security. However, prevention of sexual harassment and equal monetary benefits had remained the most preferred tasks for the UK government under this agenda. Hence, the government had taken special care for enacting various laws. The Equality Act, 2006, that established Commission for Equality and Human Rights. The Sex Discrimination Act, 1975, and the Public Authorities (Statutory Duties) Order, 2006 which ensures public authority's duty towards establishing gender equality and prevention of discrimination on any ground including gender, language, religious belief etc. The Equal Pay Act, 1970

(Amendment) Regulations 2003, and Sex Discrimination Act, 1975 (Amendment) Regulations 2003, for ensuring women's right to equal pay as well as prohibiting any sort of sexual harassment while in or even outside the workplace by employees or colleagues.[20] Other mentionable legislations which were created for eradication of discrimination for women are Criminal Justice Act, 2003 and Sexual Offences Act, 2003, etc. Both these legislations are aimed to mete out justice to victims of physical violence as well as sexual harassment by accepting evidence of "bad character" and previous sexual offences as evidences. The later provision especially broadened definitions of sexually violative activities.[21]

US, on the contrary, have not ratified the CEDAW.[22] US, as such have no specific guarantees for women's rights. The Equal rights amendment, which proposes to guarantee equal right to men and women, was first proposed in 1923. It still waits to be ratified by States.[23] The issues of equality are universally covered by the Fourteenth amendment to the constitution which says "no state shall... deny to any person within its jurisdiction the equal protection of the laws".[24] However, in a landmark case of *Roe vs. Wade*[25] women's rights were to a certain extent established when the court upheld woman's right towards her body and decision to abort. This decision was inspired by right to privacy which stemmed out from right to equality guaranteed under the Fourteenth amendment.[26] In 2005, Violence against Women and Department of Justice Reauthorization Act of 2005 came into effect, which remains a prime safeguard to women's right against violence and abuse. This Act modified relevant chapters of Title 18 of the Federal penal code considerably to regulate violence against women from domestic front, dating relationship and workplace sexual harassments; women's right to healthcare and shelter, child care and also single parent status etc.[27] This Act considerably covered cyber stalking as a part of violence against women.[28]

We note that even though many countries including those that have been discussed above, have amended their constitution or existing legislations or created new laws to safeguard women's rights, barely any country has made specific rules / regulations / laws etc to protect women's rights in the cyber space. Most countries have either stretched gender neutral laws to cover rights in the cyber space or have created new laws for the cyber space basing on the existing laws, which may not always help to preserve women's rights in the cyber space. It is painful to note that CEDAW's guidelines are quite neglected when making laws/charters for women in the cyber space.

4.4 WOMEN'S RIGHTS IN THE CYBER SPACE: AN ILLUSION?

Considering from the view points of the drafters of CEDAW,[29] International covenant on civil and political rights,[30] International covenant on economic social and cultural rights,[31] Council of Europe convention for the protection of human rights and fundamental freedoms[32] and Council of Europe's convention on cyber crime[33] etc, it could be seen that women's rights in the cyber space is nothing but a mirage. All these conventions guarantee equal rights for men and women in economic, social, political, cultural spheres. The EU convention, especially meant for regulation of cyber space, has secured child's right in the cyber space with a considerable success in the last couple of years. Sadly, human rights for women have been grossly abused in the cyber space both by the state parties as well as by individual internet users.

Our argument can be well supported by the country based statistical data of victimization of individuals in the cyber space, available in the internet,[34] various news reports, case studies etc of painstaking stories of women victims on cyber crime, some of which we have showcased in different chapters of this book through the examination of domestic cyber related laws of various countries.[35] Unless women's rights in the cyber space are identified, the saga of abusing women in the digital space will continue. Following

CEDAW's guidelines for creation of separate policy guidelines for women towards preventing abuse of rights, we can assert that women's rights in the cyber space can be created and it may not clash with the fundamental freedoms of men as well as women as has been feared by many.

We will specify the 'fear' of 'clash of interests' for securing women's rights in the cyber space as mentioned in the above paragraph, in the light of two feministic ideas; MacKinnon's ideologies against pornography[36] and Citron's (2009a, 2009b) views towards abusive communications against women in the cyber space.

Cyber space is used for simplifying communication. 'Communication' in this context is often construed in its broadest meaning which also includes human behaviors while communicating. Such human behavior tends to get corrupted especially when sexuality of women is involved and there are constant clash of fundamental freedoms and interests of women. By judging the precedents set by various reported cases, it could be seen that cyber crime against women can be of varied nature, but the inherent motive often remains misogyny and sexual exploitation of women.[37]

Feminist scholar Catherine MacKinnon started a campaign against sexual abuse of women through adult pornography and urged the US federal as well as provincial governments and the society as a whole, to consider the making / distributing / viewing of pornographic images, video clippings etc using women, as abuse of women's rights to equality. While anti-pornography group welcomed her views, MacKinnon had to face severe criticism from anti-feminist groups on the ground that she was trying to 'misbalance' the concept of individual fundamental freedom of speech and expression. Judging her ideologies, we agree that violent pornography using women and also unconsenting pornography may violate women's right to equal treatment, right to privacy, right to safe and secure life etc. According to MacKinnon, pornography formed an abuse of right to freedom of speech and expression. She specified that sexual fantasies of men especially by viewing women in the pornographic materials, might lead to abuse and physical torture of women in real life. She argued that pornography terms women in general as a sex symbol. Critics of MacKinnon felt that she was trying to obstruct individual's sexual rights which also include sexual fantasies.

We must remember that Mackinnon started her anti-pornography campaign in 1980's when communication was not as 'cyber' as it is now, and in this cyber era unfortunately her fear has turned quite true. When judging the trends of victimizing women in the cyber space, we have seen that the ways of harassing women may be new; for example, modification of her personal data, stalking, abusive communication, digital sexual abuse etc. But, the inherent motive remains ridiculing the woman victim based on her sexuality.[38] In this digital age, the concept of pornography and also obscenity is no more limited to books, print publications, adult cartoons, adult films with nude models and sexual activities of such models; but it has become a way of harassing women and exploitation of women's rights to safe and secure life in the cyber space. Further, by the term 'pornography' here we do not intend to limit our discussions only on obscenity as has been construed by many while discussing about pornography; rather we intend to cover pornography by its true meaning different from obscenity[39] and also 'obscenity' as has been legally defined.[40]

Citron (2009a, 2009b) showcased misuse of cyber communication by way of abusive, taunting language towards women; availing of anonymous cloak to attack women in the cyber space and failure of US laws to protect the interest of women in the cyber space. Citron pointed out that nothing but recognition of cyber gender harassment as gender discrimination can only bring down cyber victimization of women. She correctly opined that US concept of fundamental freedoms, in particular, the right to free speech and expression and judiciary's broader outlooks to interpret the same needs to be readjusted for upholding women's safety and interest in the cyber space.

It could be seen that what Mackinnon started as an agenda for women's rights in pre-cyber socializing era, Citron (2009a, 2009b) endorsed the same in the cyber socializing era. While the former saw adult pornography as an abuse of women's rights, the later confirmed that harassment by way of sexually teasing communications forms gender discrimination and this also includes crossing the limits of civil rights. The above discussion strongly defends our argument for creating a charter of rights for women in the cyber space. But before we formulate the charter of rights, it is essential to know what is meant by the concept of 'cyber rights of women'.

Godwin (1998) explained how constitutional guarantees for freedom of speech and expression may be extended to the cyber space. He addressed the extended free speech and the defenses to the same in the internet, problems of unlimited, unregulated speech and communication, problems of copyrights in the internet era, internet pornography and apprehended consequences of the same on 'free speech' movement in the US. This work of Godwin was one of its' first kind to establish that cyber rights exist and they are built upon the fundamental rights guaranteed by the international conventions on human rights. Logically speaking, cyber rights for women therefore can be carved out from the equality provisions guaranteed by the international conventions and also CEDAW. Hence considering from this viewpoint, we define 'cyber rights for women' as a *conglomeration of those fundamental human rights which guarantees a safe life to women in the cyber space.* By 'safe life' we signify a cyber-life which is protected against all sorts of gender abuses; which further includes verbal and also sexual abuse, abuse of general human rights like right to privacy, equal treatment, maintenance of good reputation, right to safety outside the cyber space and also right against gender discrimination towards equal protection of laws. In other words, the functional definition of cyber rights for women may mean the following:

1. Safe and protected cyber –life;
2. Rights against cyber gender harassments including online vandalism (Citron2009 a) of the virtual identity of the woman, sexually motivated or even non-sexual revengeful activities like hacking and modification of computer data specially maintained for online communications and other online purposes, modification and misusing of personal pictures of women, online abusive communications, including sending threatening mails or reaching out to peers to torment the reputation of the woman both in virtual space as well as in the real space etc;
3. Right to be recognized as a victim of cyber crime; equal treatment for legal protection against cyber crimes; right to privacy, speech and expression, free cyber movement, right to defend one's reputation in the cyberspace;
4. Right to have gender centric cyber crime preventive laws.

The above definition of 'cyber rights for women' may be used for securing justice for women victims of cyber crimes that are categorized in Chapter 2. This definition would also be useful to form a charter of model cyber rights for women.[41]

The aims and objectives of CEDAW and the fundamental rights guaranteed to human beings by Charters of Human rights could be achieved only when rights are supported by obligations. When we speak about the rights of women in the cyber space, it is essential to know that neither the users nor the developers of the internet services or the Internet service providers can excuse themselves from the "Rule of laws"[42] as in real life all individuals are bound by their respective domestic laws (Sujor,

2011). This necessarily creates responsibilities for the internet users including men and women which are analyzed in the next segment.

4.5 DUTIES OF NETIZENS

Rights imply duties and cyber space is no exception. Hence from earlier discussions on human rights and conventions of cyber crimes, we have deducted certain basic duties which needs to be carried out by both women and men netizens. These are as follows:

1. **To live and let live:** The best safety norm in the cyber space should be "live and let live". As we have shown earlier in this book, the victim-turned cyber offenders pose the biggest threat to the cyber space, who might have faced hardship and trauma due to someone else's misdeeds. Cyber space could be a real safe haven to breath afresh only when men and women live their own lives without disturbing others.

2. **Maintaining decency in the internet:** One must realize, to survive in the cyber space he or she must not cross the limits of decency. Cyber space should no way substitute real-space sex markets (Selwyn, 2008; Citron, 2009a). This implies the duty of the users to maintain decency both in the manner they opt for snap shots for showcasing themselves in the internet, as well as the language they use to communicate with absolute strangers. Maintaining decency prevents lustrous provocation and there by helps to create a safe environment for both women as well as men in the internet.

3. **Restrain from using abusive / hate / teasing words:** People entering the virtual world should never make it a battle-front (Boyd, 2008) using words as their weapons. Enmity between individuals in the real world should not be expressed in the virtual world in forms of blogs, social networking wall messages, emails, articles or even expressions through digital images.

4. **Using the electronic options to avoid further harassment:** Even when one crosses his or her limits of decency in the internet, the other person at the receiving end must not aggravate the situation by counter attacking or harassing the other person. He or she must use available electronic options like blocking the harasser, changing the profile name (in case of social networking websites or online chat rooms), renewing his / her profile, complaining to the concerned website authorities in case of defamatory statements published in the website or even copyright violations.[43] It is the duty of every people in the internet to see that the "internet culture" does not over shadow the norms of humanity in real as well as virtual life.

5. **Teaching children the norms of cyber culture:** It is needless to say, Internet has become a part of our every day lives. The cyber-generation children therefore must be taught the basic cyber values. According to Jayne Hitchcock, President, WHOA (Working for Halt Online Abuse), it is the prime duty of the parents of the kids belonging to cyber-generation to teach their children about cyber culture and further she opines: "they need to learn as much of it themselves as they can. If they don't know how to use something online, either have someone show them how to do it or take a class"[44]. The children below the age group of 13 must also be taught the dangerous part of the cyber culture, namely how not to involve in the "game" of adult pornography. They must be warned about such sites either by their parents or by their teachers or peers. This must be considered as a 'duty' towards prevention of cyber victimization of women, because many often it can be seen that young adults or teens from the age group of 15-18 get highly influenced by their

'cyber predecessors' to experiment with their cyber knowledge. Reported cases on victimization of female teachers by teenage students in the cyber space (European Trade Union Committee for Education, 2010), growing trends of teen / adult sexting (Sweetback, 2010) etc prove that these hi-tech young members of the society may turn into potential cyber perpetrators in due course.

6.   **Restrain from using the computer as well as the internet as a tool to amuse oneself by playing pranks with others:** Men, women and children must understand that cyber space is not an "amusement park" or "family get-together" where people can play pranks with strangers or even known acquaintances to amuse oneself. One must restrain oneself from mocking, teasing, bullying others, playing with personal snapshots of others or even personal reputation of others. It is only when we know our limits in the internet, our rights could be preserved.

7.   **Help the needy:** It is but essential that when a victim of cyber crime tries to reach out to his / her friends through internet or by other means of communication, the person at the receiving end must attend the SOS. He or she could refer the matter to a cyber crime counselor, cyber police cell, help centers or even the concerned website authorities. In other ways, we suggest that awareness about cyber crime, rights and rules and regulations must be spread by the internet users themselves. One must encourage others to report crime and not shy away in fear of loss of reputation.

8.   **Maintaining law and order in and outside the cyber space:** It is the duty of every internet user to maintain law and order not only in the cyber space but also outside the virtual world. Enmity between net acquaintances must not be brought outside the virtual world and neither cyber space should be used as a tool to commit heinous crimes in the real world.

9.   **Duties of the Internet service providers:** Along with the individual internet users, internet service providers (ISP) are also duty bound to make the cyber space safe for women. Almost all the ISPs follow the "safe harbor policy"[45] while framing their rights and responsibilities. Even though the ISPs may get exempted from the tortuous liabilities following Section 230 of the Communication Decency Act, this does not spare them from responsibilities to keep a watch on the deviant behavior of users (Sujor, 2011). The rights and responsibilities of every website must clearly clarify the user's limitations and expected code of conducts[46] and at the same time, the ISPs must not encourage victimization of women in the name of free speech (Citron, 2009b). The ISPs must also respond to the victim's calls for help in time to prevent escalations of victimization.

4.6 CONCLUSION

Rights and duties must be made to execute the same. Truly, absence of a universal codified charter of rights and duties for the cyber space creates a vacuum, which cyber criminals aptly use to fulfill their ulterior motives. Internet has entered in our daily life so swiftly and so deeply that we must consider it as an extended part of our life. Rights and duties as well as laws to protect and implement them, are but essential to protect the virtual life including cyber reputation and ancillary cyber rights of every woman as well as man in the cyber space.

In our next chapter when we would discuss about internet laws for women, it would be seen that certain common provisions exist in almost all the laws of various nations. Researchers may ask *why should there be uniform laws for the internet*. If the question arose in the era when internet was being used mainly for the commercial purposes, the prompt answer could be "for a smooth operation of e-commerce". But we must remember that we conceived this book in an era which is almost a decade old since the first EU convention on cyber crime was held in 2001.

REFERENCES

Boyd, D. (2008). Why youth social network sites: The role of networked publics in teenage social life. In D. Buckingham (Ed.), *Youth, identity, and digital media* (pp. 119–142). The John D. and Catherine T. MacArthur Foundation Series on Digital Media and Learning. Cambridge, MA: The MIT Press.

Cavazos, E. A., & Morin, G. (1994). *Cyberspace and the law: Your rights and duties in the on-line world*. Cambridge, MA: The MIT Press.

Citron, K. D. (2009a). Cyber civil rights. *Boston University Law Review, 89*(61), 69–75.

Citron, K. D. (2009b). Law's expressive value in combating cyber gender harassment. *Michigan Law Review, 108*, 373–415.

Convention for the Protection of Human Rights and Fundamental Freedoms. (1950). *As amended by protocols 11 and 14*. Retrieved from http://conventions.coe.int/Treaty/ EN/Treaties/html/005.htm

Convention on the Elimination of All Forms of Discrimination against Women. (1979). *Women Watch Convention*. Retrieved from http://www.un.org/womenwatch/daw/ cedaw/text/econvention.htm

Council of Europe. (2001). *Convention on cybercrime*, Budapest, 2001. Retrieved on 3rd March, 2010, from http://conventions.coe.int/Treaty/ EN/Treaties/html/185.htm

European Trade Union Committee for Education. (2010). *Cyber harassment against teachers. How to prevent cyber harassment at school?* Retrieved on February 18, 2010, from http://teachersosh.homestead.com/Publications/ Final_report_cyber-harassment_seminar_EN.pdf

Gavison, R. (1984). Privacy and the limits of law. In F. Schoeman (Ed.), *Philosophical dimensions of privacy: An anthology* (pp. 75-103). New York, NY: Cambridge.

Godwin, M. (1998). *Cyber rights: Defending free speech in the digital age*. New York, NY: Times Books.

Hauben, M. (1996). *Netizens: On the History and Impact of Usenet and the Internet*. Retrieved on February 18, 2010, from http://www.columbia.edu/~rh120/

International Covenant on Civil and Political Rights. (1966). Retrieved from http://www2.ohchr.org/english/law/ccpr.htm

International Covenant on Economic Social and Cultural Rights. (1966). Retrieved from http://www2.ohchr.org/ english/law/cescr.htm

Lessig, L. (1999). *Code and other laws of cyber space*. London, UK: Routledge.

Majury, D. (2002). The charter, equality rights, and women: Equivocation and celebration. *Osgoode Hall Law Journal, 40*(3 & 4), 298–334.

Selwyn, N. (2008). A safe haven for misbehaving? An investigation of online misbehavior among university students. *Social Science Computer Review*, *26*(4), 446–465. doi:10.1177/0894439307313515

Spinello, R. A. (2006). *Cyberethics: Morality and law in cyberspace* (3rd ed.). Boston, MA: Jones and Bartlett Publications.

Suzor, N. (forthcoming 2011). The role of the rule of law in virtual communities. *Berkeley Technology Law Journal*. Retrieved on April 22, 2011, from http://works.bepress.com/cgi/viewcontent.cgi?article=1004&context=suzor

Sweetback, S. (2010). *Another woman claims that Tony Parker was sexting her*. Retrieved on October 22, 2010, from http://hellobeautiful.com/gossip-news/sweet-sweetback/ tony-parker-was-sexting-another-woman/

ENDNOTES

[1] For more information see Introduction - Para of the 'Convention on the elimination of all forms of discrimination against women. Url: http://www.un.org/womenwatch/daw/cedaw/cedaw.htm

[2] ibid

[3] Article 1 of the Convention on the elimination of all forms of discrimination against women.

[4] Article 4(1) of the Convention on the elimination of all forms of discrimination against women.

[5] Article 4(2) of the Convention on the elimination of all forms of discrimination against women.

[6] Article 14 of the Indian constitution says "The State shall not deny to any person equality before the law or the equal protection of the laws within the territory of India". Available at page 6 of "the Constitution of India" @ http://lawmin.nic.in/coi/coiason29july08.pdf Accessed on 20.05.2010.

[7] Article 15 (1) says that "The State shall not discriminate against any citizen on grounds only of religion, race, caste, sex, place of birth or any of them". Available at page 7 of "the Constitution of India" @ http://lawmin.nic.in/coi/coiason29july08.pdf Accessed on 20.05.2010.

[8] ibid

[9] For more information see Chapter XX and XX-A of the Indian Penal Code.

[10] For more information see Equal Remunerations Act 1976 and also Mackinnon Mackenzie and Co. Ltd. vs. Audrey D'Costa and Others (1987) 2 SCC 469, Available at http://www.paycheck.in/main/articles-archives/equal-pay-for-equal-work#r2 Accessed on 20.05.2010.

[11] Section 15(1) of the Canadian Charter of freedoms and rights. Available at http://www.cejamericas.org/doc/legislacion/constituciones/can-rights-freedoms.pdf Accessed on 20.05.2010.

[12] Section 15(2), for more information, see Supra @ 11.

[13] Section 28, Charter of rights and freedoms, available at http://www.cejamericas.org/doc/legislacion/constituciones/can-rights-freedoms.pdf

[14] See *R. v. Morgentaler* [1993] 3 S.C.R. 463 for abortion rights for women; *M. v. H.* [1999] 2 S.C.R. 3, for rights of Lesbian couples. etc.

[15] 1 S.C.R. 452

[16] For more information see Obscenity: the decision of the supreme court of Canada in R. v. Butler, available at http://dsp-psd.pwgsc.gc.ca/Collection-R/LoPBdP/BP/bp289-e.htm

17   For more information see http://www.un.org/esa/gopher-data/ga/cedaw/17/country/Australia/C-AUL3.EN

18   ibid

19   ibid

20   For more information see http://daccess-dds-ny.un.org/doc/UNDOC/GEN/N07/398/67/PDF/N0739867.pdf?OpenElement

21   ibid

22   For more information see country reports on CEDAW. Available at http://www.un.org/womenwatch/daw/cedaw/reports.htm

23   Equal rights amendment, available at http://www.equalrightsamendment.org/

24   Fourteenth amendment to the US constitution.

25   410 U.S. 113 (1973)

26   Roe v. Wade. Available at http://www.law.cornell.edu/supct/html/historics/USSC_CR_0410_0113_ZS.html

27   For more information see "Violence against Women and Department of Justice Reauthorization Act of 2005".

28   We have discussed about it in detail in the later chapters.

29   Convention on the Elimination of All Forms of Discrimination against Women, 1979. The text is available at http://www.un.org/womenwatch/daw/cedaw/text/econvention.htm

30   International Covenant on Civil and Political Rights, 1966. The text is available at http://www2.ohchr.org/english/law/ccpr.htm

31   International Covenant on Economic, Social and Cultural Rights, 1966. The text is available at http://www2.ohchr.org/english/law/cescr.htm

32   Convention for the Protection of Human Rights and Fundamental Freedoms, 1950; as amended by Protocols No. 11 and No. 14. The text is available at http://conventions.coe.int/Treaty/EN/Treaties/html/005.htm

33   Council of Europe. (2001). Convention on Cybercrime, Budapest, 23.XI.2001, Text available at http://conventions.coe.int/Treaty/EN/Treaties/html/185.htm

34   See 2009 cyber stalking statistics of WHOA, available at http://www.haltabuse.org/resources/stats/2009Statistics.pdf; also see "The Garlic UK Cyber crime report, 2009", prepared by Stefan Fafinski and Neshan Minassian of Invenio Research, September 2009, available at http://www.garlik.com/cybercrime_report.php

35   Some of these laws are discussed in later chapters.

36   See Supra @14

37   See previous chapter on the discussion on motives.

38   We have discussed this broadly in Chapter 3.

39   See our discussions on pornography in chapter 2 on patterns of victimization of women in the cyber space.

40   See Miller v. California, 413 U.S. 15 (1973).

41   We have formed a model charter in Chapter 10.

42   The theory of "Rule of laws" was popularized by British Jurist A.V Dicey in 1885 in his book *An Introduction to the Study of the Law of the Constitution (1885)*. He analyzed the maxim from three angles, namely: no one can be punished except for breach of law proved in the court; no one

is above the law and every one equal before the law; the general principles on the constitutional rights of individuals are the results of judicial decisions.

43   See Online safety brochure of WHOA, available @ http://www.haltabuse.org/onlinesafety.PDF

44   This information was gathered from a private conversation with Jayne Hitchcock by the authors in March 2009.

45   See Digital Millennium Copyrights Act, 1997.

46   See http://www.facebook.com/help/?page=798. Also see http://www.myspace.com/index.cfm?fuseaction=cms.viewpage&placement=safety_pagetipshttp://www.myspace.com/index.cfm?fuseaction=misc.termshttp://www.google.com/privacypolicy.html

Chapter 5
Legal Treatment of Cyber Crimes Against Women in USA

CHAPTER OVERVIEW

US, is one country, which started the evolution of the Internet and also the first to be affected and the first to retaliate to the ugly side of the Internet, the cyber crimes. US saw a sea of growth in the cyber crimes against women and created new laws to mitigate such crime and prevent future victimization. In this chapter, we discuss about various laws developed by the US to prevent cyber victimization of women as well as conventional laws that were applied to protect women in cyber space. Regulation of crimes in cyber space such as cyber bullying, cyber stalking are examined in detail. The issue of privacy in cyber space vis-à-vis the laws related to that are identified and analyzed.

5.1 INTRODUCTION

The United States of America evidenced rapid growth of the internet and the subsequent eruption of cyber crimes. Also in the US a surge in the cyber crimes against women was seen in the new millennium. As per the WHOA statistics of 2000,[1] among 353 respondents, 87% victims of cyber crime were females and 68% of the harassers are male and only 27% harassers were females. As per this statistics, the victimization begun mostly through emails (39.5%), message boards (17.5%) and also chat rooms (15.5%), other than Instant Messaging (IM) or websites. The 2009-2010 statistics of WHOA shows that among 349 respondents, women victims still remained a majority who formed 73% of the victim ratio. Only 27% men were reported to be harassed. The statistics showed that 44.5% harassers were male and

DOI: 10.4018/978-1-60960-830-9.ch005

36% of the harassers were females. The major crime hubs still remained email communications (34%); followed by Instant Messaging (IM), chat rooms etc.[2]

The policies and terms of the various US hosted internet service providers[3] highlight the fact that freedom of speech and expression, as has been guaranteed in the First Amendment, is given highest priority when regulating "offending" contents in the sites (Citron, 2009b). Various literature reviews would show that the birth of various cyber crime regulating laws in the US, were marked by huge debates over probable clashes of constitutional rights and confusions. Laws were created one after another, publicly debated over their practical usability and constitutionality; some stood the acid test of judicial accountability by the Supreme Court, some didn't. However, none was created with a sole purpose to safeguard women's interests in the internet. In the following segment we will analyze the applicability of existing penal laws for the cause of prevention of online victimization of women.

5.2 REGULATIONS FOR MODIFICATION OF CONTENTS AND RELATED ACTIVITIES

Hacking when described in legal terms in the US, may mean unauthorized access to computer as a machine, the computer network, the data stored therein and modification of such data. Hacking in general is regulated by the Computer Fraud and Abuse Act, which is again encompassed by Title 18, USC 1030. A brief examination of the provisions therein will show that this particular legislation is made for national security and protecting financial frauds. As such, this Act safeguards "protected computers" more and not private individual's private data excluding those stored for government purposes.[4] Hence, hacking email ids, personal websites, modifying and misusing them etc, are considered more as invasion to privacy of common cyber users where unauthorized access to computer data and modification of the same are used as tools. As such, personal information of women stored in personal computers, websites, social networking profiles, email data, blog profiles etc are highly sorted after targets by miscreants, online harassers and those who set up personal enmity with the female victim(s) due to her ideologies or romantic breakups or even professional as well as personal ego-clashes. The hacking of the email id of the former Alaska Governor Sarah Palin, the then US Vice-Presidential nominee, could be taken as prime paradigm of victimization of women based on the above mentioned issues. Her Yahoo account was breached and private emails were posted online by a college student (O'Connell, 2008).

In such cases Section 2701 of Chapter 121, USC 18 (Part 1) may be applied as a preventive legislation which makes it an offence when a person (a) intentionally accesses without authorization, a facility through which an electronic communication service is provided, or in other words attacks the computer and computer networks as a whole and disrupts the right to use the electronic communications; or (b) intentionally exceeds an authorization to access that facility, or in other words hacks and cracks in other's data without the owner's permission; However, it is interesting to note how the language of the second paragraph of this provision suggests punishment depending upon the motive of the accused. As such, when the 'offence' is done with a motive to gain for "commercial purposes, malicious destruction or damage, or private commercial gain, or in furtherance of any criminal or tortuous act in violation of the Constitution or laws of the United States or any State", which may very well justify cases of hacking and morphing female victim's pictures and information for online commercial adult entertainment industry, or even defamation of the female victim and humiliating her in front of large internet audience etc. The law provides monetary fine and imprisonment sentence ranging from 5 to 10 years.[5] In other cases when such activities are not done for the purposes as stated above, and done for rather teasing the victim, harassing etc, the law provides punishment with fine and imprisonment which may range to 1 to 5 years depending upon whether the offence is a first offence or has been committed after a conviction.[6] Thus, it could be seen that both civil as well as criminal remedies are available for offences of this nature. However, it will depend upon the prosecution largely to establish the case as fit for civil or criminal remedy. These legislations may play as safety valves along with the principles of First Amendment limitations when hacking is done for furtherance of defamation including tampering the document and publishing the hacked content for portraying the victim in an indecent manner and labeling the victim in obscene fashion. Nonetheless, scale of victimization for the female victims increases when in such cases the federal laws underestimate the female victim's pains and shift the burden of proof on the victim (Citron, 2009b) to establish the infringement of her basic rights.

5.3 REGULATIONS FOR STALKING

Since the beginning of 90's, the United States Congress had been experimenting with numerous laws to prevent cyber stalking and related harassment. Cyber stalking got its first formal legal recognition in the US through Michigan Criminal Code, in 1993. This provision introduced to the term "harassment" from a new angle to cover stalking related activities. Harassment was thus defined as "conduct directed toward a victim that includes repeated or continuing unconsented contact, that would cause a reasonable individual to suffer emotional distress, and that actually causes the victim to suffer emotional distress".[7] Unconsented contact meant sending unsolicited and unwanted mail or electronic communications to the victim.[8] Even though the statute never defined "cyber stalking" with its practical and functional meanings, the Act touched the characteristics of the term "cyber stalking".

It is notable that offline stalking was long recognized in the US, and California Penal Code was the first provision to recognize harassment via telecommunication (excluding internet) as a penal offence. This was the first anti-stalking legislation of the US, and it charged a person guilty of stalking when the accused "willfully and maliciously and repeatedly follow or harass another person and make credible threats with the intent to place that person in reasonable fear for his or her safety or that of an immediate family member".[9] Following Michigan, many other states also amended the then existed laws and enacted new laws to cover cyber stalking. As such, the Alabama Code under section 13A-11-8 penalizes any harassment, threat to harass and harassing communications[10] conveyed to the victim by means of "telephone, telegraph, mail, or any other form of written or electronic communication, in a manner likely to harass or cause alarm".[11]

Similarly the Alaska Code in section 13-2921 also penalizes harassment when it is done anonymously or otherwise the harasser communicates or causes a communication with another person by verbal, electronic, mechanical, telegraphic, telephonic or written means in a manner that cause harassment.[12] The Arkansas Code in section 5-41-108 explains that, a person commits the offense of unlawful computerized communications:

if with the purpose to frighten, intimidate, threaten, abuse, or harass another person, he sends a message on an electronic mail or other computerized communication system with the reasonable expectation that the person will receive the message and in that message threatens to cause physical injury to any person or damage to the property of any person.[13]

The California Civil Code also discusses the problem of stalking under section 1708.7[14] and makes a harasser liable for stalking for carrying on harassing / threatening /abusive communications through electronic communications along with other ways of conveying the message of harassment. Section 422 of California Penal Code stretches the liability of stalking and prescribes punishment of one year imprisonment for individuals who willfully threaten to commit a crime which may result in bodily hurt, grievous hurt to the victim directly or to the immediate family members of the victims; such harasser is also liable to be punished when such threatening, which may also be through electronic communications, successfully generates fear.[15]

5.3.1 The Confusion Between the Terms "Cyber Stalking" and "Cyber Harassment"

Similar laws as those provisions discussed above were created by various States of the US to prevent and protect harassment through information technology. None of these Acts mention the term "cyber stalking" and we consider it as a glaring loophole. In most of these statutes, the existing provisions for 'harassments' have been amended to adjust the legal needs for prevention of cyber stalking. We agree with the fact that cyber stalking may include certain essential characteristics of harassment which could be online as well as offline. The online characteristics include shadowing the victim for evil purposes in the internet and sending unsolicited and unwanted mails / messages that instill fear, contacting victim's acquaintances to spread abusive messages, rumors, and defamations and informing the victim about it, etc. The other stalking characteristics may include repeated threatening telephonic calls, conversations with victim's acquaintances with intention to convey threat to the victim either face to face or via telephone and telecommunications media, following the victim outside the virtual world for inflicting harm, as well as creating fear of physical harm or emotional distress. However, cyber stalking need not necessarily be synonymous with cyber harassments; but it must be taken as another form of cyber harassment. Our arguments may be supported by the views expressed in the 1999 Report (Reno, 1999) on cyber stalking prepared by the Attorney General of the US Department of Justice. The report states as follows:

Although there is no universally accepted definition of cyber stalking, the term ... refer to the use of the Internet, e-mail, or other electronic communications devices to stalk another person. Stalking generally involves harassing or threatening behavior that an individual engages in repeatedly, such as following a person, appearing at a person's home or place of business, making harassing phone calls, leaving written messages or objects, or vandalizing a person's property. Most stalking laws require that the perpetrator make a credible threat of violence against the victim; others include threats against the victim's immediate family; and still others require only that the alleged stalker's course of conduct constitute an implied threat. While some conduct involving annoying or menacing behavior might fall short of illegal stalking, such behavior may be a prelude to stalking and violence and should be treated seriously (Para 5).

We may note that the above definition ropes in certain "harassment elements" to construct cyber stalking. It is not always essential that such harassing behavior should mean cyber stalking. The present statutes that were discussed above therefore denote a very wide arena in the name of cyber stalking. The language of these statutes suggest that they may be used for cyber stalking as well as regular cyber harassments and not particularly for cyber stalking. Does this mean that there are no particular laws targeted towards criminalizing cyber stalking? As per Pittaro (2007), a popular federal statute to deal with cyber stalking is 47 U.S.C. 223, which makes it a "crime to use a telephone or any other communication device to harass or threaten any person". Pittaro (2007) compared the statute with that in Title 18 U.S.C. 875(c) [16] by stating that the former statute is somewhat easier to apply to cyber stalking cases because it includes both harassment and threats. Further, these laws also fail to define cyber stalking with its practical meaning. Almost all the so called "cyber stalking statutes" of the US are still following the basic norms laid down in the Interstate Stalking Act of 1996 which criminalizes traveling from one state to another with the intent to injure or harass the victim (Reno, 1999). However, we agree with Pittaro (2007) that the problem with enforcing this law lies in the language used in the legislation whereby the offender must physically travel across the state line, which clearly rules out most cases of internet harassment (Reno, 1999).

5.3.2 Discussions on Federal Statute on Online Stalking

The confusion which arose due to the use of harassment related languages in the US provincial legislatures which were meant to prevent cyber stalking, was laid to rest to a great extent by the introduction of "Violence Against Women and Department of Justice Reauthorization Act, 2005."[17] This Act was the first law to penalize cyber stalking and considered women as the vulnerable victims.[18] This statute amended Section 2261A of title 18, United States Code through Section 114, to include stalking through cyber communication as a 'penal offence' and construed it as a crime as it would have been in case of physical stalking by prescribing imprisonment for minimum one year period. The amended Section 2261A of title 18, United States Code therefore successfully defines cyber stalking with three dimensional meaning. Accordingly cyber stalking will include:

(a) Traveling by the accused from one place to another: in case of physical stalking traveling from one place to another constructs stalking; in case of cyber stalking, the word "traveling" has been connoted by "following" the victim via emails or chat rooms or social networking sites etc;

(b) Such traveling or cyber movement should be done with intent to cause physical harm and /or mental distress;

(c) Physical harm or feeling of physical insecurity and/or mental distress etc must be caused to the victim, or her immediate family members or her spouse or her intimate partner.

With this amendment, certain categories of cyber crimes targeting women including cyber stalking and related cyber harassments like sending annoying messages, lewd and obscene mails / messages and defaming women or attempts through internet has been recognized as penal offences against women in the US. However, it is to be seen how far this legislation proves successful towards preventing cyber stalking against women in reality.

5.4 REGULATIONS FOR CYBER BULLYING, HATE SPEECH AND CYBER DEFAMATION OF WOMEN

A perusal of the stalking and harassment laws discussed above, would show that provincial as well as federal legislatures of the US condemn harassing, annoying and threatening communications conveyed through internet and telecommunications. However, literatures show that cyber bullying; hate speech and consequently defamatory cyber speech against women are growing irrespective of existing preventive laws (Citron, 2009a; Halder & Jaishankar, 2009; Nakashima, 2007). Prevalent cyber cultures including ridiculing women with harsh taunting languages along with elasticity of First Amendment guarantees helped cultivating cyber bullying of women and cyber hate speech targeting women as a fast growing cyber offence against women. The case of Kathy Sierra is a remarkable example of how female bloggers are attacked in the cyber space in the US because of their gender (Citron, 2009a).[19] In Sierra's website,[20] a particular comment made by her attracts our attention. She says:

Although I've learned a lot in the last few days, I still do not know who made the unclebobism photo post, or why, or whether that person is a real threat. That part of the story has continued to devolve in even scarier ways. ....So, this is the last post I'll make for some time, and I've closed comments because I cannot keep up with the hateful ones (including those that post my home address and social security number, etc.)...I'm sure I'll be back in the future.

This is one of the best examples of how a successful professional woman and an expert can be victimized because she shares her innermost feelings about the subject she literally lives in. The hardest truth is, such cyber hate and defamations against women in the US are rampant not only for bloggers, but for women in the social networking sites, chat rooms and other cyber hangouts like YouTube, personal websites etc.

Often it is felt that the reason for the growth of cyber hate speech and bullying targeting women lies in the loose interpretations of First Amendment[21] provisions. Truly, with the advent of time the expansion of the First Amendment rights has touched almost all the public communications devices like the motion pictures, radio and TV broadcastings, the print media and even the digital communication system including mobile phones, SMS and internet communications. The advantage had been enormous, but the disadvantages even more gargantuan. The courts never made this clause absolute but had put some pin holes where the congress can make laws. These are obscenity (Miller v California),[22] fighting words (Chaplinsky v. New Hampshire),[23] Commercial speech (Central Hudson Gas & Electric),[24] Incitement (clear and present danger) (Brandenburg v Ohio)[25] and Libel / Slander (New York Times co. v Sullivan),[26] (Hustler Magazine v Falwell).[27] In view of these judgments the courts in the 2007 case of United States v Sutcliff,[28] upheld a conviction of a defendant who posted threat messages in his website to kill a company's process server; uploaded the picture of the company's attorney and her daughter and published her home address. The message was accompanied by a voiceover clip played from a movie that featured the stalking of an attorney and his family. This particular case established online threats as unprotected true threats even though the defendant never sent his message directly to the recipient.

Apart from judicial interpretations of the limits of the rights guaranteed under the First Amendment; hate speech and bullying targeting women, defamation of women etc, are regulated largely by federal provisions which are meant to restraint workplace gender harassment and domestic violence or dating violence. In these provisions, harassment, stalking and sexual harassment eclipse the issues of victimization of women through online hate speech, flaming / bullying speech, defamatory gestures etc. This is evident from provisions such as Chapter 71, Part 1 of Title 18 of the US Code penalize using of obscene languages in communications through mail service and radio broadcasting. This has further been stretched to include prohibitory note for stalking violence which may include harassing the victim with obscene languages. Further, Chapter 119 of Part 1 of Title 18, US code criminalizes interception and discloser of wire, oral or electronic communications which to a long way prevents publishing of personal information and photographs for defamation purposes. But this does not provide a strong support for women who are attacked in the cyber space by anonymous perpetrators (Citron, 2009a).

We understand that regulating non-sexual offensive speech against women which do not particularly generate threat, but which creates enough scope to demean women publicly, may not be possible in the US. Women's rights in the cyber space are often looked down upon when it challenges the rights guaranteed under the First Amendment by the typical 'internet–languages' which often include slang remarks about women. It remains much as a matter of ethics in the cyber space and not a subject to be regulated by laws. Given the 'Miller test' - verdict',[29] it often seems that present young generation of internet users, including teenagers and young adults have relaxed the water mark for slang languages targeting women to be "obscene" to a great extent. Absence of any direct gender sensitive prohibitory provisions in this respect often leaves the women victims to seek justice by applying provisions for Civil Rights under Chapter 13 of the Part 1 of title 18, USC along with other related provisions on defamation and harassing communications that we have discussed above.

Critics are little cynical about the effectiveness of these legal provisions in reducing hate speech, bullying and defamation of women in the internet. Citron (2009a) expresses disappointment over the slow developments of cyber civil rights based upon the civil rights provisions. We feel that these lacunas influence heavily on the secondary victimization of women in the hands of the police who in certain cases refuse to understand the victimization involving hate speech and defamation in the social networking sites and blogs.[30]

5.5 REGULATIONS FOR ONLINE PORNOGRAPHY, OBSCENITY AND RELATED ISSUES AGAINST WOMEN

Using obscene languages and graphics in the electronic communications is considered as a crime under Section 2261A of Chapter 110A, Part 1 of Title 18USC, which speaks about domestic violence, stalking and dating violence against women. Chapter 71, Part 1 of Title 18 of the US Code further denotes creation of obscene materials for distribution as a penal offence. However, as discussed earlier, obscenity in cyber communications with women and victimizing women by soft-core pornography in the cyber space still remains a debatable issue when seen from Miller vs. California's perspective. The First Amendment remains silent about 'consented pornography' with women models and regards viewing adult pornography as an extended right for freedom of speech and expression. This is apparent from the fact that the definition of "sexually explicit conduct" in Section 2256 of title 18 of the US Code, Part 1, Chapter 110[31] does not always include obscenity but complements more with soft-core pornography and further such conducts are considered as criminal conducts only when children are victimized by such acts. Further, pornography is not defined by any specific federal provisions.

Even though the term 'pornography' has been defined by academicians from the perspective of psychological and social behaviors, philosophical aspects etc (for definitions on Pornography, see Rea, (2001); Pope et.al (2007)), none of those definitions could successfully impress the lawmakers. The reason for this could have emanated from the failed attempt of feminist activists to establish 'pornography' as an infringement of women's rights.[32] Indeed, it is a hard truth that even though pornography fails to generate legal recognition in the US, often women of cyber age fall victims of court's blind support of the rights guaranteed under the First Amendment (Citron, 2009b). However, the available legal provisions penalize unconsented filming of pornographic images of women and distribution of the same under Section 1801 of Chapter 88, Part 1 of Title 18, USC which discusses about video voyeurism and the distribution of the same.[33] We note that a broad interpretation of the language used in this provision covers unconsented capturing of sexual activities as well. We further note that several illegal activities in the cyber space including unauthorized access to personal photographs, doctoring them for pornographic purposes,[34] video voyeurisms, blackmailing with the photographs received by partners in adult sexting etc may also encourage cyber sex trade such as virtual bargaining for adult entertainment materials available in the cyber space. Even though the US laws do not recognize definitions of 'pornography', such activities as described above, may be controlled by application of penal laws available in the Title 18 USC.

Feministic interpretations of available federal laws could perhaps ascertain breach of women's fundamental rights. But how far these interpretations will sustain challenges from the rights guaranteed under the First Amendment remains a question. Apart from the laws, the society also should be sensitive to this issue. Our concern correctly reflects in Hughes's (1998) opinion:

Most adults are only concerned that their children may see pornography. They really aren't concerned about the women and children that are being exploited in the making of the pornography. In any search for a solution to pornography and prostitution it is crucial to remember that sexual exploitation starts with real people and the harm is to real people (p. 9).

5.6 ISSUES OF CYBER PRIVACY AND RELATED PROBLEMS FOR WOMEN

The cyber space regulatory laws are partly gender sensitive in the US especially for cases covering stalking, domestic violence, dating violence and the extension of the same in the cyber space. While considering general privacy issues (excluding financial crimes which are out of the scope of this book), we note that women still remain vulnerable victims. As shown in chapter 2, hacking and stalking are the most sorted crimes that invade the privacy of the victim. Video voyeurism and adult sexting are the two essential component parts of online privacy invading activities.[35] While the earlier could be regulated by existing provisions,[36] the later still needs proper legal attention. Along with these trends, privacy of women is constantly invaded through various social networking portals by the display of personal information of women.

Even though online victimization of women done through privacy invasion is not directly regulated by any provincial or federal laws except for Violence Against Women and Department of Justice Reauthorization Act of 2005,[37] several other federal legislations inspired by the the rights guaranteed under the Fourth amendment (privacy in respect to search and seizures) [38] to a certain extent protect cyber privacy of women (Halstuk, 2003). Most notable of them are: Section 2701 of Chapter 121, USC 18 (Part 1), which speaks about unauthorized access to data, Chapter 119 of Part 1 of Title 18, US code, which speaks about interception and discloser of electronic and oral communications etc; Section 1801 of Chapter 88, Part 1 of Title 18, USC, which speaks about video voyeurism, Section 2710 of Chapter 121, Part 1 of Title 18 USC which speaks about wrongful discloser of video tape rental or sale records etc. These laws definitely promise assurances for protection of private information of women stored in government records, hospital records as well as records of private organizations including workplaces, women networking sites etc. However, we noticed a strange correlation between First Amendment guarantees of free speech and the court's outlook towards exercising the same in the cyber space coupled with concerns regarding the individual's (who is practicing such rights) privacy. McIntyre v. Ohio Elections

115 S. Ct. 1511, 1516 (1995) is one of the landmark judgments which followed this norm of upholding right to free speech and right to privacy. The court has recognized 'anonymity' and political views as an additional right in the cyber space (Whitt, 1996). This goes a long way towards guaranteeing women internet users' right to privacy in the cyber space by remaining anonymous or hide under camouflaged identities, especially in cases of social networking sites and adult dating sites where risks of privacy penetration remains larger. But this judgment also opens gates for harassers to attack women under "anonymous cloaks" (Citron, 2009b). The 2004 verdict of Polito v. AOL Time Warner, Inc., 78 Pa. D. & C.4th 328 (2004) however limited this extended right of the First Amendment by attaching tortuous and criminal liability for speeches and communications made under anonymous veil with intention to harass or defame others (Arias, 2007). It is hoped that this judgment will create awareness among the internet users in respecting the privacy and dignity of others, especially women.

5.7 THE TORTUOUS LIABILITIES

Questions on cyber privacy necessarily pull out the responsibility of the ISPs towards protection given to the subscribers / customers. In the modern cyber age, mostly the US hosted ISPs rule the world. Prominent of these are Google and Google created / sponsored links like Gmail, Bloggers, YouTube, Yahoo, AOL, Facebook, MySpace, Twitter, Craiglist, SecondLife etc. Other than these prominent sites, there are thousand of other adult dating sites, matrimonial sites, commercial as well as non-commercial social networking sites, adult entertainment sites etc, which are hosted and regulated by the US laws. These search engines, email domains and social networking sites are often misused for harassing women victims. Statistical reports provided by WHOA[39] would show that harassers including ex-partners, ex-boyfriends, office colleagues, business competitors and even strangers take undue advantage of the popular sites such as those described above, to harass women. Apparently these ISPs are often considered as 'instruments' for victimization as harassers use them to convey the victimization. But the US law makers swiftly experimented the liability of the ISPs through Stratton Oakmont, Inc. v. Prodigy Services Co., 1995 WL 323710 (N.Y. Sup. Ct. 1995). This particular case held that Prodigy as an ISP is liable as a publisher as Prodigy exercised monitorial powers over the contents published in their bulletin boards. In the following year, the Congress enacted Section 230 of the Communication Decency Act, which was codified at title 47, chapter 5(II), Part 1.[40] This legislation was made to clarify the role of the ISPs keeping in view of the Stratton decision. This provision provides protection for "Good Samaritan blocking and screening of offensive material"[41] and immunes the ISPs against third party liability, conferring more responsibilities on the individual subscribers who enter into a "contractual relationship" with the ISPs through the agreements forms. Along with this, Section 512C of the Copyrights Act, inserted by Digital Millennium Copyrights Act, 1997,[42] which is hugely used by the human interactive websites to take down offensive materials in the name of infringement of copyrights, has also been used to establish the liability limitations of the ISPs. It should be noted that ISPs are not lifeless open papers to advertise about the privacy of the subscribers. The federal legislature under Title 18, part 1, chapter 121, Section 2702 predicts liability for the ISPs by stating that any person or entity providing an electronic communication service to the public and any person or entity providing remote computing service to the public, shall not divulge any contents of the electronic communications carried or maintained on that service except as provided otherwise.[43] Section 2707 further prescribes civil remedies for breach of confidentiality.[44] This indeed may protect the privacy of the women and men as well.

Given these situations, we note that it is more the liability of the users which is to be questioned than the liability of the ISPs. However, the burden lies more on the victim to prove the victimization as the provisions to save the ISPs may actually encourage enormous practice of freedom of speech. This is evident from the fact that web services such as Blogger, YouTube, Gmail, Yahoo mail etc, are hugely used to convey as well as publish abusive contents and personal information. The liability of the ISPs begins when they are notified about such misuses, which they judge in accordance with their own terms and policy guidelines to take preventive actions. Franks (2009) had thus rightly judged the situation:

Cyberspace has never been a state of perfect or even almost perfect, liberty. It has always been a realm of unequal distributions of liberty and license. The notion of cyberspace as a paradise is simply fictional, unless what one means by paradise is a place where men as a group have disproportionate access to liberty as opposed to women as a group (p. 23).

5.8 CONCLUSION

It is unfortunate to note that in spite of precautionary rules and legislations, both the judiciary as well as ISPs advocate for the free speech having little or less concern towards privacy rights of victims. For instance, when a woman victim brings her painstaking case of public defamation, exposure and publication of personal information and subsequent harassments to the notice of these ISPs, either she receives a negative response which says the case does not violate the principles of the ISP and hence she is refused any help; or she gets a cold response with practically no 'trustworthy' promise. Perhaps the drafting language of the existing provisions need to be more broadly interpreted when the victimization involves cyber space, vulnerability and sexuality of women, the patterns of using the cyber space and the gravity of *mens rea*.

We opened this chapter with statistics which show that women suffer more from cyber harassment related issues than men. Perhaps it is the vulnerability of women, the peculiar feminine trends[45] of using the internet and the laws drafted to cover limited liabilities and fast expanding meaning of First Amendment rights that make women victims more susceptible to be victimized in the internet. Further, we note that the legal definitions of gender sensitive online crimes are limited within either stalking or harassments (which also include sexual crimes like obscenity etc). We understand that online stalking is treated as a starting point of majority of online offences against women. But at the same time, perhaps the cyber crimes committed against women could be well regulated in the US if the types of victimization that we have pointed out in our 2nd chapter, were considered individually and each were analyzed in the light of the rights guaranteed under the First amendment and Fourth amendment together.

REFERENCES

Franks, M. A. (2009). Unwilling Avatars: Idealism and Discrimination in Cyberspace. *Columbia Journal of Gender and Law*, Forthcoming. (October 21, 2009). Available at SSRN: http://ssrn.com/abstract=1374533

Pittaro, M. L. (2007). Cyber stalking: An analysis of online harassment and intimidation. *International Journal of Cyber Criminology, 1*(2), 180–197.

Pope, N. K., Voges, K. E., Kuhn, K. L., & Bloxsome, E. L. (2007). Pornography and erotica: Definitions and prevalence. In M. Hume & G. Sullivan-Mort (Eds.), *Proceedings of the 2007 International Nonprofit and Social Marketing Conference: Social Entrepreneurship, Social Change and Sustainability*. Southport, Qld, Australia: Key Centre for Ethics, Law, Justice and Governance, Griffith University.

Radwanski, G. (2002). *Speech at the Spanish Data Protection Authority and Latin-American Centre of Data Protection Conference*, Madrid, Spain. May, 20, 2002. Retrieved on 6th July, 2010, from http://www.priv.gc.ca/speech/02_05_a_020520_e.cfm

Rea, M. C. (2001). What is pornography? *Nous (Detroit, Mich.), 35*(1), 118–145. doi:10.1111/0029-4624.00290

Reno, J. (1999). *1999 report on cyber stalking: A new challenge for law enforcement and industry*. Washington, D.C.: US Department of Justice.

Sandoval, G. (March 26, 2007). Blogger cancels conference appearance after death threats. *Cnet News*. Retrieved on 6th July, 2010, from http://news.cnet.com/8301-10784_3-6170683-7.html

Whitt, M. (1996). McIntyre v. Ohio elections communication: "A whole new boutique of wonderful first amendment litigation opens its doors." *Akron Law Review, 29*(2), 423-446. Retrieved on 6th July, 2010, from http://www.uakron.edu/law/lawreview/v29/docs/whitt.pdf

ENDNOTES

[1] http://www.haltabuse.org/resources/stats/2000stats.pdf
[2] http://www.haltabuse.org/resources/stats/2010Statistics.pdf
[3] See supra @ 132.
[4] For more information see Title 18, USC 1030.
[5] For further reading, please see Para (b)(1) of Section 2701 of Chapter 121, USC 18 (Part 1).
[6] For further reading, please see Para (b)(2) of Section 2701 of Chapter 121, USC 18 (Part 1).
[7] ibid
[8] Michigan Criminal Code, Stalking: Section 28.643(8). Definitions. 1993. Sec. 411h.
[9] Section 649.9 of the California Penal Code.
[10] Acts 1977, No. 607, p. 812, & Section 5530; Acts 1978, No. 770, p. 1110, & Section;1; Acts 1979, No. 79-471, p. 862, & Section;1; Acts 1996, No. 96-767, p. 1353, & Section;1; Acts 1997, No. 97-552, p. 989, & Section;1.
[11] Section 13A-11-8,Code of Alabama, 1975, available @ http://www.legislature.state.al.us/CodeofAlabama/1975/coatoc.htm
[12] Alaska Stat. §§ 11.41.260, 11.41.270
[13] ibid
[14] Cal. Civil Code § 1708.7 Retrieved on 23.04.2010 from http://www.haltabuse.org/resources/laws/california.shtml
[15] California Penal Code Section 422, Retrieved on 23.04.2010 from http://law.onecle.com/california/penal/422.html

16   Title 18 U.S.C. 875(c)states that *"Whoever transmits in interstate or foreign commerce any communication containing any threat to kidnap any person or any threat to injure the person of another, shall be fined under this title or imprisoned not more than five years, or both."* Retrieved on 10.10.10 from http://www.law.cornell.edu/uscode/18/875.html

17   Act no. 42 USC 13701.

18   Violence Against Women and Department of Justice Reauthorization Act of 2005 amends Communications Act of 1934 (47 U.S.C. 223(h) (1)) through Section 113 to include *the use of* any device or software that can be used to originate telecommunications or other types of communications that are transmitted, in whole or in part, by the Internet for the purpose of 'stalking', annoying and harassing others as penal offence.

19   Sierra, a Software developer used to write in her blogs in "Creating passionate users" http://headrush. typepad.com/creating_passionate_users/ which attracted public hate speech and bullying against her. The details of this case have been discussed in chapter 2.

20   http://headrush.typepad.com/whathappened.html

21   "Congress shall make no law respecting an establishment of religion, or prohibiting the free exercise thereof, or abridging the freedom of speech, or of the press; or the right of the people peaceably to assemble, and to petition the Government for a redress of grievances". Amendment I, The Bill of Rights

22   *Miller v. California*, 413 U.S.15 (1973), available at http://www.law.cornell.edu/supct/html/historics/ USSC_CR_0413_0015_ZS.html

23   Chaplinsky. v. New Hampshire (No. 255) 91 N.H. 310, 18 A.2d 754, available at http://www.law. cornell.edu/supct/html/historics/USSC_CR_0315_0568_ZS.html

24   Central Hudson Gas & Elec v. PUBLIC SERV. COMM'N, 447 U.S. 557 (1980) 447 U.S. 557, available at http://caselaw.lp.findlaw.com/scripts/getcase.pl?court=us&vol=447&invol=557

25   Brandenburg v Ohio 395 U.S. 444, available at http://www.law.cornell.edu/supct/html/historics/ USSC_CR_0395_0444_ZS.html

26   New York Times co. v Sullivan (No. 39) 273 Ala. 656, 144 So.2d 25, available at http://www.law. cornell.edu/supct/html/historics/USSC_CR_0376_0254_ZS.html

27   Hustler Magazine v Falwell (No. 86-1278), available at http://www.law.cornell.edu/supct/html/ historics/USSC_CR_0485_0046_ZS.html

28   505, F.3d 944, 952-53 (9th Cir.2007)

29   *Miller v. California*, 413 U.S.15 (1973), which established a three step test to prove obscenity as unprotected speech. For more information see http://www.law.cornell.edu/supct/html/historics/ USSC_CR_0413_0015_ZS.html

30   The lead author from her experiences as internet safety advocate of WHOA [1] has observed such painful experiences of the female victims from the US especially when they contacted the police for immediate redressal of hate speech, defamation or bullying remarks in the cyber space.

31   The definition explains "sexually explicit material" in Para (A) as actual or simulated sexual intercourse, including genital-genital, oral-genital, anal-genital, or oral-anal, whether between persons of the same or opposite sex; bestiality; masturbation; sadistic or masochistic abuse; or lascivious exhibition of the genitals or pubic area of any person. Para B of the same section further includes the word "graphic" to the sexual conducts mentioned in Para A to stretch the penal liability.

32 Two feminist activists, writer Andrea Dworkin and lawyer Catharine Mackinnon way back in the 1980 has prepared an ordinance to address pornography as violation of civil rights (see Dworkin & Mackinnon, 1988, 1994). Mackinnon and Dworkin (1997) argued that pornography leads to discrimination of women and denies free speech for women and therefore it should not be given umbrella protection of the First Amendment. Unfortunately, the ordinance was never born as the Mayor of Minneapolis vetoed it on the ground that it is too broad and vague. Also, the United States Court of Appeals for the Seventh Circuit in the case of *American Booksellers v. Hudnut*, 771 F.2d 323 (7th Cir. 1985), aff'd mem., 475 U.S. 1001 (1986), considered this ordinance as unconstitutional and too vague (see American Booksellers v. Hudnut).

33 See Section 1801 of Chapter 88, Part 1 of Title 18, USC, for definition of video voyeurism. Available at http://www.law.cornell.edu/uscode/18/usc_sec_18_00001801----000-.html

34 We have discussed this issue under the heading 'hacking and hacking related activities' at the beginning of this chapter.

35 Issues of privacy through adult sexting may pull legal debates since the transmission of the images are consensual. The victim has to rope in "fear factor' to establish victimization when such contents are misused by the recipient.

36 See supra @ 170

37 This considerably amended the Federal criminal law to protect women from stalking violence.

38 Fourth Amendment guarantees right to privacy and the same right has been upheld by numerous judgments, such as Griswold v. Connecticut, 381, US 479, 484 (1965), Olmstead v. United States 277, US 438, 478 (1928).

39 Available at http://www.haltabuse.org/resources/stats/index.shtml

40 See http://www.law.cornell.edu/uscode/47/230.html

41 See Clause C of Section 230 under Title 47, Chapter 5(II), Part 1, available at http://www.law.cornell.edu/uscode/47/230.html

42 Section 512C of the Digital Millennium Copyright Act states that a service provider shall not be liable for any monetary or injunctive or equitable relief for any infringement of copyright if he does not have direct knowledge of the infringing of the copyright, if he is not aware of the facts from which infringing activity is apparent and if he, upon receiving any such notice of infringement, immediately takes action to prevent such ongoing infringement activities.

43 See "Voluntary disclosure of customer communications or records" Title 18, part 1, chapter 121, Section 2702, available at http://www.law.cornell.edu/uscode/18/usc_sec_18_00002702----000-.html

44 See "Civil action" Title 18, part 1, chapter 121, Section 2707, available at http://www.law.cornell.edu/uscode/18/usc_sec_18_00002707----000-.html

45 We use the term 'feminine trends' to signify women's ways of using the internet; which may include excessive chatting with unknown persons, exposing personal informations to get more like-minded friends etc.

Chapter 6
Cyber Laws for Preventing Cyber Crimes Against Women in Canada

CHAPTER OVERVIEW

This chapter gives an overview of laws related to cyber crimes against in general and women in particular. Though there are no specific laws that were developed to mitigate crimes against women in cyber space, Canadian laws of physical space govern the cyber space crimes well. The various issues that are discussed in this chapter are: Cyber nonsexual offences against women and regulating laws in Canada, Online Stalking and related offences, Online harassment through modification of digital contents and misusing the same, Offensive communication against women, Cyber defamatory libel against women, Cyber hate propaganda against women and legal situation, Responsibilities of the ISPs, Cyber privacy and related offences against women, Regulating cyber sexual offences for women in Canada, and the problem of Obscenity and regulating laws.

6.1 INTRODUCTION

The Canadian scenario differs from the US in issues of laws on cyber crime. Canada lacks a consolidated Information technology law. The Canadian cyber crime against women scenario differs from the UK as well. It was interesting to note that even though Canada has followed British Penal system (which was a model since the late 19th century for almost all the English colonies as well as modern common-

DOI: 10.4018/978-1-60960-830-9.ch006

wealth countries like India, Australia etc) for covering offline as well as online crimes, the Canadian socio-legal approach towards generalizing various types of cyber crimes is quite similar to that of the US. Canada has no gender sensitive laws for cyber crimes like that of Women's Reauthorization Act of the US to regulate cyber stalking against women. But at the same time, the governmental efforts to spread awareness through police handbooks about cyber victimization serve similar purposes to a great extent. Notably, Canada lacks statistical data on victimization of women in the cyber space. Hence, in this segment we have tried to analyze the trends of victimization of women in the cyber space only from a legal perspective.

6.2 CYBER NONSEXUAL OFFENCES AGAINST WOMEN AND REGULATION OF LAWS

6.2.1 Online Stalking and Related Offences

The Canadian Criminal Code[1] under section 264(1) prohibits harassing activities and prescribes punishment for imprisonment for minimum 10 years or summary conviction.[2] This particular section was meant to punish offline harassment including stalking and creating fear factor in the victim's mind. The term "stalking" does not find any mention in this Section, however, the characteristics of stalking[3] are well depicted in section 264(ii) and they are termed as 'prohibited conduct'. These are:

a) Repeatedly following the other person from place to place or anyone known to them;
b) Repeatedly communicating with, either directly or indirectly, the other person or anyone known to them;
c) Besetting or watching the dwelling-house, or place where the other person, or anyone known to them, resides, works, carries on business or happens to be; or
d) Engaging in threatening conduct directed at the other person or any member of their family.

Even though this section was mainly framed to deal with offline stalking, it is now being stretched to online stalking and harassments too. The handbook for police and crown prosecutors (DOJ, Canada, 2004) has refined the concept of cyber stalking and online harassment in the meaning of section 264, when used for computer related crimes. The handbook in its opening paragraph under the title of "legislative history of criminal harassment" stated that:

On August 1, 1993, the Criminal Code was amended to create the new offence of criminal harassment. It was introduced as a specific response to violence against women, particularly to domestic violence against women. However, the offence is not restricted to domestic violence and applies equally to all victims of criminal harassment.

The statement indicates how section 264, when used for online stalking and harassment, can protect women's interest. Under Para 1.6, titled "Cyber stalking and online harassment", the Handbook admits that while applying section 264 to cyber stalking, only two requirements of the aforesaid section can be applied, namely (1) Repeatedly communicating with, either directly or indirectly, the other person or anyone known to them, which has been stated in Subsection 2(b), and (2) engaging in threatening conduct directed at the other person or any member of their family which has been stated in subsection 2(d) (DOJ, Canada, 2004). The Handbook further shows three types of 'offline stalkers' which are "erotomanic stalker", "Love obsessional stalkers" and "simple obsessional stalker" (DOJ, Canada, 2004). It is needless to say that these types of stalkers are now randomly using internet and their activities are more hi-tech. (DOJ, Canada, 2004). Online stalking would necessarily be associated with threatening mails, blackmailing and even offline physical threats. Section 264.1 regulates such threatening conducts with a punishment for 5 years imprisonment or fine. It can be noted that even though Canada does not have gender protective laws for cyber stalking, the existing Criminal Code to a certain extent protects women victims from online stalking.

Notably, unlike the US,[4] Canadian legislature attempts to cover digital stalking crimes through existing laws for regulating harassment and related offences. The Police Handbook on Stalking has created the conceptual difference between online and offline stalking and has taken only two essential characteristics from Section 264(1) to explain online stalking. We however feel that the characteristics of online stalking may also be similar to those of the offline stalking like following the victim in the internet, 'dropping in' either in her social networking profiles or chat / message box to remind her that he is there to follow and disturb etc. Given these characteristics, we feel that all the 'prohibited conducts' as mentioned in Section 264(2) may well be used for regulating online stalking too if construed from digital stalking and harassment perspective.

6.2.2 Online Harassment Through Modification of Digital Contents

Often women net users become victims of unauthorized access of their digital content, by harassers. Such hacking and hacking related activities which may also involve impersonation in web activities of the female victims are not directly regulated by any laws. However, Canadian criminal Code extends section 342.1 to regulate such activities. This provision prohibits unauthorized access to any computer data, misusing such data, preventing the original owner from accessing the contents by modifying contents etc.[5] Section 430(1.1) further puts penal sanction for creating mischief with data.[6] These sections were mainly meant for preventing hacking and offences related to e-commerce. But the wordings may very well be stretched for the purpose of protection of women from cyber crimes, such modifications of digital data, impersonations, revealing personal information etc.

Even though Canadian laws do not say anything about cyber impersonation of individuals in cases for non-economic issues, it is a hard truth that women victims in Canada face several such offences where there personal information are 'hijacked' from various computer sources, 'pretended' profiles are made and floated in the web for multi focused harassment purposes. Hacking and unauthorized access to data remain the key factor for such mischievous activities. The Criminal Code of Canada does not term section 342.1 as only for economic crimes, neither the section and related section 430(1.1) indicate that they can be used for crimes against individuals as we have mentioned above. As such when similar problems arise with women victims, often they are not provided any legal assistance because this section is presumed to be for economic offences, or the crime is booked again under section 264 which is meant for harassment and stalking. Due to these legal constraints, women victims rarely get proper justice, especially those who had been harassed by ex-spouses or ex-boyfriends. The victims also prefer not to report to the police as they do not understand the nature and gravity of such crimes.

6.2.3 Offensive Communication Against Women

The problem of online hate speech in Canada can be viewed from two angles: (a) cyber defamatory libel[7] targeted by youth, adults to other youth and adults (b) cyber hate propaganda,[8] which is generated by adults and targeted to either a community based on race, language or religion, or an individual. Neither the criminal code, nor any ordinance, rules regulations etc, nor the International Network against Cyber Hate, to which Canada is a party, describes any literature towards cyber hate speech targeted at 'only' women. It is unfortunate that women have not been projected as potential victims of cyber hate speech in Canadian legal scenario and hence no law or ordinance has been formed to protect women from cyber hate speech including defamation. However, even though there is no gender sensitive law, pulling the reference of Equality rights[9] from the Charter of rights we will discuss the existing general laws and analyze the usage of it for cases of women victims.

6.2.3.a Cyber Defamatory Libel Against Women

Defamatory libel has been termed as an offence under Part VIII of the Canadian Criminal Code under the title "Offences against the person and reputation". Section 298 (1) thus states "A defamatory libel is matter published, without lawful justification or excuse, that is likely to injure the reputation of any person by exposing him to hatred, contempt or ridicule, or that is designed to insult the person of or concerning whom it is published". Subsection 2 states that "A defamatory libel may be expressed directly or by insinuation or irony (a) in words legibly marked on any substance; or (b) by any object signifying a defamatory libel otherwise than by words". The criminal code further in section 299 states that "A person publishes a libel when he (a) exhibits it in public; (b) causes it to be read or seen; or (c) shows or delivers it, or causes it to be shown or delivered, with intent that it should be read or seen by the person whom it defames or by any other person. This section may well pull cyber defamation under sections 300 and 301 which makes defamatory libel known to be false and an offence.[10] However, even though defamatory libel through cyber technology can be brought under the criminal code, there is no specific law, sections or provisions or even ordinance to prevent online gender victimization in the form of online defamatory libels or slanders, except two provisions that broadly covers victims of both gender. These provisions are:

1.   Section 13 of the Canadian Human Rights Act, 1977, which prohibits communication by means of a telecommunication undertaking (including the Internet) of messages that are likely to expose a person to hatred or contempt on gender basis along with other basis like race, colour etc; and
2.   Section 15(1)[11] of the Canadian Charter of rights and freedoms which guarantees equality and equal protection of laws to every Canadian irrespective of sex, race, color, religion etc.

Notably, Section 13 of the Canadian Human Rights Act mentions only prohibitions of "hate" and not defamatory libel or slander. While defining defamation, Section 298 of the Criminal Code mentions "exposing" the victim "to hatred". However, we feel Section 13 of the Canadian Human Rights Act can only be brought when "hate messages" are taken in its wider sense to include online defamation of women as a type of hate message.

6.2.3.b Cyber Hate Propaganda Against Women

Online hate propaganda is dealt with in Part VIII, Section 319 under the Canadian Criminal Code which states in Para 1:

Every one who, by communicating statements in any public place, incites hatred against any identifiable group where such incitement is likely to lead to a breach of the peace is guilty of (a) an indictable offence and is liable to imprisonment for a term not exceeding two years; or (b) an offence punishable on summary conviction.

In Para 2 it states:

Every one who, by communicating statements, other than in private conversation, willfully promotes hatred against any identifiable group is guilty of (a) an indictable offence and is liable to imprisonment for a term not exceeding two years; or (b) an offence punishable on summary conviction.

Identifiable group as has been defined under section 318, includes "any section of the public distinguished by colour, race, religion, ethnic origin or sexual orientation" but not by gender. Surprisingly when the Canadian charter of human rights boasts of equal rights and equal protection of laws to men and women, and Section 13 of the *Canadian Human Rights Act* prohibits the communication by means of a telecommunication undertaking (including the Internet) of messages that are likely to expose a person to hatred or contempt on the basis of gender along with other grounds, we find no reason why the criminal code did not include gender as one of the distinguishing grounds for making "identifiable group". Canadian cyber space is no exception to the "mob attacks" on women or even targeting feminist groups for hate speech. Nonetheless, Section 13 of the Canadian Human rights Act goes a long way to fill in the vacuum, created by the Criminal Code, towards legal protection of women from hate speech and hate propaganda. However, reported cases are very few and hence hadn't created any further scope to challenge the existing laws or to propagate creation of women centric laws.

6.2.3.c Responsibilities of the ISPs

As per the Canadian Criminal Code, the proprietor of any newspaper where defamatory libel has been published with his knowledge may be pulled in for sharing the responsibility as offender[12] with that of the original writer of the defaming message. However, even though Criminal code is stretched to cover all sorts of defamation and hate propaganda, the Canadian Human Rights Act (CHRA) is more accurate on the gender based hate messages spread via internet and telecommunications. Section 13 of the CHRA thus in subsection 3 exempts ISPs from the criminal liability.[13] Hence, we feel that when a female victim reports the issue of defamation or hate propaganda on the internet to the police, the case should be judged from the angle of "discriminatory practice" as under Section 13 of the CHRA and ISPs may be exempted in that manner. However, the case should also be *read with* the provisions of the Criminal Code under Section 301 in case of defamatory libel and Section 319 in case of hate propaganda, to make it a criminal offence.

6.3 CYBER PRIVACY AND RELATED OFFENCES AGAINST WOMEN

Canadian legislature has dealt with cyber privacy in two dimensions: (a) privacy regarding information of individuals stored in personal computers as well as government records and (b) sexual privacy or voyeurism. In this segment, we will discuss privacy regarding individual information only. Voyeurism would be discussed under the title "sexual offences and laws".

Right to privacy in the cyber space has been seen as a broad spectrum under the Canadian laws. A preview of Canadian Criminal Code suggests that cyber privacy may include invasion of privacy both for economic and non economic purposes; for the purpose of our book, we will discuss issues of cyber privacy in Canadian scenario from female victim's perspective and not from economic crimes perspective. Privacy in Canada has been secured as fundamental "legal right" under Article 8 of the Canadian Charter of rights and freedom.[14] Even though this right is enacted mainly to protect privacy against unreasonable search and seizure, judicial interpretations of this right have extended the applicability of Article 8 to individual's right to privacy in other cases also which is inclusive of right against unreasonable search and seizure (Hunter v. Southam, 1984).[15] The right to privacy in Canada is also recognized as the core component for liberty and democratic nature of Canadian constitution (Lasprogata, King, & Pillay, 2004; Radwanski, 2002). This right has further covered private information stored digitally through various judicial interpretations which were delivered in the early 90's.[16] However, the present trend of theoretically interpreting cyber privacy for socio-legal researches is hugely focused on data protection, copyrights, employee's information etc (Kerr, 2007).

However, analyzing Section 184 (1) of the Criminal Code, it could be seen that privacy can be extended to private communications as well. Section 184 (1) of the Criminal Code penalizes willful interception of any private communication. Section 183 of the Criminal Code defines private communication as:

any oral communication, or any telecommunication, that is made by an originator who is in Canada or is intended by the originator to be received by a person who is in Canada and that is made under circumstances in which it is reasonable for the originator to expect that it will not be intercepted by any person other than the person intended by the originator to receive it, and includes any radio-based telephone communication that is treated electronically or otherwise for the purpose of preventing intelligible reception by any person other than the person intended by the originator to receive it.

Even though this particular definition indicates communication only within the jurisdiction of Canada and only those contents which are communicated between sender and his / her recipient, a broad analysis of section 183 and also 184 (1) may expand the meaning of communications to include emails, chats, information provided in various website for socializing, messages in social networking sites and opinions expressed in blogs etc. Further, Federal Privacy Act, 1982 under Sections 7 and 8 regulate collection, use and disclosure of personal information held by a government institution and the right to protection of such information. This legislation may go a long way towards preventing harassment of women by misusing her health / family records / bank information etc.

Even though no legislature indicates exclusive gender sensitive protections for cyber victimization, if the above mentioned laws are used along with provisions for preventing unauthorized access, unauthorized modification of data etc, online women victimization in Canada may be well prevented.

6.4 REGULATING CYBER SEXUAL OFFENCES

Canadian Criminal Code deals Cyber sexual offences from three dimensions: voyeurism, pornography and obscenity. We have noted that victimization of women is 'presumed' to be an offence through cyber sexual crimes in Canada and no law directly addresses protection of sexuality of women in the cyber space. Apparently voyeurists can attack men, women and children; laws related to pornography is mainly focused for protection of children and obscenity issues are dealt more from the perspective of moral crimes against the society and not against women victims in particular. We have therefore used this segment to experiment with the existing laws which are being used to combat voyeurism, pornography and obscenity, towards prevention of online sexual harassments against women in Canada.

Section 162(1) of the Canadian Criminal Code explains the crime of voyeurism in the following words:

Every one commits an offence who, surreptitiously, observes including by mechanical or electronic means, or makes a visual recording of a person who is in circumstances that give rise to a reasonable expectation of privacy, if (a) the person is in a place in which a person can reasonably be expected to be nude, to expose his or her genital organs or anal region or her breasts, or to be engaged in explicit sexual activity; (b) the person is nude, is exposing his or her genital organs or anal region or her breasts, or is engaged in explicit sexual activity, and the observation or recording is done for the purpose of observing or recording a person in such a state or engaged in such an activity; or (c) the observation or recording is done for a sexual purpose.

Subsection 4 penalizes distribution of voyeur pictures, clippings etc and subsection 5 prescribes punishment for the offence of voyeurism which can extend to 5 years imprisonment or summary conviction or both. Since the language of the Section carries out the criteria of "forced pornography,"[17] we have included voyeurism in this Section also, apart from the segment for discussions on privacy laws above. It criminalizes an act which is done (i) for sexual pleasure of an unwanted viewer; (ii) invades the privacy of the victim; (iii) visual recordings are captured without the consent of the victim; (iv) published / printed / circulated for the "sexual enjoyment" of a larger audience and it harms the reputation of the victim; (v) it violates the core value of right to life, security and peace as well as pulls on discrimination on the basis of sexual harassment when the victim is a female. However, for terming it a typical forced cyber pornography, we must team up the offence of voyeurism with Section 342.1 (unauthorized use of computer), when taken in its' broadest sense for application, which helps to circulate the offence to millions of cyber users.

Pornography on the other hand is interpreted as a crime happening only to children and not to adults and it is regulated by Section 163.1 of the Criminal Code. This Section not only defines child pornography, but also makes any act constituting child pornography an offence.[18] While analyzing the section, we found that the word pornography (which may be applied to adult females as well) as per Canadian law depicts:

a) photographic, film, video or other visual representation including written material;
b) which shows a person depicted in explicit sexual activities;
c) the dominant characteristics are it is for sexual purposes and reveals sexual organs of the victim;
d) the material is possessed and distributed (which is done even for monetary gain) for sexual enjoyment of others.

However, the section is complete in its legal allusion when the victim is a "child" (meaning a person who is below 18 years of age). It is surprising to note that when the legal provision is so clear in depicting the typical characteristics of pornography and when it can be "protected speech / expression"[19], why the drafters did not include "victimization of women" when discussing victimization of child and youth due to online and offline pornography? According to Vallet (2010), the simple answer for our question could be: "In Canada, the principle is that, pornography is legal, except if it is not obscene. It can be diffused on any support as from the moment that no minor takes part in it".[20]

Vallet (2010) further discussed pornography with the help of the leading case of *R c Butler.* She stated that "For Sopinka judge, in *R. c. Butler,* pornography can be divided into three categories: "(1) explicit sex with violence, (2) explicit sex without violence but which subjects people to treatment that is degrading or dehumanizing, and (3) explicit sex without violence that is neither degrading nor dehumanizing". Only, "the portrayal of sex coupled with violence will almost always constitute the undue exploitation of sex". The last category is *legal* only if no minor is put in scene sexually".[21] Vallet (2010) further opines that "The protection of women's interest is not a major preoccupation in the regulation of Internet in Canada" and this is the sharp reality which encouraged the growth of "forced pornography" of the innocent women who are used for the purpose and who are oblivion of the fact that they are used as pornographic material in the cyber space in Canada.

According to Casavant and Robertson (2007, p. 2), "A great deal of the difficulty in discussing pornography results from lack of agreement over what is meant by the term. Except for a 1993 amendment regarding "child pornography," the criminal law does not use the word "pornography" but rather "obscenity". They have further showed two contrasting definitions of pornography which makes defining pornography even more perplexing. According to one explanation, very much sexual depictions can be called "erotica" and sexual material with relatively inexplicit but demeaning content can be called "Pornography" (Casavant & Robertson, 2007). The other explanation states: "At the same time, much conventional pornography depicts naked women, and it is argued that such material perpetrates images of women as sexual objects and, thus, can victimize women directly and indirectly" (Casavant & Robertson, 2007, p. 2).

Casavant and Robertson (2007) further points out that, due to the growth of the internet, pornography has become easily accessible. "It has also been suggested that community standards have changed to the point where 30% of all Canadian newsstand sales in the mid 1980s consisted of periodicals that would have been illegal 20 years before" (Casavant & Robertson, 2007, p. 2). Casavant and Robertson (2007) have even discussed the Fraser Committee's opinion on pornography. They opine that:

The 1985 report of the Special Committee on Pornography and Prostitution (the Fraser Committee) made several significant findings on pornography in Canada. The Committee declined to give an explicit definition of what it considered "pornography," principally because there is no accepted definition in the community at large. It acknowledged the validity of the idea that pornography should be distinguished from erotica, and agreed that, although it is violent pornography that is of most concern, to some extent there is a continuum from apparently mild sexually offensive material to violent material (p. 4).

They also felt pornography may even be harmful to women when it depicts violence or even demeans women (Casavant & Robertson, 2007). Unfortunately, nothing was done to criminalize soft-core pornography, which demeans women except stretching the meaning of voyeurism to be suitably fitting for the internet era.

6.5 OBSCENITY AND REGULATIONS

Canadian Criminal Code tagged obscenity as the first offence under section 163 under the segment dealing with *"Offences Tending to Corrupt Morals"* in Part IV. Obscenity is considered as a constituting characteristic of "corrupt moral" and hence the opening sentence of section 163, subsection (1) states: "Every one commits an offence who (a) makes, prints, publishes, distributes, circulates, or has in his possession for the purpose of publication, distribution or circulation any obscene written matter, picture, model, phonograph record or other thing whatever".

The Canadian concept of standard of obscenity has gone through numerous moral as well as legal valuations since 1984. Committee reports, feminist arguments and debates and legal questions raised in various case laws helped to formulate amendments to the criminal code which finally broadened the meaning of obscenity in the legal context (Casavant & Robertson, 2007). While analyzing section 163 as a whole we can thus see that obscenity becomes an offence as per the Canadian standard when it is "published" or exposed to the world (section 163 (2)). This is further supported when Section 163 in subsection (8) defines obscene publication as any publication, a dominant characteristic of which is the undue exploitation of sex, or of sex and any one or more of the following subjects, namely, crime, horror, cruelty and violence, shall be deemed to be obscene. However, the medium of exposure or publication could vary from audio visual broadcasting system like TV or radio, printed paper, internet (section 168, subsection 1) or even through open theaters where obscene written materials are materialized by stage acting (section 167, subsections (1) and (2)).

Now, the question which arises here is: *'could cyber obscenity be taken as against women's equality right?'* After reviewing the Criminal Code, the Canadian Charter of Rights and the CHRA, we consider the answer in positive. When we take the last line of section 163(8), i.e., "......crime, horror, cruelty and violence, shall be deemed to be obscene", and read it with Right to equality as has been depicted in Canadian Charter of Rights along with women's right against discrimination as has been depicted in CHRA, we deduct that when a woman is targeted by perpetrator with the weapon of "obscenity", she does have a legal right to fight back. This is very much opposite to the case of adult pornography as literally it does not have any legal definition. But then the wordings of section 167 which criminalizes immoral theatrical performances, creates a mild confusion. As per the section the actors of the obscene performances in the stage are also liable to be punished. The following section speaks about the role of internet in spreading obscenity, and we fear that if an innocent female victim is *depicted* to be an actor in such obscene performances by digital tricks, her chances to defend herself becomes tough. However, an immediate answer to this could be that the criminal code also criminalizes unauthorized access to computer materials and voyeurism. We feel that in such situation the burden of proof falls on the female victim and that might add more agony to her trauma.

6.6 CONCLUSION

Even though Canadian laws address several sorts of cyber offences, women victim's rights still remain a far cry. Critics may argue that cyber crime is not gender neutral; hence there is no need for women centric cyber crime regulations. But when seen from female victim's perspective, the legal protections for these 'gender neutral offences' may not stand a strong protection for women. It is a hard reality that even though CHRA speaks against sexual discrimination and Charter of Rights guarantees equal rights to women, the fairer sex may not get the benefits to the fullest in the cyber space due to less awareness about legal rights of women victims and secondary victimization in the hands of government reporting agencies. The victims may feel completely handicapped due to nil or less understanding of the legal nature of the problems, and this may add to the pains of the women victims.

REFERENCES

Arias, M. L. (September 03, 2007). *The right to speak anonymously on the Internet is not absolute.* Internet Business Law Services (IBLS). Retrieved on 6th July, 2010, from http://www.ibls.com/internet_law_news_portal_ view.aspx?id=1840&s=latestnews

British Broadcasting Corporation (BBC NEWS). (Mar 27, 2007). *Blog death threats spark debate.* Retrieved on 6th July, 2010, from http://news.bbc.co.uk/1/hi/ technology/6499095.stm

Casavant, L., & Robertson, J. R. (2007). *The evolution of pornography law in Canada.* Current Issue Review, Library of Parliament, Canada. Retrieved on 6th July 2010 from http://www.parl.gc.ca/information/ library/PRBpubs/843-e.pdf

Department of Justice (DOJ). Canada. (2004). *Criminal harassment: A handbook for police and crown prosecutors.* Retrieved on 6th July, 2010, from http://www.justice.gc.ca/eng/pi/ fv-vf/pub/har/ch_e-hc_a. pdf

Dworkin, A., & Mackinnon, C. A. (1988). *Pornography and civil rights: A new day for women's equality.* Organizing Against Pornography. Retrieved on 6th July, 2010, from http://www.nostatusquo.com/ ACLU/dworkin /other/ordinance/newday/TOC.htm

Dworkin, A., & Mackinnon, C. A. (1994). *An excerpt from model anti-pornography civil rights* (pp. 138-142). Minneapolis, MN: Organizing Against Pornography. Retrieved on 6th July, 2010, from http:// www.nostatusquo.com/ACLU/dworkin /OrdinanceModelExcerpt.html

Halstuk, M. E. (2003). Shielding private lives from prying eyes: The escalating conflict between constitutional privacy and the accountability principle of democracy. *CommLaw Conspectus, 71,* 94.

Hughes, D. M. (1998). Use of the Internet for global sexual exploitation of women and children. Retrieved on 6th July, 2010, from http://www.uri.edu/artsci/wms/ hughes/internet.pdf

Kerr, I. (2007). To observe and protect? How digital rights management systems threaten privacy and what policy makers should do about it . In Yu, P. K. (Ed.), *Intellectual property and information wealth: Copyright and related rights* (pp. 321–344). Westport, CT: Praeger Publishers.

Lasprogata, G., King, N. J., & Pillay, S. (2004). Regulation of electronic employee monitoring: Identifying fundamental principles of employee privacy through a comparative study of data privacy legislation in the European Union, United States and Canada. *Stanford Technology Law Review,* 4. December 20, 2004. Retrieved on 6th July, 2010, from http://stlr.stanford.edu/pdf/Lasprogata- RegulationElectronic.pdf

Mackinnon, C. A., & Dworkin, A. (Eds.). (1997). *Harm's way: The pornography civil rights hearings.* Cambridge, MA: Harvard University Press.

Nakashima, E. (April 30, 2007). Sexual threats stifle some female bloggers. *The Washington Post*. Retrieved on 24th May, 2010, from http://www.washingtonpost.com/wp-dyn/ content/article/2007/04/29/AR2007042901555.html

O'Connell, K. (October 08, 2008). *Internet law - Governor Palin's email hack: Federal statutory law*. Retrieved on April 24, 2010, from http://www.ibls.com/internet_law_news_ portal_view.aspx?s=latestnews&id=2149

Pittaro, M. L. (2007). Cyber stalking: An analysis of online harassment and intimidation. *International Journal of Cyber Criminology*, *1*(2), 180–197.

Pope, N. K., Voges, K. E., Kuhn, K. L., & Bloxsome, E. L. (2007). Pornography and erotica: Definitions and prevalence. In M. Hume & G. Sullivan-Mort (Eds.), *Proceedings of the 2007 International Nonprofit and Social Marketing Conference: Social Entrepreneurship, Social Change and Sustainability*. Southport, Qld, Australia: Key Centre for Ethics, Law, Justice and Governance, Griffith University.

Radwanski, G. (2002). *Speech at the Spanish Data Protection Authority and Latin-American Centre of Data Protection Conference*, Madrid, Spain. May, 20, 2002. Retrieved on 6th July 2010 from http://www.priv.gc.ca/speech/ 02_05_a_020520_e.cfm

Rea, M. C. (2001). What is pornography? *Nous (Detroit, Mich.)*, *35*(1), 118–145. doi:10.1111/0029-4624.00290

Reno, J. (1999). *1999 report on cyber stalking: A new challenge for law enforcement and industry*. Washington, D.C.: US Department of Justice.

Sandoval, G. (March 26, 2007). Blogger cancels conference appearance after death threats. *Cnet News*. Retrieved on 6th July 2010 from http://news.cnet.com/8301-10784_3- 6170683-7.html

US Department of Justice. (2010). *Cybercrime and cyberstalking*. Retrieved from http://www.usdoj.gov/criminal/ cybercrime/cyberstalking.htm

Whitt, M. (1996). McIntyre V. Ohio Elections communication: "A whole new boutique of wonderful first amendment litigation opens its doors." *Akron Law Review, 29*(2), 423-446. Retrieved on 6th July, 2010, from http://www.uakron.edu/law/ lawreview/v29/docs/whitt.pdf

ENDNOTES

[1]   R.S. 1985, c, C-46, available at http://laws.justice.gc.ca/eng/C-46/index.html

[2]   Section 264 (3).

[3]   Fore more information on characteristics of stalking, see chapter 2.

[4]   See discussions about Violence against Women and Department of Justice Reauthorization Act of 2005 in chapter 5.

[5]   Section 342.1 states in Para 1: "(1) Every one who, fraudulently and without colour of right, (a) obtains, directly or indirectly, any computer service, (b) by means of an electro-magnetic, acoustic, mechanical or other device, intercepts or causes to be intercepted, directly or indirectly, any function of a computer system, (c) uses or causes to be used, directly or indirectly, a computer system with

intent to commit an offence under paragraph (a) or (b) or an offence under section 430 in relation to data or a computer system, or (d) uses, possesses, traffics in or permits another person to have access to a computer password that would enable a person to commit an offence under paragraph (a), (b) or (c) is guilty of an indictable offence and liable to imprisonment for a term not exceeding ten years, or is guilty of an offence punishable on summary conviction."

6   Section 430(1.1) states Every one commits mischief who willfully (*a*) destroys or alters data; (*b*) renders data meaningless, useless or ineffective; (*c*) obstructs, interrupts or interferes with the lawful use of data; or (*d*) obstructs, interrupts or interferes with any person in the lawful use of data or denies access to data to any person who is entitled to access thereto.

7   Section 297 of the criminal code, Canada

8   Section 319 of the criminal code, Canada.

9   Article 15(1) of the Charter of the rights says "Every individual is equal before and under the law and has the right to the equal protection and equal benefit of the law without discrimination and, in particular, without discrimination based on race, national or ethnic origin, colour, religion, sex, age or mental or physical disability". The second proviso of the article states "Subsection (1) does not preclude any law, program or activity that has as its object the amelioration of conditions of disadvantaged individuals or groups including those that are disadvantaged because of race, national or ethnic origin, colour, religion, sex, age or mental or physical disability".

10   Section 300 of the criminal code states "Every one who publishes a defamatory libel that he knows is false is guilty of an indictable offence and liable to imprisonment for a term not exceeding five years". Section 301 states "Every one who publishes a defamatory libel is guilty of an indictable offence and liable to imprisonment for a term not exceeding two years".

11   Section 15 of the Canadian Charter of rights states that (1) Every individual is equal before and under the law and has the right to the equal protection and equal benefit of the law without discrimination and, in particular, without discrimination based on race, national or ethnic origin, colour, religion, sex, age or mental or physical disability. Affirmative action programs (2) Subsection (1) does not preclude any law, program or activity that has as its object the amelioration of conditions of disadvantaged individuals or groups including those that are disadvantaged because of race, national or ethnic origin, colour, religion, sex, age or mental or physical disability.

12   Section 303 of the Canadian Criminal Code.

13   It must be noted that since the popular ISPs are mostly hosted in the US, they follow the immunity rules as established by the DMCA and the Federal Criminal Code almost universally. Even though the Dow Jones Case (DowJones & Company Inc. vs. Gutnick, (2002) HCA, 56 established rules for following law of the land where victimization is actually "seen" in cases of cyber harassments, Griffis case (discussed earlier in this chapter) gives further scope to experiment the applicability of the law of the land and the liability of the ISPs as publishers of offensive comments.

14   Article 8 of the Canadian Charter of rights and freedoms, available at http://www.cejamericas.org/doc/legislacion/constituciones/can-rights-freedoms.pdf

15   2 S.C.R. 145, 159-60

16   See R. v. Duarte, [1990] 1 S.C.R. 30, para. 27 (Can.).

17   See chapter 2.

18   Section 163.1 defines child pornography as (a) a photographic, film, video or other visual representation, whether or not it was made by electronic or mechanical means, (i) that shows a person who is or is depicted as being under the age of eighteen years and is engaged in or is depicted as

engaged in explicit sexual activity, or (ii) the dominant characteristic of which is the depiction, for a sexual purpose, of a sexual organ or the anal region of a person under the age of eighteen years; (b) any written material, visual representation or audio recording that advocates or counsels sexual activity with a person under the age of eighteen years that would be an offence under this Act; (c) any written material whose dominant characteristic is the description, for a sexual purpose, of sexual activity with a person under the age of eighteen years that would be an offence under this Act; or (d) any audio recording that has as its dominant characteristic the description, presentation or representation, for a sexual purpose, of sexual activity with a person under the age of eighteen years that would be an offence under this Act.

[19] A deep study of "defences" portion of section 163 along with the portion discussing "sexual offences" under section 150-162 and "moral corruptions" under sections 163-172 reveal that Canadian value system is more "orthodox" than the US system and hence every attempt is made to protect the child and youth from being exposed to sexual immoral activities prematurely.

[20] From personal conversation with Ms. Vallet. Source: Email conversations between Vallet and the lead author.

[21] ibid

Chapter 7
Cyber Space Regulations for Protecting Women in UK

CHAPTER OVERVIEW

This chapter describes various features of regulation of cyber space by the UK. The regulations for unauthorized access and related activities, stalking and stalking related activities, gender sensitive offensive communications and sexual offences are discussed in detail. The issue of consented and unconsented sexual exposure in the internet and various regulatory provisions related to that is also analyzed. A discussion is followed, where an emphasis is made for creation of new women centric laws for their protection in cyber space, as the current laws which are dealing with crimes against women in the cyber space, are found to be archaic.

7.1 INTRODUCTION

Recognition of gender sensitive cyber crimes as a potential danger to the society began in UK only in the late 90's with wide spread discussions in the news media about stalking female celebrities through internet (Ellison & Akdeniz, 1998). In practice, cyber crime research scenario in the UK is more oriented towards analysis including drafting of legislations, for cyber crimes targeting national safety, financial security, corporate identities and information and child safety. Cyber harassments and offences against women are comprehensively covered by the Protection of Harassment Act, 1997. When compared with the US, the UK scenario is more conservative to regulate gender centric cyber harassments except those which involve physical harm.

DOI: 10.4018/978-1-60960-830-9.ch007

This is more evident from the available statistical reports of cyber crime in the UK. Analyzing the 2008-2009 report of "Garlik", "The online experts",[1] it can be seen that among 29.7 million adult internet users in UK, there are approximately 2,374,000 instances of online harassment.[2] By online harassment, the report indicates cases of mental distress of the victim, stalking, sending unwanted abusive mails containing hate messages, racial messages, threatening messages and blackmailing mails etc)[3] This report shows that among other crimes, there were 86,900 instances of identity theft and identity fraud (which includes impersonation, using of other's identity card, identity theft etc mainly for financial gain),[4] 207,700 instances of financial frauds (which includes losses of plastic cards, bank frauds etc),[5] 137,600 instances of computer misuse (the report does not include virus infections)[6] and 609,700 instances of sexual offences which cover victimization of children mainly.[7] Apart from the Garlik report, we did not find any detailed analysis of cyber victimization, especially of women in UK. This could be an indication as how individuals, especially women are conservative about reporting the online crimes that happen to them. A victimization survey to unearth online crimes against women in the UK is the need of the hour.

7.2 UNAUTHORIZED ACCESS AND RELATED ACTIVITIES

As discussed in chapter 2, hacking and hacking related activities may not always be restricted to crimes committed against the nation or the corporate entities alone. We see it as a crime when done to stored computer data or the computer as a machine of any female victim. To access her personal information including pictures without proper authorization, with intention to misuse it, distribute it in the internet, modify the contents and give a false impression of the victim etc, are also criminal activities like stalking or bullying. Strangely enough, in UK, these sorts of cyber criminal activities against women have been never given a separate legal treatment on the pretext that these are also one of the hacking related activities which are done to individuals. We feel that the core reason for the growth of internet crimes against women could be lackluster attitude of the law and justice machinery to understand the nature of hacking related activities targeted especially to the women. Such sorts of unauthorized access towards personal data may lead to several other cyber offences including public defamation and humiliation, impersonation, unwanted exposure of the victim in adult entertainment industry etc.

Unlike the US, the UK does not have any women – special regulation to cover cyber offences originating from domestic violence or dating violence; rather the offences related to unauthorized access are regulated by a compact legislation called "Computer Misuse Act, 1990". Under this Act, three offences are penalized, namely, unauthorized access to computer material,[8] or to enable any such access to secure unauthorized access,[9] intention to create further menace with such unauthorized access[10] and unauthorized modification of the computer material.[11] As mentioned earlier, this Act was created to protect both men and women victims. Notably, the drafting of the language could very well suit the needs for preventive actions against harassment of women also when it says that the *mens rea* must be directed to the 'act' that the offender knows would successfully accomplish his intention to harm his victim.[12] In brief, the offender can be held guilty for unauthorized access if it is proved that he used his technological knowledge to access the computer material or data with intention to harm the victim.

The penalties for such offences are on a summary conviction in England and Wales to imprisonment for a term of 12 months or to a monetary fine not exceeding statutory maximum, or both. In case of summary conviction in Scotland, the law prescribes imprisonment for six months or to a fine not exceeding statutory maximum, or both.[13]

7.3 STALKING AND STALKING RELATED ACTIVITIES

UK does not have a law to address cyber stalking. The problem is dealt by other conventional laws more as a part of harassment which is stretched to imply harassment through digital publications. Firstly, it is the Protection from Harassment Act, 1997 which is construed as the main legislation for prevention of cyber stalking. Sections 1 and 4 serve the purpose when it states in section 1 that "A person must not pursue a course of conduct (a) which amounts to harassment of another, and (b) which he knows or ought to know amounts to harassment of the other." Section 4 must also be included when dealing with cyber stalking, as it mentions the "fear factor" which is essential to constitute "cyber stalking".[14] But the inherent problem of English law regarding cyber stalking is, the term 'cyber stalking' is never legally defined by the Protection from harassment Act, 1997, (Basu & Jones, 2008) or by any laws. The definition of cyber stalking provided by the Crown Prosecution Services, is: "Cyber stalking generally takes the form of threatening behavior or unwanted advances directed at another using the internet and other forms of online communications".[15]

Secondly, in cases when stalking is carried out through cyberspace, the legislations which are used as associate provisions with the Protection from Harassment Act are the Communications Act, 2003, Telecommunications Act, 1984, Malicious communications Act, 1988 etc. The purpose of these legislations in context of online stalking are however limited to sending harassing mails or messages.[16]

Also, Bocij (2003) in his study on "Victims of cyber stalking", has showed that cyber stalkers concentrate more on issuing threats, harming the victim's reputation, causing damage to data or equipment and attempting to access confidential information and computer monitoring. Nonetheless, this broad usage of the term has successfully covered not only the act of stalking, but also related activities like bullying, sending harassing mails, defaming, threatening etc.[17] Bocij's (2003) study further shows that among 169 respondents of his study, female accounted for 56.3 percent of the sample and males for 43.7 percent. The study further showed that maximum number of the respondents have experienced various dimensions of cyber stalking like receiving threatening mails, harassments via email, receiving abusive comments via mails and chat rooms and also from other known / unknown persons. Also there were several attempts to impersonate the victim both for personal communications with victim's friends and online acquaintances and also for online purchases and attempts on behalf of the stalker to monitor victim's computer activities etc (Bocij, 2003). It is understandable that in UK, stalking has remained a compact term to cover any activity which creates fear in the minds of victims; and the act of cyber stalking could be legally recognized only when it fulfills the four major fear factors that were pointed out by Bocij (2003).

This indicates the fallacy that cyber stalking is seen as quantitative assault in the UK where legislative action could be taken only when cyber stalking results in continuous harassment including receiving mails / messages / texts more than once to the victim's inbox and such communications are also made public either by sending similar defaming / harassing / threatening messages to the acquaintances of the victim or publishing them in message board or public websites. Unlike the US laws, in the UK, the concept of cyber stalking therefore must be accompanied by either defamation or bullying words or threatening or harassing mails or messages. The fear factor alone does not cause cyber stalking to be termed as crime; it must necessarily be grossly offensive communication which creates a feeling of being harassed plus the fear factor. In other words, as per UK laws, cyber shadowing and then subsequent stalking is no offence unless it gives rise to any visible harm, no matter whether such stalking behavior makes the victim apprehensive of the worst. More so, such harm must be qualified as 'harassment'. Ironically, the term 'harassment' does not find any specific legal definition in the English laws. Basu and Jones (2008, p. 144) rightly pointed out that: "the relevant UK domestic laws on harassment (of which stalking is a form) are a rag bag of statutes, many predating the explosion of internet and the development and use of mobile phones".[18] They signify the "rag bag" containing Telecommunications Act, 1984, Malicious communications Act, 1988 etc.

Cyber stalking therefore remains synonymous to harassing communications as per the UK laws and as such women victims of cyber stalking remain in the peril of being victimized both by the stalker as well as by government reporting agencies, especially the local police who may not understand the nature of the crime. Notably, some academicians of UK (Basu, 2010; Wall, 2007) feel that the legal status of cyber stalking is satisfactorily regulated. Basu (2010) feels that there is no need for a separate regulation for cyber stalking because "there can be a law or legislation for everything but society cannot work in such a way."[19] Wall (2007, p. 123-125) has pointed out that cyber stalking has often been referred to as "grooming", and are taken care by UK's law enforcement agencies.

We strongly feel that UK lacks legislation to tackle the situation especially when cyber stalking forms a crime in itself, i.e., stalking online as well as offline threatening of the female victim; and not just an "element" to form a crime like cyber gender harassment, cyber teasing, revealing the female victim's privacy to the wider audience like exposing the victim's daily cyber activities to the world, approaching her friends and acquaintances through her email / forum discussions / cyber social networking etc. This further remains a main factor for discouraging female victims to report cyber stalking in the UK. A uniform cyber stalking law in the UK, creating awareness about the nature of cyber stalking and its perilous effects towards women victims, training the police officials on cyber stalking etc are the need of the day.

7.4 GENDER BASED OFFENSIVE COMMUNICATIONS

Discussions about English stalking laws necessarily pull up the question of offensive communications. As it could be seen from the laws discussed under the heading "stalking", the laws presumed to regulate stalking in UK essentially regulates offensive communications through public network. But it is unfortunate that there are actually no separate gender protective laws to protect women from cyber offensive communication including sending defaming offensive messages or even obscene messages to female victim's inbox other than the above mentioned Acts.[20] Analyzing the Communications Act, 2003, it could be seen that this law was made to regulate cyber space[21] (which was partially fulfilled by Protection from Harassment Act, Malicious Communications Act and Telecommunications Act) and broadcasting in general. As such Chapter 1 of this Act under section 127 penalizes improper use of public network communications with 6 months imprisonment or a fine not exceeding level 5 on the standard scale or both. It is to be noted that the term "improper use" has been meant to describe offensive communication including sending offensive / threatening / harassing mails / obscene remarks / materials etc which were also formerly penalized by Malicious Communications Act.

But the question is how far communication through internet can be offensive against women as per English laws? The legislations we have discussed, prohibits grossly offensive communication which also includes obscene remarks or materials. None as such covers gender-harassing remarks, gender discriminatory remarks or even gender based bullying remarks. This could be due to less legislative concentration on the gender sensitive issues other than basic equal payment or economic security guarantees. However, the new Equality Act 2010[22] promises better management of gender based communication crimes in the cyber space from a holistic approach as this Act covers gender based harassments [23] and victimization[24] as prohibited conduct.

7.5 SEXUAL OFFENCES

Legal approach towards pornography, grooming adult females for pornographic purposes and 'forced pornography' needs renewed evaluation when it is seen from the perspective of digital age. Grooming for cyber pornographic purposes, defaming women by sexual way (by morphing her picture for defamation, putting her information in publicly accessible search engines etc) and infringement of cyber privacy of women etc, could be regulated by the Criminal Damage Act, 1977 (to cover physical damage to computer systems), Data Protection Act (for protecting personal information stored in the computer devices) the Computer Misuse Act, 1990 (related to the penetration, alteration and damage to computer systems), Protection from Harassment Act, 1997 and Malicious Communication Act 1998, Communications Act, 2003 (for the purpose of misusing public networking system and also for aiding or abetting for piercing cyber privacy in dishonest ways.[25]).The Theft Act, 1968, (for fraudulently using victim's identity) and Equality Act, 2010 (to cover harassment of sexual nature or in other words, grooming for sexual purposes). Even though some of these Acts were drafted to safeguard e-commerce and related privacy issues, post 1999 laws are remarkably focused towards individual communications and related security issues. However, voyeurism and usage of the victims' photographs for adult pornography still poses serious threat to the online privacy of the female victims. The only available legal answer could be Sexual Offences Act, 2003 which under section 67 criminalizes unconsented voyeurism and its distribution.

7.5.1 Consented and Unconsented Sexual Exposure in the Internet

Interestingly, some of the laws like Police and Justices Act, Sexual offences Act etc were targeted to control child pornography and not specifically to save women's interest. However, Section 63 of the Criminal Justice and Immigration Act, 2008, criminalize possession of extreme porn images in one's personal computer.[26] The origin of the above provision could be traced to the heinous murder of a young female school teacher Jane Longhurst in 2003, which was suspected to be the result of one of the internet based atrocity, the violent pornography. The conviction of the accused Graham Coutt in 2004 made a huge impact in UK, demanding a ban of extreme internet sites promoting violence against women in the name of sexual gratification. This forced the government to pressurize shutting of the violent pornographic websites. But it was seemingly an impossible task for the government to ban such sites especially when many such sites originate outside UK where performers perhaps legally consented for the pornographic acts. Hence to eradicate the problem of 'importing' illegal sites, Criminal Justice and Immigration Act 2008 was drafted to ban possession of such sites. It highlighted pornography and the possession of it, rather than obscenity and took a successful attempt to legally distinguish pornography and obscenity and victimization of women.

Section 63 of the Act explicitly discusses the problem. To start with, the section in its opening subsection criminalizes possession of an extreme pornographic image.[27] The law further analyzes the meaning of "extreme pornographic image" which is both pornographic and extreme. The law in UK recognizes an image as "pornographic" if it is of such a nature that it must reasonably be assumed to have been produced solely or principally for the purpose of sexual arousal" (subsection 3 of section 63). An extreme pornographic image therefore is defined as an image which is both pornographic and extreme (section 2 (a) and (b)). This particular law has minutely answered several questions as, could an image which is part of a series be considered as falling within the meaning of subsection 3 (pornographic)? Also, what is meant by "extreme image"? Subsection (4) thus clarifies:

Where (as found in the person's possession) an image forms part of a series of images, the question whether the image is of such a nature as is mentioned in subsection (3) is to be determined by reference to— (a) The image itself, and (b) (if the series of images is such as to be capable of providing a context for the image) the context in which it occurs in the series of images.

Subsection 5 is used as an aid to subsection (4) and it provides an example. It says, where an image forms an integral part of a narrative constituted by a series of images, and having regard to those images as a whole, they are not of such a nature that they must reasonably be assumed to have been produced solely or principally for the purpose of sexual arousal (paras (a) and (b)), the image may, by virtue of being part of that narrative, could fall apart from the definition "pornographic", even though the image if taken by itself, may satisfy the conditions to be 'pornographic".

Both subsections 6 and 7 define and clarify the meaning of extreme pornography according to which, an image to be categorized as extreme image[28] must fulfill two conditions, namely:

1. the image must fall within the meaning of subsection (7), i.e., it portrays, in an explicit and realistic way, any of the following, (a) an act which threatens a person's life, (b) an act which results, or is likely to result, in serious injury to a person's anus, breasts or genitals, (c) an act which involves sexual intercourse with a human corpse, or (d) a person performing an act of intercourse or oral sex with an animal (whether dead or alive), and a reasonable person looking at the image would think that any such person or animal was real; and
2. it is grossly offensive, disgusting or otherwise of an obscene character.

This is to be noted that this law does not include extracted images from a classified films (section 64)[29]. The law further rules in section 67, that possessor of such extreme pornographic images is liable: (a) on summary conviction, to imprisonment for a term not exceeding the relevant period or a fine not exceeding the statutory maximum or both; (b) on conviction on indictment, to imprisonment for a term not exceeding 3 years or a fine or both.[30] Subsection (3) states that if the offence relates to an image that does not portray any act within section 63(7) (a) or (b), which refers to violent pornography, causing serious bodily injury to the "models" (the language of subsection and, Para 1 and 2 suggests that it is targeted to both male and female bodies), the offender is liable (a) on summary conviction, to imprisonment for a term not exceeding the relevant period or a fine not exceeding the statutory maximum or both; (b) on conviction on indictment, to imprisonment for a term not exceeding 2 years or a fine or both.

The law further clarifies the stand of the recipient when he/she receives such contents through mails/ messages etc. In such case, the liabilities could be exempted if he/she was in possession of such material for (i) legitimate reason, (ii) had not seen, did not know the contents of the message and (iii) received the material without request and did not keep for an unreasonable time.[31]

The critical analysis of the above, may further open a question as where do women victims stand as per this law? Victims who have been "forced" to give consent to be portrayed in extreme porno images, or whose digital images have been doctored to make them / her appear as a "consenting" model may find it extremely difficult to prove their victimization especially when they are threatened by their perpetrators or when they are completely unaware of the fact that they had been portrayed in this fashion. Also, it should be noted that no law punishes adult models or photographer or the crew behind it as it satisfies the contract laws between the model and the agency who is filming the porno images.[32] However, this specific provision remotely punishes distribution of such extreme pornographic videos in the internet as penalizing accessing and possessing such contents in personal computers may not be possible unless distribution of the same is also controlled.

The Criminal Justice Immigration Act revamped legal provisions for certain "social offences" for good. Thus apart from managing pornography and extreme pornography in a very subtle way, the Act also touched the Protection of Children's Act, 1978, for ruling over cases of indecent photographs of children in England and Wales[33] and Northern Ireland;[34] as well as Obscene Publication Act, 1959, decreasing punishment for publication of obscene material from five years to three years;[35] and the Sexual offences Act, for offences committed outside the United Kingdom by a national of United Kingdom and its extension to Wales and Northern England,[36] as well as amending section 15 of the sexual Offences Act to have more stringent monitoring on the child grooming.[37] Indeed all these offences relate directly to victimization of women in the cyber space and the law has taken positive steps to control it.

7.6 CONCLUSION

The above mentioned criminal laws in UK must be read together to understand the UK approach towards saving the interest of female users of the cyber space. But then it becomes really a difficult job for an educated, well informed, female victim to understand why and how the "attack" should be considered an "offence". Moreover the presence of the actual rule through numerous legislations could make it more confusing for the civilians as well as law enforcement officers of remote areas to understand the legal nature of the offence. It cannot be ruled out that due to lack of proper understanding, the victim might be rejected by the police from lodging a formal complaint. Could the Prevention of Harassment Act really save women from stalking and hate crimes? Could Equality Act really prove women's rights in the cyber space? Do these Acts guarantee that women will not be ridiculed for being "women" in the cyber space? Are these laws failing to prevent such crimes or rather encouraging these crimes due to back dated "phrases" or age old way of punishing the offender? Perhaps, Yes. Most of these laws have been drafted in the pre-internet era and they are being amended, modified, and refined to suit the needs of the cyber era. Hence, we feel that a woman centric law is the need of the day in the UK which could cover all the cyber offences where women form majority part of the victims.

REFERENCES

Adam, A. (2002). Cyberstalking and Internet pornography: Gender and the gaze. *Ethics and Information Technology, 4*, 133–142. doi:10.1023/A:1019967504762

Basu, S., & Jones, R. (2008). Regulating cyberstalking. In F. Schmallager, & M. Pittaro (Eds.), *Crimes of the Internet* (pp. 141–165). Upper Saddle River, NJ: Prentice Hall.

Bocij, P. (2003). Victims of cyberstalking: An exploratory study of harassment perpetrated via the Internet. *First Monday*. Retrieved on 28th June, 2010, from http://firstmonday.org/htbin/cgiwrap/bin/ojs/index.php/fm/article/view/1086/1006

Ellison, L., & Akdeniz, Y. (1998). Cyber-stalking: The regulation of harassment on the Internet. *Criminal Law Review*, December Special Edition: Crime, Criminal Justice and the Internet, 29-48.

Wall, D. S. (2007). *Cybercrimes: The transformation of crime in the information age*. Cambridge, UK: Polity.

ENDNOTES

[1]   http://www.garlik.com

[2]   Report is available at http://www.garlik.com/cybercrime_report.php

[3]   For more information see http://www.garlik.com/cybercrime_report.php

[4]   ibid

[5]   ibid

[6]   ibid

[7]   ibid

[8]   Section 1 of the Computer Misuse Act, 1990.

[9]   As has been amended by the Police and Justice Act, 2006 (c.48).

[10] Section 2 ibid.

[11] Section 3 ibid.

[12] Section 1 of the CMA 1990 states in subsection 1C that a person would be guilty of an offence of unauthorized access to computer material if he knows at the time when he causes the computer to perform the function that that is the case; again, under subsection 2 it is said that the intent a person has to have to commit an offence under this section need not be directed at any particular program or data; a program or data of any particular kind; or a program or data held in any particular computer.

[13] As has been amended by the Police and Justice Act, 2006 (c.48).

[14] Section 4(1&2) states that a person whose course of conduct causes another to fear, on at least two occasions, that violence will be used against him is guilty of an offence if he knows or ought to know that his course of conduct will cause the other so to fear on each of those occasions. Further, the person whose course of conduct is in question ought to know that it will cause another to fear that violence will be used against him on any occasion if a reasonable person in possession of the same information would think the course of conduct would cause the other so to fear on that occasion.

[15] ibid

[16] Section 127 of the Communications Act, 2003 makes it an offence to send or cause to be sent any message or other matter that is grossly offensive or of an indecent, obscene or menacing character by means of public electronic communications network; The Malicious Communications Act also makes it an offence under section 1 to send any mail /message which is grossly offensive, threatening in character or carrying an intention to defame the victim.

[17] Resources gathered from http://www.bullyonline.org/related/stalking.htm

18   ibid

19   From a private conversation with Subhajit Basu, 2010.

20   Communications Act 2003, Telecommunications Act 1984, Malicious Communications Act 1988, Protection from Harassment Act.

21   The preamble to the Act says this is "An Act to confer functions on the Office of Communications; to make provision about the regulation of the provision of electronic communications networks and services and of the use of the electro-magnetic spectrum; to make provision about the regulation of broadcasting and of the provision of television and radio services; to make provision about mergers involving newspaper and other media enterprises and, in that connection, to amend the Enterprise Act 2002; and for connected purposes."

22   2010 Chapter 15

23   Section 26 of the Act includes one's conducts violating other's dignity or harassment of sexual nature against women as harassment. For more information see Section 26 of the Equality Act, 2010, available @ http://www.opsi.gov.uk/acts/acts2010/ukpga

24   Section 27 speaks about victimization irrespective of gender when the perpetrator victimizes the concerned victim who is doing a protected act. For more information see Section 27 of the Equality Act.

25   For more information see sections 125-127 of the Communications Act, 2003.

26   Section 63 of the Criminal Justice and Immigrations Act, 2008.

27   Subsection 1 of the section 63

28   According subsection (8) of section 63 image means (a) a moving or still image (produced by any means); or b) data (stored by any means) which is capable of conversion into an image within paragraph (a).

29   Section 64 excludes extracted images from classified films in subsection (1). the section runs as follows: (2) An "excluded image" is an image, which forms part of a series of images contained in a recording of the whole or part of a classified work. (3) But such an image is not an "excluded image" if— (a) it is contained in a recording of an extract from a classified work, and (b) it is of such a nature that it must reasonably be assumed to have been extracted (whether with or without other images) solely or principally for the purpose of sexual arousal. (4) Where an extracted image is one of a series of images contained in the recording, the question whether the image is of such a nature as is mentioned in subsection (3)(b) is to be determined by reference to— (a) the image itself, and (b) (if the series of images is such as to be capable of providing a context for the image) the context in which it occurs in the series of images; and section 63(5) applies in connection with determining that question as it applies in connection with determining whether an image is pornographic. (5) In determining for the purposes of this section whether a recording is a recording of the whole or part of a classified work, any alteration attributable to— (a) a defect caused for technical reasons or by inadvertence on the part of any person, or (b) the inclusion in the recording of any extraneous material (such as advertisements), is to be disregarded. (6) Nothing in this section is to be taken as affecting any duty of a designated authority to have regard to section 63 (along with other enactments creating criminal offences) in determining whether a video work is suitable for a classification certificate to be issued in respect of it. (7) In this section— "classified work" means (subject to subsection (8)) a video work in respect of which a classification certificate has been issued by a designated authority (whether before or after the commencement of this section); "classification certificate" and "video work" have the same meanings as in the Video Recordings

Act 1984 (c. 39); "designated authority" means an authority which has been designated by the Secretary of State under section 4 of that Act; "extract" includes an extract consisting of a single image; "image" and "pornographic" have the same meanings as in section 63; "recording" means any disc, tape or other device capable of storing data electronically and from which images may be produced (by any means).(8) Section 22(3) of the Video Recordings Act 1984 (effect of alterations) applies for the purposes of this section as it applies for the purposes of that Act.

[30] Section 67, subsections 1 and 2

[31] Section 65

[32] Criminal Justice and Immigrations Act, 2008 very swiftly exempts the creator and actor(s) from liabilities of being part of violent pornographic clippings in the jurisdiction of English courts through section 66.This provision specifies that when the filming of violent pornography is done as consensual act of the partners and when models consent to act as "corpses", neither the creator nor the actors could be held liable.

[33] Section 69

[34] Section 70

[35] Section 71

[36] Section 72

[37] Section 73

Chapter 8
Cyber Crime Against Women and Regulations in Australia

CHAPTER OVERVIEW

This chapter deals with the legal regulations that protect Australian women in cyber space. Various issues that are discussed in this chapter are: Cyber harassments including hacking and hacking related offences against women and regulatory provisions, stalking women and the concerned laws, harassments, threatening, blackmailing, defamation and related laws. Legal approach to problems of 'forced pornography', obscenity and the liability of the ISPs as per the Australian laws are also discussed. The chapter ends with a discussion. In this chapter a strong emphasis is made on the need for new laws that will protect Australian women in cyber space.

8.1 INTRODUCTION

Cyber crime against women in Australia deserves a better analytical treatment from law and justice machinery as well as cyber criminologists, socio-legal researchers and activists. Ironically, most surveys show economic loss as the highest rated cyber crime happening in Australia, closely followed by virus infections, hacking, child pornography and cyber bullying among children (Rust, 2008; Arias, 2007, Roberts, 2008). Even though stalking has been enlisted as a crime,[1] besides other general cyber crimes listed above, we could find no good survey results of stalking by intimate partners to women or cyber victimizations of women including cyber bullying, privacy-penetration, cyber gender sensitive defamation, forced pornography etc. More emphasis is given to child grooming, crimes against children and

DOI: 10.4018/978-1-60960-830-9.ch008

youth belonging to the age group of 16-19 and identity theft (in relation to monetary crimes especially) in Australia (Roberts, 2008). In Australia, century old laws have been amended and adjusted to prevent cyber crimes and cyber borne crimes against the society as a whole. Even though victimization of women have taken a technical turn since long, little thought has been given to draft gender sensitive penal laws to save women from being abused and tormented. However, the good news is, several such 'adjusted' laws do help women victims while in 'cyber –distress'. In the following sections, we will discuss some of these federal and provincial laws, which are being used to prevent and protect cyber victimization of women in Australia and the government, and non-government initiatives, which are being taken to prevent cyber harassments of women.

8.2 CYBER HARASSMENTS

As per our typology discussed in the chapter 2, hacking may constitute a separate gender sensitive cyber crime even if it is not necessarily related to financial crimes. Hacking may lead to various other cyber crimes such as destroying personal information and blocking others to contact the victim, leaving her completely isolated in a cyber - imprisonment state; accessing the individual's personal and professional information and creating cloned web profiles to impersonate the victim; misusing the information of the female victim(s) including her pictures for illegal financial gains, especially by making her website / public profile look like hard core adult entertainer's profile; intentionally destroying her professional identity and make her a 'laughing stock', etc. As such, these sorts of harassments, which involve hacking, hacking and cloning, hacking and morphing, hacking and impersonation etc, are well controlled by the Federal Criminal Code Act, 1995, as has been amended by Cyber Crime Act, 2001.[2] The Cyber Crime Act, 2001, prohibits unauthorized access, modification or impairment of computer data, which is done with intent to commit a serious offence under section 477.1,[3] 2, 3, and 4.[4] However, these provisions are used maximum for preventing crimes against governments and corporations (Smith, Grobosky & Urbas, 2004). We found no literature to show that these provisions have also been used to prevent hacking and hacking related problems targeted towards women.

According to the Australian laws, hacking and hacking related problems are construed more as an offence towards the computer as a machine, towards the network and towards the government and financial data. In short, hacking is termed as "computer offence" done through 'carriage service.'[5] These provisions especially when read with provisions regarding invasions to privacy under the Privacy Act, 1988, may well be used as preventive legislation to prohibit harassing women when hacking and hacking related activities are done to publicly humiliate the victim by publishing her personal information, religious, feministic and sexual opinions and beliefs. Even though the main objective of the Privacy Act, 1988, is to secure financial, health and government identity related information, "sensitive records" as has been interpreted by Section 6 of the Act, could be extended to cover information or opinion about any individual's racial or ethnic origin, political opinion and belief, membership to unions and associations, religious opinions and favoritisms, sexual practices and preferences, criminal records, health records and also genetic records. It is presumed that women and men as well, may be victimized when the harasser hacks and cracks such information and uses it to fulfill revengeful or other harmful activities.

However, it must be noted that Privacy Act, 1988, does not provide protection to information which are generally available to public, including information "however published".[6] In such cases the provisions enacted in divisions 477 and 478 of the Criminal Code Act, 1995, must be used to protect women when their online profiles including personal websites, social networking profiles, pictures provided there in and blogs etc are engineered for wrongful gains. In such cases, women may face perennial problems especially when their personal information is available in any web host or social networking sites.

8.3 STALKING

Stalking seems to be a well-recognized problem, by which a majority of Australian women in the cyber space becomes victim (Ogilvie, 2000). According to Ogilvie (2000), women are stalked in different dimensions such as stalking by strangers, former intimate partners, male friends who are obsessive lovers etc. Even though the Federal Criminal Code does not address the subject directly, the use of Part 10.6, especially divisions 474.17 which deals with usage of internet and telecommunication services for harassing, creating menace or causing offence and 474.15 which deals with usage of internet and telecommunication services for creating threat, can very well combat online stalking and stalking related harassments. The later provision is better equipped to deal with the issues when the stalker is obsessive about harming his victim and the victim apprehends physical threat from online behaviors of the stalker. It is to be noted here that the language of division 474.15 extends the applicability of the law to the cyber space as well. The provision thus specifically mentions three sets of offences, namely, 'threat to kill', 'threat to cause serious harm' and offence which causes to believe that harm can be done but which may or may not generate 'actual fear'. The last set of offence could be seen to be happening against women in the internet often. As such stalking, including cyber stalking is regulated in Australian Capital Territory by section 34A of Crimes Act, 1900 (as inserted in 1996), in Northern Territory by section 189 of Criminal Code Act, (as inserted in 1994), in New South Wales by Section 562 AB of Crimes Act, 1900 (as inserted in 1994), in Queensland by section 359A of Criminal Code Act, (as inserted in 1993 and again amended in 1998); in South Australia by section 19AA of Criminal Law Consolidation Act, 1935 (as inserted in 1994); in Tasmania section 192 of Criminal Code Act, 1924 (as inserted in 1995 and again amended in 1999) and in Victoria by Section 21 A of the Crimes Act, 1958, (as inserted in 1995). All these provisions particularly mention applicability for mental threat as well.

Stalking may often lead to intrusion in to the privacy of female colleagues or even official networks containing professional information of female workers. In such cases, these regulations work well when read with Privacy Act 1988 along with the national privacy principles (extracted from the Privacy Act 1988)[7] and Guidelines on Workplace E-mail, Web Browsing and Privacy, provided by Australian Government, Office of the Privacy Commissioner.[8] Nonetheless, workplace gender abuse, cyber harassment and stalking are there to stay. With judicious use of the preventive principles and precautionary laws, it is hoped that such harassments will be lesser.

8.4 HARASSMENTS, THREATENING, BLACKMAILING, AND DEFAMATION

As has been stated in the typology in the second chapter, threatening, blackmailing to publish personal information and obscene pictures of the victim in the internet, continuously sending harassing, teasing or threatening messages, etc, are some forms of cyber crime against women. In Australia, such sorts of cyber crimes have not fully been approached from women victim's viewpoints, even though such harassments are rampant (Ogilvie, 2000). However, federal criminal code does manage these crimes universally through divisions 474.17 and 474.15, which deal with usage of internet and telecommunication services for harassing, creating menace or causing offence and usage of internet and telecommunication services for creating threat and online blackmailing. But these legislations may not be enough especially when the harassment turns up as continuous bullying (which may also turn into violent verbal abuse through internet communications) of the adult female victim or sexual as well as non sexual defamation of the victim (including publishing or threat to publish misleading information, false stories, morphed pictures etc of the victim).

Defamation by publishing modified contents of the victim and related harassment are dealt with by division 474.17 of the Federal Criminal Code. This provision deals with menace, harassments or causing offences through internet and telecommunication services. In 2006, NSW, Victoria, QLD, Tasmania, ACT, Western Australia etc had uniform defamation laws for the purpose of regulating defamatory publications both in print media as well as in the electronic media. Reviewing the uniform provincial laws, it can be seen that most States have accepted the meaning of 'electronic communication' as exchange of any data, text, image or video image.[9] This gives a wider meaning to 'defamatory statement' which may cover potential defamatory victimization woman victim where her image may be used with obscene sexual remarks to spoil her reputation. Even in cases where the textual remarks are derogatory and they are not accompanied by photo or cartoon images, these legislations can well be stretched to be used to combat the menace. But it must noted that defamation in the cyber space in Australia does not form a strict penal fault as per the criminal laws, and it is approached more as civil dispute.[10] However, the legislation strictly rules that wrongdoer cannot escape his liabilities by simply processing apology for the published offensive comments.[11] The law further establishes two ways to redress the grievances of the victim; by way of resolution of civil dispute without litigation where by the publisher may offer to amend the disputed publication[12] and if the victim accepts apology and the offer to the amendment, he/she will no more be eligible to continue with formal court procedures.[13] However, in case the victim does not accept the offer for amendment; the court must consider the offers made by the publisher to amend disputed part while awarding damages.[14] In cases of litigations of civil dispute, the court may award damages as remedy to the victim depending upon the gravity of the harm suffered by the victim.[15]

Defamation may essentially involve adult bullying also. It is disheartening to note that exclusive gender / race based online bullying prohibitory policy guidelines for adults have not yet gained much attention. Such menaces are however controlled by Sex Discrimination Act, 1984, Race Discrimination Act, 1975, and Australian Human Rights Commission Act, 1986 along with provisions of Federal Criminal Code Act, 1995. But these legislations are still inadequate to protect women online.

From the perusal of the federal and provincial laws mentioned above, we understand that victimization of women by way of offensive communications has been dealt from a very broad angle. Gender sensitive offensive communications targeted to women are treated more as 'sexual harassment'. As such, offensive communications which involves fear factor or which damages the female victim's reputation from non sexual perspective, are hardly given any separate legal recognition as an offence breaching women's fundamental rights. The root cause could be traced to the basic frame work of Human Rights Charter which promised special treatment to women in cases where, due to physical needs, they may not be able to claim equal opportunities as their male counterparts. Australian constitution also adopted equality provision in the same lines as that of Human Rights Charter and CEDAW. We feel that this concept of 'physical inabilities' has motivated for the creation of laws whose foremost aims should be protection of financial equality and protection of women from the perception of sex, and sexual harassment only. Australian laws are no exception and resultant, nonsexual defamation or harassment to women never gets any serious consideration from the law makers. The constitutional concern for freedom of thought and expression almost always overshadows the need of exclusive rights for women to live a dignified life.

8.5 FORCED PORNOGRAPHY AND OBSCENITY

Sexual defamation, publishing of morphed pictures; creating obscene images with obscene captions to describe a woman in an offensive way etc are not very well covered by Australian Federal Criminal Code or by any compact internet harassment related laws. Several commonwealth laws like the Federal Criminal Code, Broadcasting Services Amendment (online services) Act, 1999 etc do not actually prevent such online victimization on women, where the victim may be groomed, abused or threatened in sexual ways. The existing laws take more precautionary steps towards child pornography and related harassments than protecting adult victims of potential online sexual harassments. This could be considered as a crime only when the act is determined as "offensive" as subdivision 473.4 of the Federal Criminal Code lays down the category as what can be called 'offensive' in the following language:

The matters to be taken into account in deciding for the purposes of this part whether reasonable persons would regard particular material, or a particular use of a carriage service, as being, in all the circumstances, offensive, includes: (a) the standards of morality, decency and propriety generally accepted by reasonable adults; and (b) the literary, artistic or educational merit (if any) of the material; and (c) the general character of the material (including whether it is of a medical, legal or scientific character).

Therefore we understand that such issues like 'forced pornography' against adult females, sexual grooming, sending obscene mail/messages or publishing obscene images of the victim in the internet and thereby victimizing her, depends much upon the social morality, decency and propriety standards. The burden of proof falls very much upon the victim to establish as to how mischievous acts have crossed the red line of morality and decency. We note that this particular legislation clears all sorts of potential doubts about individual's right to explore sexual concepts through internet in the similar fashion as that of the 'Miller's test'[16] in the USA;

A brief examination of the existing Australian laws in this issue would show that these issues are generally approached from three aspects:

1. In cases when such pornographic and obscene images are made, morphed or created and distributed to wider audience with defamatory notes about the victim for the purpose of defaming her, the provincial defamation laws could be used along with federal provisions such as Division 474.17 of the Criminal Code Act, 1955 to penalize the act. However, as we have discussed earlier, law gives enough scope to bury the rage once the wrongdoer apologizes and withdraws the comments and offensive images.

2. In cases when such pictures and information are accessed by hacking the victim's personal computer data, such information are tampered and then distributed for mischievous gain including online sex trade, the Federal Criminal Code may be used through Divisions 477 (serious computer offences) and 478 (other computer offences), where the wrongdoer may be punished for unauthorized access of computer data and modifying it; along with provisions such as subdivision 474.14 and 474.17

which speak about using telecommunication network with intention to commit serious crime and using telecommunication network for harassing, creating menace, blackmailing etc.

3.   Cases of video voyeurism including capturing private parts of the victim's body, full or parts of her naked body, sexual activities performed by the victim etc, and then publishing it in the web, blackmailing the victim with such stored pictures or video graphs etc are dealt with by provincial law such as, section 91J of the Crimes Act, 1900, NSW,[17] and also Subdivision 474.15 of the Federal Criminal Code which deals with threatening and blackmailing communications.

8.6 LIABILITY OF THE ISPs

It could be noted that subdivision 474.25 of the Federal Criminal Code Act makes the internet service providers and internet content hosts liable for punishment in cases of distributing child pornography materials. But for distribution of adult offensive pornographic and obscene materials, the federal law makes the user of the internet service more liable and not the internet service provider / internet content hosts directly. However, the internet service provider may be liable only when distribution of such material is prohibited by Broadcasting services amendment (online services) Act, 1999 (Penfold, 2001). The execution of the prohibition order is a three phased function: (i) the complaints must be made to the Australian Broadcasting Authority (ABA), (ii) the ABA refers the controversial content to the Classification Board for their clarification, (iii) Once the Classification Board approves the content as liable to be removed, the ABA may order the concerned internet content host and service provider to take down the 'prohibited content'. However, if the content host fails to comply with the orders, ABA can take legal action against such internet service provider in case the content is hosted in Australia.

In this context Dow Jone's case must mentioned to explain the Australian judicial interpretation of applicability of the law of the land in cases of cyber defamation and liability of the users and the ISPs. In the landmark judgment of Dow Jones and Company Inc v Gutnick [2002][18] the High Court of Australia upheld Supreme Court of Victoria's findings that the content of the website was comprehended and downloaded in Victoria and as such, the Victorian laws will govern the suit and the laws of the place of uploading (i.e., the law of New Jersey or US federal laws) will not be applicable. Even though this verdict threw a strong blow to the virtual colonization of the cyber space by US hosted popular ISPs and their policies and terms which incline to the US principles of promotion of free speech and due process clause to suit the need of digital era, the subsequent US judgment in the Griffis Case (2002)[19] renewed the challenge for acceptance of foreign judgments in case of liabilities of the users and the ISPs who belong to the foreign jurisdictions outside the jurisdiction of the complainant's place of residence.

8.7 CONCLUSION

The above discussions lead us to the understanding that there is a severe lacuna in the Australian internet related laws for victimization of women by way of personal emotional injuries, emotional cheating, impersonation and adult cyber grooming. Even though stalking and harassment related laws are being used to blanket cover these menaces, certain cases of such issues with women need to be addressed as proper crimes and not simply nuisances. The federal law strictly addresses issues of grooming children for pornographic purposes. What happens when a woman who prefers to be cyber savvy, is groomed for similar harassments and finally falls in the cyber trap? The law has no answer because it is often presumed that adults will be more matured to save themselves. Australia tries to cater the needs of adult and teenage victims through several government initiatives like Australia High-tech Crime Centre (AHTCC) (Smith, Grabosky & Urbas, 2004), Australian Federal Police, Crime stoppers, [20] etc. However, it is disheartening to note that problems of adult female victims remain largely neglected in all these initiatives. At the same time, crime reporting in this arena seems to be very poor which could be one of the causes for having less legal concern. Numerous policy guidelines may well create awareness, but we strongly feel that issues of cyber victimization of women must be addressed by separate legislations which will bind morally and legally the offenders, the victims as well as the government reporting agencies.

REFERENCES

Arias, M. L. (March, 06, 2007). *Internet law- Cybercrime statistics in Australia*. Internet Business Law Services (IBLS). Retrieved on 6th July, 2010, from http://www.ibls.com/internet_law_news_portal_view.aspx?id=1840&s=latestnews

Ogilvie, E. (2000). *Stalking: Legislative, policing and prosecution patterns in Australia*. (Research and public policy series no. 34). Canberra, Australia: Australian Institute of Criminology. Retrieved on 6th July, 2010, from http://www.aic.gov.au/documents/3/D/D/ %7B3DDEC8F8-7ECC-4DC3-9E92-CCD62DA463EE%7DRPP34.pdf

Penfold, C. (2001). Nazis, porn and politics: Asserting control over Internet content. *The Journal of Information, Law and Technology (JILT)*, 2001(2). Retrieved on 6th July, 2010, from http://www2.warwick.ac.uk/fac/soc/law/elj/jilt/2001_2/penfold/

Roberts, L. (2008). *Cyber-victimization in Australia: Extent, impact on individuals and responses*. Briefing paper no.6, June, 2008. Retrieved on 14.12.2010 from http://www.utas.edu.au/tiles/publications_and_reports/briefing_papers/briefing_papers_pdf/Briefing_Paper_No_6.pdf

Rust, L. (June, 20, 2008). *Australia tops cyber crime list*. Retrieved on 6th July, 2010, from http://www.crime-research.org/news/20.06.2008/3422/

Smith, R. G., Grabosky, P., & Urbas, G. (2004). *Cyber Criminals on Trial*. Cambridge: Cambridge University Press. doi:10.1017/CBO9780511481604

Whitty, M., & Carr, A. (2006). *Cyberspace romance: The psychology of online relationships*. Hampshire, UK: Palgrave Macmillan.

ENDNOTES

[1]   "Cyber crime" @ http://ken-g.webado.net/cybercrime.shtml

[2]   Act No. 12 of 1995 as amended taking into account amendments up to Act No. 127 of 2005.

[3]   This particular section imposes criminal liability in such cases with life imprisonment or imprisonment for 5 years depending upon the seriousness of the crime.

4   Further, sections 477.2 and 3 of this Act prohibit unauthorised modification of data to cause impairment and unauthorised impairment of electronic communications with maximum punishment for 10 years. Apart from these offences of hacking, which are considered as "serious offences", this Act also prohibits unauthorised access to, or modification of, restricted data under section 478.1, unauthorised impairment of data held on a computer disk etc. (s. 478.2). Both these offences are punishable with imprisonment for maximum of 2 years; Possession or control of data with intent to commit a computer offence (s. 478.3), which is punishable with imprisonment for 3 years maximum and producing, supplying or obtaining data with intent to commit a computer offence (s. 478.4) with punishment for maximum 3 years.

5   Telecommunication Act, 1997, under Section 7 defines 'carriage services' as "service for carrying communications by means of guided and/or unguided electromagnetic energy'.

6   Section 6, Privacy Act 1988.

7   Collected from http://www.privacy.gov.au/materials/types/infosheets/view/6583

8   http://www.privacy.gov.au/materials/types/guidelines/view/6056

9   For further reading please see Defamation Act 2005 (QLD), Defamation Act 2005 (NSW) etc.

10   For more information see Defamation Acts 2005, NSW

11   Section 20, Defamation Acts 2005, NSW

12   Section 13, Defamations Act, 2005, NSW

13   Section 17, Defamations Act, 2005, NSW

14   Section 18, Defamation Act 2005, NSW

15   Section 34, Defamation Act 2005, NSW

16   *Miller v. California*, 413 U.S. 15 (1973).

17   Section 91J addresses video voyeurism and prescribes punishment for producing and distributing voyeur videos in the media including the internet;

18   HCA 56; 210 CLR 575; 194 ALR 433; 77 ALJR 255 (decided on 10 December 2002), retrieved from http://www.austlii.edu.au/au/cases/cth/high_ct/2002/56.html on 12.06.2010

19   Katherine Griffis vs. Mariane Luban [2002], retrieved from http://www.lawlibrary.state.mn.us/archive/supct/0207/c301296.htm on 13.06.2010

20   http://www.crimestoppers.com.au/cs/home.jsp

Chapter 9
Cyber Victimization of Women and Cyber Laws in India

CHAPTER OVERVIEW

This chapter provides a situational analysis of cyber crimes against women in India and laws that prevent cyber victimization in general and women in particular. The chapter is divided into three parts. The part one provides a situational analysis of cyber victimization of women in India, where a pilot study on cyber victimization is also discussed. The part two of this chapter deals with the current legal protection that are available to women victims in India for cyber crimes such as offensive communication, offences against cyber privacy, hacking, stalking and related crimes, cheating by impersonation, voyeurism, pornography, obscenity and indecent representation of women in the cyber space. The part three discusses on various loopholes that exist in Indian laws, especially the Indian Information Technology Act, and suitable solutions are provided.

9.1 INTRODUCTION

In India, cyber crime against women is relatively a new concept. It can be noted that when India started her journey in the field of Information Technology, the immediate need that was felt is to protect the electronic commerce and related communications and not cyber socializing communications. The drafters of the Indian Information Technology Act, 2000, created it on the influence of the Model Law on Electronic Commerce, which was adopted by the resolution of the General Assembly of the United Nations in 1997. The Act turned out to be a half baked law as the operating area of the law stretched

DOI: 10.4018/978-1-60960-830-9.ch009

beyond electronic commerce to cover cyber attacks of non-commercial nature on individuals as well. While commercial crimes and economic crimes were moderately managed by this Act, it miserably failed to prevent the growth of cyber crime against individuals, including women (Halder & Jaishankar, 2008). However, it took nearly eight years for the Indian parliament to create a modified all exclusive information technology law which tries to regulate illegal cyber activities with prime focus towards protection of electronic commerce. During this gap of eight years of the chaotic lawless situation, India witnessed growth of cyber crimes and watched helplessly the perpetration of cyber crime against women in particular. Often the laws that were used to combat such crimes set a wrong example and confusion; women victims were hugely discouraged to report the crimes by peers; immediate media attention and the attitude of confused government reporting agencies made women victims more traumatized than their cyber crime victimization.

PART I: SITUATIONAL ANALYSIS OF CYBER VICTIMIZATION OF WOMEN

9.2 The 'Gestation Period'

In India, 'cyber crime against women' was an issue of which few talked about and few worked on and which was suffered by huge numbers of victims helplessly. The term 'cyber crime against women' in India is mostly used to cover sexual crimes and sexual abuses in the internet, such as morphing the picture and using it for purposes of pornography, harassing women with sexually blackmailing / harassing mails or messages etc, or cyber stalking (Balakrishnan, 2009; Mohan, 2004). This is also evident from the fact that majority of the cases reported to the police are of the nature of sexual crimes and most of them are booked under the erstwhile Section 67 (which was meant to cover pornography and obscenity in the internet) of the Information Technology Act, 2000. The following examples depict the situation on this issue:

In the case of 'Sex Doctor', the accused, an orthopedic surgeon named Dr. Prakash, was found guilty under Section 506 (part II of the section which prescribes punishment for criminal intimidation to cause death or grievous hurt), 367 (which deals with kidnapping or abduction for causing death or grievous hurt) and 120-B (criminal conspiracy) of the IPC and Section 67 of Information Technology Act, 2000 (which dealt with obscene publication in the internet). Dr. Prakash was accused of taking obscene pictures and videos by forcing women to perform sexual acts and then later uploading and selling these videos as adult entertainment materials abroad. He was sentenced for life imprisonment and a pecuniary fine of Rupees. 1,25,000 under the Immoral Trafficking (Prevention) Act, 1956 (CNN-IBN, 2008).

In the case of *State of Tamil Nadu vs. Suhas Katti*, which is considered as one of the first cases to be booked under the Information Technology Act, 2000 (IT Act); the accused Katti posted obscene, defamatory messages about a divorced woman in the Yahoo message group. The accused advertised the victim as one who solicits for sex. The accused was convicted under sections 469, 509 of Indian Penal Code (IPC) and 67 of IT Act 2000 and was sentenced to undergo 2 years rigorous imprisonment and fine (India News, 2010).

The above-mentioned cases were the first of its kind that were reported in India after the IT Act 2000 came into existence. Halder and Jaishankar (2008) have explored ten basic types of cyber crimes that happen to Indian women in the cyber space. These are: Harassment via e-mail, Cyber-stalking, Cyber defamation, Hacking, Morphing, Email spoofing, Cyber pornography, Cyber sexual defamation, Cyber flirting and Cyber bullying. However, the Indian criminal justice machineries, media and the victims limit their outlook only to sexual crimes, harassing mails and stalking and the awareness of other crimes targeting Indian women in the cyber space remain limited. The rate of reporting of the crimes was low as the present legal infrastructure often failed to mete out justice (Halder & Jaishankar, 2008). Halder and Jaishankar (2008) also noted that Indian laws were unequipped to regulate these trends of crime in the cyber space (also see Halder, 2007). This was apparent in the case of Ritu Kohli (Cyberlaw Consultant, 2000). This case dates back to 2000-2001 when Ms. Kohli complained to the Delhi police about being disturbed by numerous phone calls of malicious nature. It was found that Kohli's online identity was being used in a website called www.mirc.com where 'she' was having online chats with everyone in obscene, vulgar languages; 'she' also distributed her residential phone number and address apparently to entertain men for sexual activities. When Delhi police swung into action, it was found that the perpetrator Manish Kathuria impersonated Ms. Kohli in the chat rooms, and he was found stalking her also. Even though this case was termed as 'India's first case on stalking,' the accused was not booked under any laws relating to stalking as the IT Act does not recognize stalking. He was finally booked under Section 509 of the IPC, which punishes for harming the modesty of women.

9.3 The Transition Period

The situation related to the prevention of cyber crimes against women and their protection changed during the period of 2006-2008. This could be called a transition period in the field of cyber crime regulation in India. With the introduction of the Bill for the amended Information Technology Act in 2006, India witnessed installation of cyber crime police cells in various States of India.[1] This encouraged the victims to approach the cyber crime cells through online form-fill up facilities, which to a certain extent enhanced the awareness and reporting of the crimes by the victims. However, the concept of cyber victimization remained to be used mainly for covering financial data theft and cyber sexual offences including stalking. In these situations, cyber crime related laws were hardly used due to lack of suitable provisions in the Information Technology Act. In 2009, Indian actor Celena Jaitley had registered a complaint with the Mumbai cyber crime cell that during one of her photo shoot someone had captured her images and published it in the web after morphing it in a vulgar manner. The complaint also mentioned that those morphed pictures were being used to sell products though websites. The case was considered fit case to be tried under provisions for obscenity and pornography of the IT Act (Dnaindia, 2009).

9.4 Pilot Study on Cyber Victimization

On behalf of our organization 'Centre for Cyber Victim Counselling' (CCVC), we conducted a pilot study with a sample size of 73 respondents (60 respondents were women) from all over India on cyber victimization of women and related awareness among women and men in India.[2] The following are some of the results of the pilot study:

9.4.a Women Respondents' Knowledge on Their Victimization

The study covered adult male and female respondents and 74% of respondents felt that women are more vulnerable in the cyber space than men. This study covered 60 female respondents. Among these 60 respondents, only 11.7% are aware that they had bad encounters in the cyber space. 85% of these respondents have received abusive mails containing pornographic images / erotic messages etc from known / not so known / known through friends of social networking sites / unknown individuals. Only 15% respondents are aware that these messages are 'trashes' and are never bothered by these mails. Hence, these respondents said NO when they were asked whether they had received any abusive messages etc that bothers them. Almost 50% of these respondents have received threatening / blackmailing / abusive mails from their ex-boyfriends / ex-husbands.

When asked about their awareness about traditional cyber crimes like hacking, stalking etc, we found that 48.3% had felt that they had been victims of hacking, 41.7% responded that they had never been victims of hacking and 10.0% responded that they are not aware. 40% of these respondents felt that they had been stalked, 46.7% responded negatively, while 13.3% responded that they are not aware. 61.7% had been victims of impersonation, 26.7% responded negatively while 11.6% responded that they are not aware whether they had been victimized by impersonated profiles of others. Interestingly, 50% have seen their cloned profiles, identities etc, 40% have never seen such things and 10% are not aware that their profile could be or had been cloned. 71.7% had confirmed that they had been defamed in the cyber space by various modes and in the real life, due to cyber assisted defamation; 18.3% responded that they had never been defamed and 10.0% told they are not aware. 41.7% said that they had received messages either in the emails or in their social networking profiles which amount to hate messages, 46.7% reported that they had never received such messages in their inbox and 11.6% are stated that they were not aware. 45.0% responded that they had been targeted in the cyber space (emails, blogs, social networking sites, community walls etc) due to their gender and / or feminine ideologies; 53.3% reported that they had never been targeted and 1.7% told they are not aware. 33.3% have seen their morphed pictures and are aware that such pictures have been misused; 58.3% had never seen their morphed pictures and 8.4% are not aware of such things. 33.3% have been bullied, 56.7% responded that they had not been bullied and they do not consider any teasing / flaming remarks as something, which could be qualified as "bullying message". 10% responded that they are not aware what is meant by bullying. 40% responded that they had been victimized by their known or not so known virtual friends; 58.3% confirmed that they had never been victimized by their virtual friends and 1.7% said they are not aware that virtual acquaintances can victimize individuals.

9.4.b Awareness of Cyber Cultures

Among the 73 respondents (including 60 Men and 13 Women), 56.2% are aware of the basic age limit for joining any cyber community / groups / social networking sites. 46.6% of these 73 respondents allow others like spouse, children, intimate partners etc to use their own id and password. Strangely enough, the group of respondents who form this 46.6%, also includes a fraction of those who belong to those 56.2% of the respondents who are aware of minimum age for joining cyber-networking communities. It is interesting to note that this group of respondents, knowing well about the minimum age limit of users for joining social networking sites etc, allows their children besides spouses, to use their internet ids, which we understand, is a risky act. This may motivate child victimization when the child is approached by acquaintances of the parents who may send adult contents to the child user unknowingly, thinking that the internet identity is actually being used by the original owner, i.e, an adult. 69.9% of these respondents are aware of various self protection tools in the internet like filtering emails, blocking unwanted persons, locking one's personal walls, albums and information in the social networking sites etc. 30.1% do not believe in restricting their emails / chat boxes / social networking sites only to known friends and they do not use any safety options to hide their email ids, chat ids, social networking sites in sites which may allow public search of individuals and their personal information on the basis of emails, social networking ids etc. 37.0% respondents mail / message back to any mails / messages that they receive from unknown sources including strangers, spammers etc. These respondents communicate with such strangers more out of curiosity than necessity. 74.0% respondents share their personal information such as: actual residential place, telephone numbers, personal favorites, personal pictures, mood swings, thoughts about other friends, political ideologies, non political events, cinemas, holiday-places, children's schoolings and spouse's job and related information with virtual friends in social networking comminutes, chat partners etc whom they have never seen in real life. We found out that only 37.0% respondents believe in exercising right to speech in a controlled and measured way and as many as 63.0% respondents feel that there is no need to be formal or control speech or expressions in the written form. Among these 73 respondents, only 27.4% take the risk of chatting with unknown chatroom participants. 71.2% respondents feel it is risky to chat with unknown people and 1.4% respondents do not chat with unknown persons.

9.4.c Awareness of Legal Rights / Laws

In our research, we noted that along with awareness of cyber crimes common legal knowledge also plays a great role in encouraging victims to report crime. Among the 73 respondents, 80.8% are aware that hacking, creation of pornography / distributing the same, distribution obscene materials etc are criminal offences; 19.2% are not aware about these. 78.1% are aware of his / her legal right to protect privacy in the cyber space; and only 19.2% are aware that cyber bullying, cyber stalking, sending annoying, defaming messages etc can be penalized.

9.4.d Reporting Behavior of Female Victims

Our research study showed that 35% of women respondents have reported abuse in the cyber space to social networking sites and ISPs; some of them were happy with the response from the ISPs, some were not happy with nonchalant attitude of the ISPs. However, they did not feel that police complaint was necessary. 46.7% respondents were never bothered either with any sort of victimization or with reporting any such incidences. They preferred to stay 'as they are' and 18.3% responded that are not aware of any reporting agencies including the ISPs. Further, only 8.3% had felt confident to refer the victimization to the police, while 91.7% victims felt it is safer to not to sought for police help. They apprehended more harassment once they report the crimes.

In this connection, it may be noted that Orkut and Facebook being some of the most favorite cyber hubs for many Indians, especially women, maximum victimizations in the social networking sites generate from either Orkut and / or Facebook.[3] Many victims had seemingly received reply from Orkut authorities for their complaints, stating that their complaint contained "no serious activities" as per Orkut policies. It is apparent that Orkut policies were drafted on US based laws and concept of free speech value system and hence Indian concepts as well as social value system on pornography, obscene speech gender harassments etc may not be always be accepted as 'crimes' under Orkut policies. On behalf of our organization CCVC, we had preferred an open petition to Google and Orkut for responding positively to complaints lodged by Indian users.[4] The petition had as many as 128 Indian respondents and this proves the seriousness of the situation. Incidentally, Indian government simultaneously took serious note of the situation from various reported cases in cyber crimes cells of different parts of India and sent as many as 142 requests to Google to remove impersonated or defamatory contents from Google's social networking site Orkut (The Statesman, 2010). In response to this issue, Orkut has also rectified their complaint response policies.

Several respondents had also contacted Facebook. Even though Facebook is also governed by policies based upon US laws and US constitutional principles of freedom of speech and expression, we noted from these respondents that Facebook had opted to dismiss accused profiles basing on the evidences provide by the victims and their own guidelines about prevention of harassment and anti bullying policies.

PART II: LEGAL PROTECTIONS TO WOMEN CYBER VICTIMS

9.5 Non-Sexual Offences

Indian Information Technology Act (amended), 2008, have recognized several nonsexual offences such as offensive communications, cheating by impersonation, identity theft, unauthorized access to computers etc. However, it is to be noted that the Indian chapter of cyber law began its formal journey way back in 2000 with the drafting and implementation of Information Technology Act, 2000. However, the Act was drafted mainly for protecting e-commerce, hence the law was not well equipped to deal with other cyber menaces, leave the security of women in the cyber space. The Act was armed with only two sections to fight for women, section 67 on obscenity and section 72 on breach of privacy. Nevertheless, these were rarely used. After much criticism, came the amended version of the information technology Act 2008, which largely saves the interest of net surfers. In this section the utility of the Act and the penal laws towards prevention of cyber atrocities against women are examined as below:

9.5.1 Offensive Communication

From the pilot study of the Centre for Cyber Victim Counselling, it could be seen that adult bullying, hate propaganda against feministic ideas, mailing / messaging women with threatening, blackmailing contents etc are growing in number in India. Offensive communication while cyber socializing in India is actually the result of huge following of western cyber etiquettes by the Indian net users, which has an inherent cultural conflict. Indeed, women are the scapegoats for such experimentation of right to speech and expression in the cyber space. Apart from using English slang words towards women in open public forums, it has become a 'fashion' to use colloquial vernacular slang for attacking women.

Similarly 'dropping in' for teasing, name calling etc for women are also rampant in Indian social networking sites, chatting sites etc. Such offensive communications are compactly regulated by section 66A of the Information Technology Act (amended), 2008, which includes grossly offensive communications, information containing menacing character, defamatory statements which the sender knows to be false, but are communicated for the purpose of causing annoyance, inconvenience, danger, obstruction, insult, injury, criminal intimidation, enmity, hatred, or ill will etc. This section also covers misleading mails with attachments of any documents including audio / video clippings etc.[5] Section 66A prescribes 3 years imprisonment or fine for such offensive communications. In practice, the IPC is also applied to book the offender under Sections 500, which prescribes punishment for defamation with simple imprisonment, which may extend to two years or with fine or with both. Section 502 (b) of the IPC further prohibits sale of printed or engraved substance containing defamatory matter knowing it to contain such matter in any other case and terms it as a non cognizable offence with simple imprisonment for 2 years or with fine or with both. It can be seen that this particular provision may serve purposes for preventing adult bullying, hate propaganda or offensive mails, but harassment of women are not mentioned here. In such case, Section 509 of IPC may be engaged to prevent such harassments. This provision prohibits uttering any word or making any gesture intended to insult the modesty of a woman and considers it as a cognizable offence punishable with simple imprisonment for one year or with fine or with both.

Offensive communication also includes blackmailing or threatening mails or messages. However, Section 66A does not specifically mention about such atrocities. On the other hand, it tends to club all such communications together under one umbrella term "offensive communication". In such cases, predominantly Section 383 of the IPC is also used to combat the crime. This section addresses the 'fear factor' and terms it a crime to put any person in fear of any injury by dishonestly inducing the victim to deliver to any person any property or valuable security. It may be noted that this particular crime is defined by the modus operandi, i.e., "extortion" and is more focused towards the harasser's conduct of creating fear and the victim's presumed compulsiveness to satisfy the harasser's demand. In cases of harassing the women victim with threatening / blackmailing mails, this section may well play the role of savior if the course of conduct of the harasser carries the inherent meaning of provisions of Section 509 of the IPC, i.e., an intention to insult the modesty of woman.

9.5.2 Offences Against Cyber Privacy, Hacking, Stalking, and Related Crimes

As per the IT Act 2008, cyber privacy is interpreted only to cover commercial privacy and not necessarily individual's right to privacy in the cyber space.[6] Privacy has not been guaranteed as a direct fundamental right under the Indian constitution, but it is the judicial interpretations of Right to life (Article 21 of the Constitution of India) which has extended the meaning of right to life to cover right to privacy of common individuals. The legal meaning of right to life and liberty[7] may be expanded to cover vast areas of the technical meaning of "life" and "livelihood", but for the purpose of this segment, we would confide our discussions to two rights, namely right to privacy and right to live with dignity. The historic verdict in the case of *Kharak Singh vs. State of UP*, AIR 1963, SC 1295 by the Supreme Court of India expanded the meaning of "life" to cover privacy as a basic fundamental need to enjoy life: "By the term life as used here, something more is meant than mere animal existence. The inhibition against its deprivation extends to all those limits and faculties by which the life is enjoyed." We feel this particular explanation by the Supreme Court defines an individual's basic right in the internet also. However, this right is very much interrelated with right to live with human dignity.

Right to life was first interpreted to cover life with dignity in the case of *Maneka Gandhi vs. Union of India*, AIR 1981, SC 746. In this case, the court held that: "right to live is not merely confined to physical existence, but it includes within its ambit the right to live with human dignity". This stands true for life in the cyber space. Various sorts of cyber offences of the nature of invading privacy, such as stalking, floating private information in the web without consent, unauthorized accessing and modifying digital contents and misusing them etc, may crop up only when these two basic rights are hampered. Unauthorized access to computers is regulated by Section 43 of the IT Act, 2008, which penalizes unauthorized access, downloads, prohibitions for original owner to access the digital contents etc. Section 65 further prohibits tampering or modification of such data that were accessed unauthorized. The other provision, which we feel, could be very aptly used in cases where the victim's account is 'taken over' and misused, would be section 66 C of the Information Technology Act (amended), 2008. This section states:

Whoever, fraudulently or dishonestly make use of the electronic signature, password or any other unique identification feature of any other person, shall be punished with imprisonment of either description for a term which may extend to three years and shall also be liable to fine which may extend to rupees one lakh.

The language of this section was meant to control bank frauds, credit card frauds and email account hackings. We feel that this section can suitably be used for the purpose of covering offences described in this chapter, namely hacking and modification.

Unauthorized access may lead to revealing of personal data to the wider audience, which has become a chosen trend for many men as an extended revenge taking activity on women in the cyber space over split affairs. Similarly, stalking women online, especially ex-spouses or ex-partners or girlfriends has also become a disturbing trend in the Indian cyber crime scenario. Since stalking has no direct legal definition in Indian laws, awareness among victims that they were being stalked remained relatively less than women victims of UK or US. Many of them thought that their ex-partners are continuing the abuse in the 'cyber way' which included following the internet activities of the victims, and contacting the victim's friends and acquaintances with threatening and /or defamatory contents about the victim etc. We observe that even though stalking is not directly addressed by any legal provisions, Section 72 of the IT Act could be stretched to cover stalking menaces. This Section states that:

any person who, in pursuant of any of the powers conferred under this Act, rules or regulations made there under, has secured access to any electronic record, book, register, correspondence, information, document or other material without the consent of the person concerned discloses such electronic record, book, register, correspondence, information, document or other material to any other person shall be punished with imprisonment for a term which may extend to two years, or with fine which may extend to one lakh rupees, or with both.

However, in reality, this section is mainly used to focus on cyber privacy and not the fear factor that has been highlighted by the US laws. It can be thus noted that Indian laws consider stalking as invasion of cyber privacy, which is offensive to the victim. Several reported cases suggest that Section 509 of the Indian Penal code may also be pulled in to cover online stalking (Duggal, 2001; Cyberlaw Consultant, 2000). We feel that there is a huge confusion in the Indian mindset about the characteristics of stalking. It is often felt that stalking ultimately leads to sexual defamation of female victims.[8] Most reported cases show women as the victims. Most of the online stalking incidences start by disturbing mails from the harasser who may had a emotional split up with the victim or other similar reasons. The harasser may spread rumors about her to her peers, which finally ends in either revealing the victim's personal information to strangers to enable them to contact her and disturb her; or presenting her in an indecent manner with morphed pictures / modified web contents showing her as 'sex-item'. Since there are no legal clarifications of online stalking in India, it has become a legal trend to pull up provisions of Section 509 of the IPC along with section 72 of the IT Act to technically establish the damage to the modesty of female victims. The other provision, which could also be included to clarify characteristics of stalking, is Section 441 of the IPC, (which speaks about physical trespass to annoy or insult individuals). We prefer to include Section 441 of the IPC for stalking activities in India, because the inherent meaning of stalking is following the victim and crossing the harasser's own physical boundaries and entering the victim's physical space to cause harm to the victim or creating fear of harm in the mind of victim. Indeed, cyber space has no geographical boundaries, but when stalking also involves invasion of digital privacy by way of tapping / monitoring the victim's online activities or modification of data etc to create fear factor, it is but natural to assume that digital trespass has happened. However, the ambiguity can only be set at rest if a consolidated online stalking law is created.

9.6 Sexual Offences

9.6.1 Voyeurism

Section 66E of the Information Technology Act, 2008, deals with intervention of sexual privacy of individuals and distribution of the same in the internet. This section says:

Whoever, intentionally or knowingly captures, publishes or transmits the image of a private area of any person without his or her consent, under circumstances violating the privacy of that person, shall be punished with imprisonment which may extend to three years or with fine not exceeding two lakh rupees, or with both.

This section however does not speak about sexual activities of the victim unlike the Canadian, British or American anti voyeurism laws. We presume that the words "private body parts" also cover nude body parts and usage of such body parts for sexual activities. Section 67A may also be used to prohibit such voyeur sexual activities, as the wordings of Section 67A strongly prohibit distribution of sexually explicit acts or conduct.[9]

We must remember that before the amended version of the Information Technology Act was drafted; the Indian cyber crime scenario had witnessed some western style usage of the information technology by adults as well as young adults in taking revenge of petty verbal fights, insults or even broken romantic affairs.[10] Such instances may include capturing intimate moments of the victim(s) along with her / their partners whereby the victim(s) may or may not have given the consent. When the relationship between the victim and the harasser did not stand good, the harasser published such intimate moments in the web and / or listing such clippings in adult entertainment sites to portray the victim as regular porno-model, to take revenge (Halder, 2010). Prior to the present amended Act, such cases were mute evidences of lawlessness in the Indian cyber space and were dealt with by IPC with a tinge of color of cyber law (the Section 67 of the erstwhile Information Technology Act, 2000 that dealt with pornography and Section 72 of the Act dealing with breach of privacy). However, the situation has improved after Section 66E became functional to dealt with this situation through the amended version of the Information Technology Act, 2008. The explanations to this section[11] have set all doubts and confusions at rest and have successfully covered privacy issues for women, especially in the internet.

9.6.2 Pornography, Obscenity, and Indecent Representation of Women in the Cyber Space

Prior to the present I.T. Act 2008, Indecent Representation of Women (Prohibition) Act, 1986,[12] was used along with sections 293 and 509 of the IPC and erstwhile section 67 of the I.T Act 2000 to prevent obscenity and pornography targeting women in the cyber space. However, except the Indecent Representation of Women (Prohibition) Act, 1986, none of the provisions mentioned above were particularly focused on creation and distribution of adult porno materials or obscene materials using innocent women in the cyber space. Publications of unconsented sexual materials in the cyber space were prohibited in the true sense only after the new I.T. Act came into force.

Sections 67 and 67 A of the I.T Act 2008 deal with obscenity and sexually explicit materials in the internet. Section 67 says:

whoever publishes or transmits or causes to be published in the electronic form, any material which is lascivious or appeals to the prurient interest or if its effect is such as to tend to deprave and corrupt persons who are likely, having regard to all relevant circumstances, to read, see or hear the matter contained or embodied in it, shall be punished on first conviction with imprisonment of either description for a term which may extend to three years and with fine which may extend to five lakh rupees and in the event of a second or subsequent conviction with imprisonment of either description for a term which may extend to five years and also with fine which may extend to ten lakh rupees.

Section 67 A says:

whoever publishes or transmits or causes to be published or transmitted in the electronic form any material which contains sexually explicit act or conduct shall be punished on first conviction with imprisonment of either description for a term which may extend to five years and with fine which may extend to ten lakh rupees and in the event of second or subsequent conviction with imprisonment of either description for a term which may extend to seven years and also with fine which may extend to ten lakh rupees.[13]

We may note that the drafters of this Act have carefully retained the hairline difference between the meaning of obscenity and sexually explicit materials. Britton, Maguire and Nathanson (1993) differentiate the core notions of obscenity and pornography for legal understanding of the two:

....Obscenity is sexual words and images, which are not protected by Constitutional guarantees of free speech. To be illegally obscene, a work must appeal to the prurient interests, depict sex in a patently offensive way, and lack serious literary, artistic, political or scientific value. Pornography is material designed to arouse and has no legal or consistent definition. Each person's definition depends on her upbringing, sexual preference and viewing context. One woman's "trash" may be another's treasure or boredom (Para 3).

Even though this differentiation was made in view of American constitutional guarantees on freedom of speech, the Indian laws hardly differentiated between the two. The Indian Supreme Court has adopted Cockburn's definition of obscenity, i.e., "the test of obscenity is this, whether the tendency of the matter charged as obscene is to deprave and corrupt those whose minds are open to such immoral influences and into whose hands a publication of this sort may fall".[14] The Indian Supreme Court addressed obscenity as a social crime in the case of *Ranjit D. Udeshi vs. State of Maharashtra*[15] and stated, "When treatment of sex becomes offensive to public decency and morality as judged by the prevailing standards of morality in the society in the society, then only the work may be regarded as an obscene production". This may lead to the presumption that the Indian laws address (in a very technical sense) only obscenity and not pornography.

Pope, Voges, Kuhn and Bloxsome (2007, p. 168) defines "intentional pornography" as: "a communication material provided for the purpose of sexually arousing or gratifying a user in isolation from others". However, we must remember that this present law, i.e., the Information Technology Act, 2000 (amended in 2008) has used the term "sexually explicit material" and not "pornography" We have noticed that there is a huge tendency in the Indian scenario to use pornography as a synonym to obscenity.[16] However, no legal provision had defined the term pornography in a typical legal term and the confusion still exists. Analyzing Section 67 and 67A of the Information Technology Act, 2000 (amended in 2008), we may get clear definitions of internet obscenity and internet pornography in the Indian context. Hence as per Section 67 of the I.T. Act, internet obscenity may mean:

1. any material, which is audible and visible.
2. which must be in the electronic form.
3. it should be lascivious or appeals to the prurient interest.
4. its effect is such as to tend to deprave and corrupt persons.
5. the material must be such as to be read, seen or heard of the matter contained or embodied in it.

Again, a material to be qualified as "sexually explicit material" (as has been termed by the section 67A of the I.T. Act (amended) 2008) in the Indian cyber scenario must have the following conditions:

1. The material must contain sexually explicit acts or conducts.
2. It must contain uncensored sexual acts like sexual intercourse.
3. It must reveal uncovered private parts.
4. If we go very technical on the language of the section, the material must be only "acts or conducts" which is enough to arouse sexual feelings.
5. It must be published or transmitted in the web.

When we follow these differences minutely along with the discussions on characteristics of pornography as has been discussed above, we may note the following:

a) Obscenity is a broader term which may even include pornographic acts, lascivious writings, and sex-cartoons with filthy remarks;
b) 'Sexually explicit material' becomes pornography when it is used for arousing sexual intentions and erotica in human beings;
c) When sexually explicit material is published or transmitted in the web, and becomes 'cyber pornography', the Indian I.T. Act punishes the publisher or transmitter.
d) Similarly, the publisher or transmitter of obscene materials in the internet is liable to be punished.

It is evident from the above that the Indian laws prohibit that communication/distribution of both obscene as well as sexually explicit materials. These provisions of the I.T. Act can be successfully used to book the offender, when a woman in victimized by way of defamation in the sexual way (i.e., her modified profile is floated or she is presented as 'online call girl' with indecent pictures), or when she receives indecent mails with image attachments etc. In other words, the woman victim may hope to get justice even if the harassing content does not qualify as obscene but qualifies as sexually explicit material. However, neither this provision promises complete protection to women victims as it does not recognize offences against women that may happen in the cyber space.

PART III: LACUNAS IN THE CYBER LAWS

9.7 Loopholes

In the Indian I.T. (Amended) Act 2008, we found several lacunas, which strengthen our argument that this present Act is also not fully capable of protecting women victims in the cyber space. These are:

1. *No mention of women investigating officer or "reporting cell" for women exclusively in the I.T Act, 2000 (amended in 2008):* It is indeed unfortunate to note that there is no mention of gender centric victim assistance cell by the present Act. Section 78 of the I.T Act, 2000 (amended in 2008) and Section 80(1) mentions only about an officer in a gender-neutral term and not specifically mention whether a male or female officer is eligible to investigate or search or arrest in certain cases.[17] Due to the fear of social stigmas the female victims prefer not to seek police or judicial assistance. Hence, it is very essential that there should be a women's wing in the cyber police cells for reporting victimization of women exclusively and victims must be encouraged to contact this cell for procedural help.

2. *No mention of the word "women" in the Act:* The amended version of the I.T. Act differentiates child pornography from adult obscenity and pornography but there is no mention of any provision in this Act to protect women exclusively. Notably, IPC has provision to penalize offences against "modesty of women"(Section 509 of the IPC). If similar ideologies were incorporated for IT Act, protection of women in the Indian cyber space would become easier for the law and justice machinery.

3. *Responsibility of the ISPs are ambiguous:* Section 79 of the I.T. Act, 2008, specifies the grounds of immunity for intermediaries from the third party liability in the similar lines of "due diligence" clause of the US federal Provision i.e., Section 512C of the Digital millennium Copyright Act.[18] We also note that victimization of women happen mostly in the sites such as Google, Yahoo (including the email services, chat room and social networking sites provided and supported by the Google and Yahoo etc), Facebook, My Space, Twitter etc and adult entertainment sites which are hosted and guided by US rules. Unless the responsibilities of the ISPs are clarified from the Indian laws and the Australian federal laws that are based on social perspectives,[19] usage of ISPs as a medium to victimize women in India may not be fully prevented.

9.8 CONCLUSION

Cyber crime scenario in India has gone through a huge metamorphosis since the inception of the first Information Technology Act in 2000. However, India still needs to recognize that cyber crime against women does not only signify sexual crimes but it can be of various non-sexual types as well. Even though present Indian laws are capable to prevent such activities in the cyber space, such non-sexual crimes are less reported and rarely recognized. We also note that the biggest drawback in preventing cyber crime against women in India is less reporting and lack of awareness. This was perhaps caused due to fear of media attention, refusal to register the case by the police and inherent threat, which are generated by the perpetrator with dire consequences if the victim reports the incidences. We understand that lack of awareness among common people, especially women victims is the main reason, which instigates less reporting and almost nil usage of provisions meant for crimes other than pornography and obscenity.

The above discussions on cyber victimization of women reveal that the situation in India is no less severe than that in the US, UK, Canada or Australia. It must also be noted that the Indian social system is more orthodox than the social system of the US or UK. The US standard of obscenity may not always be successful for meting out justice to the Indian victims. We note that many Indians join US based social networking sites, open email accounts with US based ISPs or join online chat rooms, which are guided by US rules and regulations. Many often, when victimization occurs in these sites, the victims get to see 'strange responses' from the ISPs as well as law and justice machinery. This is because either such victimization do not qualify as crimes as per the norms of the policy guidelines of the ISPs or are not recognized as crimes by the Indian laws. It can be noted that India manages most gender harassment cases in the cyber space with the help of century old laws, which were created during the British colonization period. India needs more specific laws to cover cyber crimes including stalking, adult grooming, emotional cheating and subsequent harassments etc. We also feel that the US has completely colonized the cyber space. In such case when the foreign websites are involved in generating crimes against women in India, the questions of application of proper laws also arise. Also, the need to define cyber crimes against women from an international perspective becomes imperative.

REFERENCES

Balakrishnan, K. G. (2009). *Speech at seminar on cyber crimes against women - Public awareness meeting*, Maharaja College, Ernakulam, August 1, 2009. Retrieved on 6th July, 2010, from http://www.supremecourtofindia.nic.in/speeches/ speeches_2009/Seminar_-_Cyber_crimes_against_ women_1-08-09.pdf

Britton, P. O., Maguire, J., & Nathanson, B. (1993). *Feminism and free speech: Pornography*. Feminists for Free Expression. Retrieved from http://www.ffeusa.org/html/statements /Pornographybrochure.pdf

CNN IBN. (Feb 07, 2008). *Sex doctor gets life in cyber-porn case*. Retrieved on 15th April, 2010, from http://ibnlive.in.com/news/sex-doctor-gets-life-in- cyberporn-case/58375-3.html?xml

Cyber Lawyer. (November 14, 2009). *Anoushka Shankar blackmail case update*. Retrieved on 15th December, 2009, from http://www.cyberlawtimes.com/2009/11/14/ anoushka-shankar-blackmail-case-update/

Cyberlaw Consultant. (2000). *Legislation to check cyber stalking needed urgently*. Retrieved on 15th May, 2010, from http://www.expressindia.com/news/fe/ daily/20000727/efe27021.html

DNAIndia. (May 16, 2009). *Celina Jaitley complains*. Retrieved on 15th December, 2009, from http://movies.indiainfo.com/article/0905161058_ celina_jaitley_complains/356286.html

Duggal, P. (2001). *India's first cyberstalking case: Some cyberlaw perspectives*. Retrieved on 15th May, 2010, from http://cyberlaws.net/cyberindia/ 2CYBER27.htm

Halder, D. (2007). Cyber crime against women in India. *CyberLawTimes.com Monthly Newsletter, 2*(6). June 2007. Retrieved on 15th June, 2008, from http://www.cyberlawtimes.com/articles/103.html

Halder, D. (2010). Abuse of intimate moments in the cyber ways. Retrieved June 2010, from http://debaraticyberspace.blogspot.com

Halder, D., & Jaishankar, K. (2008, June). Cyber crimes against women in India: Problems, perspectives and solutions. *TMC Academy Journal, 3*(1), 48–62.

Halder, D., & Jaishankar, K. (2010). *Cyber victimization in India: A baseline survey report*. Tirunelveli, India: Centre for Cyber Victim Counselling.

India News. (30 March, 2010). *Indian approach towards the fight against cyber crime*. Retrieved on 15th April, 2010, from http://www.desitoob.com/indian-approach- towards-the-fight-against-cyber-crime/

Kuhn, K.-A., Voges, K., Pope, N., & Bloxsome, E. (2007). Pornography and erotica: Definitions and prevalence. In *Proceedings of the 2007 International Nonprofit and Social Marketing Conference Social entrepreneurship, Social Change and Sustainability* (pp. 165-173). 27 and 28 September, 2007. Brisbane, Australia: Griffith University.

Mohan, V. (January 08, 2004). Cyber crime against woman. *Chandigarh Newsline*. Retrieved on 25th May, 2010, from http://www.crime-research.org/news/2004/ 01/Mess0801.html

The Statesman. (21 April, 2010). *Google gets 142 requests from Indian government to remove info*. Retrieved on 15th May, 2010, from http://www.thestatesman.net/index.php?option= com_content&view=article&show=archive&id=325867& catid=36&year=2010&month=04&day=21&Itemid=66

ENDNOTES

[1]   For more information see http://infosecawareness.in/cyber-crime-cells-in-india

[2]   See http://www.cybervictims.org/CCVCresearchreport2010.pdf

[3]   From personal experiences of the lead author as a counselor for cyber crime victims.

[4]   The petition can be seen at http://www.petitiononline.com/ccvc123/petition.html

[5]   Section 66A of the IT Act, 2008 states any electronic mail or electronic mail message for the purpose of causing annoyance or inconvenience or to deceive or to mislead the addressee or recipient about the origin of such messages (Inserted vide ITAA 2008).

[6]   Section 72 of the IT Act, 2008 speaks about breach of privacy as follows "Save as otherwise provided in this Act or any other law for the time being in force, any person who, in pursuant of any of the powers conferred under this Act, rules or regulations made there under, has secured access to any electronic record, book, register, correspondence, information, document or other material without the consent of the person concerned discloses such electronic record, book, register, correspondence, information, document or other material to any other person shall be punished with imprisonment for a term which may extend to two years, or with fine which may extend to one lakh rupees, or with both."; Section 72 A further states "Save as otherwise provided in this Act or any other law for the time being in force, any person including an intermediary who, while providing services under the terms of lawful contract, has secured access to any material containing personal

information about another person, with the intent to cause or knowing that he is likely to cause wrongful loss or wrongful gain discloses, without the consent of the person concerned, or in breach of a lawful contract, such material to any other person shall be punished with imprisonment for a term which may extend to three years, or with a fine which may extend to five lakh rupees, or with both". Both these provisions were enacted mainly to protect electronic commercial privacy issues.

7   Article 21 of the constitution says: "no person shall be deprived of his life and liberty except according to the procedure established by law".

8   See discussions on the case of Ritu Kohli under the sub-heading, gestation period.

9   For more information see section 67A of the I.T Act 2008, available at http://cybercrime.planetindia. net/ch11_2008.htm

10   Some of these cases are discussed in chapter 2.

11   The explanation reads as follows: For the purposes of this section--(a) "transmit" means to electronically send a visual image with the intent that it be viewed by a person or persons; (b) "capture", with respect to an image, means to videotape, photograph, film or record by any means; (c) "private area" means the naked or undergarment clad genitals, pubic area, buttocks or female breast; (d) "publishes" means reproduction in the printed or electronic form and making it available for public; e) "under circumstances violating privacy" means circumstances in which a person can have a reasonable expectation that-- (i) he or she could disrobe in privacy, without being concerned that an image of his private area was being captured; or (ii) any part of his or her private area would not be visible to the public, regardless of whether that person is in a public or private place

12   For more information see supra @ 8

13   The exception to this section says: This section and section 67 does not extend to any book, pamphlet, paper, writing, drawing, painting, representation or figure in electronic form- (i) the publication of which is proved to be justified as being for the public good on the ground that such book, pamphlet, paper, writing, drawing, painting, representation or figure is in the interest of science, literature, art, or learning or other objects of general concern; or (ii) which is kept or used bona fide for religious purposes.

14   Per Cockbern C.J., in Hicklin, (1868), LR 3 QB360, 371.

15   Ranjit. D. Udeshi. (1965) 1SCR65 SC.

16   See discussions on pornography and Indian laws in articles such as *India's fight against pornography*, retrieved from http://netsafety.nic.in/cyberlaws.htm on 12.10.2010; *Fine Tune law on pornography*, retrieved from http://timesofindia.indiatimes.com/city/pune/Fine-tune-law-on-pornography/ articleshow/1019510.cms; etc

17   "Notwithstanding anything contained in the Code of Criminal Procedure, 1973, a police officer not below the rank of Inspector shall investigate any offence under this Act". Section 80(1) of this Act is a corollary provision to this section which states "Notwithstanding anything contained in the Code of Criminal Procedure, 1973, any police officer, not below the rank of a Inspector or any other officer of the Central Government or a State Government authorized by the Central Government in this behalf may enter any public place and search and arrest without warrant any person found therein who is reasonably suspected of having committed or of committing or of being about to commit any offence under this Act. [1] The section further says: 2) Where any person is arrested under sub-section (1) by an officer other than a police officer, such officer shall, without unnecessary delay, take or send the person arrested before a magistrate having jurisdiction in the case or before the officer-in-charge of a police station. (3) The provisions of the Code of Criminal

Procedure, 1973 shall, subject to the provisions of this section, apply, so far as may be, in relation to any entry, search or arrest, made under this section.

[18] Section 79 of the Information Technology Act, 2008 states: "Notwithstanding anything contained in any law for the time being in force but subject to the provisions of sub-sections (2) and (3), an intermediary shall not be liable for any third party information, data, or communication link hosted by him. (corrected vide Information Technology Act (Amended) (ITAA), 2008)". Subsection 2 of this provision states that the provisions of sub-section (1) shall apply if- (a) the function of the intermediary is limited to providing access to a communication system over which information made available by third parties is transmitted or temporarily stored; or (b) the intermediary does not- (i) initiate the transmission, (ii) select the receiver of the transmission, and (iii) select or modify the information contained in the transmission (c) the intermediary observes due diligence while discharging his duties under this Act and also observes such other guidelines as the Central Government may prescribe in this behalf (Inserted Vide ITAA, 2008) Subsection 3 specifies that the provisions of sub-section (1) shall not apply if- (a) the intermediary has conspired or abetted or aided or induced whether by threats or promise or otherwise in the commission of the unlawful act (ITAA 2008) (b) upon receiving actual knowledge, or on being notified by the appropriate Government or its agency that any information, data or communication link residing in or connected to a computer resource controlled by the intermediary is being used to commit the unlawful act, the intermediary fails to expeditiously remove or disable access to that material on that resource without vitiating the evidence in any manner.

[19] See discussion regarding Australian laws in Chapter 8.

Chapter 10
Model Charter and Conclusion

CHAPTER OVERVIEW

This chapter provides a model charter and a conclusion to the book. The contents of the Model charter to prevent online victimization of women are: Part I: Definition, Part II: Proposal for cyber rights for women, and Part III: Proposal for a code of conduct in the cyber space. In the conclusion we have strongly emphasized the need for new laws related to cyber crimes against women, both in developed and less developed nations. In addition, the need for more research works that analyzes cyber victimization of women is emphasized.

10.1 INTRODUCTION

The discussions in the earlier chapters establish that the core problem related to cyber victimization of women lies in four main factors, namely:

1. **Cyber behaviors of the users:** When in the cyber space, adult users may behave in a strange fashion, which might be different from the behaviors in the real space. Many men and also women use the internet as a platform to express personal frustrations and angers in a language, which may not be treated as 'protected speech' in real life. Cyber space does not victimize individuals' suo motu. It is the manner of usage of the cyber space by the users that generates victimizations. Seeing from a feministic perspective, which is well supported by the international surveys, it could be assumed that women are the worst sufferers of atrocious behaviors of frustrated lovers and ex-partners, jealous colleagues, habitual bullies and antifeminist debaters in the cyber space.

DOI: 10.4018/978-1-60960-830-9.ch010

2. **The cyber ethics and etiquettes developed by the users as well as the ISPs:** Cyber behaviors of users may influence the development of cyber ethics and etiquettes that are followed by various popular ISPs, which may lay down their own terms and conditions for monitoring ethics and etiquettes. Free speech notion may be expanded to recognize the digital norms of speech and expressions. However, these ethics and etiquettes may not always reflect the expected social behaviors especially when the users belong to comparatively orthodox societies. In such cases, perpetrators belonging to these societies may take these ethics and etiquettes as the supportive elements to attack their female victims in the digital way in a manner that may not be legally or socially possible in their offline social and legal structure. Resultant to this, ISPs and social networking sites may get transformed in to platforms to practice several ethics and etiquettes such as publishing demeaning words targeting women, portraying women in indecent words, expressing personal feelings against women or users who are professing feminist ideologies through blogs in critical manner etc, which may be considered bad ethics and etiquettes in real life societies.

3. **Awareness among users:** Victimization begins due to less or nil awareness among users about the advantages and disadvantages of using cyber space as a platform to express one's thoughts and expressions. The more the users are aware of cyber norms, safety measures and good cyber ethics, the less will be the victimization rate in the cyber space.

4. Less or nil legal recognition of the types of crimes and subsequently poor cooperation from the police and law and justice machinery could cause more victimization to women and may set very bad precedent for the next generation cyber perpetrators.

Analyzing the above contentions, we understand that a model charter for prevention of victimization of women in the cyber space is the need of the day. In the following segment, we have formulated a model charter, which could help to understand the nature of victimization and simultaneously prevent further victimizations of women in the cyber space.

10.2 MODEL CHARTER

We propose a universal model charter for prevention of online victimization of women that could be used for the lawmakers to draft gender centric cyber crime preventive laws or even policy makers to create model guidelines for prohibiting cyber atrocities against women.

Title: Model charter to prevent online victimization of women

Contents:

Part I: Definition
Part II: Proposal for cyber rights for women
Part III: Proposal for a code of conduct in the cyber space

Purpose: This model charter may be used to prevent online victimization of women, define various cyber offences that may happen to women online, prohibit several conducts as unethical and illegal and against the interest of women, spread awareness among men and women about cyber crimes affecting women, encourage government reporting agencies to understand the nature of the crime and thereby help the women victims.

Part I: Definition

For the purpose of this model charter, the following definitions are derived and these terms are defined from feministic perspective.

1. **Hacking:** Hacking may mean unauthorized access to the digital contents of the original owner, and also includes blocking the original author of such digital contents from accessing it. The term may also cover modification of such digital contents and / or re-publishing the modified or altered digital contents for mischievous purposes.

2. **Digital contents:** Digital contents may mean any content, material, personal information, including personal photograph / images / video clippings etc of the original owner or her family members, which are used by the original owner as her identity in the web world for the purpose professional as well as personal usage; or are created by the original owner to express her views in the web world.

3. **Cyber privacy:** Cyber privacy may mean 'right to be left alone' regarding any digital content owned by the original owner; and / or information about the original owner stored either in a government computer or corporate data for health, social security, professional records or monetary data.

4. **Online defamation:** Online defamation may mean publication in the internet of information about any individual, which the creator of such information knows to be false; and the act is done to harm the reputation of said person. Publication in this context may mean spreading the false information about the victim to others, other than the victim.

5. **Cyber bullying:** Cyber bullying may mean attacking anyone with harsh or rude words in the cyber space, including public bulletin boards, chat rooms, emails, blogs etc, and such harsh or rude words are particularly made to ridicule one's body shape, gender, physical or mental incapability, race, colour, opinion, educational background, language etc.

6. **Cyber grooming:** Cyber grooming may mean constant interactions / communications with any individual focusing on sexual conducts or other unethical or illegal conducts in a camouflaged manner with a purpose to misuse the digital presence and / or identity of the respondent herself or personal information provided by her.

7. **Cyber stalking:** Cyber stalking may mean monitoring the internet activity of any individual, finding out the peers of the victim with whom she interacts the most, mailing or messaging either her or her peers with threatening / abusive / defamatory contents or invading in her personal cyber space and creating fear.

8. **Cyber harassment:** Cyber harassments may mean and include sending unwanted mails to one's inbox, forcefully including one's id for chatting, sending abusive / harassing / teasing / bullying mails / messages, cyber stalking, invasion of cyber privacy, spreading hate propaganda, sending-defamatory information about the victim to others in the internet, unauthorized usage of digital identity and digital contents of the original owners for the purpose of adult entertainment etc.

9. **Cyber blackmailing:** Cyber blackmailing may mean and include sending mails / messages to one's inbox with threatening words, asking the recipient to obey the demands of the sender, or

blackmails the victim by informing her that her private information will be revealed or portrayed in false manner, thereby tries to harm her reputation etc.

10. **Forced pornography:** Forced pornography may mean and include publishing or using pictures of any individuals which may or may not be modified / voyeured images of one's naked body parts / video clippings of sexual activities of the individual / private residential information etc of the individual without consent or knowledge of the said individual either in any adult entertainment site or through any website or blog etc, with a mischievous intention to portray such individual as porn-model or commercial sex worker; and thereby forcing the said individual against her wishes or knowledge, to be part of the adult entertainment industry or soft core pornography.

11. **Cyber hate propaganda:** Cyber hate propaganda may mean offensive communication between the sender and multiple recipients with intent to spread hatred against a particular individual for her opinion, race, gender etc.

12. **Obscenity:** Obscenity may mean any cyber communication or content which is published in the internet and which contains images, materials, contents etc which creates 'prurient interests' and which is against social value system of the 'physical' place where it is downloaded and seen.

13. **Offensive communications:** Offensive communication may mean and include communications between the sender and the recipient(s), which carries offensive contents including threatening / bullying / defamatory / obscene messages.

Part II: Proposal of Cyber Rights for Women

1. **Right to equality**: Right to equality includes right against discrimination of any sort. This right must be acknowledged as the primary right for women in the cyber space.

2. **Right to live safely with dignity**: this right may include the following:
   (a) Right against 'forced pornography'
   (b) Right against hateful communications including defamations.
   (c) Right against hacking for the purpose of sexual as well as nonsexual crimes in the cyber space.
   (d) Right against stalking and following harassments.
   (e) Right against being abused in all the ways as discussed above in the internet.
   (f) Right against blackmailing, threatening and cheating, and
   (g) Right to live safely with dignity in the real space along with a clean virtual identity

3. **Right to speech and expression**: Women must have right to speech and expression of their views about feminism and various other subjects.

4. **Right to information in the cyber space**: This right may include right to information in cyber space and right to view other websites.

5. **Right to communicate with others:** This right may mean and include right to free speech and right to choose individuals with whom the woman feels comfortable to communicate. This may also include right to block or remove unwanted individuals who tries to communicate with her against her wish.

6. **Right to make a livelihood from the cyber space and with the assistance of cyber space:** This may include right to express her views and carry on her profession for a livelihood with the aid of cyber space. However this right also includes right to be protected from being used as a trade item for pornographic websites, obscene contents without the consent of the woman in concern.

7. **Right to have "own space" in the internet:** This right may include right to access and create a domain, right to create email ids, blogs and also access social networking sites and create profiles etc.

8. **Right to assemble and association:** This right may include right to create any web based association, women-only forums etc

9. **Right to privacy:** Right to privacy may mean and include right against invasions in her digital contents, private information and also private offline activities, which may be published online.

10. **Right to defend self-reputation:** This right may mean right to speech and expression and also right to protect cyber privacy. This right extends to contacting the police or the cyber – crime cells or cyber security experts and or lawyers.

Part III: Proposal for Code of Conduct in the Cyber Space

Code of conduct for internet users: For the purpose of this policy guideline, we propose a set of code conducts for male and female internet users towards safeguarding women's interest in the cyber space. These are as follows:

1. To respect other's right to privacy;
2. Restraining from indecent conducts in the cyber space;
3. Restraining from using cyber space as a verbal warfare and restraining from using abusive languages;
4. Restraining from using, modifying, republishing others contents without proper permission

10.3 CONCLUSION

The issue of cyber crimes against women has remained a delicate subject and will remain the same forever. In the cyber space, women are victims not only in the hands of individuals, but also in the hands of technology as well as the law and governmental systems. Women are humiliated, made fun of and left to be an object to be ridiculed. The reason lies in the volume of rapid growth of a typical 'cyber culture' where basic fundamental rights are given least importance. This volume of growth could not be matched by law makers of any country or any global organizations. Indeed, when the law fails to take note of the ongoing victimization, the harm escalates more. It can be seen that there is a peculiar trend of the law makers to approach cyber crimes from three basic angles, namely crime against government, financial crime and crime against children. Further, crime against government and financial crimes are often clubbed by creating numerous hacking related laws as well as anti money laundering laws. Crimes against children however are gaining highlights due to increased legal barricades through laws on child pornography and bullying etc. Millions of women and men, who use internet as a way of life from other aspects, like leisure, non economic communications, socializing etc also continue to experience the curse of technology in a lawless state. Users create their own rules and regulations to carry on their virtual lives. No one bothers about the wrongs that can be done to others and prolong in exercising their own free rights without knowing any limits. The cyber space turns as a Utopia to some and hell to others. Sadly enough online victimization and subsequent damage to reputation harms women more than men. This is mainly because damage to reputation may often lead to piercing of privacy and women are more susceptible in such cases

While preparing the definition chapter, the question that was raised in our discussion was *Is there any need for grouping women as a minority community and defining specific crimes that can happen to them online?* From a feministic view point we found this particular issue relevant and pertinent as most surveys showed women victims outnumbering men. We were surprised to note that even when hacking, identity related crimes and cyber terrorism are on the growth, women still formed majority of the victims of interpersonal cyber crimes. Unfortunately, many of these crimes against women are over looked. These instances of victimizations do constitute several characteristics to be termed as, 'crimes' and they very much violate fundamental rights of women. We are disheartened to note that many luminaries in the field of law, criminology and victimology refuse to call them 'crimes'. The factors that we have mentioned as reasons for the growth of victimization also ring the alarm. Many women are oblivious of the fact that they had been victimized and many harassers apparently do not understand their 'crimes'. The survey results of WHOA for last ten years will also show that cyber harassments for women in many cases begin and end with the up or down scales of emotional attachments with men. Holistically it can be said that many women do not use their rights in the cyber space and their harassers including men and women, abuse their rights. This lack of awareness concerns us as in the age of digital communication where many cyber guardians continuously volunteer with cyber tips, it can very well be expected that net savvy women will practice their rights to privacy. We feel in most cases of cyber victimization of women, victimization escalated because victims knowingly had unsafe cyber communications, which in turn, may have made them victim-turned-perpetrators.

Among the countries that we have covered, we were saddened to note the failure of legal drafters to define several hi-tech crimes. For instance, online stalking still remains a bizarre term for English laws. Adult bullying and in some cases gender based bullying towards adult females are still being considered as extended freedom of speech as per the US freedom charters. The term 'harassment' is being used by domestic laws of many countries to umbrella cover several gender based online atrocities and the problems of cyber grooming adult females for mischievous purposes still remain a relatively unknown fact. Similarly 'soft porno' remains unregulated in many countries irrespective of the fact whether the adult female models have consented with free will or their digital images are being used to satisfy millions of viewers of adult entertainment sites.

Unfortunately, the hard truth is that, the contemporary cyberspace is turning every pre-cyber age setup obsolete. No law can sustain the challenges of web 2.0 if it is not amended to suite the digital civilization. Ironically, even when the basic norms of human civilization have been elevated to digital era, women continue to live in an obnoxious space. This situation could be improved only if more researches are done to understand the applicability of the existing laws to the crimes done to the victims online and also gender sensitive laws are created to prevent further harm. To meet the objectives of the model charter presented in chapter 10, international bodies like the United Nations, academic institutions, industry etc may promote researches on offensive cyber conducts targeting women. This will further help to formulate the laws and typologies on gender sensitive victimizations in the cyber space and assist in the protection of women.

Appendices

APPENDIX 1

Council of Europe Convention on Cybercrime, Budapest, 23.XI.2001

Preamble

The member States of the Council of Europe and the other States signatory hereto,

Considering that, the aim of the Council of Europe is to achieve a greater unity between its members;

Recognising the value of fostering co-operation with the other States parties to this Convention;

Convinced of the need to pursue, as a matter of priority, a common criminal policy aimed at the protection of society against cybercrime, *inter alia,* by adopting appropriate legislation and fostering international co-operation;

Conscious of the profound changes brought about by the digitalisation, convergence and continuing globalisation of computer networks;

Concerned by the risk that computer networks and electronic information may also be used for committing criminal offences and that evidence relating to such offences may be stored and transferred by these networks;

Recognising the need for co-operation between States and private industry in combating cybercrime and the need to protect legitimate interests in the use and development of information technologies;

Believing that an effective fight against cybercrime requires increased, rapid and well-functioning international co-operation in criminal matters;

Convinced that the present Convention is necessary to deter action directed against the confidentiality, integrity and availability of computer systems, networks and computer data as well as the misuse of such systems, networks and data by providing for the criminalisation of such conduct, as described in this Convention, and the adoption of powers sufficient for effectively combating such criminal offences, by facilitating their detection, investigation and prosecution at both the domestic and international levels and by providing arrangements for fast and reliable international co-operation;

Mindful of the need to ensure a proper balance between the interests of law enforcement and respect for fundamental human rights as enshrined in the 1950 Council of Europe Convention for the Protection of Human Rights and Fundamental Freedoms, the 1966 United Nations International Covenant on Civil and Political Rights and other applicable international human rights treaties, which reaffirm the right of everyone to hold opinions without interference, as well as the right to freedom of expression, including the freedom to seek, receive, and impart information and ideas of all kinds, regardless of frontiers, and the rights concerning the respect for privacy;

Mindful also of the right to the protection of personal data, as conferred, for example, by the 1981 Council of Europe Convention for the Protection of Individuals with regard to Automatic Processing of Personal Data;

Considering the 1989 United Nations Convention on the Rights of the Child and the 1999 International Labour Organization Worst Forms of Child Labour Convention;

Taking into account the existing Council of Europe conventions on co-operation in the penal field, as well as similar treaties which exist between Council of Europe member States and other States, and stressing that the present Convention is intended to supplement those conventions in order to make criminal investigations and proceedings concerning criminal offences related to computer systems and data more effective and to enable the collection of evidence in electronic form of a criminal offence;

Welcoming recent developments which further advance international understanding and co-operation in combating cybercrime, including action taken by the United Nations, the OECD, the European Union and the G8;

Recalling Committee of Ministers Recommendations No. R (85) 10 concerning the practical application of the European Convention on Mutual Assistance in Criminal Matters in respect of letters rogatory for the interception of telecommunications, No. R (88) 2 on piracy in the field of copyright and neighbouring rights, No. R (87) 15 regulating the use of personal data in the police sector, No. R (95) 4 on the protection of personal data in the area of telecommunication services, with particular reference to telephone services, as well as No. R (89) 9 on computer-related crime providing guidelines for national legislatures concerning the definition of certain computer crimes and No. R (95) 13 concerning problems of criminal procedural law connected with information technology;

Having regard to Resolution No. 1 adopted by the European Ministers of Justice at their 21st Conference (Prague, 10 and 11 June 1997), which recommended that the Committee of Ministers support the work on cybercrime carried out by the European Committee on Crime Problems (CDPC) in order to bring domestic criminal law provisions closer to each other and enable the use of effective means of investigation into such offences, as well as to Resolution No. 3 adopted at the 23rd Conference of the European Ministers of Justice (London, 8 and 9 June 2000), which encouraged the negotiating parties to pursue their efforts with a view to finding appropriate solutions to enable the largest possible number of States to become parties to the Convention and acknowledged the need for a swift and efficient system of international co-operation, which duly takes into account the specific requirements of the fight against cybercrime;

Having also regard to the Action Plan adopted by the Heads of State and Government of the Council of Europe on the occasion of their Second Summit (Strasbourg, 10 and 11 October 1997), to seek common responses to the development of the new information technologies based on the standards and values of the Council of Europe;

Have agreed as follows:

Chapter I: Use of Terms

Article 1: Definitions

For the purposes of this Convention:

a. "computer system" means any device or a group of interconnected or related devices, one or more of which, pursuant to a program, performs automatic processing of data;

b. "computer data" means any representation of facts, information or concepts in a form suitable for processing in a computer system, including a program suitable to cause a computer system to perform a function;

c. "service provider" means:

   i. any public or private entity that provides to users of its service the ability to communicate by means of a computer system, and

   ii. any other entity that processes or stores computer data on behalf of such communication service or users of such service.

d. "traffic data" means any computer data relating to a communication by means of a computer system, generated by a computer system that formed a part in the chain of communication, indicating the communication's origin, destination, route, time, date, size, duration, or type of underlying service.

Chapter II: Measures to be Taken at the National Level

Section 1: Substantive Criminal Law

Title 1: Offences against the Confidentiality, Integrity and Availability of Computer Data and Systems

Article 2: Illegal Access

Each Party shall adopt such legislative and other measures as may be necessary to establish as criminal offences under its domestic law, when committed intentionally, the access to the whole or any part of a computer system without right. A Party may require that the offence be committed by infringing security measures, with the intent of obtaining computer data or other dishonest intent, or in relation to a computer system that is connected to another computer system.

Article 3: Illegal Interception

Each Party shall adopt such legislative and other measures as may be necessary to establish as criminal offences under its domestic law, when committed intentionally, the interception without right, made by technical means, of non-public transmissions of computer data to, from or within a computer system, including electromagnetic emissions from a computer system carrying such computer data. A Party may require that the offence be committed with dishonest intent, or in relation to a computer system that is connected to another computer system.

Article 4: Data Interference

1. Each Party shall adopt such legislative and other measures as may be necessary to establish as criminal offences under its domestic law, when committed intentionally, the damaging, deletion, deterioration, alteration or suppression of computer data without right.

2. A Party may reserve the right to require that the conduct described in paragraph 1 result in serious harm.

Article 5: System Interference

Each Party shall adopt such legislative and other measures as may be necessary to establish as criminal offences under its domestic law, when committed intentionally, the serious hindering without right of the functioning of a computer system by inputting, transmitting, damaging, deleting, deteriorating, altering or suppressing computer data.

Article 6: Misuse of Devices

1. Each Party shall adopt such legislative and other measures as may be necessary to establish as criminal offences under its domestic law, when committed intentionally and without right:
    a. the production, sale, procurement for use, import, distribution or otherwise making available of:
        i.   a device, including a computer program, designed or adapted primarily for the purpose of committing any of the offences established in accordance with Articles 2 through 5;
        ii. a computer password, access code, or similar data by which the whole or any part of a computer system is capable of being accessed, with intent that it be used for the purpose of committing any of the offences established in Articles 2 through 5; and
    b. the possession of an item referred to in paragraphs a.i or ii above, with intent that it be used for the purpose of committing any of the offences established in Articles 2 through 5. A Party may require by law that a number of such items be possessed before criminal liability attaches.
2. This article shall not be interpreted as imposing criminal liability where the production, sale, procurement for use, import, distribution or otherwise making available or possession referred to in paragraph 1 of this article is not for the purpose of committing an offence established in accordance with Articles 2 through 5 of this Convention, such as for the authorised testing or protection of a computer system.
3. Each Party may reserve the right not to apply paragraph 1 of this article, provided that the reservation does not concern the sale, distribution or otherwise making available of the items referred to in paragraph 1 a.ii of this article.

Title 2: Computer-Related Offences

Article 7: Computer-Related Forgery

Each Party shall adopt such legislative and other measures as may be necessary to establish as criminal offences under its domestic law, when committed intentionally and without right, the input, alteration, deletion, or suppression of computer data, resulting in inauthentic data with the intent that it be considered or acted upon for legal purposes as if it were authentic, regardless whether or not the data is directly readable and intelligible. A Party may require an intent to defraud, or similar dishonest intent, before criminal liability attaches.

Article 8: Computer-Related Fraud

Each Party shall adopt such legislative and other measures as may be necessary to establish as criminal offences under its domestic law, when committed intentionally and without right, the causing of a loss of property to another person by:

a.   any input, alteration, deletion or suppression of computer data,

b.   any interference with the functioning of a computer system, with fraudulent or dishonest intent of procuring, without right, an economic benefit for oneself or for another person.

Title 3: Content-Related Offences

Article 9:Offences Related to Child Pornography

1.   Each Party shall adopt such legislative and other measures as may be necessary to establish as criminal offences under its domestic law, when committed intentionally and without right, the following conduct:
    a.   producing child pornography for the purpose of its distribution through a computer system;
    b.   offering or making available child pornography through a computer system;
    c.   distributing or transmitting child pornography through a computer system;
    d.   procuring child pornography through a computer system for oneself or for another person;
    e.   possessing child pornography in a computer system or on a computer-data storage medium.
2.   For the purpose of paragraph 1 above, the term "child pornography" shall include pornographic material that visually depicts:
    a.   a minor engaged in sexually explicit conduct;
    b.   a person appearing to be a minor engaged in sexually explicit conduct;
    c.   realistic images representing a minor engaged in sexually explicit conduct.
3.   For the purpose of paragraph 2 above, the term "minor" shall include all persons under 18 years of age. A Party may, however, require a lower age-limit, which shall be not less than 16 years.
4.   Each Party may reserve the right not to apply, in whole or in part, paragraphs 1, sub-paragraphs d. and e, and 2, sub-paragraphs b. and c.

Title 4: Offences Related to Infringements of Copyright and Related Rights

Article 10: Offences Related to Infringements of Copyright and Related Rights

1.   Each Party shall adopt such legislative and other measures as may be necessary to establish as criminal offences under its domestic law the infringement of copyright, as defined under the law of that Party, pursuant to the obligations it has undertaken under the Paris Act of 24 July 1971 revising the Bern Convention for the Protection of Literary and Artistic Works, the Agreement on Trade-Related Aspects of Intellectual Property Rights and the WIPO Copyright Treaty, with the exception of any moral rights conferred by such conventions, where such acts are committed wilfully, on a commercial scale and by means of a computer system.

2. Each Party shall adopt such legislative and other measures as may be necessary to establish as criminal offences under its domestic law the infringement of related rights, as defined under the law of that Party, pursuant to the obligations it has undertaken under the International Convention for the Protection of Performers, Producers of Phonograms and Broadcasting Organisations (Rome Convention), the Agreement on Trade-Related Aspects of Intellectual Property Rights and the WIPO Performances and Phonograms Treaty, with the exception of any moral rights conferred by such conventions, where such acts are committed wilfully, on a commercial scale and by means of a computer system.

3. A Party may reserve the right not to impose criminal liability under paragraphs 1 and 2 of this article in limited circumstances, provided that other effective remedies are available and that such reservation does not derogate from the Party's international obligations set forth in the international instruments referred to in paragraphs 1 and 2 of this article.

Title 5: Ancillary Liability and Sanctions

Article 11: Attempt and Aiding or Abetting

1. Each Party shall adopt such legislative and other measures as may be necessary to establish as criminal offences under its domestic law, when committed intentionally, aiding or abetting the commission of any of the offences established in accordance with Articles 2 through 10 of the present Convention with intent that such offence be committed.

2. Each Party shall adopt such legislative and other measures as may be necessary to establish as criminal offences under its domestic law, when committed intentionally, an attempt to commit any of the offences established in accordance with Articles 3 through 5, 7, 8, and 9.1.a and c. of this Convention.

3. Each Party may reserve the right not to apply, in whole or in part, paragraph 2 of this article.

Article 12: Corporate Liability

1. Each Party shall adopt such legislative and other measures as may be necessary to ensure that legal persons can be held liable for a criminal offence established in accordance with this Convention, committed for their benefit by any natural person, acting either individually or as part of an organ of the legal person, who has a leading position within it, based on:
    a. a power of representation of the legal person;
    b. an authority to take decisions on behalf of the legal person;
    c. an authority to exercise control within the legal person.

2. In addition to the cases already provided for in paragraph 1 of this article, each Party shall take the measures necessary to ensure that a legal person can be held liable where the lack of supervision or control by a natural person referred to in paragraph 1 has made possible the commission of a criminal offence established in accordance with this Convention for the benefit of that legal person by a natural person acting under its authority.

3. Subject to the legal principles of the Party, the liability of a legal person may be criminal, civil or administrative.

4. Such liability shall be without prejudice to the criminal liability of the natural persons who have committed the offence.

Article 13: Sanctions and Measures

1. Each Party shall adopt such legislative and other measures as may be necessary to ensure that the criminal offences established in accordance with Articles 2 through 11 are punishable by effective, proportionate and dissuasive sanctions, which include deprivation of liberty.
2. Each Party shall ensure that legal persons held liable in accordance with Article 12 shall be subject to effective, proportionate and dissuasive criminal or non-criminal sanctions or measures, including monetary sanctions.

Section 2: Procedural Law

Title 1: Common Provisions

Article 14: Scope of Procedural Provisions

1. Each Party shall adopt such legislative and other measures as may be necessary to establish the powers and procedures provided for in this section for the purpose of specific criminal investigations or proceedings.
2. Except as specifically provided otherwise in Article 21, each Party shall apply the powers and procedures referred to in paragraph 1 of this article to:
    a. the criminal offences established in accordance with Articles 2 through 11 of this Convention;
    b. other criminal offences committed by means of a computer system; and
    c. the collection of evidence in electronic form of a criminal offence.
3.
    a. Each Party may reserve the right to apply the measures referred to in Article 20 only to offences or categories of offences specified in the reservation, provided that the range of such offences or categories of offences is not more restricted than the range of offences to which it applies the measures referred to in Article 21. Each Party shall consider restricting such a reservation to enable the broadest application of the measure referred to in Article 20.
    b. Where a Party, due to limitations in its legislation in force at the time of the adoption of the present Convention, is not able to apply the measures referred to in Articles 20 and 21 to communications being transmitted within a computer system of a service provider, which system:
        i.   is being operated for the benefit of a closed group of users, and
        ii. does not employ public communications networks and is not connected with another computer system, whether public or private, that Party may reserve the right not to apply these measures to such communications. Each Party shall consider restricting such a reservation to enable the broadest application of the measures referred to in Articles 20 and 21.

Article 15: Conditions and Safeguards

1. Each Party shall ensure that the establishment, implementation and application of the powers and procedures provided for in this Section are subject to conditions and safeguards provided for under its domestic law, which shall provide for the adequate protection of human rights and liberties, including rights arising pursuant to obligations it has undertaken under the 1950 Council of Europe Convention for the Protection of Human Rights and Fundamental Freedoms, the 1966 United Nations International Covenant on Civil and Political Rights, and other applicable international human rights instruments, and which shall incorporate the principle of proportionality.

2. Such conditions and safeguards shall, as appropriate in view of the nature of the procedure or power concerned, *inter alia,* include judicial or other independent supervision, grounds justifying application, and limitation of the scope and the duration of such power or procedure.

3. To the extent that it is consistent with the public interest, in particular the sound administration of justice, each Party shall consider the impact of the powers and procedures in this section upon the rights, responsibilities and legitimate interests of third parties.

Title 2: Expedited Preservation of Stored Computer Data

Article 16: Expedited Preservation of Stored Computer Data

1. Each Party shall adopt such legislative and other measures as may be necessary to enable its competent authorities to order or similarly obtain the expeditious preservation of specified computer data, including traffic data, that has been stored by means of a computer system, in particular where there are grounds to believe that the computer data is particularly vulnerable to loss or modification.

2. Where a Party gives effect to paragraph 1 above by means of an order to a person to preserve specified stored computer data in the person's possession or control, the Party shall adopt such legislative and other measures as may be necessary to oblige that person to preserve and maintain the integrity of that computer data for a period of time as long as necessary, up to a maximum of ninety days, to enable the competent authorities to seek its disclosure. A Party may provide for such an order to be subsequently renewed.

3. Each Party shall adopt such legislative and other measures as may be necessary to oblige the custodian or other person who is to preserve the computer data to keep confidential the undertaking of such procedures for the period of time provided for by its domestic law.

4. The powers and procedures referred to in this article shall be subject to Articles 14 and 15.

Article 17: Expedited Preservation and Partial Disclosure of Traffic Data

1. Each Party shall adopt, in respect of traffic data that is to be preserved under Article 16, such legislative and other measures as may be necessary to:
    a. ensure that such expeditious preservation of traffic data is available regardless of whether one or more service providers were involved in the transmission of that communication; and
    b. ensure the expeditious disclosure to the Party's competent authority, or a person designated by that authority, of a sufficient amount of traffic data to enable the Party to identify the service providers and the path through which the communication was transmitted.

2. The powers and procedures referred to in this article shall be subject to Articles 14 and 15.

Title 3: Production Order

Article 18: Production Order

1. Each Party shall adopt such legislative and other measures as may be necessary to empower its competent authorities to order:
   a. a person in its territory to submit specified computer data in that person's possession or control, which is stored in a computer system or a computer-data storage medium; and
   b. a service provider offering its services in the territory of the Party to submit subscriber information relating to such services in that service provider's possession or control.
2. The powers and procedures referred to in this article shall be subject to Articles 14 and 15.
3. For the purpose of this article, the term "subscriber information" means any information contained in the form of computer data or any other form that is held by a service provider, relating to subscribers of its services other than traffic or content data and by which can be established:
   a. the type of communication service used, the technical provisions taken thereto and the period of service;
   b. the subscriber's identity, postal or geographic address, telephone and other access number, billing and payment information, available on the basis of the service agreement or arrangement;
   c. any other information on the site of the installation of communication equipment, available on the basis of the service agreement or arrangement.

Title 4: Search and Seizure of Stored Computer Data

Article 19: Search and seizure of Stored Computer Data

1. Each Party shall adopt such legislative and other measures as may be necessary to empower its competent authorities to search or similarly access:
   a. a computer system or part of it and computer data stored therein; and
   b. a computer-data storage medium in which computer data may be stored in its territory.
2. Each Party shall adopt such legislative and other measures as may be necessary to ensure that where its authorities search or similarly access a specific computer system or part of it, pursuant to paragraph 1.a, and have grounds to believe that the data sought is stored in another computer system or part of it in its territory, and such data is lawfully accessible from or available to the initial system, the authorities shall be able to expeditiously extend the search or similar accessing to the other system.
3. Each Party shall adopt such legislative and other measures as may be necessary to empower its competent authorities to seize or similarly secure computer data accessed according to paragraphs 1 or 2. These measures shall include the power to:
   a. seize or similarly secure a computer system or part of it or a computer-data storage medium;
   b. make and retain a copy of those computer data;
   c. maintain the integrity of the relevant stored computer data;
   d. render inaccessible or remove those computer data in the accessed computer system.
4. Each Party shall adopt such legislative and other measures as may be necessary to empower its competent authorities to order any person who has knowledge about the functioning of the computer

system or measures applied to protect the computer data therein to provide, as is reasonable, the necessary information, to enable the undertaking of the measures referred to in paragraphs 1 and 2.

5. The powers and procedures referred to in this article shall be subject to Articles 14 and 15.

Title 5: Real-Time Collection of Computer Data

Article 20: Real-Time Collection of Traffic Data

1. Each Party shall adopt such legislative and other measures as may be necessary to empower its competent authorities to:
    a. collect or record through the application of technical means on the territory of that Party, and
    b. compel a service provider, within its existing technical capability:
        i. to collect or record through the application of technical means on the territory of that Party; or
        ii. to co-operate and assist the competent authorities in the collection or recording of, traffic data, in real-time, associated with specified communications in its territory transmitted by means of a computer system.
2. Where a Party, due to the established principles of its domestic legal system, cannot adopt the measures referred to in paragraph 1.a, it may instead adopt legislative and other measures as may be necessary to ensure the real-time collection or recording of traffic data associated with specified communications transmitted in its territory, through the application of technical means on that territory.
3. Each Party shall adopt such legislative and other measures as may be necessary to oblige a service provider to keep confidential the fact of the execution of any power provided for in this article and any information relating to it.
4. The powers and procedures referred to in this article shall be subject to Articles 14 and 15.

Article 21: Interception of Content Data

1. Each Party shall adopt such legislative and other measures as may be necessary, in relation to a range of serious offences to be determined by domestic law, to empower its competent authorities to:
    a. collect or record through the application of technical means on the territory of that Party, and
    b. compel a service provider, within its existing technical capability:
        i. to collect or record through the application of technical means on the territory of that Party, or
        ii. to co-operate and assist the competent authorities in the collection or recording of, content data, in real-time, of specified communications in its territory transmitted by means of a computer system.
2. Where a Party, due to the established principles of its domestic legal system, cannot adopt the measures referred to in paragraph 1.a, it may instead adopt legislative and other measures as may be necessary to ensure the real-time collection or recording of content data on specified communications in its territory through the application of technical means on that territory.

3. Each Party shall adopt such legislative and other measures as may be necessary to oblige a service provider to keep confidential the fact of the execution of any power provided for in this article and any information relating to it.
4. The powers and procedures referred to in this article shall be subject to Articles 14 and 15.

Section 3: Jurisdiction

Article 22: Jurisdiction

1. Each Party shall adopt such legislative and other measures as may be necessary to establish jurisdiction over any offence established in accordance with Articles 2 through 11 of this Convention, when the offence is committed:
   a. in its territory; or
   b. on board a ship flying the flag of that Party; or
   c. on board an aircraft registered under the laws of that Party; or
   d. by one of its nationals, if the offence is punishable under criminal law where it was committed or if the offence is committed outside the territorial jurisdiction of any State.
2. Each Party may reserve the right not to apply or to apply only in specific cases or conditions the jurisdiction rules laid down in paragraphs 1.b through 1.d of this article or any part thereof.
3. Each Party shall adopt such measures as may be necessary to establish jurisdiction over the offences referred to in Article 24, paragraph 1, of this Convention, in cases where an alleged offender is present in its territory and it does not extradite him or her to another Party, solely on the basis of his or her nationality, after a request for extradition.
4. This Convention does not exclude any criminal jurisdiction exercised by a Party in accordance with its domestic law.
5. When more than one Party claims jurisdiction over an alleged offence established in accordance with this Convention, the Parties involved shall, where appropriate, consult with a view to determining the most appropriate jurisdiction for prosecution.

Chapter III: International Co-Operation

Section 1: General Principles

Title 1: General Principles Relating to International Co-Operation

Article 23: General Principles Relating to International Co-Operation

The Parties shall co-operate with each other, in accordance with the provisions of this chapter, and through the application of relevant international instruments on international co-operation in criminal matters, arrangements agreed on the basis of uniform or reciprocal legislation, and domestic laws, to the widest extent possible for the purposes of investigations or proceedings concerning criminal offences related to computer systems and data, or for the collection of evidence in electronic form of a criminal offence.

Title 2: Principles Relating to Extradition

Article 24: Extradition

1.
   a.   This article applies to extradition between Parties for the criminal offences established in accordance with Articles 2 through 11 of this Convention, provided that they are punishable under the laws of both Parties concerned by deprivation of liberty for a maximum period of at least one year, or by a more severe penalty.
   b.   Where a different minimum penalty is to be applied under an arrangement agreed on the basis of uniform or reciprocal legislation or an extradition treaty, including the European Convention on Extradition (ETS No. 24), applicable between two or more parties, the minimum penalty provided for under such arrangement or treaty shall apply.

2.   The criminal offences described in paragraph 1 of this article shall be deemed to be included as extraditable offences in any extradition treaty existing between or among the Parties. The Parties undertake to include such offences as extraditable offences in any extradition treaty to be concluded between or among them.

3.   If a Party that makes extradition conditional on the existence of a treaty receives a request for extradition from another Party with which it does not have an extradition treaty, it may consider this Convention as the legal basis for extradition with respect to any criminal offence referred to in paragraph 1 of this article.

4.   Parties that do not make extradition conditional on the existence of a treaty shall recognise the criminal offences referred to in paragraph 1 of this article as extraditable offences between themselves.

5.   Extradition shall be subject to the conditions provided for by the law of the requested Party or by applicable extradition treaties, including the grounds on which the requested Party may refuse extradition.

6.   If extradition for a criminal offence referred to in paragraph 1 of this article is refused solely on the basis of the nationality of the person sought, or because the requested Party deems that it has jurisdiction over the offence, the requested Party shall submit the case at the request of the requesting Party to its competent authorities for the purpose of prosecution and shall report the final outcome to the requesting Party in due course. Those authorities shall take their decision and conduct their investigations and proceedings in the same manner as for any other offence of a comparable nature under the law of that Party.

7.
   a.   Each Party shall, at the time of signature or when depositing its instrument of ratification, acceptance, approval or accession, communicate to the Secretary General of the Council of Europe the name and address of each authority responsible for making or receiving requests for extradition or provisional arrest in the absence of a treaty.
   b.   The Secretary General of the Council of Europe shall set up and keep updated a register of authorities so designated by the Parties. Each Party shall ensure that the details held on the register are correct at all times.

Title 3: General Principles Relating to Mutual Assistance

Article 25: General Principles Relating to Mutual Assistance

1. The Parties shall afford one another mutual assistance to the widest extent possible for the purpose of investigations or proceedings concerning criminal offences related to computer systems and data, or for the collection of evidence in electronic form of a criminal offence.

2. Each Party shall also adopt such legislative and other measures as may be necessary to carry out the obligations set forth in Articles 27 through 35.

3. Each Party may, in urgent circumstances, make requests for mutual assistance or communications related thereto by expedited means of communication, including fax or e-mail, to the extent that such means provide appropriate levels of security and authentication (including the use of encryption, where necessary), with formal confirmation to follow, where required by the requested Party. The requested Party shall accept and respond to the request by any such expedited means of communication.

4. Except as otherwise specifically provided in articles in this chapter, mutual assistance shall be subject to the conditions provided for by the law of the requested Party or by applicable mutual assistance treaties, including the grounds on which the requested Party may refuse co-operation. The requested Party shall not exercise the right to refuse mutual assistance in relation to the offences referred to in Articles 2 through 11 solely on the ground that the request concerns an offence, which it considers a fiscal offence.

5. Where, in accordance with the provisions of this chapter, the requested Party is permitted to make mutual assistance conditional upon the existence of dual criminality, that condition shall be deemed fulfilled, irrespective of whether its laws place the offence within the same category of offence or denominate the offence by the same terminology as the requesting Party, if the conduct underlying the offence for which assistance is sought is a criminal offence under its laws.

Article 26: Spontaneous Information

1. A Party may, within the limits of its domestic law and without prior request, forward to another Party information obtained within the framework of its own investigations when it considers that the disclosure of such information might assist the receiving Party in initiating or carrying out investigations or proceedings concerning criminal offences established in accordance with this Convention or might lead to a request for co-operation by that Party under this chapter.

2. Prior to providing such information, the providing Party may request that it be kept confidential or only used subject to conditions. If the receiving Party cannot comply with such request, it shall notify the providing Party, which shall then determine whether the information should nevertheless be provided. If the receiving Party accepts the information subject to the conditions, it shall be bound by them.

Title 4: Procedures Pertaining to Mutual Assistance Requests in the Absence of Applicable International Agreements

Article 27: Procedures Pertaining to Mutual Assistance Requests in the Absence of Applicable International Agreements

1. Where there is no mutual assistance treaty or arrangement on the basis of uniform or reciprocal legislation in force between the requesting and requested Parties, the provisions of paragraphs 2 through 9 of this article shall apply. The provisions of this article shall not apply where such treaty, arrangement or legislation exists, unless the Parties concerned agree to apply any or all of the remainder of this article in lieu thereof.

2.
   a. Each Party shall designate a central authority or authorities responsible for sending and answering requests for mutual assistance, the execution of such requests or their transmission to the authorities competent for their execution.
   b. The central authorities shall communicate directly with each other;
   c. Each Party shall, at the time of signature or when depositing its instrument of ratification, acceptance, approval or accession, communicate to the Secretary General of the Council of Europe the names and addresses of the authorities designated in pursuance of this paragraph;
   d. The Secretary General of the Council of Europe shall set up and keep updated a register of central authorities designated by the Parties. Each Party shall ensure that the details held on the register are correct at all times.

3. Mutual assistance requests under this article shall be executed in accordance with the procedures specified by the requesting Party, except where incompatible with the law of the requested Party.

4. The requested Party may, in addition to the grounds for refusal established in Article 25, paragraph 4, refuse assistance if:
   a. the request concerns an offence which the requested Party considers a political offence or an offence connected with a political offence, or
   b. it considers that execution of the request is likely to prejudice its sovereignty, security, *ordre public* or other essential interests.

5. The requested Party may postpone action on a request if such action would prejudice criminal investigations or proceedings conducted by its authorities.

6. Before refusing or postponing assistance, the requested Party shall, where appropriate after having consulted with the requesting Party, consider whether the request may be granted partially or subject to such conditions as it deems necessary.

7. The requested Party shall promptly inform the requesting Party of the outcome of the execution of a request for assistance. Reasons shall be given for any refusal or postponement of the request. The requested Party shall also inform the requesting Party of any reasons that render impossible the execution of the request or are likely to delay it significantly.

8. The requesting Party may request that the requested Party keep confidential the fact of any request made under this chapter as well as its subject, except to the extent necessary for its execution. If the requested Party cannot comply with the request for confidentiality, it shall promptly inform the requesting Party, which shall then determine whether the request should nevertheless be executed.

9.

    a.   In the event of urgency, requests for mutual assistance or communications related thereto may be sent directly by judicial authorities of the requesting Party to such authorities of the requested Party. In any such cases, a copy shall be sent at the same time to the central authority of the requested Party through the central authority of the requesting Party.

    b.   Any request or communication under this paragraph may be made through the International Criminal Police Organisation (Interpol).

    c.   Where a request is made pursuant to sub-paragraph a. of this article and the authority is not competent to deal with the request, it shall refer the request to the competent national authority and inform directly the requesting Party that it has done so.

    d.   Requests or communications made under this paragraph that do not involve coercive action may be directly transmitted by the competent authorities of the requesting Party to the competent authorities of the requested Party.

    e.   Each Party may, at the time of signature or when depositing its instrument of ratification, acceptance, approval or accession, inform the Secretary General of the Council of Europe that, for reasons of efficiency, requests made under this paragraph are to be addressed to its central authority.

Article 28: Confidentiality and Limitation on Use

1.   When there is no mutual assistance treaty or arrangement on the basis of uniform or reciprocal legislation in force between the requesting and the requested Parties, the provisions of this article shall apply. The provisions of this article shall not apply where such treaty, arrangement or legislation exists, unless the Parties concerned agree to apply any or all of the remainder of this article in lieu thereof.

2.   The requested Party may make the supply of information or material in response to a request dependent on the condition that it is:

    a.   kept confidential where the request for mutual legal assistance could not be complied with in the absence of such condition, or

    b.   not used for investigations or proceedings other than those stated in the request.

3.   If the requesting Party cannot comply with a condition referred to in paragraph 2, it shall promptly inform the other Party, which shall then determine whether the information should nevertheless be provided. When the requesting Party accepts the condition, it shall be bound by it.

4.   Any Party that supplies information or material subject to a condition referred to in paragraph 2 may require the other Party to explain, in relation to that condition, the use made of such information or material.

Section 2: Specific Provisions

Title 1: Mutual Assistance Regarding Provisional Measures

Article 29: Expedited Preservation of Stored Computer Data

1. A Party may request another Party to order or otherwise obtain the expeditious preservation of data stored by means of a computer system, located within the territory of that other Party and in respect of which the requesting Party intends to submit a request for mutual assistance for the search or similar access, seizure or similar securing, or disclosure of the data.
2. A request for preservation made under paragraph 1 shall specify:
    a. the authority seeking the preservation;
    b. the offence that is the subject of a criminal investigation or proceedings and a brief summary of the related facts;
    c. the stored computer data to be preserved and its relationship to the offence;
    d. any available information identifying the custodian of the stored computer data or the location of the computer system;
    e. the necessity of the preservation; and
    f. that the Party intends to submit a request for mutual assistance for the search or similar access, seizure or similar securing, or disclosure of the stored computer data.
3. Upon receiving the request from another Party, the requested Party shall take all appropriate measures to preserve expeditiously the specified data in accordance with its domestic law. For the purposes of responding to a request, dual criminality shall not be required as a condition to providing such preservation.
4. A Party that requires dual criminality as a condition for responding to a request for mutual assistance for the search or similar access, seizure or similar securing, or disclosure of stored data may, in respect of offences other than those established in accordance with Articles 2 through 11 of this Convention, reserve the right to refuse the request for preservation under this article in cases where it has reasons to believe that at the time of disclosure the condition of dual criminality cannot be fulfilled.
5. In addition, a request for preservation may only be refused if:
    a. the request concerns an offence which the requested Party considers a political offence or an offence connected with a political offence, or
    b. the requested Party considers that execution of the request is likely to prejudice its sovereignty, security, *ordre public* or other essential interests.
6. Where the requested Party believes that preservation will not ensure the future availability of the data or will threaten the confidentiality of or otherwise prejudice the requesting Party's investigation, it shall promptly so inform the requesting Party, which shall then determine whether the request should nevertheless be executed.
7. Any preservation effected in response to the request referred to in paragraph 1 shall be for a period not less than sixty days, in order to enable the requesting Party to submit a request for the search or similar access, seizure or similar securing, or disclosure of the data. Following the receipt of such a request, the data shall continue to be preserved pending a decision on that request.

Article 30: Expedited Disclosure of Preserved Traffic Data

1. Where, in the course of the execution of a request made pursuant to Article 29 to preserve traffic data concerning a specific communication, the requested Party discovers that a service provider in another State was involved in the transmission of the communication, the requested Party shall expeditiously disclose to the requesting Party a sufficient amount of traffic data to identify that service provider and the path through which the communication was transmitted.

2. Disclosure of traffic data under paragraph 1 may only be withheld if:
   a. the request concerns an offence which the requested Party considers a political offence or an offence connected with a political offence; or
   b. the requested Party considers that execution of the request is likely to prejudice its sovereignty, security, *ordre public* or other essential interests.

Title 2: Mutual Assistance Regarding Investigative Powers

Article 31: Mutual Assistance Regarding Accessing of Stored Computer Data

1. A Party may request another Party to search or similarly access, seize or similarly secure, and disclose data stored by means of a computer system located within the territory of the requested Party, including data that has been preserved pursuant to Article 29.

2. The requested Party shall respond to the request through the application of international instruments, arrangements and laws referred to in Article 23, and in accordance with other relevant provisions of this chapter.

3. The request shall be responded to on an expedited basis where:
   a. there are grounds to believe that relevant data is particularly vulnerable to loss or modification; or
   b. the instruments, arrangements and laws referred to in paragraph 2 otherwise provide for expedited co-operation.

Article 32: Trans-Border Access to Stored Computer Data with Consent or Where Publicly Available

A Party may, without the authorisation of another Party:

a. access publicly available (open source) stored computer data, regardless of where the data is located geographically; or
b. access or receive, through a computer system in its territory, stored computer data located in another Party, if the Party obtains the lawful and voluntary consent of the person who has the lawful authority to disclose the data to the Party through that computer system.

Article 33: Mutual Assistance Regarding the Real-Time Collection of Traffic Data

1. The Parties shall provide mutual assistance to each other in the real-time collection of traffic data associated with specified communications in their territory transmitted by means of a computer

system. Subject to the provisions of paragraph 2, this assistance shall be governed by the conditions and procedures provided for under domestic law.

2.   Each Party shall provide such assistance at least with respect to criminal offences for which real-time collection of traffic data would be available in a similar domestic case.

Article 34: Mutual Assistance Regarding the Interception of Content Data

The Parties shall provide mutual assistance to each other in the real-time collection or recording of content data of specified communications transmitted by means of a computer system to the extent permitted under their applicable treaties and domestic laws.

Title 3: 24/7 Network

Article 35: 24/7 Network

1.   Each Party shall designate a point of contact available on a twenty-four hour, seven-day-a-week basis, in order to ensure the provision of immediate assistance for the purpose of investigations or proceedings concerning criminal offences related to computer systems and data, or for the collection of evidence in electronic form of a criminal offence. Such assistance shall include facilitating, or, if permitted by its domestic law and practice, directly carrying out the following measures:
     a.   the provision of technical advice;
     b.   the preservation of data pursuant to Articles 29 and 30;
     c.   the collection of evidence, the provision of legal information, and locating of suspects.

2.
     a.   A Party's point of contact shall have the capacity to carry out communications with the point of contact of another Party on an expedited basis.
     b.   If the point of contact designated by a Party is not part of that Party's authority or authorities responsible for international mutual assistance or extradition, the point of contact shall ensure that it is able to co-ordinate with such authority or authorities on an expedited basis.

3.   Each Party shall ensure that trained and equipped personnel are available, in order to facilitate the operation of the network.

Chapter IV: Final Provisions

Article 36: Signature and Entry into Force

1.   This Convention shall be open for signature by the member States of the Council of Europe and by non-member States which have participated in its elaboration.

2.   This Convention is subject to ratification, acceptance or approval. Instruments of ratification, acceptance or approval shall be deposited with the Secretary General of the Council of Europe.

3.   This Convention shall enter into force on the first day of the month following the expiration of a period of three months after the date on which five States, including at least three member States of

the Council of Europe, have expressed their consent to be bound by the Convention in accordance with the provisions of paragraphs 1 and 2.

4. In respect of any signatory State which subsequently expresses its consent to be bound by it, the Convention shall enter into force on the first day of the month following the expiration of a period of three months after the date of the expression of its consent to be bound by the Convention in accordance with the provisions of paragraphs 1 and 2.

Article 37: Accession to the Convention

1. After the entry into force of this Convention, the Committee of Ministers of the Council of Europe, after consulting with and obtaining the unanimous consent of the Contracting States to the Convention, may invite any State which is not a member of the Council and which has not participated in its elaboration to accede to this Convention. The decision shall be taken by the majority provided for in Article 20.d. of the Statute of the Council of Europe and by the unanimous vote of the representatives of the Contracting States entitled to sit on the Committee of Ministers.

2. In respect of any State acceding to the Convention under paragraph 1 above, the Convention shall enter into force on the first day of the month following the expiration of a period of three months after the date of deposit of the instrument of accession with the Secretary General of the Council of Europe.

Article 38: Territorial Application

1. Any State may, at the time of signature or when depositing its instrument of ratification, acceptance, approval or accession, specify the territory or territories to which this Convention shall apply.

2. Any State may, at any later date, by a declaration addressed to the Secretary General of the Council of Europe, extend the application of this Convention to any other territory specified in the declaration. In respect of such territory the Convention shall enter into force on the first day of the month following the expiration of a period of three months after the date of receipt of the declaration by the Secretary General.

3. Any declaration made under the two preceding paragraphs may, in respect of any territory specified in such declaration, be withdrawn by a notification addressed to the Secretary General of the Council of Europe. The withdrawal shall become effective on the first day of the month following the expiration of a period of three months after the date of receipt of such notification by the Secretary General.

Article 39: Effects of the Convention

1. The purpose of the present Convention is to supplement applicable multilateral or bilateral treaties or arrangements as between the Parties, including the provisions of:
   - the European Convention on Extradition, opened for signature in Paris, on 13 December 1957 (ETS No. 24);
   - the European Convention on Mutual Assistance in Criminal Matters, opened for signature in Strasbourg, on 20 April 1959 (ETS No. 30);
   - the Additional Protocol to the European Convention on Mutual Assistance in Criminal Matters, opened for signature in Strasbourg, on 17 March 1978 (ETS No. 99).

2. If two or more Parties have already concluded an agreement or treaty on the matters dealt with in this Convention or have otherwise established their relations on such matters, or should they in future do so, they shall also be entitled to apply that agreement or treaty or to regulate those relations accordingly. However, where Parties establish their relations in respect of the matters dealt with in the present Convention other than as regulated therein, they shall do so in a manner that is not inconsistent with the Convention's objectives and principles.

3. Nothing in this Convention shall affect other rights, restrictions, obligations and responsibilities of a Party.

Article 40: Declarations

By a written notification addressed to the Secretary General of the Council of Europe, any State may, at the time of signature or when depositing its instrument of ratification, acceptance, approval or accession, declare that it avails itself of the possibility of requiring additional elements as provided for under Articles 2, 3, 6 paragraph 1.b, 7, 9 paragraph 3, and 27, paragraph 9.e.

Article 41: Federal Clause

1. A federal State may reserve the right to assume obligations under Chapter II of this Convention consistent with its fundamental principles governing the relationship between its central government and constituent States or other similar territorial entities provided that it is still able to co-operate under Chapter III.

2. When making a reservation under paragraph 1, a federal State may not apply the terms of such reservation to exclude or substantially diminish its obligations to provide for measures set forth in Chapter II. Overall, it shall provide for a broad and effective law enforcement capability with respect to those measures.

3. With regard to the provisions of this Convention, the application of which comes under the jurisdiction of constituent States or other similar territorial entities, that are not obliged by the constitutional system of the federation to take legislative measures, the federal government shall inform the competent authorities of such States of the said provisions with its favourable opinion, encouraging them to take appropriate action to give them effect.

Article 42: Reservations

By a written notification addressed to the Secretary General of the Council of Europe, any State may, at the time of signature or when depositing its instrument of ratification, acceptance, approval or accession, declare that it avails itself of the reservation(s) provided for in Article 4, paragraph 2, Article 6, paragraph 3, Article 9, paragraph 4, Article 10, paragraph 3, Article 11, paragraph 3, Article 14, paragraph 3, Article 22, paragraph 2, Article 29, paragraph 4, and Article 41, paragraph 1. No other reservation may be made.

Article 43: Status and Withdrawal of Reservations

1. A Party that has made a reservation in accordance with Article 42 may wholly or partially withdraw it by means of a notification addressed to the Secretary General of the Council of Europe. Such

withdrawal shall take effect on the date of receipt of such notification by the Secretary General. If the notification states that the withdrawal of a reservation is to take effect on a date specified therein, and such date is later than the date on which the notification is received by the Secretary General, the withdrawal shall take effect on such a later date.

2. A Party that has made a reservation as referred to in Article 42 shall withdraw such reservation, in whole or in part, as soon as circumstances so permit.

3. The Secretary General of the Council of Europe may periodically enquire with Parties that have made one or more reservations as referred to in Article 42 as to the prospects for withdrawing such reservation(s).

Article 44: Amendments

1. Amendments to this Convention may be proposed by any Party, and shall be communicated by the Secretary General of the Council of Europe to the member States of the Council of Europe, to the non-member States which have participated in the elaboration of this Convention as well as to any State which has acceded to, or has been invited to accede to, this Convention in accordance with the provisions of Article 37.

2. Any amendment proposed by a Party shall be communicated to the European Committee on Crime Problems (CDPC), which shall submit to the Committee of Ministers its opinion on that proposed amendment.

3. The Committee of Ministers shall consider the proposed amendment and the opinion submitted by the CDPC and, following consultation with the non-member States Parties to this Convention, may adopt the amendment.

4. The text of any amendment adopted by the Committee of Ministers in accordance with paragraph 3 of this article shall be forwarded to the Parties for acceptance.

5. Any amendment adopted in accordance with paragraph 3 of this article shall come into force on the thirtieth day after all Parties have informed the Secretary General of their acceptance thereof.

Article 45: Settlement of Disputes

1. The European Committee on Crime Problems (CDPC) shall be kept informed regarding the interpretation and application of this Convention.

2. In case of a dispute between Parties as to the interpretation or application of this Convention, they shall seek a settlement of the dispute through negotiation or any other peaceful means of their choice, including submission of the dispute to the CDPC, to an arbitral tribunal whose decisions shall be binding upon the Parties, or to the International Court of Justice, as agreed upon by the Parties concerned.

Article 46: Consultations of the Parties

1. The Parties shall, as appropriate, consult periodically with a view to facilitating:
    a. the effective use and implementation of this Convention, including the identification of any problems thereof, as well as the effects of any declaration or reservation made under this Convention;

b.   the exchange of information on significant legal, policy or technological developments pertaining to cybercrime and the collection of evidence in electronic form;

c.   consideration of possible supplementation or amendment of the Convention.

2.   The European Committee on Crime Problems (CDPC) shall be kept periodically informed regarding the result of consultations referred to in paragraph 1.

3.   The CDPC shall, as appropriate, facilitate the consultations referred to in paragraph 1 and take the measures necessary to assist the Parties in their efforts to supplement or amend the Convention. At the latest three years after the present Convention enters into force, the European Committee on Crime Problems (CDPC) shall, in co-operation with the Parties, conduct a review of all of the Convention's provisions and, if necessary, recommend any appropriate amendments.

4.   Except where assumed by the Council of Europe, expenses incurred in carrying out the provisions of paragraph 1 shall be borne by the Parties in the manner to be determined by them.

5.   The Parties shall be assisted by the Secretariat of the Council of Europe in carrying out their functions pursuant to this article.

Article 47: Denunciation

1.   Any Party may, at any time, denounce this Convention by means of a notification addressed to the Secretary General of the Council of Europe.

2.   Such denunciation shall become effective on the first day of the month following the expiration of a period of three months after the date of receipt of the notification by the Secretary General.

Article 48: Notification

The Secretary General of the Council of Europe shall notify the member States of the Council of Europe, the non-member States which have participated in the elaboration of this Convention as well as any State which has acceded to, or has been invited to accede to, this Convention of:

a.   any signature;

b.   the deposit of any instrument of ratification, acceptance, approval or accession;

c.   any date of entry into force of this Convention in accordance with Articles 36 and 37;

d.   any declaration made under Article 40 or reservation made in accordance with Article 42;

e.   any other act, notification or communication relating to this Convention.

In witness whereof the undersigned, being duly authorised thereto, have signed this Convention.

Done at Budapest, this 23rd day of November 2001, in English and in French, both texts being equally authentic, in a single copy which shall be deposited in the archives of the Council of Europe. The Secretary General of the Council of Europe shall transmit certified copies to each member State of the Council of Europe, to the non-member States which have participated in the elaboration of this Convention, and to any State invited to accede to it.

APPENDIX 2

Relevant Provisions from USC 18, Part-1: Crimes (Sections 1-2725)
Title 18, Part-1, Chapter 71:

§ 1460. Possession with Intent to Sell, and Sale, of Obscene Matter on Federal Property

a.   Whoever, either—
1.   in the special maritime and territorial jurisdiction of the United States, or on any land or building owned by, leased to, or otherwise used by or under the control of the Government of the United States; or
2.   in the Indian country as defined in section 1151 of this title,

knowingly sells or possesses with intent to sell an obscene visual depiction shall be punished by a fine in accordance with the provisions of this title or imprisoned for not more than 2 years, or both.

b.   For the purposes of this section, the term "visual depiction" includes undeveloped film and video-tape but does not include mere words.

§ 1461. Mailing Obscene or Crime-Inciting Matter

Every obscene, lewd, lascivious, indecent, filthy or vile article, matter, thing, device, or substance; and—
   Every article or thing designed, adapted, or intended for producing abortion, or for any indecent or immoral use; and
   Every article, instrument, substance, drug, medicine, or thing which is advertised or described in a manner calculated to lead another to use or apply it for producing abortion, or for any indecent or immoral purpose; and
   Every written or printed card, letter, circular, book, pamphlet, advertisement, or notice of any kind giving information, directly or indirectly, where, or how, or from whom, or by what means any of such mentioned matters, articles, or things may be obtained or made, or where or by whom any act or operation of any kind for the procuring or producing of abortion will be done or performed, or how or by what means abortion may be produced, whether sealed or unsealed; and
   Every paper, writing, advertisement, or representation that any article, instrument, substance, drug, medicine, or thing may, or can, be used or applied for producing abortion, or for any indecent or immoral purpose; and
   Every description calculated to induce or incite a person to so use or apply any such article, instrument, substance, drug, medicine, or thing—
   Is declared to be nonmailable matter and shall not be conveyed in the mails or delivered from any post office or by any letter carrier.
   Whoever knowingly uses the mails for the mailing, carriage in the mails, or delivery of anything declared by this section or section 3001 (e) of title 39 to be nonmailable, or knowingly causes to be delivered by mail according to the direction thereon, or at the place at which it is directed to be delivered by the person to whom it is addressed, or knowingly takes any such thing from the mails for the purpose

of circulating or disposing thereof, or of aiding in the circulation or disposition thereof, shall be fined under this title or imprisoned not more than five years, or both, for the first such offense, and shall be fined under this title or imprisoned not more than ten years, or both, for each such offense thereafter.

The term "indecent", as used in this section includes matter of a character tending to incite arson, murder, or assassination.

§ 1462. Importation or Transportation of Obscene Matters

Whoever brings into the United States, or any place subject to the jurisdiction thereof, or knowingly uses any express company or other common carrier or interactive computer service (as defined in section 230(e)(2) [1] of the Communications Act of 1934), for carriage in interstate or foreign commerce—

a. any obscene, lewd, lascivious, or filthy book, pamphlet, picture, motion-picture film, paper, letter, writing, print, or other matter of indecent character; or

b. any obscene, lewd, lascivious, or filthy phonograph recording, electrical transcription, or other article or thing capable of producing sound; or

c. any drug, medicine, article, or thing designed, adapted, or intended for producing abortion, or for any indecent or immoral use; or any written or printed card, letter, circular, book, pamphlet, advertisement, or notice of any kind giving information, directly or indirectly, where, how, or of whom, or by what means any of such mentioned articles, matters, or things may be obtained or made; or

Whoever knowingly takes or receives, from such express company or other common carrier or interactive computer service (as defined in section 230(e)(2) of the Communications Act of 1934) any matter or thing the carriage or importation of which is herein made unlawful—

Shall be fined under this title or imprisoned not more than five years, or both, for the first such offense and shall be fined under this title or imprisoned not more than ten years, or both, for each such offense thereafter.

§ 1464. Broadcasting Obscene Language

Whoever utters any obscene, indecent, or profane language by means of radio communication shall be fined under this title or imprisoned not more than two years, or both.

§ 1465. Production and Transportation of Obscene Matters for Sale or Distribution

Whoever knowingly produces with the intent to transport, distribute, or transmit in interstate or foreign commerce, or whoever knowingly transports or travels in, or uses a facility or means of, interstate or foreign commerce or an interactive computer service (as defined in section 230(e)(2) of the Communications Act of 1934) in or affecting such commerce, for the purpose of sale or distribution of any obscene, lewd, lascivious, or filthy book, pamphlet, picture, film, paper, letter, writing, print, silhouette, drawing, figure, image, cast, phonograph recording, electrical transcription or other article capable of producing sound or any other matter of indecent or immoral character, shall be fined under this title or imprisoned not more than five years, or both.

The transportation as aforesaid of two or more copies of any publication or two or more of any article of the character described above, or a combined total of five such publications and articles, shall create a presumption that such publications or articles are intended for sale or distribution, but such presumption shall be rebuttable.

§ 1466. Engaging in the Business of Selling or Transferring Obscene Matter

a. Whoever is engaged in the business of producing with intent to distribute or sell, or selling or transferring obscene matter, who knowingly receives or possesses with intent to distribute any obscene book, magazine, picture, paper, film, videotape, or phonograph or other audio recording, which has been shipped or transported in interstate or foreign commerce, shall be punished by imprisonment for not more than 5 years or by a fine under this title, or both.

b. As used in this section, the term "engaged in the business" means that the person who produces sells or transfers or offers to sell or transfer obscene matter devotes time, attention, or labor to such activities, as a regular course of trade or business, with the objective of earning a profit, although it is not necessary that the person make a profit or that the production, selling or transferring or offering to sell or transfer such material be the person's sole or principal business or source of income. The offering for sale of or to transfer, at one time, two or more copies of any obscene publication, or two or more of any obscene article, or a combined total of five or more such publications and articles, shall create a rebuttable presumption that the person so offering them is "engaged in the business" as defined in this subsection.

§ 1466A. Obscene Visual Representations of the Sexual Abuse of Children

a. In General.— Any person who, in a circumstance described in subsection (d), knowingly produces, distributes, receives, or possesses with intent to distribute, a visual depiction of any kind, including a drawing, cartoon, sculpture, or painting, that—

    1.
        A. depicts a minor engaging in sexually explicit conduct; and
        B. is obscene; or

    2.
        A. depicts an image that is, or appears to be, of a minor engaging in graphic bestiality, sadistic or masochistic abuse, or sexual intercourse, including genital-genital, oral-genital, anal-genital, or oral-anal, whether between persons of the same or opposite sex; and
        B. lacks serious literary, artistic, political, or scientific value; or attempts or conspires to do so, shall be subject to the penalties provided in section 2252A (b)(1), including the penalties provided for cases involving a prior conviction.

b. Additional Offenses.— Any person who, in a circumstance described in subsection (d), knowingly possesses a visual depiction of any kind, including a drawing, cartoon, sculpture, or painting, that—

    1.
        A. depicts a minor engaging in sexually explicit conduct; and
        B. is obscene; or

2.
- A. depicts an image that is, or appears to be, of a minor engaging in graphic bestiality, sadistic or masochistic abuse, or sexual intercourse, including genital-genital, oral-genital, anal-genital, or oral-anal, whether between persons of the same or opposite sex; and
- B. lacks serious literary, artistic, political, or scientific value; or attempts or conspires to do so, shall be subject to the penalties provided in section 2252A (b)(2), including the penalties provided for cases involving a prior conviction.

c. Nonrequired Element of Offense.— It is not a required element of any offense under this section that the minor depicted actually exist.

d. Circumstances.— The circumstance referred to in subsections (a) and (b) is that—
1. any communication involved in or made in furtherance of the offense is communicated or transported by the mail, or in interstate or foreign commerce by any means, including by computer, or any means or instrumentality of interstate or foreign commerce is otherwise used in committing or in furtherance of the commission of the offense;
2. any communication involved in or made in furtherance of the offense contemplates the transmission or transportation of a visual depiction by the mail, or in interstate or foreign commerce by any means, including by computer;
3. any person travels or is transported in interstate or foreign commerce in the course of the commission or in furtherance of the commission of the offense;
4. any visual depiction involved in the offense has been mailed, or has been shipped or transported in interstate or foreign commerce by any means, including by computer, or was produced using materials that have been mailed, or that have been shipped or transported in interstate or foreign commerce by any means, including by computer; or
5. the offense is committed in the special maritime and territorial jurisdiction of the United States or in any territory or possession of the United States.

e. Affirmative Defense.— It shall be an affirmative defense to a charge of violating subsection (b) that the defendant—
1. possessed less than 3 such visual depictions; and
2. promptly and in good faith, and without retaining or allowing any person, other than a law enforcement agency, to access any such visual depiction—
   - A. took reasonable steps to destroy each such visual depiction; or
   - B. reported the matter to a law enforcement agency and afforded that agency access to each such visual depiction.

f. Definitions.— For purposes of this section—
1. the term "visual depiction" includes undeveloped film and videotape, and data stored on a computer disk or by electronic means which is capable of conversion into a visual image, and also includes any photograph, film, video, picture, digital image or picture, computer image or picture, or computer generated image or picture, whether made or produced by electronic, mechanical, or other means;
2. the term "sexually explicit conduct" has the meaning given the term in section 2256 (2)(A) or 2256 (2)(B); and
3. the term "graphic", when used with respect to a depiction of sexually explicit conduct, means that a viewer can observe any part of the genitals or pubic area of any depicted person or animal during any part of the time that the sexually explicit conduct is being depicted.

§ 1467. Criminal Forfeiture

a. Property Subject to Criminal Forfeiture.— A person who is convicted of an offense involving obscene material under this chapter shall forfeit to the United States such person's interest in—

    1. any obscene material produced, transported, mailed, shipped, or received in violation of this chapter;

    2. any property, real or personal, constituting or traceable to gross profits or other proceeds obtained from such offense; and

    3. any property, real or personal, used or intended to be used to commit or to promote the commission of such offense.

b. The provisions of section 413 of the Controlled Substances Act (21 U.S.C. 853), with the exception of subsections (a) and (d), shall apply to the criminal forfeiture of property pursuant to subsection (a).

c. Any property subject to forfeiture pursuant to subsection (a) may be forfeited to the United States in a civil case in accordance with the procedures set forth in chapter 46 of this title.

Chapter 88

§ 1801. Video Voyeurism

a. Whoever, in the special maritime and territorial jurisdiction of the United States, has the intent to capture an image of a private area of an individual without their consent, and knowingly does so under circumstances in which the individual has a reasonable expectation of privacy, shall be fined under this title or imprisoned not more than one year, or both.

b. In this section—

    1. the term "capture", with respect to an image, means to videotape, photograph, film, record by any means, or broadcast;

    2. the term "broadcast" means to electronically transmit a visual image with the intent that it be viewed by a person or persons;

    3. the term "a private area of the individual" means the naked or undergarment clad genitals, pubic area, buttocks, or female breast of that individual;

    4. the term "female breast" means any portion of the female breast below the top of the areola; and

    5. the term "under circumstances in which that individual has a reasonable expectation of privacy" means—

        A. circumstances in which a reasonable person would believe that he or she could disrobe in privacy, without being concerned that an image of a private area of the individual was being captured; or

        B. circumstances in which a reasonable person would believe that a private area of the individual would not be visible to the public, regardless of whether that person is in a public or private place.

c. This section does not prohibit any lawful law enforcement, correctional, or intelligence activity.

Chapter 121

§ 2701. Unlawful Access to Stored Communications

a. Offense.— Except as provided in subsection (c) of this section whoever—

    1.   intentionally accesses without authorization a facility through which an electronic communication service is provided; or

    2.   intentionally exceeds an authorization to access that facility; and thereby obtains, alters, or prevents authorized access to a wire or electronic communication while it is in electronic storage in such system shall be punished as provided in subsection (b) of this section.

b. Punishment.— The punishment for an offense under subsection (a) of this section is—

    1.   if the offense is committed for purposes of commercial advantage, malicious destruction or damage, or private commercial gain, or in furtherance of any criminal or tortuous act in violation of the Constitution or laws of the United States or any State—

        A.   a fine under this title or imprisonment for not more than 5 years, or both, in the case of a first offense under this subparagraph; and

        B.   a fine under this title or imprisonment for not more than 10 years, or both, for any subsequent offense under this subparagraph; and

    2.   in any other case—

        A.   a fine under this title or imprisonment for not more than 1 year or both, in the case of a first offense under this paragraph; and

        B.   a fine under this title or imprisonment for not more than 5 years, or both, in the case of an offense under this subparagraph that occurs after a conviction of another offense under this section.

c. Exceptions.— Subsection (a) of this section does not apply with respect to conduct authorized—

    1.   by the person or entity providing a wire or electronic communications service;

    2.   by a user of that service with respect to a communication of or intended for that user; or

    3.   in section 2703, 2704 or 2518 of this title.

§ 2702. Voluntary Disclosure of Customer Communications or Records

a. Prohibitions.— Except as provided in subsection (b) or (c)—

    1.   a person or entity providing an electronic communication service to the public shall not knowingly divulge to any person or entity the contents of a communication while in electronic storage by that service; and

    2.   a person or entity providing remote computing service to the public shall not knowingly divulge to any person or entity the contents of any communication which is carried or maintained on that service—

        A.   on behalf of, and received by means of electronic transmission from (or created by means of computer processing of communications received by means of electronic transmission from), a subscriber or customer of such service;

        B.   solely for the purpose of providing storage or computer processing services to such subscriber or customer, if the provider is not authorized to access the contents of any such communications for purposes of providing any services other than storage or computer processing; and

  3. a provider of remote computing service or electronic communication service to the public shall not knowingly divulge a record or other information pertaining to a subscriber to or customer of such service (not including the contents of communications covered by paragraph (1) or (2)) to any governmental entity.

b. Exceptions for disclosure of communications.—A provider described in subsection (a) may divulge the contents of a communication—

  1. to an addressee or intended recipient of such communication or an agent of such addressee or intended recipient;

  2. as otherwise authorized in section 2517, 2511 (2)(a), or 2703 of this title;

  3. with the lawful consent of the originator or an addressee or intended recipient of such communication, or the subscriber in the case of remote computing service;

  4. to a person employed or authorized or whose facilities are used to forward such communication to its destination;

  5. as may be necessarily incident to the rendition of the service or to the protection of the rights or property of the provider of that service;

  6. to the National Center for Missing and Exploited Children, in connection with a report submitted thereto under section 2258A;

  7. to a law enforcement agency—

    A. if the contents—

      i. were inadvertently obtained by the service provider; and

      ii. appear to pertain to the commission of a crime; or [(B) Repealed. Pub. L. 108–21, title V, § 508(b)(1)(A), Apr. 30, 2003, 117 Stat. 684]

  8. to a governmental entity, if the provider, in good faith, believes that an emergency involving danger of death or serious physical injury to any person requires disclosure without delay of communications relating to the emergency.

c. Exceptions for Disclosure of Customer Records.— A provider described in subsection (a) may divulge a record or other information pertaining to a subscriber to or customer of such service (not including the contents of communications covered by subsection (a)(1) or (a)(2))—

  1. as otherwise authorized in section 2703;

  2. with the lawful consent of the customer or subscriber;

  3. as may be necessarily incident to the rendition of the service or to the protection of the rights or property of the provider of that service;

  4. to a governmental entity, if the provider, in good faith, believes that an emergency involving danger of death or serious physical injury to any person requires disclosure without delay of information relating to the emergency;

  5. to the National Center for Missing and Exploited Children, in connection with a report submitted thereto under section 2258A; or

  6. to any person other than a governmental entity.

d. Reporting of Emergency Disclosures.— On an annual basis, the Attorney General shall submit to the Committee on the Judiciary of the House of Representatives and the Committee on the Judiciary of the Senate a report containing—

1. the number of accounts from which the Department of Justice has received voluntary disclosures under subsection (b)(8); and
2. a summary of the basis for disclosure in those instances where—
    A. voluntary disclosures under subsection (b)(8) were made to the Department of Justice; and
    B. the investigation pertaining to those disclosures was closed without the filing of criminal charges.

§ 2707. Civil Action

a. Cause of Action.— Except as provided in section 2703 (e), any provider of electronic communication service, subscriber, or other person aggrieved by any violation of this chapter in which the conduct constituting the violation is engaged in with a knowing or intentional state of mind may, in a civil action, recover from the person or entity, other than the United States, which engaged in that violation such relief as may be appropriate.
b. Relief.— In a civil action under this section, appropriate relief includes—
    1. such preliminary and other equitable or declaratory relief as may be appropriate;
    2. damages under subsection c; and
    3 a reasonable attorney's fee and other litigation costs reasonably incurred.
c. Damages.— The court may assess as damages in a civil action under this section the sum of the actual damages suffered by the plaintiff and any profits made by the violator as a result of the violation, but in no case shall a person entitled to recover receive less than the sum of $1,000. If the violation is willful or intentional, the court may assess punitive damages. In the case of a successful action to enforce liability under this section, the court may assess the costs of the action, together with reasonable attorney fees determined by the court.
d. Administrative Discipline.— If a court or appropriate department or agency determines that the United States or any of its departments or agencies has violated any provision of this chapter, and the court or appropriate department or agency finds that the circumstances surrounding the violation raise serious questions about whether or not an officer or employee of the United States acted willfully or intentionally with respect to the violation, the department or agency shall, upon receipt of a true and correct copy of the decision and findings of the court or appropriate department or agency promptly initiate a proceeding to determine whether disciplinary action against the officer or employee is warranted. If the head of the department or agency involved determines that disciplinary action is not warranted, he or she shall notify the Inspector General with jurisdiction over the department or agency concerned and shall provide the Inspector General with the reasons for such determination.
e. Defense.— A good faith reliance on—
    1. a court warrant or order, a grand jury subpoena, a legislative authorization, or a statutory authorization (including a request of a governmental entity under section 2703 (f) of this title);
    2. a request of an investigative or law enforcement officer under section 2518 (7) of this title; or

3. a good faith determination that section 2511 (3) of this title permitted the conduct complained of; is a complete defense to any civil or criminal action brought under this chapter or any other law.

f. Limitation.— A civil action under this section may not be commenced later than two years after the date upon which the claimant first discovered or had a reasonable opportunity to discover the violation.

g. Improper Disclosure.— Any willful disclosure of a "record", as that term is defined in section 552a (a) of title 5, United States Code, obtained by an investigative or law enforcement officer, or a governmental entity, pursuant to section 2703 of this title, or from a device installed pursuant to section 3123 or 3125 of this title, that is not a disclosure made in the proper performance of the official functions of the officer or governmental entity making the disclosure, is a violation of this chapter. This provision shall not apply to information previously lawfully disclosed (prior to the commencement of any civil or administrative proceeding under this chapter) to the public by a Federal, State, or local governmental entity or by the plaintiff in a civil action under this chapter.

APPENDIX 3

Relevant Provisions from Violence Against Women and Department of Justice Reauthorization Act, 2005, Regarding Stalking and Related Violence against Women

SEC. 113. Preventing Cyberstalking

a. IN GENERAL.—Paragraph (1) of section 223(h) of the Communications Act of 1934 (47 U.S.C. 223(h)(1)) is amended—

1. in subparagraph (A), by striking "and" at the end;
2. in subparagraph (B), by striking the period at the end and inserting "; and"; and
3. by adding at the end the following new subparagraph: "(c)in the case of subparagraph (c) of subsection (a)(1), includes any device or software that can be used to originate telecommunications or other types of communications that are transmitted, in whole or in part, by the Internet (as such term is defined in section 1104 of the Internet Tax Freedom Act (47 U.S.C. 151 note)).".

b. RULE OF CONSTRUCTION.—This section and the amendment made by this section may not be construed to affect the meaning given the term "telecommunications device" in section 223(h)(1) of the Communications Act of 1934, as in effect before the date of the enactment of this section.

SEC. 114. Criminal Provision Relating to Stalking

a. INTERSTATE STALKING.—Section 2261A of title 18, United States Code, is amended to read as follows:

"§ 2261A. Stalking
"Whoever—

"1. travels in interstate or foreign commerce or within the special maritime and territorial jurisdiction of the United States, or enters or leaves Indian country, with the intent to kill, injure, harass, or place under surveillance with intent to kill, injure, harass, or intimidate another person, and in the course of, or as a result of, such travel places that person in reasonable fear of the death of, or serious bodily injury to, or causes substantial emotional distress to that person, a member of the immediate family (as defined in section 115) of that person, or the spouse or intimate partner of that person;

or
"2. with the intent—
"A. to kill, injure, harass, or place under surveillance with intent to kill, injure, harass, or intimidate, or cause substantial emotional distress to a person in another State or tribal jurisdiction or within the special maritime and territorial jurisdiction of the United States; or

"B. to place a person in another State or tribal jurisdiction, or within the special maritime and territorial jurisdiction of the United States, in reasonable fear of the death of, or serious bodily injury to—

"i. that person;

"ii. a member of the immediate family (as defined in section 115 of that person; or

"iii. a spouse or intimate partner of that person; uses the mail, any interactive computer service, or any facility of interstate or foreign commerce to engage in a course of conduct that causes substantial emotional distress to that person or places that person in reasonable fear of the death of, or serious bodily injury to, any of the persons described in clauses (i) through (iii) of subparagraph (B); shall be punished as provided in section 2261(b) of this title. ".

b.   ENHANCED PENALTIES FOR STALKING.—Section 2261(b) of title 18, United States Code, is amended by adding at the end the following:

"6. Whoever commits the crime of stalking in violation of a temporary or permanent civil or criminal injunction restraining order, no-contact order, or other order described in section 2266 of title 18, United States Code, shall be punished by imprisonment for not less than 1 year. ".

SEC. 115. Repeat Offender Provision

Chapter 110A of title 18, United States Code, is amended by adding after section 2265 the following:

"§ 2265A. Repeat offenders

"a. MAXIMUM TERM OF IMPRISONMENT.—The maximum term of imprisonment for a violation of this chapter after a prior domestic violence or stalking offense shall be twice the term otherwise provided under this chapter.

"b. DEFINITION.—For purposes of this section—

"1. the term 'prior domestic violence or stalking offense' means a conviction for an offense—

"A. under section 2261, 2261A, or 2262 of this chapter;

or

"B. under State law for an offense consisting of conduct that would have been an offense under a section referred to in subparagraph (A) if the conduct had occurred within the special maritime and territorial jurisdiction of the United States, or in interstate or foreign commerce;

and

"2. the term 'State' means a State of the United States, the District of Columbia, or any commonwealth, territory, or possession of the United States."

APPENDIX 4

Relevant Provisions from Canadian Criminal Code (R.S. 1985, c, C-46)[1]

PART VI

Invasion of Privacy

Section 183

Definitions

"*authorization*" means an authorization to intercept a private communication given under section 186 or subsection 184.2(3), 184.3(6) or 188(2);

"*electro-magnetic, acoustic, mechanical or other device*" means any device or apparatus that is used or is capable of being used to intercept a private communication, but does not include a hearing aid used to correct subnormal hearing of the user to not better than normal hearing;

"*intercept*" includes listen to, record or acquire a communication or acquire the substance, meaning or purport thereof;

"*offence*" means an offence contrary to, any conspiracy or attempt to commit or being an accessory after the fact in relation to an offence contrary to, or any counselling in relation to an offence contrary to

a. any of the following provisions of this Act, namely,

i.		section 47 (high treason),
ii.		section 51 (intimidating Parliament or a legislature),
iii.		section 52 (sabotage),
	iii.1.	section 56.1 (identity documents),
iv.		section 57 (forgery, etc.),
v.		section 61 (sedition),
vi.		section 76 (hijacking),
vii.		section 77 (endangering safety of aircraft or airport),
viii.		ection 78 (offensive weapons, etc., on aircraft),
ix.		section 78.1 (offences against maritime navigation or fixed platforms),
x.		section 80 (breach of duty),
xi.		section 81 (using explosives),
xii.		section 82 (possessing explosives),
	xii.1.	section 83.02 (providing or collecting property for certain activities),
	xii.2.	section 83.03 (providing, making available, etc., property or services for terrorist purposes),
	xii.3.	section 83.04 (using or possessing property for terrorist purposes),
	xii.4.	section 83.18 (participation in activity of terrorist group),
	xii.5.	section 83.19 (facilitating terrorist activity),
	xii.6.	section 83.2 (commission of offence for terrorist group),
	xii.7.	section 83.21 (instructing to carry out activity for terrorist group),
	xii.8.	section 83.22 (instructing to carry out terrorist activity),

xii.9.	section 83.23 (harbouring or concealing),

xii.91.	section 83.231 (hoax — terrorist activity),

xiii.	section 96 (possession of weapon obtained by commission of offence),

xiii.1.	section 98 (breaking and entering to steal firearm),

xiii.2.	section 98.1 (robbery to steal firearm),

xiv.	section 99 (weapons trafficking),

xv.	section 100 (possession for purpose of weapons trafficking),

xvi.	section 102 (making automatic firearm),

xvii.	section 103 (importing or exporting knowing it is unauthorized),

xviii.	section 104 (unauthorized importing or exporting),

xix.	section 119 (bribery, etc.),

xx.	section 120 (bribery, etc.),

xxi.	section 121 (fraud on government),

xxii.	section 122 (breach of trust),

xxiii.	section 123 (municipal corruption),

xxiv.	section 132 (perjury),

xxv.	section 139 (obstructing justice),

xxvi.	section 144 (prison breach),

xxvii.	subsection 145(1) (escape, etc.),

xxvii.1.	section 162 (voyeurism),

xxviii.	paragraph 163(1)(a) (obscene materials),

xxix.	section 163.1 (child pornography),

xxx.	section 184 (unlawful interception),

xxxi.	section 191 (possession of intercepting device),

xxxii.	subsection 201(1) (keeping gaming or betting house),

xxxiii.	paragraph 202(1)(e) (pool-selling, etc.),

xxxiv.	subsection 210(1) (keeping common bawdy house),

xxxv.	subsection 212(1) (procuring),

xxxvi.	subsection 212(2) (procuring),

xxxvii.	subsection 212(2.1) (aggravated offence in relation to living on the avails of prostitution of a person under the age of eighteen years),

xxxviii.	subsection 212(4) (offence — prostitution of person under eighteen),

xxxix.	section 235 (murder),

xxxix.1.	section 244 (discharging firearm with intent),

xxxix.2.	section 244.2 (discharging firearm — recklessness),

xl.	section 264.1 (uttering threats),

xli.	section 267 (assault with a weapon or causing bodily harm),

xlii.	section 268 (aggravated assault),

xliii.	section 269 (unlawfully causing bodily harm),

xliii.1.	section 270.01 (assaulting peace officer with weapon or causing bodily harm),

xliii.2.	section 270.02 (aggravated assault of peace officer),

xliv.	section 271 (sexual assault),

xlv.	section 272 (sexual assault with a weapon, threats to a third party or causing bodily harm),

xlvi.	section 273 (aggravated sexual assault),

xlvii.	section 279 (kidnapping),

xlvii.1.   section 279.01 (trafficking in persons),

xlvii.2.   section 279.02 (material benefit),

xlvii.3.   section 279.03 (withholding or destroying documents),

xlviii.   section 279.1 (hostage taking),

xlix.   section 280 (abduction of person under sixteen),

l.   section 281 (abduction of person under fourteen),

li.   section 282 (abduction in contravention of custody order),

lii.   section 283 (abduction),

liii.   section 318 (advocating genocide),

liv.   section 327 (possession of device to obtain telecommunication facility or service),

lv.   section 334 (theft),

lvi.   section 342 (theft, forgery, etc., of credit card),

lvi.1.   section 342.01 (instruments for copying credit card data or forging or falsifying credit cards),

lvii.   section 342.1 (unauthorized use of computer),

lviii.   section 342.2 (possession of device to obtain computer service),

lix.   section 344 (robbery),

lx.   section 346 (extortion),

lxi.   section 347 (criminal interest rate),

lxii.   section 348 (breaking and entering),

lxiii.   section 354 (possession of property obtained by crime),

lxiv.   section 356 (theft from mail),

lxv.   section 367 (forgery),

lxvi.   section 368 (use, trafficking or possession of forged document),

lxvi.1.   section 368.1 (forgery instruments),

lxvii.   section 372 (false messages),

lxviii.   section 380 (fraud),

lxix.   section 381 (using mails to defraud),

lxx.   section 382 (fraudulent manipulation of stock exchange transactions),

lxx.1.   subsection 402.2(1) (identity theft),

lxx.2.   subsection 402.2(2) (trafficking in identity information),

lxx.3.   section 403 (identity fraud),

lxxi.   section 423.1 (intimidation of justice system participant or journalist),

lxxii.   section 424 (threat to commit offences against internationally protected person),

lxxii.1.   section 424.1 (threat against United Nations or associated personnel),

lxxiii.   section 426 (secret commissions),

lxxiv.   section 430 (mischief),

lxxv.   section 431 (attack on premises, residence or transport of internationally protected person),

lxxv.1.   section 431.1 (attack on premises, accommodation or transport of United Nations or associated personnel),

lxxv.2.   subsection 431.2(2) (explosive or other lethal device),

lxxvi.   section 433 (arson),

lxxvii.   section 434 (arson),

lxxviii.   section 434.1 (arson),

lxxix.	section 435 (arson for fraudulent purpose),
lxxx.	section 449 (making counterfeit money),
lxxxi.	section 450 (possession, etc., of counterfeit money),
lxxxii.	section 452 (uttering, etc., counterfeit money),
lxxxiii.	section 462.31 (laundering proceeds of crime),
lxxxiv.	subsection 462.33(11) (acting in contravention of restraint order),
lxxxv.	section 467.11 (participation in criminal organization),
lxxxvi.	section 467.12 (commission of offence for criminal organization), or
lxxxvii.	section 467.13 (instructing commission of offence for criminal organization),

b. section 198 (fraudulent bankruptcy) of the Bankruptcy and Insolvency Act,

    b.1. any of the following provisions of the Biological and Toxin Weapons Convention Implementation Act, namely,

        i. section 6 (production, etc., of biological agents and means of delivery), or

        ii. section 7 (unauthorized production, etc., of biological agents),

c. any of the following provisions of the Competition Act, namely,

    i. section 45 (conspiracies, agreements or arrangements between competitors),

    ii. section 47 (bid-rigging), or

    iii. subsection 52.1(3) (deceptive telemarketing),

d. any of the following provisions of the Controlled Drugs and Substances Act, namely,

    i. section 5 (trafficking),

    ii. section 6 (importing and exporting), or

    iii. section 7 (production),

e. section 3 (bribing a foreign public official) of the Corruption of Foreign Public Officials Act,

    e.1. the Crimes Against Humanity and War Crimes Act,

f. either of the following provisions of the Customs Act, namely,

    i. section 153 (false statements), or

    ii. section 159 (smuggling),

g. any of the following provisions of the Excise Act, 2001, namely,

    i. section 214 (unlawful production, sale, etc., of tobacco or alcohol),

    ii. section 216 (unlawful possession of tobacco product),

    iii. section 218 (unlawful possession, sale, etc., of alcohol),

    iv. section 219 (falsifying or destroying records),

    v. section 230 (possession of property obtained by excise offences), or

    vi. section 231 (laundering proceeds of excise offences),

h. any of the following provisions of the Export and Import Permits Act, namely,

    i. section 13 (export or attempt to export),

    ii. section 14 (import or attempt to import),

    iii. section 15 (diversion, etc.),

    iv. section 16 (no transfer of permits),

    v. section 17 (false information), or

    vi. section 18 (aiding and abetting),

i. any of the following provisions of the Immigration and Refugee Protection Act, namely,

    i. section 117 (organizing entry into Canada),

    ii. section 118 (trafficking in persons),

    iii. section 119 (disembarking persons at sea),

iv.   section 122 (offences related to documents),

v.   section 126 (counselling misrepresentation), or

vi.   section 129 (offences relating to officers), or

j.   any offence under the Security of Information Act, and includes any other offence that there are reasonable grounds to believe is a criminal organization offence or any other offence that there are reasonable grounds to believe is an offence described in paragraph (b) or (c) of the definition "terrorism offence" in section 2;

"private communication" means any oral communication, or any telecommunication, that is made by an originator who is in Canada or is intended by the originator to be received by a person who is in Canada and that is made under circumstances in which it is reasonable for the originator to expect that it will not be intercepted by any person other than the person intended by the originator to receive it, and includes any radio-based telephone communication that is treated electronically or otherwise for the purpose of preventing intelligible reception by any person other than the person intended by the originator to receive it;

"public switched telephone network" means a telecommunication facility the primary purpose of which is to provide a land line-based telephone service to the public for compensation;

"radio-based telephone communication" means any radiocommunication within the meaning of the Radiocommunication Act that is made over apparatus that is used primarily for connection to a public switched telephone network;

"sell" includes offer for sale, expose for sale, have in possession for sale or distribute or advertise for sale;

Consent to Interception

Section 183.1

Where a private communication is originated by more than one person or is intended by the originator thereof to be received by more than one person, a consent to the interception thereof by any one of those persons is sufficient consent for the purposes of any provision of this Part.

Interception of Communications

Interception

Section 184

1.   Every one who, by means of any electro-magnetic, acoustic, mechanical or other device, wilfully intercepts a private communication is guilty of an indictable offence and liable to imprisonment for a term not exceeding five years.

Saving Provision

2.   Subsection (1) does not apply to

a. a person who has the consent to intercept, express or implied, of the originator of the private communication or of the person intended by the originator thereof to receive it;

b. a person who intercepts a private communication in accordance with an authorization or pursuant to section 184.4 or any person who in good faith aids in any way another person who the aiding person believes on reasonable grounds is acting with an authorization or pursuant to section 184.4;

c. a person engaged in providing a telephone, telegraph or other communication service to the public who intercepts a private communication,
   i. if the interception is necessary for the purpose of providing the service,
   ii. in the course of service observing or random monitoring necessary for the purpose of mechanical or service quality control checks, or
   iii. if the interception is necessary to protect the person's rights or property directly related to providing the service;

d. an officer or servant of Her Majesty in right of Canada who engages in radio frequency spectrum management, in respect of a private communication intercepted by that officer or servant for the purpose of identifying, isolating or preventing an unauthorized or interfering use of a frequency or of a transmission; or

e. a person, or any person acting on their behalf, in possession or control of a computer system, as defined in subsection 342.1(2), who intercepts a private communication originating from, directed to or transmitting through that computer system, if the interception is reasonably necessary for
   i. managing the quality of service of the computer system as it relates to performance factors such as the responsiveness and capacity of the system as well as the integrity and availability of the system and data, or
   ii. protecting the computer system against any act that would be an offence under subsection 342.1(1) or 430(1.1).

Use or Retention

3. A private communication intercepted by a person referred to in paragraph (2)(e) can be used or retained only if
   a. it is essential to identify, isolate or prevent harm to the computer system; or
   b. it is to be disclosed in circumstances referred to in subsection 193(2).

PART VIII: OFFENCE AGAINST THE PERSON AND REPUTATION

Criminal Harassment

Section 264

1. No person shall, without lawful authority and knowing that another person is harassed or recklessly as to whether the other person is harassed, engage in conduct referred to in subsection (2) that

causes that other person reasonably, in all the circumstances, to fear for their safety or the safety of anyone known to them.

Prohibited Conduct

2. The conduct mentioned in subsection (1) consists of
    a. repeatedly following from place to place the other person or anyone known to them;
    b. repeatedly communicating with, either directly or indirectly, the other person or anyone known to them;
    c. besetting or watching the dwelling-house, or place where the other person, or anyone known to them, resides, works, carries on business or happens to be; or
    d. engaging in threatening conduct directed at the other person or any member of their family.

Punishment

3. Every person who contravenes this section is guilty of
    a. an indictable offence and is liable to imprisonment for a term not exceeding ten years; or
    b. an offence punishable on summary conviction.

Factors to be Considered

4. Where a person is convicted of an offence under this section, the court imposing the sentence on the person shall consider as an aggravating factor that, at the time the offence was committed, the person contravened
    a. the terms or conditions of an order made pursuant to section 161 or a recognizance entered into pursuant to section 810, 810.1 or 810.2; or
    b. the terms or conditions of any other order or recognizance made or entered into under the common law or a provision of this or any other Act of Parliament or of a province that is similar in effect to an order or recognizance referred to in paragraph (a).

Reasons

5. Where the court is satisfied of the existence of an aggravating factor referred to in subsection (4), but decides not to give effect to it for sentencing purposes, the court shall give reasons for its decision.

Blasphemous Libel

Section 296

Offence

1. Every one who publishes a blasphemous libel is guilty of an indictable offence and liable to imprisonment for a term not exceeding two years.

Question of Fact

2. It is a question of fact whether or not any matter that is published is a blasphemous libel.

Saving

3. No person shall be convicted of an offence under this section for expressing in good faith and in decent language, or attempting to establish by argument used in good faith and conveyed in decent language, an opinion on a religious subject.

Defamatory Libel

Section 298

Definition

1. A defamatory libel is matter published, without lawful justification or excuse, that is likely to injure the reputation of any person by exposing him to hatred, contempt or ridicule, or that is designed to insult the person of or concerning whom it is published.

Mode of Expression

2. A defamatory libel may be expressed directly or by insinuation or irony
   a. in words legibly marked on any substance; or
   b. by any object signifying a defamatory libel otherwise than by words.

Publishing

Section 299

A person publishes a libel when he

a. exhibits it in public;
b. causes it to be read or seen; or
c. shows or delivers it, or causes it to be shown or delivered, with intent that it should be read or seen by the person whom it defames or by any other person.

Punishment of Libel Known to be False

Section 300

Every one who publishes a defamatory libel that he knows is false is guilty of an indictable offence and liable to imprisonment for a term not exceeding five years.

Punishment for Defamatory Libel

Section 301

Every one who publishes a defamatory libel is guilty of an indictable offence and liable to imprisonment for a term not exceeding two years.

APPENDIX 5

Relevant Provisions from Protection from Harassment Act 1997, C-40[2]

An Act to make provision for protecting persons from harassment and similar conduct.

[21st March 1997]

Be it enacted by the Queen's most Excellent Majesty, by and with the advice and consent of the Lords Spiritual and Temporal, and Commons, in this present Parliament assembled, and by the authority of the same, as follows:—

England and Wales

Section 1: Prohibition of Harassment

1. A person must not pursue a course of conduct—
   a. which amounts to harassment of another, and
   b. which he knows or ought to know amounts to harassment of the other.
2. For the purposes of this section, the person whose course of conduct is in question ought to know that it amounts to harassment of another if a reasonable person in possession of the same information would think the course of conduct amounted to harassment of the other.
3. Subsection (1) does not apply to a course of conduct if the person who pursued it shows—
   a. that it was pursued for the purpose of preventing or detecting crime,
   b. that it was pursued under any enactment or rule of law or to comply with any condition or requirement imposed by any person under any enactment, or
   c. that in the particular circumstances the pursuit of the course of conduct was reasonable.

Section 2: Offence of Harassment

1. A person who pursues a course of conduct in breach of section 1 is guilty of an offence.
2. A person guilty of an offence under this section is liable on summary conviction to imprisonment for a term not exceeding six months, or a fine not exceeding level 5 on the standard scale, or both.
3. In section 24(2) of the [1984 c. 60.] Police and Criminal Evidence Act 1984 (arrestable offences), after paragraph (m) there is inserted—

"(n) an offence under section 2 of the Protection from Harassment Act 1997 (harassment).".

Section 3: Civil Remedy

1. An actual or apprehended breach of section 1 may be the subject of a claim in civil proceedings by the person who is or may be the victim of the course of conduct in question.
2. On such a claim, damages may be awarded for (among other things) any anxiety caused by the harassment and any financial loss resulting from the harassment.
3. Where—

a.   in such proceedings the High Court or a county court grants an injunction for the purpose of restraining the defendant from pursuing any conduct which amounts to harassment, and

b.   the plaintiff considers that the defendant has done anything which he is prohibited from doing by the injunction, the plaintiff may apply for the issue of a warrant for the arrest of the defendant.

4.   An application under subsection (3) may be made—

a.   where the injunction was granted by the High Court, to a judge of that court, and

b.   where the injunction was granted by a county court, to a judge or district judge of that or any other county court.

5.   The judge or district judge to whom an application under subsection (3) is made may only issue a warrant if—

a.   the application is substantiated on oath, and

b.   the judge or district judge has reasonable grounds for believing that the defendant has done anything which he is prohibited from doing by the injunction.

6.   Where—

a.   the High Court or a county court grants an injunction for the purpose mentioned in subsection (3)(a), and

b.   without reasonable excuse the defendant does anything which he is prohibited from doing by the injunction, he is guilty of an offence.

7.   Where a person is convicted of an offence under subsection (6) in respect of any conduct, that conduct is not punishable as a contempt of court.

8.   A person cannot be convicted of an offence under subsection (6) in respect of any conduct which has been punished as a contempt of court.

9.   A person guilty of an offence under subsection (6) is liable—

a.   on conviction on indictment, to imprisonment for a term not exceeding five years, or a fine, or both, or

b.   on summary conviction, to imprisonment for a term not exceeding six months, or a fine not exceeding the statutory maximum, or both.

Section 4: Putting People in Fear of Violence

1.   A person whose course of conduct causes another to fear, on at least two occasions, that violence will be used against him is guilty of an offence if he knows or ought to know that his course of conduct will cause the other so to fear on each of those occasions.

2.   For the purposes of this section, the person whose course of conduct is in question ought to know that it will cause another to fear that violence will be used against him on any occasion if a reasonable person in possession of the same information would think the course of conduct would cause the other so to fear on that occasion.

3.   It is a defence for a person charged with an offence under this section to show that—

a.   his course of conduct was pursued for the purpose of preventing or detecting crime,

b.   his course of conduct was pursued under any enactment or rule of law or to comply with any condition or requirement imposed by any person under any enactment, or

c.   the pursuit of his course of conduct was reasonable for the protection of himself or another or for the protection of his or another's property.

4. A person guilty of an offence under this section is liable—
   a. on conviction on indictment, to imprisonment for a term not exceeding five years, or a fine, or both, or
   b. on summary conviction, to imprisonment for a term not exceeding six months, or a fine not exceeding the statutory maximum, or both.
5. If on the trial on indictment of a person charged with an offence under this section the jury find him not guilty of the offence charged, they may find him guilty of an offence under section 2.
6. The Crown Court has the same powers and duties in relation to a person who is by virtue of subsection (5) convicted before it of an offence under section 2 as a magistrates' court would have on convicting him of the offence.

Section 5: Restraining Orders

1. A court sentencing or otherwise dealing with a person ("the defendant") convicted of an offence under section 2 or 4 may (as well as sentencing him or dealing with him in any other way) make an order under this section.
2. The order may, for the purpose of protecting the victim of the offence, or any other person mentioned in the order, from further conduct which—
   a. amounts to harassment, or
   b. will cause a fear of violence, prohibit the defendant from doing anything described in the order.
3. The order may have effect for a specified period or until further order.
4. The prosecutor, the defendant or any other person mentioned in the order may apply to the court which made the order for it to be varied or discharged by a further order.
5. If without reasonable excuse the defendant does anything which he is prohibited from doing by an order under this section, he is guilty of an offence.
6. A person guilty of an offence under this section is liable—
   a. on conviction on indictment, to imprisonment for a term not exceeding five years, or a fine, or both, or
   b. on summary conviction, to imprisonment for a term not exceeding six months, or a fine not exceeding the statutory maximum, or both.

Section 6: Limitation

In section 11 of the [1980 c. 58.] Limitation Act 1980 (special time limit for actions in respect of personal injuries), after subsection (1) there is inserted—

   "(1A) This section does not apply to any action brought for damages under section 3 of the Protection from Harassment Act 1997."

Section 7: Interpretation of this Group of Sections

1. This section applies for the interpretation of sections 1 to 5.
2. References to harassing a person include alarming the person or causing the person distress.

3. A "course of conduct" must involve conduct on at least two occasions.
4. "Conduct" includes speech.

Section 8: Harassment

1. Every individual has a right to be free from harassment and, accordingly, a person must not pursue a course of conduct which amounts to harassment of another and—
   a. is intended to amount to harassment of that person; or
   b. occurs in circumstances where it would appear to a reasonable person that it would amount to harassment of that person.
2. An actual or apprehended breach of subsection (1) may be the subject of a claim in civil proceedings by the person who is or may be the victim of the course of conduct in question; and any such claim shall be known as an action of harassment.
3. For the purposes of this section—

   "conduct" includes speech;
   "harassment" of a person includes causing the person alarm or distress; and a course of conduct must involve conduct on at least two occasions.

4. It shall be a defence to any action of harassment to show that the course of conduct complained of—
   a. was authorised by, under or by virtue of any enactment or rule of law;
   b. was pursued for the purpose of preventing or detecting crime; or
   c. was, in the particular circumstances, reasonable.
5. In an action of harassment the court may, without prejudice to any other remedies which it may grant—
   a. award damages;
   b. grant—
      i. interdict or interim interdict;
      ii. if it is satisfied that it is appropriate for it to do so in order to protect the person from further harassment, an order, to be known as a "non-harassment order", requiring the defender to refrain from such conduct in relation to the pursuer as may be specified in the order for such period (which includes an indeterminate period) as may be so specified, but a person may not be subjected to the same prohibitions in an interdict or interim interdict and a non-harassment order at the same time.
6. The damages which may be awarded in an action of harassment include damages for any anxiety caused by the harassment and any financial loss resulting from it.
7. Without prejudice to any right to seek review of any interlocutor, a person against whom a non-harassment order has been made, or the person for whose protection the order was made, may apply to the court by which the order was made for revocation of or a variation of the order and, on any such application, the court may revoke the order or vary it in such manner as it considers appropriate.

8.   In section 10(1) of the [1976 c. 13.] Damages (Scotland) Act 1976 (interpretation), in the definition of "personal injuries", after "to reputation" there is inserted ", or injury resulting from harassment actionable under section 8 of the Protection from Harassment Act 1997".

Section 9: Breach of Non-Harassment Order

1.   Any person who is found to be in breach of a non-harassment order made under section 8 is guilty of an offence and liable—
    a.   on conviction on indictment, to imprisonment for a term not exceeding five years or to a fine, or to both such imprisonment and such fine; and
    b.   on summary conviction, to imprisonment for a period not exceeding six months or to a fine not exceeding the statutory maximum, or to both such imprisonment and such fine.
2.   A breach of a non-harassment order shall not be punishable other than in accordance with subsection (1).

Section 10: Limitation

1.   After section 18A of the [1973 c. 52.] Prescription and Limitation (Scotland) Act 1973 there is inserted the following section—

"18B Actions of harassment

1.   *This section applies to actions of harassment (within the meaning of section 8 of the Protection from Harassment Act 1997) which include a claim for damages.*
2.   *Subject to subsection (3) below and to section 19A of this Act, no action to which this section applies shall be brought unless it is commenced within a period of 3 years after—*
    a.   *the date on which the alleged harassment ceased; or*
    b.   *the date, (if later than the date mentioned in paragraph (a) above) on which the pursuer in the action became, or on which, in the opinion of the court, it would have been reasonably practicable for him in all the circumstances to have become, aware, that the defender was a person responsible for the alleged harassment or the employer or principal of such a person.*
3.   *In the computation of the period specified in subsection (2) above there shall be disregarded any time during which the person who is alleged to have suffered the harassment was under legal disability by reason of nonage or unsoundness of mind.".*
2.   In subsection (1) of section 19A of that Act (power of court to override time-limits), for "section 17 or section 18 and section 18A" there is substituted "section 17, 18, 18A or 18B".

Section 11: Non-Harassment Order Following Criminal Offence

After section 234 of the [1995 c. 46.] Criminal Procedure (Scotland) Act 1995 there is inserted the following section—
    "Non-harassment orders
    234A Non-harassment orders

1. *Where a person is convicted of an offence involving harassment of a person ("the victim"), the prosecutor may apply to the court to make a non-harassment order against the offender requiring him to refrain from such conduct in relation to the victim as may be specified in the order for such period (which includes an indeterminate period) as may be so specified, in addition to any other disposal which may be made in relation to the offence.*

2. *On an application under subsection (1) above the court may, if it is satisfied on a balance of probabilities that it is appropriate to do so in order to protect the victim from further harassment, make a non-harassment order.*

3. *A non-harassment order made by a criminal court shall be taken to be a sentence for the purposes of any appeal and, for the purposes of this subsection "order" includes any variation or revocation of such an order made under subsection (6) below.*

4. *Any person who is found to be in breach of a non-harassment order shall be guilty of an offence and liable—*

    a. *on conviction on indictment, to imprisonment for a term not exceeding 5 years or to a fine, or to both such imprisonment and such fine; and*

    b. *on summary conviction, to imprisonment for a period not exceeding 6 months or to a fine not exceeding the statutory maximum, or to both such imprisonment and such fine.*

5. *The Lord Advocate, in solemn proceedings, and the prosecutor, in summary proceedings, may appeal to the High Court against any decision by a court to refuse an application under subsection (1) above; and on any such appeal the High Court may make such order as it considers appropriate.*

6. *The person against whom a non-harassment order is made, or the prosecutor at whose instance the order is made, may apply to the court which made the order for its revocation or variation and, in relation to any such application the court concerned may, if it is satisfied on a balance of probabilities that it is appropriate to do so, revoke the order or vary it in such manner as it thinks fit, but not so as to increase the period for which the order is to run.*

7. *For the purposes of this section "harassment" shall be construed in accordance with section 8 of the Protection from Harassment Act 1997.".*

General

Section 12: National Security, etc

1. If the Secretary of State certifies that in his opinion anything done by a specified person on a specified occasion related to—

    a. national security,

    b. the economic well-being of the United Kingdom, or

    c. the prevention or detection of serious crime, and was done on behalf of the Crown, the certificate is conclusive evidence that this Act does not apply to any conduct of that person on that occasion.

2. In subsection (1), "specified" means specified in the certificate in question.

3. A document purporting to be a certificate under subsection (1) is to be received in evidence and, unless the contrary is proved, be treated as being such a certificate.

Section 13: Corresponding Provision for Northern Ireland

An Order in Council made under paragraph 1(1)(b) of Schedule 1 to the [1974 c. 28.] Northern Ireland Act 1974 which contains a statement that it is made only for purposes corresponding to those of sections 1 to 7 and 12 of this Act—

a. shall not be subject to sub-paragraphs (4) and (5) of paragraph 1 of that Schedule (affirmative resolution of both Houses of Parliament), but
b. shall be subject to annulment in pursuance of a resolution of either House of Parliament.

Section 14: Extent

1. Sections 1 to 7 extend to England and Wales only.
2. Sections 8 to 11 extend to Scotland only.
3. This Act (except section 13) does not extend to Northern Ireland.

Section 15: Commencement

1. Sections 1, 2, 4, 5 and 7 to 12 are to come into force on such day as the Secretary of State may by order made by statutory instrument appoint.
2. Sections 3 and 6 are to come into force on such day as the Lord Chancellor may by order made by statutory instrument appoint.
3. Different days may be appointed under this section for different purposes.

APPENDIX 6

Relevant Provisions from Equality Act, 2010[3]

Part 2 Equality: Key Concepts

Chapter 1 Protected Characteristics

Section 4: The Protected Characteristics

The following characteristics are protected characteristics—

- age;
- disability;
- gender reassignment;
- marriage and civil partnership;
- pregnancy and maternity;
- race;
- religion or belief;
- sex;
- sexual orientation.

Section 7: Gender Reassignment

1. A person has the protected characteristic of gender reassignment if the person is proposing to undergo, is undergoing or has undergone a process (or part of a process) for the purpose of reassigning the person's sex by changing physiological or other attributes of sex.
2. A reference to a transsexual person is a reference to a person who has the protected characteristic of gender reassignment.
3. In relation to the protected characteristic of gender reassignment—
    a. a reference to a person who has a particular protected characteristic is a reference to a transsexual person;
    b. a reference to persons who share a protected characteristic is a reference to transsexual persons.

Section 8: Marriage and Civil Partnership

1. A person has the protected characteristic of marriage and civil partnership if the person is married or is a civil partner.
2. In relation to the protected characteristic of marriage and civil partnership—
    a. a reference to a person who has a particular protected characteristic is a reference to a person who is married or is a civil partner;
    b. a reference to persons who share a protected characteristic is a reference to persons who are married or are civil partners.

Section 9: Race

1. Race includes—
   a. colour;
   b. nationality;
   c. ethnic or national origins.
2. In relation to the protected characteristic of race—
   a. a reference to a person who has a particular protected characteristic is a reference to a person of a particular racial group;
   b. a reference to persons who share a protected characteristic is a reference to persons of the same racial group.
3. A racial group is a group of persons defined by reference to race; and a reference to a person's racial group is a reference to a racial group into which the person falls.
4. The fact that a racial group comprises two or more distinct racial groups does not prevent it from constituting a particular racial group.
5. A Minister of the Crown may by order—
   a. amend this section so as to provide for caste to be an aspect of race;
   b. amend this Act so as to provide for an exception to a provision of this Act to apply, or not to apply, to caste or to apply, or not to apply, to caste in specified circumstances.
6. The power under section 207(4)(b), in its application to subsection (5), includes power to amend this Act.

Section 10: Religion or Belief

1. Religion means any religion and a reference to religion includes a reference to a lack of religion.
2. Belief means any religious or philosophical belief and a reference to belief includes a reference to a lack of belief.
3. In relation to the protected characteristic of religion or belief—
   a. a reference to a person who has a particular protected characteristic is a reference to a person of a particular religion or belief;
   b. a reference to persons who share a protected characteristic is a reference to persons who are of the same religion or belief.

Section 11: Sex

In relation to the protected characteristic of sex—

a. a reference to a person who has a particular protected characteristic is a reference to a man or to a woman;
b. a reference to persons who share a protected characteristic is a reference to persons of the same sex.

Section 12: Sexual Orientation

1. Sexual orientation means a person's sexual orientation towards—
    a. persons of the same sex,
    b. persons of the opposite sex, or
    c. persons of either sex.
2. In relation to the protected characteristic of sexual orientation—
    a. a reference to a person who has a particular protected characteristic is a reference to a person who is of a particular sexual orientation;
    b. a reference to persons who share a protected characteristic is a reference to persons who are of the same sexual orientation.

Chapter 2: Prohibited Conduct

Discrimination

Section 13: Direct Discrimination

1. A person (A) discriminates against another (B) if, because of a protected characteristic, A treats B less favourably than A treats or would treat others.
2. If the protected characteristic is age, A does not discriminate against B if A can show A's treatment of B to be a proportionate means of achieving a legitimate aim.
3. If the protected characteristic is disability, and B is not a disabled person, A does not discriminate against B only because A treats or would treat disabled persons more favourably than A treats B.
4. If the protected characteristic is marriage and civil partnership, this section applies to a contravention of Part 5 (work) only if the treatment is because it is B who is married or a civil partner.
5. If the protected characteristic is race, less favourable treatment includes segregating B from others.
6. If the protected characteristic is sex—
    a. less favourable treatment of a woman includes less favourable treatment of her because she is breast-feeding;
    b. in a case where B is a man, no account is to be taken of special treatment afforded to a woman in connection with pregnancy or childbirth.
7. Subsection (6)(a) does not apply for the purposes of Part 5 (work).
8. This section is subject to sections 17(6) and 18(7).

Section 14: Combined Discrimination: Dual Characteristics

1. A person (A) discriminates against another (B) if, because of a combination of two relevant protected characteristics, A treats B less favourably than A treats or would treat a person who does not share either of those characteristics.
2. The relevant protected characteristics are—

    a.   age;

    b.   disability;

    c.   gender reassignment;

    d.   race

    e.   religion or belief;

    f.   sex;

    g.   sexual orientation.

3.   For the purposes of establishing a contravention of this Act by virtue of subsection (1), B need not show that A's treatment of B is direct discrimination because of each of the characteristics in the combination (taken separately).

4.   But B cannot establish a contravention of this Act by virtue of subsection (1) if, in reliance on another provision of this Act or any other enactment, A shows that A's treatment of B is not direct discrimination because of either or both of the characteristics in the combination.

5.   Subsection (1) does not apply to a combination of characteristics that includes disability in circumstances where, if a claim of direct discrimination because of disability were to be brought, it would come within section 116 (special educational needs).

6.   A Minister of the Crown may by order amend this section so as to—

    a.   make further provision about circumstances in which B can, or in which B cannot, establish a contravention of this Act by virtue of subsection (1);

    b.   specify other circumstances in which subsection (1) does not apply.

7.   The references to direct discrimination are to a contravention of this Act by virtue of section 13.

Section 19: Indirect Discrimination

1.   A person (A) discriminates against another (B) if A applies to B a provision, criterion or practice which is discriminatory in relation to a relevant protected characteristic of B's.

2.   For the purposes of subsection (1), a provision, criterion or practice is discriminatory in relation to a relevant protected characteristic of B's if—

    a.   A applies, or would apply, it to persons with whom B does not share the characteristic,

    b.   it puts, or would put, persons with whom B shares the characteristic at a particular disadvantage when compared with persons with whom B does not share it,

    c.   it puts, or would put, B at that disadvantage, and

    d.   A cannot show it to be a proportionate means of achieving a legitimate aim.

3.   The relevant protected characteristics are—

    ◦   age;

    ◦   disability;

    ◦   gender reassignment;

    ◦   marriage and civil partnership;

    ◦   race;

    ◦   religion or belief;

    ◦   sex;

    ◦   sexual orientation.

Adjustments for Disabled Persons

Section 20: Duty to Make Adjustments

1. Where this Act imposes a duty to make reasonable adjustments on a person, this section, sections 21 and 22 and the applicable Schedule apply; and for those purposes, a person on whom the duty is imposed is referred to as A.
2. The duty comprises the following three requirements.
3. The first requirement is a requirement, where a provision, criterion or practice of A's puts a disabled person at a substantial disadvantage in relation to a relevant matter in comparison with persons who are not disabled, to take such steps as it is reasonable to have to take to avoid the disadvantage.
4. The second requirement is a requirement, where a physical feature puts a disabled person at a substantial disadvantage in relation to a relevant matter in comparison with persons who are not disabled, to take such steps as it is reasonable to have to take to avoid the disadvantage.
5. The third requirement is a requirement, where a disabled person would, but for the provision of an auxiliary aid, be put at a substantial disadvantage in relation to a relevant matter in comparison with persons who not disabled, to take such steps as it is reasonable to have to take to provide the auxiliary aid.
6. Where the first or third requirement relates to the provision of information, the steps which it is reasonable for A to have to take include steps for ensuring that in the circumstances concerned the information is provided in an accessible format.
7. A person (A) who is subject to a duty to make reasonable adjustments is not (subject to express provision to the contrary) entitled to require a disabled person, in relation to whom A is required to comply with the duty, to pay to any extent A's costs of complying with the duty.
8. A reference in section 21 or 22 or an applicable Schedule to the first, second or third requirement is to be construed in accordance with this section.
9. In relation to the second requirement, a reference in this section or an applicable Schedule to avoiding a substantial disadvantage includes a reference to—
    a. removing the physical feature in question,
    b. altering it, or
    c. providing a reasonable means of avoiding it.
10. A reference in this section, section 21 or 22 or an applicable Schedule (apart from paragraphs 2 to 4 of Schedule 4) to a physical feature is a reference to—
    a. a feature arising from the design or construction of a building,
    b. a feature of an approach to, exit from or access to a building,
    c. a fixture or fitting, or furniture, furnishings, materials, equipment or other chattels, in or on premises, or
    d. any other physical element or quality.
11. A reference in this section, section 21 or 22 or an applicable Schedule to an auxiliary aid includes a reference to an auxiliary service.
12. A reference in this section or an applicable Schedule to chattels is to be read, in relation to Scotland, as a reference to moveable property.
13. The applicable Schedule is, in relation to the Part of this Act specified in the first column of the Table, the Schedule specified in the second column.

Table 1.

Part of this Act	Applicable Schedule
Part 3 (services and public functions)	Schedule 2
Part 4 (premises)	Schedule 4
Part 5 (work)	Schedule 8
Part 6 (education)	Schedule 13
Part 7 (associations)	Schedule 15
Each of the Parts mentioned above	Schedule 21

Section 21: Failure to Comply with Duty

1. A failure to comply with the first, second or third requirement is a failure to comply with a duty to make reasonable adjustments.
2. A discriminates against a disabled person if A fails to comply with that duty in relation to that person.
3. A provision of an applicable Schedule which imposes a duty to comply with the first, second or third requirement applies only for the purpose of establishing whether A has contravened this Act by virtue of subsection (2); a failure to comply is, accordingly, not actionable by virtue of another provision of this Act or otherwise.

Section 22: Regulations

1. Regulations may prescribe—
   a. matters to be taken into account in deciding whether it is reasonable for A to take a step for the purposes of a prescribed provision of an applicable Schedule;
   b. descriptions of persons to whom the first, second or third requirement does not apply.
2. Regulations may make provision as to—
   a. circumstances in which it is, or in which it is not, reasonable for a person of a prescribed description to have to take steps of a prescribed description;
   b. what is, or what is not, a provision, criterion or practice;
   c. things which are, or which are not, to be treated as physical features;
   d. things which are, or which are not, to be treated as alterations of physical features;
   e. things which are, or which are not, to be treated as auxiliary aids.
3. Provision made by virtue of this section may amend an applicable Schedule.

Discrimination: Supplementary

Section 23: Comparison by Reference to Circumstances

1. On a comparison of cases for the purposes of section 13, 14, or 19 there must be no material difference between the circumstances relating to each case.
2. The circumstances relating to a case include a person's abilities if—

a. on a comparison for the purposes of section 13, the protected characteristic is disability;

b. on a comparison for the purposes of section 14, one of the protected characteristics in the combination is disability.

3. If the protected characteristic is sexual orientation, the fact that one person (whether or not the person referred to as B) is a civil partner while another is married is not a material difference between the circumstances relating to each case.

Section 24: Irrelevance of Alleged Discriminator's Characteristics

1. For the purpose of establishing a contravention of this Act by virtue of section 13(1), it does not matter whether A has the protected characteristic.

2. For the purpose of establishing a contravention of this Act by virtue of section 14(1), it does not matter—

a. whether A has one of the protected characteristics in the combination;

b. whether A has both.

Section 25: References to Particular Strands of Discrimination

1. Age discrimination is—

a. discrimination within section 13 because of age;

b. discrimination within section 19 where the relevant protected characteristic is age.

2. Disability discrimination is—

a. discrimination within section 13 because of disability;

b. discrimination within section 15;

c. discrimination within section 19 where the relevant protected characteristic is disability;

d. discrimination within section 21.

3. Gender reassignment discrimination is—

a. discrimination within section 13 because of gender reassignment;

b. discrimination within section 16;

c. discrimination within section 19 where the relevant protected characteristic is gender reassignment.

4. Marriage and civil partnership discrimination is—

a. discrimination within section 13 because of marriage and civil partnership;

b. discrimination within section 19 where the relevant protected characteristic is marriage and civil partnership.

5. Pregnancy and maternity discrimination is discrimination within section 17 or 18.

6. Race discrimination is—

a. discrimination within section 13 because of race;

b. discrimination within section 19 where the relevant protected characteristic is race.

7. Religious or belief-related discrimination is—

a. discrimination within section 13 because of religion or belief;

b. discrimination within section 19 where the relevant protected characteristic is religion or belief.

8. Sex discrimination is—

a. discrimination within section 13 because of sex;

b. discrimination within section 19 where the relevant protected characteristic is sex.

9. Sexual orientation discrimination is—

a. discrimination within section 13 because of sexual orientation;

b. discrimination within section 19 where the relevant protected characteristic is sexual orientation.

Other Prohibited Conduct

Section 26: Harassment

1. A person (A) harasses another (B) if—

a. A engages in unwanted conduct related to a relevant protected characteristic, and

b. the conduct has the purpose or effect of—

i. violating B's dignity, or

ii. creating an intimidating, hostile, degrading, humiliating or offensive environment for B.

2. A also harasses B if—

a. A engages in unwanted conduct of a sexual nature, and

b. the conduct has the purpose or effect referred to in subsection (1)(b).

3. A also harasses B if—

a. A or another person engages in unwanted conduct of a sexual nature or that is related to gender reassignment or sex,

b. the conduct has the purpose or effect referred to in subsection (1)(b), and

c. because of B's rejection of or submission to the conduct, A treats B less favourably than A would treat B if B had not rejected or submitted to the conduct.

4. In deciding whether conduct has the effect referred to in subsection (1)(b), each of the following must be taken into account—

a. the perception of B;

b. the other circumstances of the case;

c. whether it is reasonable for the conduct to have that effect.

5. The relevant protected characteristics are—

- age;
- disability;
- gender reassignment;
- race;
- religion or belief;
- sex;
- sexual orientation.

Section 27: Victimisation

1. A person (A) victimises another person (B) if A subjects B to a detriment because—

a. B does a protected act, or

b. A believes that B has done, or may do, a protected act.

2. Each of the following is a protected act—
   a. bringing proceedings under this Act;
   b. giving evidence or information in connection with proceedings under this Act;
   c. doing any other thing for the purposes of or in connection with this Act;
   d. making an allegation (whether or not express) that A or another person has contravened this Act.
3. Giving false evidence or information, or making a false allegation, is not a protected act if the evidence or information is given, or the allegation is made, in bad faith.
4. This section applies only where the person subjected to a detriment is an individual.
5. The reference to contravening this Act includes a reference to committing a breach of an equality clause or rule.

APPENDIX 7

Relevant Provisions from the Computer Misuse Act, 1990 (C 18)[4]

An Act to make provision for securing computer material against unauthorised access or modification; and for connected purposes.

[29th June 1990]

Be it enacted by the Queen's most Excellent Majesty, by and with the advice and consent of the Lords Spiritual and Temporal, and Commons, in this present Parliament assembled, and by the authority of the same, as follows:—

Computer Misuse Offences

Section 1: Unauthorised Access to Computer Material

1. A person is guilty of an offence if—
   a. he causes a computer to perform any function with intent to secure access to any program or data held in any computer;
   b. the access he intends to secure is unauthorised; and
   c. he knows at the time when he causes the computer to perform the function that that is the case.
2. The intent a person has to have to commit an offence under this section need not be directed at—
   a. any particular program or data;
   b. a program or data of any particular kind; or
   c. a program or data held in any particular computer.
3. A person guilty of an offence under this section shall be liable on summary conviction to imprisonment for a term not exceeding six months or to a fine not exceeding level 5 on the standard scale or to both.

Section 2: Unauthorised Access with Intent to Commit or Facilitate Commission of Further Offences

1. A person is guilty of an offence under this section if he commits an offence under section 1 above ("the unauthorised access offence") with intent—
   a. to commit an offence to which this section applies; or
   b. to facilitate the commission of such an offence (whether by himself or by any other person); and the offence he intends to commit or facilitate is referred to below in this section as the further offence.
2. This section applies to offences—
   a. for which the sentence is fixed by law; or
   b. for which a person of twenty-one years of age or over (not previously convicted) may be sentenced to imprisonment for a term of five years (or, in England and Wales, might be so sentenced but for the restrictions imposed by section 33 of the [1980 c. 43.] Magistrates' Courts Act 1980).

3. It is immaterial for the purposes of this section whether the further offence is to be committed on the same occasion as the unauthorised access offence or on any future occasion.
4. A person may be guilty of an offence under this section even though the facts are such that the commission of the further offence is impossible.
5. A person guilty of an offence under this section shall be liable—
    a. on summary conviction, to imprisonment for a term not exceeding six months or to a fine not exceeding the statutory maximum or to both; and
    b. on conviction on indictment, to imprisonment for a term not exceeding five years or to a fine or to both.

Section 3: Unauthorised Modification of Computer Material

1. A person is guilty of an offence if—
    a. he does any act which causes an unauthorised modification of the contents of any computer; and
    b. at the time when he does the act he has the requisite intent and the requisite knowledge.
2. For the purposes of subsection (1)(b) above the requisite intent is an intent to cause a modification of the contents of any computer and by so doing—
    a. to impair the operation of any computer;
    b. to prevent or hinder access to any program or data held in any computer; or
    c. to impair the operation of any such program or the reliability of any such data.
3. The intent need not be directed at—
    a. any particular computer;
    b. any particular program or data or a program or data of any particular kind; or
    c. any particular modification or a modification of any particular kind.
4. For the purposes of subsection (1)(b) above the requisite knowledge is knowledge that any modification he intends to cause is unauthorised.
5. It is immaterial for the purposes of this section whether an unauthorised modification or any intended effect of it of a kind mentioned in subsection (2) above is, or is intended to be, permanent or merely temporary.
6. For the purposes of the [1971 c. 48.] Criminal Damage Act 1971 a modification of the contents of a computer shall not be regarded as damaging any computer or computer storage medium unless its effect on that computer or computer storage medium impairs its physical condition.
7. A person guilty of an offence under this section shall be liable—
    a. on summary conviction, to imprisonment for a term not exceeding six months or to a fine not exceeding the statutory maximum or to both; and
    b. on conviction on indictment, to imprisonment for a term not exceeding five years or to a fine or to both.

Jurisdiction

Section 4: Territorial Scope of Offences under this Act

1. Except as provided below in this section, it is immaterial for the purposes of any offence under section 1 or 3 above—

a.   whether any act or other event proof of which is required for conviction of the offence occurred in the home country concerned; or

b.   whether the accused was in the home country concerned at the time of any such act or event.

2.   Subject to subsection (3) below, in the case of such an offence at least one significant link with domestic jurisdiction must exist in the circumstances of the case for the offence to be committed.

3.   There is no need for any such link to exist for the commission of an offence under section 1 above to be established in proof of an allegation to that effect in proceedings for an offence under section 2 above.

4.   Subject to section 8 below, where—

a.   any such link does in fact exist in the case of an offence under section 1 above; and

b.   commission of that offence is alleged in proceedings for an offence under section 2 above; section 2 above shall apply as if anything the accused intended to do or facilitate in any place outside the home country concerned which would be an offence to which section 2 applies if it took place in the home country concerned were the offence in question.

5.   This section is without prejudice to any jurisdiction exercisable by a court in Scotland apart from this section.

6.   References in this Act to the home country concerned are references—

a.   in the application of this Act to England and Wales, to England and Wales;

b.   in the application of this Act to Scotland, to Scotland; and

c.   in the application of this Act to Northern Ireland, to Northern Ireland.

Section 5: Significant Links with Domestic Jurisdiction

1.   The following provisions of this section apply for the interpretation of section 4 above.

2.   In relation to an offence under section 1, either of the following is a significant link with domestic jurisdiction—

a.   that the accused was in the home country concerned at the time when he did the act which caused the computer to perform the function; or

b.   that any computer containing any program or data to which the accused secured or intended to secure unauthorised access by doing that act was in the home country concerned at that time.

3.   In relation to an offence under section 3, either of the following is a significant link with domestic jurisdiction—

a.   that the accused was in the home country concerned at the time when he did the act which caused the unauthorised modification; or

b.   that the unauthorised modification took place in the home country concerned.

Section 6: Territorial Scope of Inchoate Offences Related to Offences under this Act

1.   On a charge of conspiracy to commit an offence under this Act the following questions are immaterial to the accused's guilt—

a.   the question where any person became a party to the conspiracy; and

b.   the question whether any act, omission or other event occurred in the home country concerned.

2. On a charge of attempting to commit an offence under section 3 above the following questions are immaterial to the accused's guilt—
   a. the question where the attempt was made; and
   b. the question whether it had an effect in the home country concerned.
3. On a charge of incitement to commit an offence under this Act the question where the incitement took place is immaterial to the accused's guilt.
4. This section does not extend to Scotland.

Section 7: Territorial Scope of Inchoate Offences Related to Offences under External Law Corresponding to Offences under this Act

1. The following subsections shall be inserted after subsection (1) of section 1 of the [1977 c. 45.] Criminal Law Act 1977—

   "1A. Subject to section 8 of the Computer Misuse Act 1990 (relevance of external law), if this subsection applies to an agreement, this Part of this Act has effect in relation to it as it has effect in relation to an agreement falling within subsection (1) above.

   1B. Subsection (1A) above applies to an agreement if—
   a. *a party to it, or a party's agent, did anything in England and Wales in relation to it before its formation; or*
   b. *a party to it became a party in England and Wales (by joining it either in person or through an agent); or*
   c. *a party to it, or a party's agent, did or omitted anything in England and Wales in pursuance of it; and the agreement would fall within subsection (1) above as an agreement relating to the commission of a computer misuse offence but for the fact that the offence would not be an offence triable in England and Wales if committed in accordance with the parties' intentions.".*

2. The following subsections shall be inserted after subsection (4) of that section—

   "5. In the application of this Part of this Act to an agreement to which subsection (1A) above applies any reference to an offence shall be read as a reference to what would be the computer misuse offence in question but for the fact that it is not an offence triable in England and Wales.
   6. *In this section "computer misuse offence" means an offence under the Computer Misuse Act 1990.".*

3. The following subsections shall be inserted after section 1(1) of the [1981 c. 47.] Criminal Attempts Act 1981—

   "1A. Subject to section 8 of the Computer Misuse Act 1990 (relevance of external law), if this subsection applies to an act, what the person doing it had in view shall be treated as an offence to which this section applies.

   1B. Subsection (1A) above applies to an act if—
   a. *it is done in England and Wales; and*
   b. *it would fall within subsection (1) above as more than merely preparatory to the commission of an offence under section 3 of the Computer Misuse Act 1990 but for the fact that the offence, if completed, would not be an offence triable in England and Wales.".*

4. Subject to section 8 below, if any act done by a person in England and Wales would amount to the offence of incitement to commit an offence under this Act but for the fact that what he had in view would not be an offence triable in England and Wales—

    a. what he had in view shall be treated as an offence under this Act for the purposes of any charge of incitement brought in respect of that act; and

    b. any such charge shall accordingly be triable in England and Wales.

Section 8: Relevance of External Law

1. A person is guilty of an offence triable by virtue of section 4(4) above only if what he intended to do or facilitate would involve the commission of an offence under the law in force where the whole or any part of it was intended to take place.

2. A person is guilty of an offence triable by virtue of section 1(1A) of the [1977 c. 45.] Criminal Law Act 1977 only if the pursuit of the agreed course of conduct would at some stage involve—

    a. an act or omission by one or more of the parties; or

    b. the happening of some other event; constituting an offence under the law in force where the act, omission or other event was intended to take place.

3. A person is guilty of an offence triable by virtue of section 1(1A) of the [1981 c. 47.] Criminal Attempts Act 1981 or by virtue of section 7(4) above only if what he had in view would involve the commission of an offence under the law in force where the whole or any part of it was intended to take place.

4. Conduct punishable under the law in force in any place is an offence under that law for the purposes of this section, however it is described in that law.

5. Subject to subsection (7) below, a condition specified in any of subsections (1) to (3) above shall be taken to be satisfied unless not later than rules of court may provide the defence serve on the prosecution a notice—

    a. stating that, on the facts as alleged with respect to the relevant conduct, the condition is not in their opinion satisfied;

    b. showing their grounds for that opinion; and

    c. requiring the prosecution to show that it is satisfied.

6. In subsection (5) above "the relevant conduct" means—

    a. where the condition in subsection (1) above is in question, what the accused intended to do or facilitate;

    b. where the condition in subsection (2) above is in question, the agreed course of conduct; and

    c. where the condition in subsection (3) above is in question, what the accused had in view.

7. The court, if it thinks fit, may permit the defence to require the prosecution to show that the condition is satisfied without the prior service of a notice under subsection (5) above.

8. If by virtue of subsection (7) above a court of solemn jurisdiction in Scotland permits the defence to require the prosecution to show that the condition is satisfied, it shall be competent for the prosecution for that purpose to examine any witness or to put in evidence any production not included in the lists lodged by it.

9. In the Crown Court the question whether the condition is satisfied shall be decided by the judge alone.

10. In the High Court of Judiciary and in the sheriff court the question whether the condition is satisfied shall be decided by the judge or, as the case may be, the sheriff alone.

Section 9: British Citizenship Immaterial

1. In any proceedings brought in England and Wales in respect of any offence to which this section applies it is immaterial to guilt whether or not the accused was a British citizen at the time of any act, omission or other event proof of which is required for conviction of the offence.
2. This section applies to the following offences—
   a. any offence under this Act;
   b. conspiracy to commit an offence under this Act;
   c. any attempt to commit an offence under section 3 above; and
   d. incitement to commit an offence under this Act.

Miscellaneous and General

Section 10: Saving for Certain Law Enforcement Powers

Section 1(1) above has effect without prejudice to the operation—

a. in England and Wales of any enactment relating to powers of inspection, search or seizure; and
b. in Scotland of any enactment or rule of law relating to powers of examination, search or seizure.

Section 11: Proceedings for Offences under Section 1

1. A magistrates' court shall have jurisdiction to try an offence under section 1 above if—
   a. the accused was within its commission area at the time when he did the act which caused the computer to perform the function; or
   b. any computer containing any program or data to which the accused secured or intended to secure unauthorised access by doing that act was in its commission area at that time.
2. Subject to subsection (3) below, proceedings for an offence under section 1 above may be brought within a period of six months from the date on which evidence sufficient in the opinion of the prosecutor to warrant the proceedings came to his knowledge.
3. No such proceedings shall be brought by virtue of this section more than three years after the commission of the offence.
4. For the purposes of this section, a certificate signed by or on behalf of the prosecutor and stating the date on which evidence sufficient in his opinion to warrant the proceedings came to his knowledge shall be conclusive evidence of that fact.
5. A certificate stating that matter and purporting to be so signed shall be deemed to be so signed unless the contrary is proved.
6. In this section "commission area" has the same meaning as in the Justices of the [1979 c. 55.] Peace Act 1979.
7. This section does not extend to Scotland.

Section 12: Conviction of an Offence Under Section 1 in Proceedings for an Offence Under Section 2 or 3

1. If on the trial on indictment of a person charged with—
   a. an offence under section 2 above; or
   b. an offence under section 3 above or any attempt to commit such an offence; the jury find him not guilty of the offence charged, they may find him guilty of an offence under section 1 above if on the facts shown he could have been found guilty of that offence in proceedings for that offence brought before the expiry of any time limit under section 11 above applicable to such proceedings.

2. The Crown Court shall have the same powers and duties in relation to a person who is by virtue of this section convicted before it of an offence under section 1 above as a magistrates' court would have on convicting him of the offence.

3. This section is without prejudice to section 6(3) of the [1967 c. 58.] Criminal Law Act 1967 (conviction of alternative indictable offence on trial on indictment).

4. This section does not extend to Scotland.

Section 13: Proceedings in Scotland

1. A sheriff shall have jurisdiction in respect of an offence under section 1 or 2 above if—
   a. the accused was in the sheriffdom at the time when he did the act which caused the computer to perform the function; or
   b. any computer containing any program or data to which the accused secured or intended to secure unauthorised access by doing that act was in the sheriffdom at that time.

2. A sheriff shall have jurisdiction in respect of an offence under section 3 above if—
   a. the accused was in the sheriffdom at the time when he did the act which caused the unauthorised modification; or
   b. the unauthorised modification took place in the sheriffdom.

3. Subject to subsection (4) below, summary proceedings for an offence under section 1, 2 or 3 above may be commenced within a period of six months from the date on which evidence sufficient in the opinion of the procurator fiscal to warrant proceedings came to his knowledge.

4. No such proceedings shall be commenced by virtue of this section more than three years after the commission of the offence.

5. For the purposes of this section, a certificate signed by or on behalf of the procurator fiscal and stating the date on which evidence sufficient in his opinion to warrant the proceedings came to his knowledge shall be conclusive evidence of that fact.

6. A certificate stating that matter and purporting to be so signed shall be deemed to be so signed unless the contrary is proved.

7. Subsection (3) of section 331 of the [1975 c. 21.] Criminal Procedure (Scotland) Act 1975 (date of commencement of proceedings) shall apply for the purposes of this section as it applies for the purposes of that section.

8. In proceedings in which a person is charged with an offence under section 2 or 3 above and is found not guilty or is acquitted of that charge, he may be found guilty of an offence under section 1 above if on the facts shown he could have been found guilty of that offence in proceedings for

that offence commenced before the expiry of any time limit under this section applicable to such proceedings.

9.   Subsection (8) above shall apply whether or not an offence under section 1 above has been libelled in the complaint or indictment.

10.   A person found guilty of an offence under section 1 above by virtue of subsection (8) above shall be liable, in respect of that offence, only to the penalties set out in section 1.

11.   This section extends to Scotland only.

Section 14: Search Warrants for Offences Under Section 1

1.   Where a circuit judge is satisfied by information on oath given by a constable that there are reasonable grounds for believing—
   a.   that an offence under section 1 above has been or is about to be committed in any premises; and
   b.   that evidence that such an offence has been or is about to be committed is in those premises; he may issue a warrant authorising a constable to enter and search the premises, using such reasonable force as is necessary.

2.   The power conferred by subsection (1) above does not extend to authorising a search for material of the kinds mentioned in section 9(2) of the [1984 c. 60.] Police and Criminal Evidence Act 1984 (privileged, excluded and special procedure material).

3.   A warrant under this section—
   a.   may authorise persons to accompany any constable executing the warrant; and
   b.   remains in force for twenty-eight days from the date of its issue.

4.   In executing a warrant issued under this section a constable may seize an article if he reasonably believes that it is evidence that an offence under section 1 above has been or is about to be committed.

5.   In this section "premises" includes land, buildings, movable structures, vehicles, vessels, aircraft and hovercraft.

6.   This section does not extend to Scotland.

Section 15: Extradition Where Schedule 1 to the Extradition Act 1989 Applies

The offences to which an Order in Council under section 2 of the [1870 c. 52.] Extradition Act 1870 can apply shall include—

a.   offences under section 2 or 3 above;
b.   any conspiracy to commit such an offence; and
c.   any attempt to commit an offence under section 3 above.

Section 16: Application to Northern Ireland

1.   The following provisions of this section have effect for applying this Act in relation to Northern Ireland with the modifications there mentioned.

2.   In section 2(2)(b)—

a.   the reference to England and Wales shall be read as a reference to Northern Ireland; and

b.   the reference to section 33 of the [1980 c. 43.] Magistrates' Courts Act 1980 shall be read as a reference to Article 46(4) of the [S.I. 1981/1675 (N.I.26).] Magistrates' Courts (Northern Ireland) Order 1981.

3.   The reference in section 3(6) to the [1971 c. 48.] Criminal Damage Act 1971 shall be read as a reference to the [S.I. 1977/426 (N.I.4).] Criminal Damage (Northern Ireland) Order 1977.

4.   Subsections (5) to (7) below apply in substitution for subsections (1) to (3) of section 7; and any reference in subsection (4) of that section to England and Wales shall be read as a reference to Northern Ireland.

5.   The following paragraphs shall be inserted after paragraph (1) of Article 9 of the [S.I. 1983/1120 (N.I.13).] Criminal Attempts and Conspiracy (Northern Ireland) Order 1983—

"1A. Subject to section 8 of the Computer Misuse Act 1990 (relevance of external law), if this paragraph applies to an agreement, this Part has effect in relation to it as it has effect in relation to an agreement falling within paragraph (1).

1B. Paragraph (1A) applies to an agreement if—

a.   *a party to it, or a party's agent, did anything in Northern Ireland in relation to it before its formation;*

b.   *a party to it became a party in Northern Ireland (by joining it either in person or through an agent); or*

c.   *a party to it, or a party's agent, did or omitted anything in Northern Ireland in pursuance of it; and the agreement would fall within paragraph (1) as an agreement relating to the commission of a computer misuse offence but for the fact that the offence would not be an offence triable in Northern Ireland if committed in accordance with the parties' intentions.".*

6.   The following paragraph shall be inserted after paragraph (4) of that Article—

"5. In the application of this Part to an agreement to which paragraph (1A) applies any reference to an offence shall be read as a reference to what would be the computer misuse offence in question but for the fact that it is not an offence triable in Northern Ireland.

6.   *In this Article "computer misuse offence" means an offence under the Computer Misuse Act 1990.".*

7.   The following paragraphs shall be inserted after Article 3(1) of that Order—

"1A. Subject to section 8 of the Computer Misuse Act 1990 (relevance of external law), if this paragraph applies to an act, what the person doing it had in view shall be treated as an offence to which this Article applies.

1B. Paragraph (1A) above applies to an act if—

a.   *it is done in Northern Ireland; and*

b.   *it would fall within paragraph (1) as more than merely preparatory to the commission of an offence under section 3 of the Computer Misuse Act 1990 but for the fact that the offence, if completed, would not be an offence triable in Northern Ireland.".*

8.   In section 8—

a.   the reference in subsection (2) to section 1(1A) of the [1977 c. 45.] Criminal Law Act 1977 shall be read as a reference to Article 9(1A) of that Order; and

b.   the reference in subsection (3) to section 1(1A) of the [1981 c. 47.] Criminal Attempts Act 1981 shall be read as a reference to Article 3(1A) of that Order.

9.   The references in sections 9(1) and 10 to England and Wales shall be read as references to Northern Ireland.

10.   In section 11, for subsection (1) there shall be substituted—

"1. A magistrates' court for a county division in Northern Ireland may hear and determine a complaint charging an offence under section 1 above or conduct a preliminary investigation or preliminary inquiry into an offence under that section if—

    a.   the accused was in that division at the time when he did the act which caused the computer to perform the function; or

    b.   any computer containing any program or data to which the accused secured or intended to secure unauthorised access by doing that act was in that division at that time. "; and subsection (6) shall be omitted.

11.   The reference in section 12(3) to section 6(3) of the [1967 c. 58.] Criminal Law Act 1967 shall be read as a reference to section 6(2) of the [1967 c. 18 (N.I.).] Criminal Law Act (Northern Ireland) 1967.

12.   In section 14—

    a.   the reference in subsection (1) to a circuit judge shall be read as a reference to a county court judge; and

    b.   the reference in subsection (2) to section 9(2) of the [1984 c. 60.] Police and Criminal Evidence Act 1984 shall be read as a reference to Article 11(2) of the [S.I. 1989/1341 (N.I. 12).] Police and Criminal Evidence (Northern Ireland) Order 1989.

Section 17: Interpretation

1.   The following provisions of this section apply for the interpretation of this Act.

2.   A person secures access to any program or data held in a computer if by causing a computer to perform any function he—

    a.   alters or erases the program or data;

    b.   copies or moves it to any storage medium other than that in which it is held or to a different location in the storage medium in which it is held;

    c.   uses it; or

    d.   has it output from the computer in which it is held (whether by having it displayed or in any other manner); and references to access to a program or data (and to an intent to secure such access) shall be read accordingly.

3.   For the purposes of subsection (2)(c) above a person uses a program if the function he causes the computer to perform—

    a.   causes the program to be executed; or

    b.   is itself a function of the program.

4.   For the purposes of subsection (2)(d) above—

    a.   a program is output if the instructions of which it consists are output; and

    b.   the form in which any such instructions or any other data is output (and in particular whether or not it represents a form in which, in the case of instructions, they are capable of being executed or, in the case of data, it is capable of being processed by a computer) is immaterial.

5. Access of any kind by any person to any program or data held in a computer is unauthorised if—
   a. he is not himself entitled to control access of the kind in question to the program or data; and
   b. he does not have consent to access by him of the kind in question to the program or data from any person who is so entitled.
6. References to any program or data held in a computer include references to any program or data held in any removable storage medium which is for the time being in the computer; and a computer is to be regarded as containing any program or data held in any such medium.
7. A modification of the contents of any computer takes place if, by the operation of any function of the computer concerned or any other computer—
   a. any program or data held in the computer concerned is altered or erased; or
   b. any program or data is added to its contents; and any act which contributes towards causing such a modification shall be regarded as causing it.
8. Such a modification is unauthorised if—
   a. the person whose act causes it is not himself entitled to determine whether the modification should be made; and
   b. he does not have consent to the modification from any person who is so entitled.
9. References to the home country concerned shall be read in accordance with section 4(6) above.
10. References to a program include references to part of a program.

APPENDIX 8

Relevant Provisions from Police and Justice Act, 2006, C-48[5]

Preamble: An Act to establish a National Policing Improvement Agency; to make provision about police forces and police authorities and about police pensions; to make provision about police powers and about the powers and duties of community support officers, weights and measures inspectors and others; to make provision about the supply to the police and others of information contained in registers of death; to make further provision for combatting crime and disorder; to make further provision about certain inspectorates; to amend Part 12 of the Criminal Justice Act 2003; to amend the Computer Misuse Act 1990; to make provision about the forfeiture of indecent images of children; to provide for the conferring of functions on the Independent Police Complaints Commission in relation to the exercise of enforcement functions by officials involved with immigration and asylum; to amend the Extradition Act 2003; to make further provision about the use of live links in criminal proceedings; and for connected purposes.

[8th November 2006]

Be it enacted by the Queen's most Excellent Majesty, by and with the advice and consent of the Lords Spiritual and Temporal, and Commons, in this present Parliament assembled, and by the authority of the same, as follows:—

Part 5

Computer Misuse

Section 35: Unauthorised Access to Computer Material

1. In the Computer Misuse Act 1990 (c. 18) ("the 1990 Act"), section 1 (offence of unauthorised access to computer material) is amended as follows.
2. In subsection (1)—
    a. in paragraph (a), after "any computer" there is inserted ", or to enable any such access to be secured";
    b. in paragraph (b), after "secure" there is inserted ", or to enable to be secured,".
3. For subsection (3) there is substituted—
    "3. A person guilty of an offence under this section shall be liable—
    a. *on summary conviction in England and Wales, to imprisonment for a term not exceeding 12 months or to a fine not exceeding the statutory maximum or to both;*
    b. *on summary conviction in Scotland, to imprisonment for a term not exceeding six months or to a fine not exceeding the statutory maximum or to both;*
    c. *on conviction on indictment, to imprisonment for a term not exceeding two years or to a fine or to both."*

Section 36: Unauthorised Acts with Intent to Impair Operation of Computer, Etc

For section 3 of the 1990 Act (unauthorised modification of computer material) there is substituted—
    "3 Unauthorised acts with intent to impair, or with recklessness as to impairing, operation of computer, etc.

1. *A person is guilty of an offence if—*
   a. *he does any unauthorised act in relation to a computer;*
   b. *at the time when he does the act he knows that it is unauthorised; and*
   c. *either subsection (2) or subsection (3) below applies.*
2. *This subsection applies if the person intends by doing the act—*
   a. *to impair the operation of any computer;*
   b. *to prevent or hinder access to any program or data held in any computer;*
   c. *to impair the operation of any such program or the reliability of any such data; or*
   d. *to enable any of the things mentioned in paragraphs (a) to (c) above to be done.*
3. *This subsection applies if the person is reckless as to whether the act will do any of the things mentioned in paragraphs (a) to (d) of subsection (2) above.*
4. *The intention referred to in subsection (2) above, or the recklessness referred to in subsection 3. above, need not relate to—*
   a. *any particular computer;*
   b. *any particular program or data; or*
   c. *a program or data of any particular kind.*
5. *In this section—*
   a. *a reference to doing an act includes a reference to causing an act to be done;*
   b. *"act" includes a series of acts;*
   c. *a reference to impairing, preventing or hindering something includes a reference to doing so temporarily.*
6. *A person guilty of an offence under this section shall be liable—*
   a. *on summary conviction in England and Wales, to imprisonment for a term not exceeding 12 months or to a fine not exceeding the statutory maximum or to both;*
   b. *on summary conviction in Scotland, to imprisonment for a term not exceeding six months or to a fine not exceeding the statutory maximum or to both;*
   c. *on conviction on indictment, to imprisonment for a term not exceeding ten years or to a fine or to both."*

Section 37: Making, Supplying or Obtaining Articles for use in Computer Misuse Offences

After section 3 of the 1990 Act there is inserted—
   "3A Making, supplying or obtaining articles for use in offence under section 1 or 3

1. A person is guilty of an offence if he makes, adapts, supplies or offers to supply any article intending it to be used to commit, or to assist in the commission of, an offence under section 1 or 3.
2. A person is guilty of an offence if he supplies or offers to supply any article believing that it is likely to be used to commit, or to assist in the commission of, an offence under section 1 or 3.
3. A person is guilty of an offence if he obtains any article with a view to its being supplied for use to commit, or to assist in the commission of, an offence under section 1 or 3.
4. In this section "article" includes any program or data held in electronic form.
5. A person guilty of an offence under this section shall be liable—

a. on summary conviction in England and Wales, to imprisonment for a term not exceeding 12 months or to a fine not exceeding the statutory maximum or to both;

b. on summary conviction in Scotland, to imprisonment for a term not exceeding six months or to a fine not exceeding the statutory maximum or to both;

c. on conviction on indictment, to imprisonment for a term not exceeding two years or to a fine or to both."

Section 38: Transitional and Saving Provision

1. The amendments made by—
   a. subsection (2) of section 35, and
   b. paragraphs 19(2), 25(2) and 29(2) of Schedule 14, apply only where every act or other event proof of which is required for conviction of an offence under section 1 of the 1990 Act takes place after that subsection comes into force.
2. The amendments made by—
   a. subsection (3) of section 35, and
   b. paragraphs 23, 24, 25(4) and (5), 26, 27(2) and (7) and 28 of Schedule 14, do not apply in relation to an offence committed before that subsection comes into force.
3. An offence is not committed under the new section 3 unless every act or other event proof of which is required for conviction of the offence takes place after section 36 above comes into force.
4. In relation to a case where, by reason of subsection (3), an offence is not committed under the new section 3—
   a. section 3 of the 1990 Act has effect in the form in which it was enacted;
   b. paragraphs 19(3), 25(3) to (5), 27(4) and (5) and 29(3) and (4) of Schedule 14 do not apply.
5. An offence is not committed under the new section 3A unless every act or other event proof of which is required for conviction of the offence takes place after section 37 above comes into force.
6. In the case of an offence committed before section 154(1) of the Criminal Justice Act 2003 (c. 44) comes into force, the following provisions have effect as if for "12 months" there were substituted "six months"—
   a. paragraph (a) of the new section 1(3);
   b. paragraph (a) of the new section 2(5);
   c. subsection (6)(a) of the new section 3;
   d. subsection (5)(a) of the new section 3A.
7. In this section—
   a. "the new section 1(3)" means the subsection (3) substituted in section 1 of the 1990 Act by section 35 above;
   b. "the new section 2(5)" means the subsection (5) substituted in section 2 of the 1990 Act by paragraph 17 of Schedule 14 to this Act;
   c. "the new section 3" means the section 3 substituted in the 1990 Act by section 36 above;
   d. "the new section 3A" means the section 3A inserted in the 1990 Act by section 37 above.

Forfeiture of Indecent Photographs of Children

Section 39: Forfeiture of Indecent Photographs of Children: England and Wales

1. The Protection of Children Act 1978 (c. 37) is amended as follows.
2. In section 4 (entry, search and seizure)—
   a. subsection (3) is omitted;
   b. for subsection (4) there is substituted—
      "4. In this section "premises" has the same meaning as in the Police and Criminal Evidence Act 1984 (see section 23 of that Act)."
3. For section 5 (forfeiture) there is substituted—

   "5 Forfeiture
   The Schedule to this Act makes provision about the forfeiture of indecent photographs and pseudo-photographs."

4. At the end of the Act there is inserted the Schedule set out in Schedule 11 to this Act.
5. The amendment made by paragraph (b) of subsection (2) has effect only in relation to warrants issued under section 4 of the Protection of Children Act 1978 after the commencement of that paragraph.
6. The amendments made by subsections (2)(a), (3) and (4) and Schedule 11 have effect whether the property in question was lawfully seized before or after the coming into force of those provisions.

   This is subject to subsection (7).

7. Those amendments do not have effect in a case where the property has been brought before a justice of the peace under section 4(3) of the Protection of Children Act 1978 before the coming into force of those provisions.

Section 40: Forfeiture of Indecent Photographs of Children: Northern Ireland

1. The Protection of Children (Northern Ireland) Order 1978 (S.I. 1978/1047 (N.I. 17)) is amended as follows.
2. In Article 4 (entry, search and seizure), for paragraph (2) there is substituted—
   "2. In this Article "premises" has the same meaning as in the Police and Criminal Evidence (Northern Ireland) Order 1989 (S.I. 1989/1341 (N.I. 12)) (see Article 25 of that Order)."
3. For Articles 5 and 6 (forfeiture) there is substituted—

   "5 Forfeiture
   The Schedule to this Order makes provision about the forfeiture of indecent photographs and pseudo-photographs."

4. At the end of the Order there is inserted the Schedule set out in Schedule 12.

5. The amendment made by subsection (2) has effect only in relation to warrants granted under Article 4(1) of the Protection of Children (Northern Ireland) Order 1978 after the commencement of that subsection.

6. The amendments made by subsections (3) and (4) and Schedule 12 have effect whether the property in question was lawfully seized before or after the coming into force of those provisions.

   This is subject to subsection (7).

7. Those amendments do not have effect in a case where the property has been brought before a resident magistrate under Article 5(1) of the Protection of Children (Northern Ireland) Order 1978 (S.I. 1978/1047 (N.I. 17)) before the coming into force of those provisions.

APPENDIX 9

Relevant Provisions of Criminal Code Act, 1995, of Australia, Act no 12 of 1995, as Amended[6] and Cyber Crime Act, 2001,[7] of Australia

Relevant Provisions of Criminal Code Act, 1995, of Australia

Part 10.6—Telecommunications Services

Division 473—Preliminary

Section 473.1: Definitions

In this Part:

access in relation to material includes:

a.   the display of the material by a computer or any other output of the material from a computer; or
b.   the copying or moving of the material to any place in a computer or to a data storage device; or
c.   in the case of material that is a program—the execution of the program.

account identifier means:

a.   something that:
    i.   contains subscription-specific secure data; and
    ii. is installed, or capable of being installed, in a mobile telecommunications device; or
b.   anything else that:
    i.   allows a particular mobile telecommunications account to be identified; and
    ii. is prescribed by the regulations as an account identifier for the purposes of this Part.

    Note: Paragraph (a)—This would include a SIM card.
    carriage service provider has the same meaning as in the Telecommunications Act 1997.
    Note: See also section 474.3 respecting persons who are taken to be carriage service providers in relation to certain matters.
    carrier has the same meaning as in the Telecommunications Act 1997.
    Note: See also section 474.3 respecting persons who are taken to be carriers in relation to certain matters.
    carry includes transmit, switch and receive.
    child abuse material means:

a.   material that depicts a person, or a representation of a person,

who:
    i.   is, or appears to be, under 18 years of age; and

ii.   is, or appears to be, a victim of torture, cruelty or physical abuse; and does this in a way that reasonable persons would regard as being, in all the circumstances, offensive; or

b.   material that describes a person who:

i.   is, or is implied to be, under 18 years of age; and

ii.   is, or is implied to be, a victim of torture, cruelty or physical abuse; and does this in a way that reasonable persons would regard as being, in all the circumstances, offensive.

child pornography material means:

a.   material that depicts a person, or a representation of a person, who is, or appears to be, under 18 years of age and who:

i.   is engaged in, or appears to be engaged in, a sexual pose or sexual activity (whether or not in the presence of other persons); or

ii.   is in the presence of a person who is engaged.in, or appears to be engaged in, a sexual pose or sexual activity; and does this in a way that reasonable persons would regard as being, in all the circumstances, offensive; or

b.   material the dominant characteristic of which is the depiction, for a sexual purpose, of:

i.   a sexual organ or the anal region of a person who is, or appears to be, under 18 years of age; or

ii.   a representation of such a sexual organ or anal region;

or

iii.   the breasts, or a representation of the breasts, of a female person who is, or appears to be, under 18 years of age; in a way that reasonable persons would regard as being, in all the circumstances, offensive; or

c.   material that describes a person who is, or is implied to be, under 18 years of age and who:

i.   is engaged in, or is implied to be engaged in, a sexual pose or sexual activity (whether or not in the presence of other persons); or

ii.   is in the presence of a person who is engaged in, or is implied to be engaged in, a sexual pose or sexual activity; and does this in a way that reasonable persons would regard as being, in all the circumstances, offensive; or

d.   material that describes:

i.   a sexual organ or the anal region of a person who is, or is implied to be, under 18 years of age; or

ii.   the breasts of a female person who is, or is implied to be, under 18 years of age; and does this in a way that reasonable persons would regard as being, in all the circumstances, offensive.

communication in the course of telecommunications carriage means a communication that is being carried by a carrier or carriage service provider, and includes a communication that has been collected or received by a carrier or carriage service provider for carriage, but has not yet been delivered by the carrier or carriage service provider.

connected, in relation to a telecommunications network, includes connection otherwise than by means of physical contact (for example, a connection by means of radiocommunication).

control of data, or material that is in the form of data, has the meaning given by section473.2.

depict includes contain data from which a visual image (whether still or moving) can be generated.

describe includes contain data from which text or sounds can be generated.

emergency call person has the same meaning as in the Telecommunications Act 1997.

emergency service number has the same meaning as in the Telecommunications Act 1997.

emergency service organisation has the same meaning as in section 147 of the Telecommunications (Consumer Protection and Service Standards) Act 1999.

facility has the same meaning as in the Telecommunications Act 1997.

interception device means an apparatus or device that:

a. is of a kind that is capable of being used to enable a person to intercept a communication passing over a telecommunications system; and

b. could reasonably be regarded as having been designed:

    i. for the purpose of; or

    ii. for purposes including the purpose of; using it in connection with the interception of communications passing over a telecommunications system;

    and

c. is not designed principally for the reception of communications transmitted by radiocommunications.

Internet content host has the same meaning as in Schedule 5 to the Broadcasting Services Act 1992.

Internet service provider has the same meaning as in Schedule 5 to the Broadcasting Services Act 1992.

mobile telecommunications account means an account with a carriage service provider for the supply of a public mobile telecommunications service to an end-user.

mobile telecommunications device means an item of customer equipment (within the meaning of the Telecommunications Act 1997) that is used, or is capable of being used, in connection with a public mobile telecommunications service. nominated carrier has the same meaning as in the Telecommunications Act 1997.

Section 473.2 Possession or Control of Data or Material in the Form of Data

A reference in this Part to a person having possession or control of data, or material that is in the form of data, includes a reference to the person:

a. having possession of a computer or data storage device that holds or contains the data; or

b. having possession of a document in which the data is recorded; or

c. having control of data held in a computer that is in the possession of another person (whether inside or outside Australia).

Section 473.3 Producing, Supplying or Obtaining Data or Material in the Form of Data

A reference in this Part to a person producing, supplying or obtaining data, or material that is in the form of data, includes a reference to the person:

a. producing, supplying or obtaining data held or contained in a computer or data storage device; or
b. producing, supplying or obtaining a document in which the data is recorded.

Section 473.4 Determining Whether Material is Offensive

The matters to be taken into account in deciding for the purposes of this Part whether reasonable persons would regard particular material, or a particular use of a carriage service, as being, in all the circumstances, offensive, include:

a. the standards of morality, decency and propriety generally accepted by reasonable adults; and
b. the literary, artistic or educational merit (if any) of the material; and
c. the general character of the material (including whether it is of a medical, legal or scientific character).

473.5 Use of a Carriage Service

For the purposes of this Part, a person is taken not to use a carriage service by engaging in particular conduct if:

a. the person is a carrier and, in engaging in that conduct, is acting solely in the person's capacity as a carrier; or
b. the person is a carriage service provider and, in engaging in that conduct, is acting solely in the person's capacity as a carriage service provider; or
c. the person is an internet service provider and, in engaging in that conduct, is acting solely in the person's capacity as an internet service provider; or
d. the person is an internet content host and, in engaging in that conduct, is acting solely in the person's capacity as an internet content host.

Division 474—Telecommunications Offences

Subdivision A–Dishonesty with Respect to Carriage Services

Section 474.1 Dishonesty

1. For the purposes of this Subdivision, dishonest means:
   a. dishonest according to the standards of ordinary people; and
   b. known by the defendant to be dishonest according to the standards of ordinary people.
2. In a prosecution for an offence against this Subdivision, the determination of dishonesty is a matter for the trier of fact.

Section 474.2 General Dishonesty with Respect to a Carriage Service Provider

Obtaining a gain

1.   A person is guilty of an offence if the person does anything with the intention of dishonestly obtaining a gain from a carriage service provider by way of the supply of a carriage service.

    Penalty: Imprisonment for 5 years.
    Causing a loss

2.   A person is guilty of an offence if the person does anything with the intention of dishonestly causing a loss to a carriage service provider in connection with the supply of a carriage service. Penalty: Imprisonment for 5 years.
3.   A person is guilty of an offence if:
    a.   the person dishonestly causes a loss, or dishonestly causes a risk of loss, to a carriage service provider in connection with the supply of a carriage service; and
    b.   the person knows or believes that the loss will occur or that there is a substantial risk of the loss occurring.

    Penalty: Imprisonment for 5 years.

Subdivision B—Interference with Telecommunications

Section 474.3 Person Acting for a Carrier or Carriage Service Provider

1.   For the purposes of this Subdivision, a person who does any thing for or on behalf of a carrier, or on behalf of persons at least one of whom is a carrier, is, in respect of:
    a.   the doing by that person of that thing; or
    b.   any rental, fee or charge payable for or in relation to the doing by that person of that thing; or
    c.   the operation by that person of a facility in connection with the doing of that thing; or
    d.   a facility belonging to that person; or
    e.   the operation by that person of a satellite; taken to be a carrier.
2.   For the purposes of this Subdivision, a person who does any thing for or on behalf of a carriage service provider, or on behalf of persons at least one of whom is a carriage service provider, is, in respect of:
    a.   the doing by that person of that thing; or
    b.   any rental, fee or charge payable for or in relation to the doing by that person of that thing; or
    c.   the operation by that person of a facility in connection with the doing of that thing; or
    d.   a facility belonging to that person; or
    e.   the operation by that person of a satellite; taken to be a carriage service provider.

Section 474.4 Interception Devices

1. A person is guilty of an offence if:
    a. the person:
        i.   manufactures; or
        ii.   advertises, displays or offers for sale; or
        iii. sells; or
        iv.   possesses; an apparatus or device (whether in an assembled or unassembled form); and
    b. the apparatus or device is an interception device.

    Penalty: Imprisonment for 5 years.

2. A person is not criminally responsible for an offence against subsection (1) if the person possesses the interception device in the course of the person's duties relating to the interception of communications that does not constitute a contravention of subsection 7(1) of the Telecommunications (Interception) Act 1979.

    Note: A defendant bears an evidential burden in relation to the matter in this subsection, see subsection 13.3(3).

3. A person is not criminally responsible for an offence against subsection (1) if the applicable conduct mentioned in subparagraphs (1)(a)(i) to (iv) is in circumstances specified in regulations made for the purposes of this subsection.

    Note: A defendant bears an evidential burden in relation to the matter in this subsection, see subsection 13.3(3).

Section 474.5. Wrongful Delivery of Communications

1. A person is guilty of an offence if:
    a. a communication is in the course of telecommunications carriage; and
    b. the person causes the communication to be received by a person or carriage service other than the person or service to whom it is directed.

    Penalty: Imprisonment for 1 year.

2. A person is not criminally responsible for an offence against subsection (1) if the person engages in the conduct referred to in paragraph (1)(b) with the consent or authorisation of the person to whom, or the person operating the carriage service to which, the communication is directed.

    Note: A defendant bears an evidential burden in relation to the matter in this subsection, see subsection 13.3(3).

Section 474.6. Interference with Facilities

1. A person is guilty of an offence if the person tampers with, or interferes with, a facility owned or operated by:
   a. a carrier; or
   b. a carriage service provider; or
   c. a nominated carrier.

   Penalty: Imprisonment for 1 year.

2. For the purposes of an offence against subsection (1), absolute liability applies to the physical element of circumstance of the offence, that the facility is owned or operated by a carrier, a carriage service provider or a nominated carrier.

3. A person is guilty of an offence if:
   a. the person tampers with, or interferes with, a facility owned or operated by:
      i. a carrier; or
      ii. a carriage service provider; or
      iii. a nominated carrier; and
   b. this conduct results in hindering the normal operation of a carriage service supplied by a carriage service provider.

   Penalty: Imprisonment for 2 years.

4. For the purposes of an offence against subsection (3), absolute liability applies to the following physical elements of circumstance of the offence:
   a. that the facility is owned or operated by a carrier, a carriage service provider or a nominated carrier;
   b. that the carriage service is supplied by a carriage service provider.

5. A person is guilty of an offence if:
   a. the person uses or operates any apparatus or device (whether or not it is comprised in, connected to or used in connection with a telecommunications network); and
   b. this conduct results in hindering the normal operation of a carriage service supplied by a carriage service provider. Penalty: Imprisonment for 2 years.

6. For the purposes of an offence against subsection (5), absolute liability applies to the physical element of circumstance of the offence, that the carriage service is supplied by a carriage service provider.

7. A person is not criminally responsible for an offence against subsection (5) if:
   a. the person is, at the time of the offence, a law enforcement officer, or an intelligence or security officer, acting in good faith in the course of his or her duties; and
   b. the conduct of the person is reasonable in the circumstances for the purpose of performing that duty.

   Note 1: A defendant bears an evidential burden in relation to the matter in this subsection, see subsection 13.3(3).

Note 2: See also subsection 475.1(2) for the interaction between this defence and the Radiocommunications Act 1992.

8. For the purposes of this section, a facility is taken to be owned or operated by a nominated carrier if the Telecommunications Act 1997 applies, under section 81A of that Act, as if that facility were owned or operated by the nominated carrier.

Section 474.7 Modification etc. of a Telecommunications Device Identifier

1. A person is guilty of an offence if the person:
   a. modifies a telecommunications device identifier; or
   b. interferes with the operation of a telecommunications device identifier.

   Penalty: Imprisonment for 2 years.

2. A person is not criminally responsible for an offence against subsection (1) if the person is:
   a. the manufacturer of the mobile telecommunications device in which the telecommunications device identifier is installed;

   or

   b. an employee or agent of the manufacturer who is acting on behalf of the manufacturer; or
   c. acting with the consent of the manufacturer.

   Note: A defendant bears an evidential burden in relation to the matter in this subsection, see subsection 13.3(3).

3. A person is not criminally responsible for an offence against subsection (1) if:
   a. the person is, at the time of the offence, a law enforcement officer, or an intelligence or security officer, acting in the course of his or her duties; and
   b. the conduct of the person is reasonable in the circumstances for the purpose of performing that duty.

   Note 1: A defendant bears an evidential burden in relation to the matter in this subsection, see subsection 13.3(3).
   Note 2: This subsection merely creates a defence to an offence against subsection (1) and does not operate to authorise any conduct that requires a warrant under some other law.

Section 474.8 Possession or Control of Data or a Device with Intent to Modify a Telecommunications Device Identifier

1. A person is guilty of an offence if:
   a. the person has possession or control of any thing or data; and
   b. the person has that possession or control with the intention that the thing or data be used:

      i.   by the person; or

     ii.   by another person;

in committing an offence against subsection 474.7(1) (modification of a telecommunications device identifier).

   Penalty: Imprisonment for 2 years.

2.   A person may be found guilty of an offence against subsection (1) even if committing the offence against subsection 474.7(1) (modification of a telecommunications device identifier) is impossible.

3.   It is not an offence to attempt to commit an offence against subsection (1).

4.   A person is not criminally responsible for an offence against subsection (1) if the person is:

    a.   the manufacturer of the mobile telecommunications device in which the telecommunications device identifier is installed; or

    b.   an employee or agent of the manufacturer who is acting on behalf of the manufacturer; or

    c.   acting with the consent of the manufacturer.

       Note: A defendant bears an evidential burden in relation to the matter in this subsection, see subsection 13.3(3).

5.   A person is not criminally responsible for an offence against subsection (1) if:

    a.   the person is, at the time of the offence, a law enforcement officer, or an intelligence or security officer, acting in the course of his or her duties; and

    b.   the conduct of the person is reasonable in the circumstances for the purpose of performing that duty.

       Note 1: A defendant bears an evidential burden in relation to the matter in this subsection, see subsection 13.3(3).

       Note 2: This subsection merely creates a defence to an offence against subsection (1) and does not operate to authorise any conduct that requires a warrant under some other law.

Section 474.9 Producing, Supplying or Obtaining Data or a Device with Intent to Modify a Telecommunications Device Identifier

1.   A person is guilty of an offence if:

    a.   the person produces, supplies or obtains any thing or data; and

    b.   the person does so with the intention that the thing or data be used:

      i.   by the person; or

     ii.   by another person;

in committing an offence against subsection 474.7(1) (modification of a telecommunications device identifier).

   Penalty: Imprisonment for 2 years.

2. A person may be found guilty of an offence against subsection (1) even if committing the offence against subsection 474.7(1) (modification of a telecommunications device identifier) is impossible.
3. It is not an offence to attempt to commit an offence against subsection (1).
4. A person is not criminally responsible for an offence against subsection (1) if the person is:
   a. the manufacturer of the mobile telecommunications device in which the telecommunications device identifier is installed; or
   b. an employee or agent of the manufacturer who is acting on behalf of the manufacturer; or
   c. acting with the consent of the manufacturer.

   Note: A defendant bears an evidential burden in relation to the matter in this subsection, see subsection 13.3(3).

5. A person is not criminally responsible for an offence against subsection (1) if:
   a. the person is, at the time of the offence, a law enforcement officer, or an intelligence or security officer, acting in the course of his or her duties; and
   b. the conduct of the person is reasonable in the circumstances for the purpose of performing that duty.

   Note 1: A defendant bears an evidential burden in relation to the matter in this subsection, see subsection 13.3(3).
   Note 2: This subsection merely creates a defence to an offence against subsection (1) and does not operate to authorise any conduct that requires a warrant under some other law.

Section 474.10 Copying Subscription-Specific Secure Data

Copying subscription-specific secure data from an existing account identifier

1. A person is guilty of an offence if the person:
   a. copies the subscription-specific secure data from an account identifier; and
   b. does so with the intention that the data will be copied (whether by the person or by someone else) onto something that:
      i. is an account identifier; or
      ii. will, once the data is copied onto it, be capable of operating as an account identifier.

Penalty: Imprisonment for 2 years.

Copying subscription-specific secure data onto a new account identifier

2. A person is guilty of an offence if:
   a. subscription-specific secure data is copied from an account identifier (whether by the person or by someone else); and
   b. the person copies that data onto something that:
      i. is an account identifier; or
      ii. will, once the data is copied onto it, be capable of operating as an account identifier.

This is so whether or not the person knows which particular account identifier the subscription-specific secure data is copied from.

Penalty: Imprisonment for 2 years.

Defences

3. A person is not criminally responsible for an offence against subsection (1) or (2) if the person is:
    a. the carrier who operates the facilities used, or to be used, in the supply of the public mobile telecommunications service to which the subscription-specific secure data relates; or
    b. an employee or agent of that carrier who is acting on behalf of that carrier; or
    c. acting with the consent of that carrier.

    Note: A defendant bears an evidential burden in relation to the matter in this subsection, see subsection 13.3(3).

4. A person is not criminally responsible for an offence against subsection (1) or (2) if:
    a. the person is, at the time of the offence, a law enforcement officer, or an intelligence or security officer, acting in the course of his or her duties; and
    b. the conduct of the person is reasonable in the circumstances for the purpose of performing that duty.

    Note 1: A defendant bears an evidential burden in relation to the matter in this subsection, see subsection 13.3(3).
    Note 2: This subsection merely creates a defence to an offence against subsection (1) or (2) and does not operate to authorise any conduct that requires a warrant under some other law.

Section 474.11 Possession or Control of Data or a Device with Intent to Copy an Account Identifier

1. A person is guilty of an offence if:
    a. the person has possession or control of any thing or data; and
    b. the person has that possession or control with the intention that the thing or data be used:
        i.   by the person; or
        ii. by another person;

    in committing an offence against subsection 474.10(1) (copying subscription-specific secure data from an account identifier) or 474.10(2) (copying subscription-specific secure data onto an account identifier).
    Penalty: Imprisonment for 2 years.

2. A person may be found guilty of an offence against subsection (1) even if committing the offence against subsection 474.10(1) (copying subscription-specific secure data from an account identifier) or 474.10(2) (copying subscription-specific secure data onto an account identifier) is impossible.
3. It is not an offence to attempt to commit an offence against subsection (1).

Defences

4. A person is not criminally responsible for an offence against subsection (1) if the person is:
    a. the carrier who operates the facilities used, or to be used, in the supply of the public mobile telecommunications service to which the subscription-specific secure data relates; or
    b. an employee or agent of that carrier who is acting on behalf of that carrier; or
    c. acting with the consent of that carrier.

    Note: A defendant bears an evidential burden in relation to the matter in this subsection, see subsection 13.3(3).

5. A person is not criminally responsible for an offence against subsection (1) if:
    a. the person is, at the time of the offence, a law enforcement officer, or an intelligence or security officer, acting in the course of his or her duties; and
    b. the conduct of the person is reasonable in the circumstances for the purpose of performing that duty.

    Note 1: A defendant bears an evidential burden in relation to the matter in this subsection, see subsection 13.3(3).
    Note 2: This subsection merely creates a defence to an offence against subsection (1) and does not operate to authorise any conduct that requires a warrant under some other law.

Section 474.12 Producing, Supplying or Obtaining Data or a Device with Intent to Copy an Account Identifier

1. A person is guilty of an offence if:
    a. the person produces, supplies or obtains any thing or data; and
    b. the person does so with the intention that the thing or data be used:
        i. by the person; or
        ii. by another person;

    in committing an offence against subsection 474.10(1) (copying subscription-specific secure data from an account identifier) or 474.10(2) (copying subscription-specific secure data onto an account identifier).
    Penalty: Imprisonment for 2 years.

2. A person may be found guilty of an offence against subsection (1) even if committing the offence against subsection 474.10(1) (copying subscription-specific secure data from an account identifier) or 474.10(2) (copying subscription-specific secure data onto an account identifier) is impossible.
3. It is not an offence to attempt to commit an offence against subsection (1).

Defences

4. A person is not criminally responsible for an offence against subsection (1) if the person is:

a.   the carrier who operates the facilities used, or to be used, in the supply of the public mobile telecommunications service to which the subscription-specific secure data relates; or

b.   an employee or agent of that carrier who is acting on behalf of that carrier; or

c.   acting with the consent of that carrier.

Note: A defendant bears an evidential burden in relation to the matter in this subsection, see subsection 13.3(3).

5.   A person is not criminally responsible for an offence against subsection (1) if:

a.   the person is, at the time of the offence, a law enforcement officer, or an intelligence or security officer, acting in the course of his or her duties; and

b.   the conduct of the person is reasonable in the circumstances for the purpose of performing that duty.

Note 1: A defendant bears an evidential burden in relation to the matter in this subsection, see subsection 13.3(3).

Note 2: This subsection merely creates a defence to an offence against subsection (1) and does not operate to authorise any conduct that requires a warrant under some other law.

Subdivision C—General Offences Relating to use of Telecommunications

Section 474.14 Using a Telecommunications Network with Intention to Commit a Serious Offence

1.   A person is guilty of an offence if:
   a.   the person:
      i.   connects equipment to a telecommunications network; and
      ii. intends by this to commit, or to facilitate the commission of, an offence (whether by that person or another person); and
   b.   the offence is:
      i.   a serious offence against a law of the Commonwealth, a State or a Territory; or
      ii. a serious offence against a foreign law.

2.   A person is guilty of an offence if:
   a.   the person uses equipment connected to a telecommunications network in the commission of, or to facilitate the commission of, an offence (whether by that person or another person); and
   b.   the offence is:
      i.   a serious offence against a law of the Commonwealth, a State or a Territory; or
      ii. a serious offence against a foreign law.

3.   A person who is guilty of an offence against subsection (1) or (2) is punishable, on conviction, by a penalty not exceeding the penalty applicable to the serious offence.

4.   Absolute liability applies to paragraphs (1)(b) and (2)(b).

Note: For *absolute liability*, see section 6.2.

5.   A person may be found guilty of an offence against subsection (1) or (2) even if committing the serious offence is impossible.

6.   It is not an offence to attempt to commit an offence against subsection (1) or (2).

Section 474.15 Using a Carriage Service to Make a Threat

Threat to kill

1.   A person (the *first person*) is guilty of an offence if:
     a.   the first person uses a carriage service to make to another person (the *second person*) a threat to kill the second person or a third person; and
     b.   the first person intends the second person to fear that the threat will be carried out.

Penalty: Imprisonment for 10 years.

Threat to cause serious harm

2.   A person (the *first person*) is guilty of an offence if:
     a.   the first person uses a carriage service to make to another person (the *second person*) a threat to cause serious harm to the second person or a third person; and
     b.   the first person intends the second person to fear that the threat will be carried out.

Penalty: Imprisonment for 7 years.

Actual fear not necessary

3.   In a prosecution for an offence against this section, it is not necessary to prove that the person receiving the threat actually feared that the threat would be carried out.

Definitions

4.   In this section:

fear includes apprehension.
threat to cause serious harm to a person includes a threat to substantially contribute to serious harm to the person.

Section 474.16 Using a Carriage Service for a Hoax Threat

A person is guilty of an offence if:

a.   the person uses a carriage service to send a communication; and
b.   the person does so with the intention of inducing a false belief that an explosive, or a dangerous or harmful substance or thing, has been or will be left in any place.

Penalty: Imprisonment for 10 years.

Section 474.17 Using a Carriage Service to Menace, Harass or Cause Offence

1. A person is guilty of an offence if:
   a. the person uses a carriage service; and
   b. the person does so in a way (whether by the method of use or the content of a communication, or both) that reasonable persons would regard as being, in all the circumstances, menacing, harassing or offensive.

   Penalty: Imprisonment for 3 years.

2. Without limiting subsection (1), that subsection applies to menacing, harassing or causing offence to:
   a. an employee of the NRS provider; or
   b. an emergency call person; or
   c. an employee of an emergency service organisation; or
   d. an APS employee in the Attorney-General's Department acting as a National Security Hotline call taker.

Section 474.18 Improper use of Emergency Call Service

1. A person is guilty of an offence if the person:
   a. makes a call to an emergency service number; and
   b. does so with the intention of inducing a false belief that an emergency exists.

   Penalty: Imprisonment for 3 years.

2. A person is guilty of an offence if:
   a. the person makes a call to an emergency service number; and
   b. the person makes the call otherwise than for the purpose of reporting an emergency; and
   c. the call is a vexatious one.

   Penalty: Imprisonment for 3 years.

3. In determining whether a call by a person to an emergency service number is a vexatious one, have regard to:
   a. the content of the call; and
   b. the number, frequency and content of previous calls the person has made to emergency service numbers otherwise than for the purpose of reporting emergencies; and
   c. any other relevant matter.

Subdivision D—Offences Relating to use of Carriage Service for Child Pornography Material or Child Abuse Material

Section 474.19 Using a Carriage Service for Child Pornography Material

1. A person is guilty of an offence if:
    a. the person: distributes, advertises or promotes material; or
        iv. solicits material; and
            aa. the person does so using a carriage service; and
    b. the material is child pornography material.

    Penalty: Imprisonment for 15 years.

2. To avoid doubt, the following are the fault elements for the physical elements of an offence against subsection (1):
    a. intention is the fault element for the conduct referred to in paragraph (1)(a);
    b. recklessness is the fault element for the circumstances referred to in paragraph (1)(b).

    Note: For the meaning of ***intention*** and ***recklessness*** see sections 5.2 and 5.4.
    2A. Absolute liability applies to paragraph (1)(aa).

    Note: For absolute liability, see section 6.2.

3. As well as the general defences provided for in Part 2.3, defences are provided for under section 474.21 in relation to this section.

Section 474.20 Possessing, Controlling, Producing, Supplying or Obtaining Child Pornography Material for use Through a Carriage Service

1. A person is guilty of an offence if:
    a. the person:
        i. has possession or control of material; or
        ii. produces, supplies or obtains material; and
    b. the material is child pornography material; and
    c. the person has that possession or control, or engages in that production, supply or obtaining, with the intention that the material be used:
        i. by that person; or
        ii. by another person;
    in committing an offence against section 474.19 (using a carriage service for child pornography material).
    Penalty: Imprisonment for 15 years.

2. A person may be found guilty of an offence against subsection (1) even if committing the offence against section 474.19 (using a carriage service for child pornography material) is impossible.

3. It is not an offence to attempt to commit an offence against subsection (1).

Section 474.21 Defences in Respect of Child Pornography Material

1. A person is not criminally responsible for an offence against section 474.19 (using a carriage service for child pornography material) or 474.20 (possessing etc. child pornography material for use through a carriage service) because of engaging in particular conduct if the conduct:

   a. is of public benefit; and

   b. does not extend beyond what is of public benefit.

   In determining whether the person is, under this subsection, not criminally responsible for the offence, the question whether the conduct is of public benefit is a question of fact and the person's motives in engaging in the conduct are irrelevant.

   Note: A defendant bears an evidential burden in relation to the matter in this subsection, see subsection 13.3(3).

2. For the purposes of subsection (1), conduct is of public benefit if, and only if, the conduct is necessary for or of assistance in:

   a. enforcing a law of the Commonwealth, a State or a Territory; or

   b. monitoring compliance with, or investigating a contravention of, a law of the Commonwealth, a State or a Territory; or

   c. the administration of justice; or

   d. conducting scientific, medical or educational research that has been approved by the Minister in writing for the purposes of this section.

3. A person is not criminally responsible for an offence against section 474.19 (using a carriage service for child pornography material) or 474.20 (possessing etc. child pornography material for use through a carriage service) if:

   a. the person is, at the time of the offence, a law enforcement officer, or an intelligence or security officer, acting in the course of his or her duties; and

   b. the conduct of the person is reasonable in the circumstances for the purpose of performing that duty.

   Note: A defendant bears an evidential burden in relation to the matter in this subsection, see subsection 13.3(3).

4. A person is not criminally responsible for an offence against section 474.19 (using a carriage service for child pornography material) or 474.20 (possessing etc. child pornography material for use through a carriage service) if the person engages in the conduct in good faith for the sole purpose of:

   a. assisting the Australian Communications and Media Authority to detect:

      i. prohibited content (within the meaning of Schedule 7 to the *Broadcasting Services Act 1992*); or

ii. potential prohibited content (within the meaning of that Schedule); in the performance of the Authority's functions under Schedule 5 or Schedule 7 to that Act; or

b. manufacturing or developing, or updating, content filtering technology (including software) in accordance with:

 i. a recognised alternative access-prevention arrangement (within the meaning of clause 40 of Schedule 5 to the *Broadcasting Services Act 1992*); or

 ii. a designated alternative access-prevention arrangement (within the meaning of clause 60 of that Schedule).

Note: A defendant bears an evidential burden in relation to the matter in this subsection, see subsection 13.3(3).

Section 474.22 Using a Carriage Service for Child Abuse Material

1. A person is guilty of an offence if:

 a. the person:

  i. accesses material; or

  ii. causes material to be transmitted to himself or herself; or

  iii. transmits, makes available, publishes, distributes, advertises or promotes material; or

  iv. solicits material; and

  aa. the person does so using a carriage service; and

 b. the material is child abuse material.

Penalty: Imprisonment for 15 years.

2. To avoid doubt, the following are the fault elements for the physical elements of an offence against subsection (1):

 a. intention is the fault element for the conduct referred to in paragraph (1)(a);

 b. recklessness is the fault element for the circumstances referred to in paragraph (1)(b).

Note: For the meaning of *intention* and *recklessness* see sections 5.2 and 5.4.

2A. Absolute liability applies to paragraph (1)(aa).

Note: For absolute liability, see section 6.2.

3. As well as the general defences provided for in Part 2.3, defences are provided for under section 474.24 in relation to this section.

Section 474.23 Possessing, Controlling, Producing, Supplying or Obtaining Child Abuse Material for use through a Carriage Service

1. A person is guilty of an offence if:

 a. the person:

  i. has possession or control of material; or

  ii. produces, supplies or obtains material; and

b. the material is child abuse material; and

c. the person has that possession or control, or engages in that production, supply or obtaining, with the intention that the material be used:

i. by that person; or

ii. by another person; in committing an offence against section 474.22 (using a carriage service for child abuse material).

Penalty: Imprisonment for 15 years.

2. A person may be found guilty of an offence against subsection (1) even if committing the offence against section 474.22 (using a carriage service for child abuse material) is impossible.

3. It is not an offence to attempt to commit an offence against subsection (1).

Section 474.24 Defences in Respect of Child Abuse Material

1. A person is not criminally responsible for an offence against section 474.22 (using a carriage service for child abuse material) or 474.23 (possessing etc. child abuse material for use through a carriage service) because of engaging in particular conduct if the conduct:

a. is of public benefit; and

b. does not extend beyond what is of public benefit.

In determining whether the person is, under this subsection, not criminally responsible for the offence, the question whether the conduct is of public benefit is a question of fact and the person's motives in engaging in the conduct are irrelevant.

Note: A defendant bears an evidential burden in relation to the matter in this subsection, see subsection 13.3(3).

2. For the purposes of subsection (1), conduct is of public benefit if, and only if, the conduct is necessary for or of assistance in:

a. enforcing a law of the Commonwealth, a State or a Territory; or

b. monitoring compliance with, or investigating a contravention of, a law of the Commonwealth, a State or a Territory; or

c. the administration of justice; or

d. conducting scientific, medical or educational research that has been approved by the Minister in writing for the purposes of this section.

3. A person is not criminally responsible for an offence against section 474.22 (using a carriage service for child abuse material) or 474.23 (possessing etc. child abuse material for use through a carriage service) if:

a. the person is, at the time of the offence, a law enforcement officer, or an intelligence or security officer, acting in the course of his or her duties; and

b. the conduct of the person is reasonable in the circumstances for the purpose of performing that duty.

Note: A defendant bears an evidential burden in relation to the matter in this subsection, see subsection 13.3(3).

4. A person is not criminally responsible for an offence against section 474.22 (using a carriage service for child abuse material) or 474.23 (possessing etc. child abuse material for use through a carriage service) if the person engages in the conduct in good faith for the sole purpose of:
   a. assisting the Australian Communications and Media Authority to detect:
      i. prohibited content (within the meaning of Schedule 7 to the *Broadcasting Services Act 1992*); or
      ii. potential prohibited content (within the meaning of that Schedule); in the performance of the Authority's functions under Schedule 5 or Schedule 7 to that Act; or
   b. manufacturing or developing, or updating, content filtering technology (including software) in accordance with:
      i. a recognised alternative access-prevention arrangement (within the meaning of clause 40 of Schedule 5 to the *Broadcasting Services Act 1992*); or
      ii. a designated alternative access-prevention arrangement (within the meaning of clause 60 of that Schedule).

   Note: A defendant bears an evidential burden in relation to the matter in this subsection, see subsection 13.3(3).

Section 474.24A Aggravated Offence—Offence Involving Conduct on 3 or More Occasions and 2 or More People

1. A person commits an offence against this section if:
   a. the person commits an offence against one or more of the following provisions on 3 or more separate occasions:
      i. section 474.19 (using a carriage service for child pornography material);
      ii. section 474.20 (possessing etc. child pornography material for use through a carriage service);
      iii. section 474.22 (using a carriage service for child abuse material);
      iv. section 474.23 (possessing etc. child abuse material for use through a carriage service); and
   b. the commission of each such offence involves 2 or more people.

   Penalty: Imprisonment for 25 years.
2. There is no fault element for any of the physical elements described in paragraph (1)(a) other than the fault elements (however described), if any, for the offence against section 474.19, 474.20, 474.22 or 474.23.
3. To avoid doubt, a person does not commit an offence against section 474.19, 474.20, 474.22 or 474.23 for the purposes of paragraph (1)(a) if the person has a defence to that offence.

Offence or conduct need not be the same

4. For the purposes of subsection (1), it is immaterial whether the offence, or the conduct constituting the offence, is the same on each occasion.

Double jeopardy etc.

5. A person who has been convicted or acquitted of an offence (the ***aggravated offence***) against this section may not be convicted of an offence against section 474.19, 474.20, 474.22 or 474.23 in relation to the conduct that constituted the aggravated offence.
6. Subsection (5) does not prevent an alternative verdict under section 474.24B.
7. A person who has been convicted or acquitted of an offence (the ***underlying offence***) against section 474.19, 474.20, 474.22 or 474.23 may not be convicted of an offence against this section in relation to the conduct that constituted the underlying offence.

Section 474.24B Alternative Verdict if Aggravated Offence not Proven

If, on a trial for an offence (the ***aggravated offence***) against subsection 474.24A(1), the trier of fact:

a. is not satisfied that the defendant is guilty of the aggravated offence; but
b. is satisfied beyond reasonable doubt that he or she is guilty of an offence (the ***underlying offence***) against section 474.19, 474.20, 474.22 or 474.23;

it may find the defendant not guilty of the aggravated offence but guilty of the underlying offence, so long as the defendant has been accorded procedural fairness in relation to that finding of guilt.

Section 474.24C Consent to Commencement of Proceedings where Defendant under 18

1. Proceedings for an offence against this Subdivision must not be commenced without the consent of the Attorney-General if the defendant was under 18 at the time he or she allegedly engaged in the conduct constituting the offence.
2. However, a person may be arrested for, charged with, or remanded in custody or on bail in connection with, such an offence before the necessary consent has been given.

Subdivision E—Offence Relating to Obligations of Internet Service Providers and Internet Content Hosts

Section 474.25 Obligations of Internet Service Providers and Internet Content Hosts

A person commits an offence if the person:

a. is an internet service provider or an internet content host; and
b. is aware that the service provided by the person can be used to access particular material that the person has reasonable grounds to believe is:
    i.   child pornography material; or
    ii. child abuse material; and
c. does not refer details of the material to the Australian Federal Police within a reasonable time after becoming aware of the existence of the material.

Penalty: 100 penalty units.

Subdivision F—Offences Relating to Use of Carriage Service Involving Sexual Activity with Person under 16

Section 474.25A Using a Carriage Service for Sexual Activity with Person under 16 Years of Age

Engaging in sexual activity with child using a carriage service

1. A person commits an offence if:
    a. the person engages in sexual activity with another person (the *child*) using a carriage service; and
    b. the child is under 16 years of age; and
    c. the person is at least 18 years of age.

    Penalty: Imprisonment for 15 years.

Causing child to engage in sexual activity with another person

2. A person (the *defendant*) commits an offence if:
    a. the defendant engages in conduct in relation to another person (the *child*); and
    b. that conduct causes the child to engage in sexual activity with another person (the *participant*) using a carriage service; and
    c. the child is under 16 years of age when the sexual activity is engaged in; and
    d. the participant is at least 18 years of age when the sexual activity is engaged in.

    Penalty: Imprisonment for 15 years.

3. The fault element for paragraph (2)(b) is intention.

Defence—child present but defendant does not intend to derive gratification

4. It is a defence to a prosecution for an offence against subsection (1) or (2) if:
    a. the conduct constituting the offence consists only of the child being in the presence of a person while sexual activity is engaged in; and
    b. the defendant proves that he or she did not intend to derive gratification from the presence of the child during that activity.

    > Note 1: A defendant bears a legal burden in relation to the matter in this subsection, see section 13.4.
    > Note 2: For other defences relating to this offence, see section 474.29.

Section 474.25B Aggravated Offence—Child with Mental Impairment or under Care, Supervision or Authority of Defendant

1. A person commits an offence against this section if:
   a. the person commits an offence against either of the following provisions in relation to another person (the *child*):
      i. subsection 474.25A(1) (engaging in sexual activity with child using a carriage service);
      ii. subsection 474.25A(2) (causing child to engage in sexual activity with another person); and
   b. either or both of the following apply at the time the person commits the offence:
      i. the child has a mental impairment;
      ii. the person is in a position of trust or authority in relation to the child, or the child is otherwise under the care, supervision or authority of the person.

   Penalty: Imprisonment for 25 years.

2. To avoid doubt, a person does not commit the offence against subsection 474.25A(1 or 2) for the purposes of paragraph (1)(a) if the person has a defence to that offence.

   Alternative verdicts

3. If, on a trial for an offence (the *aggravated offence*) against subsection (1), the trier of fact:
   a. is not satisfied that the defendant is guilty of the aggravated offence; but
   b. is satisfied beyond reasonable doubt that he or she is guilty of an offence (the *underlying offence*) against subsection 474.25A(1) or (2); it may find the defendant not guilty of the aggravated offence but guilty of the underlying offence, so long as the defendant has been accorded procedural fairness in relation to that finding of guilt.

Section 474.26 Using a Carriage Service to Procure Persons under 16 Years of Age

1. A person (the *sender*) commits an offence if:
   a. the sender uses a carriage service to transmit a communication to another person (the *recipient*); and
   b. the sender does this with the intention of procuring the recipient to engage in sexual activity with the sender; and
   c. the recipient is someone who is, or who the sender believes to be, under 16 years of age; and
   d. the sender is at least 18 years of age.

   Penalty: Imprisonment for 15 years.

2. A person (the *sender*) commits an offence if:
    a. the sender uses a carriage service to transmit a communication to another person (the *recipient*); and
    b. the sender does this with the intention of procuring the recipient to engage in sexual activity with another person (the *participant*); and
    c. the recipient is someone who is, or who the sender believes to be, under 16 years of age; and
    d. the participant is someone who is, or who the sender believes to be, at least 18 years of age.

    Penalty: Imprisonment for 15 years.

3. A person (the *sender*) commits an offence if:
    a. the sender uses a carriage service to transmit a communication to another person (the *recipient*); and
    b. the sender does this with the intention of procuring the recipient to engage in sexual activity with another person; and
    c. the recipient is someone who is, or who the sender believes to be, under 16 years of age; and
    d. the other person referred to in paragraph (b) is someone who is, or who the sender believes to be, under 18 years of age; and
    e. the sender intends that the sexual activity referred to in paragraph (b) will take place in the presence of:
        i. the sender; or
        ii. another person (the *participant*) who is, or who the sender believes to be, at least 18 years of age.

    Penalty: Imprisonment for 15 years.

Section 474.27 Using a Carriage Service to "Groom" Persons under 16 Years of Age

1. A person (the *sender*) commits an offence if:
    a. the sender uses a carriage service to transmit a communication to another person (the *recipient*); and
    c. the sender does this with the intention of making it easier to procure the recipient to engage in sexual activity with the sender; and
    d. the recipient is someone who is, or who the sender believes to be, under 16 years of age; and
    e. the sender is at least 18 years of age.

    Penalty: Imprisonment for 12 years.

2. A person (the *sender*) commits an offence if:
    a. the sender uses a carriage service to transmit a communication to another person (the *recipient*); and
    c. the sender does this with the intention of making it easier to procure the recipient to engage in sexual activity with another person (the *participant*); and
    d. the recipient is someone who is, or who the sender believes to be, under 16 years of age; and
    e. the participant is someone who is, or who the sender believes to be, at least 18 years of age.

Penalty: Imprisonment for 12 years.

3.   A person (the *sender*) commits an offence if:
  a.   the sender uses a carriage service to transmit a communication to another person (the *recipient*); and
  c.   the sender does this with the intention of making it easier to procure the recipient to engage in sexual activity with another person; and
  d.   the recipient is someone who is, or who the sender believes to be, under 16 years of age; and
  e.   the other person referred to in paragraph (c) is someone who is, or who the sender believes to be, under 18 years of age; and
  f.   the sender intends that the sexual activity referred to in paragraph (c) will take place in the presence of:
    i.   the sender; or
    ii.   another person (the *participant*) who is, or who the sender believes to be, at least 18 years of age.

Penalty: Imprisonment for 15 years.

Section 474.27A. Using a Carriage Service to Transmit Indecent Communication to Person under 16 Years of Age

1.   A person (the *sender*) commits an offence if:
  a.   the sender uses a carriage service to transmit a communication to another person (the *recipient*); and
  b.   the communication includes material that is indecent; and
  c.   the recipient is someone who is, or who the sender believes to be, under 16 years of age; and
  d.   the sender is at least 18 years of age.

Penalty: Imprisonment for 7 years.

2.   In a prosecution for an offence against subsection (1), whether material is indecent is a matter for the trier of fact.
3.   In this section:
  indecent means indecent according to the standards of ordinary people.

Section 474.28 Provisions Relating to Offences against this Subdivision

Age-related issues—application of absolute liability

1.   For the purposes of an offence against this Subdivision, absolute liability applies to the physical element of circumstance of the offence that:
  a.   in the case of an offence against section 474.25A—the child is under 16 years of age; and
  b.   in the case of an offence against section 474.26, 474.27 or 474.27A—the recipient is someone who is under 16 years of age.

Note 1: For ***absolute liability***, see section 6.2.

Note 2: For a defence based on belief about age, see section 474.29.

2. For the purposes of an offence against subsection 474.25A(2), 474.26(2) or (3) or 474.27(2) or (3), absolute liability applies to the physical elements of circumstance of the offence that the participant is at least 18 years of age.

    Note 1: For ***absolute liability***, see section 6.2.

    Note 2: For a defence based on belief about age, see section 474.29.

Proof of belief about age—evidence of representation

3. For the purposes of sections 474.26, 474.27 and 474.27A, evidence that the recipient was represented to the sender as being under or of a particular age is, in the absence of evidence to the contrary, proof that the sender believed the recipient to be under or of that age.

4. For the purposes of sections 474.25A, 474.26 and 474.27, evidence that the participant was represented to the sender as being:

    a. at least 18 years of age; or

    b. over or of a particular age;

is, in the absence of evidence to the contrary, proof that the sender believed the participant to be at least 18 years of age or over or of that age.

Determining age—admissible evidence

5. In determining for the purposes of this Subdivision how old a person is or was at a particular time, a jury or court may treat any of the following as admissible evidence:

    a. the person's appearance;

    b. medical or other scientific opinion;

    c. a document that is or appears to be an official or medical record from a country outside Australia;

    d. a document that is or appears to be a copy of such a record.

6. Subsection (5) does not make any other kind of evidence inadmissible, and does not affect a prosecutor's duty to do all he or she can to adduce the best possible evidence for determining the question.

7. If, on a trial for an offence against a provision of this Subdivision, evidence may be treated as admissible because of subsection (5), the court must warn the jury that it must be satisfied beyond reasonable doubt in determining the question.

Issues relating to aggravated offence involving sexual activity

7A. For the purposes of an offence against subsection 474.25B(1):

    a. there is no fault element for the physical element described in paragraph (a) of that subsection other than the fault elements (however described), if any, for the underlying offence; and

     b.   absolute liability applies to the physical element of circumstance of the offence that the child has a mental impairment; and

     c.   strict liability applies to the physical element of circumstance of the offence that the defendant is in a position of trust or authority in relation to the child, or the child is otherwise under the care, supervision or authority of the defendant.

Note 1: For absolute liability, see section 6.2.

Note 2: For strict liability, see section 6.1.

Note 3: For a defence based on belief that the child did not have a mental impairment, see section 474.29.

Impossibility of sexual activity taking place

8.   A person may be found guilty of an offence against section 474.26 or 474.27 even if it is impossible for the sexual activity referred to in that section to take place.

Fictitious recipient

9.   For the purposes of sections 474.26, 474.27 and 474.27A, it does not matter that the recipient to whom the sender believes the sender is transmitting the communication is a fictitious person represented to the sender as a real person.

Attempt not offence

10.   It is not an offence to attempt to commit an offence against section 474.26 or 474.27.

Section 474.29 Defences to Offences against this Subdivision

Offences involving sexual activity—belief that child at least 16 years of age

1.   It is a defence to a prosecution for an offence against section 474.25A if the defendant proves that, at the time the sexual activity was engaged in, he or she believed that the child was at least 16 years of age.

Note: A defendant bears a legal burden in relation to the matter in this subsection, see section 13.4.

Offences involving sexual activity with other participant—belief that participant under 18 years of age

2.   It is a defence to a prosecution for an offence against subsection 474.25A(2) if the defendant proves that, at the time the sexual activity was engaged in, he or she believed that the participant was under 18 years of age.

Note: A defendant bears a legal burden in relation to the matter in this subsection, see section 13.4.

Aggravated offence involving sexual activity—belief that child did not have mental impairment

3.   It is a defence to a prosecution for an offence against subsection 474.25B(1) (as that subsection applies because of subparagraph 474.25B(1)(b)(i)) if the defendant proves that, at the time the defendant committed the offence, he or she believed that the child did not have a mental impairment.

Note: A defendant bears a legal burden in relation to the matter in this subsection, see section 13.4.

Offences involving procuring or "grooming" person for sexual activity with other participant—belief that participant under 18 years of age

4.   It is a defence to a prosecution for an offence against subsection 474.26(2) or (3) or 474.27(2) or (3) if the defendant proves that, at the time the communication was transmitted, he or she believed that the participant was under 18 years of age.

Note: A defendant bears a legal burden in relation to the matter in this subsection, see section 13.4.

Offences involving transmission of communication—belief that recipient at least 16 years of age

5.   It is a defence to a prosecution for an offence against section 474.26, 474.27 or 474.27A if the defendant proves that, at the time the communication was transmitted, he or she believed that the recipient was at least 16 years of age.

Note: A defendant bears a legal burden in relation to the matter in this subsection, see section 13.4.

Trier of fact may take into account whether belief reasonable

6.   In determining whether the defendant had the belief mentioned in one of the preceding subsections of this section, the trier of fact may take into account whether the alleged belief was reasonable in the circumstances.

Subdivision G—Offences Relating to Use of Carriage Service for Suicide Related Material

Section 474.29A Using a Carriage Service for Suicide Related Material

1.   A person is guilty of an offence if:
    a.   the person:
        i.   uses a carriage service to access material; or
        ii.   uses a carriage service to cause material to be transmitted to the person; or
        iii.   uses a carriage service to transmit material; or
        iv.   uses a carriage service to make material available; or
        v.   uses a carriage service to publish or otherwise distribute material; and

    b.   the material directly or indirectly counsels or incites committing or attempting to commit suicide; and

    c.   the person:

        i.   intends to use the material to counsel or incite committing or attempting to commit suicide; or

        ii.   intends that the material be used by another person to counsel or incite committing or attempting to commit suicide.

Penalty: 1,000 penalty units.

2.   A person is guilty of an offence if:

    a.   the person:

        i.   uses a carriage service to access material; or

        ii.   uses a carriage service to cause material to be transmitted to the person; or

        iii.   uses a carriage service to transmit material; or

        iv.   uses a carriage service to make material available; or

        v.   uses a carriage service to publish or otherwise distribute material; and

    b.   the material directly or indirectly:

        i.   promotes a particular method of committing suicide; or

        ii.   provides instruction on a particular method of committing suicide; and

    c.   the person:

        i.   intends to use the material to promote that method of committing suicide or provide instruction on that method of committing suicide; or

        ii.   intends that the material be used by another person to promote that method of committing suicide or provide instruction on that method of committing suicide; or

        iii.   intends the material to be used by another person to commit suicide.

Penalty: 1,000 penalty units.

3.   To avoid doubt, a person is not guilty of an offence against subsection (1) merely because the person uses a carriage service to:

    a.   engage in public discussion or debate about euthanasia or suicide; or

    b.   advocate reform of the law relating to euthanasia or suicide;

if the person does not:

    c.   intend to use the material concerned to counsel or incite committing or attempting to commit suicide; or

    d.   intend that the material concerned be used by another person to counsel or incite committing or attempting to commit suicide.

4.   To avoid doubt, a person is not guilty of an offence against subsection (2) merely because the person uses a carriage service to:

    a.   engage in public discussion or debate about euthanasia or suicide; or

    b.   advocate reform of the law relating to euthanasia or suicide;

if the person does not:

    c.   intend to use the material concerned to promote a method of committing suicide or provide instruction on a method of committing suicide; or

    d.   intend that the material concerned be used by another person to promote a method of committing suicide or provide instruction on a method of committing suicide; or

    e.   intend the material concerned to be used by another person to commit suicide.

Section 474.29B Possessing, Controlling, Producing, Supplying or Obtaining Suicide Related Material for Use through a Carriage Service

1.   A person is guilty of an offence if:

    a.   the person:

        i.   has possession or control of material; or

        ii.   produces, supplies or obtains material; and

    b.   the material directly or indirectly:

        i.   counsels or incites committing or attempting to commit suicide; or

        ii.   promotes a particular method of committing suicide; or

        iii.   provides instruction on a particular method of committing suicide; and

    c.   the person has that possession or control, or engages in that production, supply or obtaining, with the intention that the material be used:

        i.   by that person; or

        ii.   by another person;

in committing an offence against section 474.29A (using a carriage service for suicide related material). Penalty: 1,000 penalty units.

2.   A person may be found guilty of an offence against subsection (1) even if committing the offence against section 474.29A (using a carriage service for suicide related material) is impossible.

3.   It is not an offence to attempt to commit an offence against subsection (1).

Part 10.7—Computer Offences

Division 476—Preliminary

Section 476.1 Definitions

1.   In this Part:

access to data held in a computer means:

    a.   the display of the data by the computer or any other output of the data from the computer; or

    b.   the copying or moving of the data to any other place in the computer or to a data storage device; or

    c.   in the case of a program—the execution of the program.

Commonwealth computer means a computer owned, leased or operated by a Commonwealth entity.

electronic communication means a communication of information in any form by means of guided or unguided electromagnetic energy.

impairment of electronic communication to or from a computer includes:

    a.   the prevention of any such communication; or

    b.   the impairment of any such communication on an electronic link or network used by the computer;

but does not include a mere interception of any such communication.

modification, in respect of data held in a computer, means:

    a.   the alteration or removal of the data; or

    b.   an addition to the data.

unauthorised access, modification or impairment has the meaning given in section 476.2.

2.   In this Part, a reference to:

    a.   access to data held in a computer; or

    b.   modification of data held in a computer; or

    c.   the impairment of electronic communication to or from a computer;

is limited to such access, modification or impairment caused, whether directly or indirectly, by the execution of a function of a computer.

Section 476.2 Meaning of Unauthorised Access, Modification or Impairment

1.   In this Part:

    a.   access to data held in a computer; or

    b.   modification of data held in a computer; or

    c.   the impairment of electronic communication to or from a computer; or

    d.   the impairment of the reliability, security or operation of any data held on a computer disk, credit card or other device used to store data by electronic means;

by a person is unauthorised if the person is not entitled to cause that access, modification or impairment.

2.   Any such access, modification or impairment caused by the person is not unauthorised merely because he or she has an ulterior purpose for causing it.

3.   For the purposes of an offence under this Part, a person causes any such unauthorised access, modification or impairment if the person's conduct substantially contributes to it.

4.   For the purposes of subsection (1), if:

    a.   a person causes any access, modification or impairment of a kind mentioned in that subsection; and

    b.   the person does so:

        i.   under a warrant issued under the law of the Commonwealth, a State or a Territory; or

ii.   under an emergency authorisation given to the person under Part 3 of the *Surveillance Devices Act 2004* or under a law of a State or Territory that makes provision to similar effect; or

iii.   under a tracking device authorisation given to the person under section 39 of that Act;

the person is entitled to cause that access, modification or impairment.

Section 476.3 Geographical Jurisdiction

Section 15.1 (extended geographical jurisdiction—Category A) applies to offences under this Part.

476.4 Saving of Other Laws

1 This Part is not intended to exclude or limit the operation of any other law of the Commonwealth, a State or a Territory.

2 Subsection (1) has effect subject to section 476.5.

Section 476.5 Liability for Certain Acts

1.   A staff member or agent of ASIS, DIGO or DSD (the *agency*) is not subject to any civil or criminal liability for any computer-related act done outside Australia if the act is done in the proper performance of a function of the agency.

2.   A person is not subject to any civil or criminal liability for any act done inside Australia if:

    a.   the act is preparatory to, in support of, or otherwise directly connected with, overseas activities of the agency concerned; and

    b.   the act:

        i.   taken together with a computer-related act, event, circumstance or result that took place, or was intended to take place, outside Australia, could amount to an offence; but

        ii.   in the absence of that computer-related act, event, circumstance or result, would not amount to an offence; and

    c.   the act is done in the proper performance of a function of the agency.

        2A. Subsection (2) is not intended to permit any act in relation to premises, persons, computers, things, or carriage services in Australia, being:

        a.   an act that ASIO could not do without a Minister authorising it by warrant issued under Division 2 of Part III of the *Australian Security Intelligence Organisation Act 1979* or under Part 2-2 of the *Telecommunications (Interception and Access) Act 1979*; or

        b.   an act to obtain information that ASIO could not obtain other than in accordance with Division 3 of Part 4-1 of the *Telecommunications (Interception and Access) Act 1979*.

        2B. The Inspector-General of Intelligence and Security may give a certificate in writing certifying any fact relevant to the question of whether an act was done in the proper performance of a function of an agency.

2C. In any proceedings, a certificate given under subsection (2B) is prima facie evidence of the facts certified.

3.   In this section:

ASIS means the Australian Secret Intelligence Service.

civil or criminal liability means any civil or criminal liability (whether under this Part, under another law or otherwise).

computer-related act, event, circumstance or result means an act, event, circumstance or result involving:
- a.   the reliability, security or operation of a computer; or
- b.   access to, or modification of, data held in a computer or on a data storage device; or
- c.   electronic communication to or from a computer; or
- d.   the reliability, security or operation of any data held in or on a computer, computer disk, credit card, or other data storage device; or
- e.   possession or control of data held in a computer or on a data storage device; or
- f.   producing, supplying or obtaining data held in a computer or on a data storage device.

DIGO means that part of the Department of Defence known as the Defence Imagery and Geospatial Organisation.

DSD means that part of the Department of Defence known as the Defence Signals Directorate.

staff member means:
- a.   in relation to ASIS—the Director-General of ASIS or a member of the staff of ASIS (whether an employee of ASIS, a consultant or contractor to ASIS, or a person who is made available by another Commonwealth or State authority or other person to perform services for ASIS); and
- b.   in relation to DSD—the Director of DSD or a member of the staff of DSD (whether an employee of DSD, a consultant or contractor to DSD, or a person who is made available by another Commonwealth or State authority or other person to perform services for DSD); and
- c.   in relation to DIGO—the Director of DIGO or a member of the staff of DIGO (whether an employee of DIGO, a consultant or contractor to DIGO, or a person who is made available by another Commonwealth or State authority or other person to perform services for DIGO).

Division 477—Serious Computer Offences

Section 477.1 Unauthorised Access, Modification or Impairment with Intent to Commit a Serious Offence

Intention to commit a serious Commonwealth, State or Territory offence

1.   A person is guilty of an offence if:
- a.   the person causes:
  - i.   any unauthorised access to data held in a computer; or
  - ii.   any unauthorised modification of data held in a computer; or

iii.   any unauthorised impairment of electronic communication to or from a computer; and
    b.   the unauthorised access, modification or impairment is caused by means of a carriage service; and
    c.   the person knows the access, modification or impairment is unauthorised; and
    d.   the person intends to commit, or facilitate the commission of, a serious offence against a law of the Commonwealth, a State or a Territory (whether by that person or another person) by the access, modification or impairment.

2.   Absolute liability applies to paragraph (1)(b).

3.   In a prosecution for an offence against subsection (1), it is not necessary to prove that the defendant knew that the offence was:
    a.   an offence against a law of the Commonwealth, a State or a Territory; or
    b.   a serious offence.

Intention to commit a serious Commonwealth offence

4.   A person is guilty of an offence if:
    a.   the person causes:
       i.   any unauthorised access to data held in a computer; or
       ii.   any unauthorised modification of data held in a computer; or
   iii any unauthorised impairment of electronic communication to or from a computer; and
    b.   the person knows the access, modification or impairment is unauthorised; and
    c.   the person intends to commit, or facilitate the commission of, a serious offence against a law of the Commonwealth (whether by that person or another person) by the access, modification or impairment.

5.   In a prosecution for an offence against subsection (3), it is not necessary to prove that the defendant knew that the offence was:
    a.   an offence against a law of the Commonwealth; or
    b.   a serious offence.

Penalty

6.   A person who is guilty of an offence against this section is punishable, on conviction, by a penalty not exceeding the penalty applicable to the serious offence.

Impossibility

7.   A person may be found guilty of an offence against this section even if committing the serious offence is impossible.

No offence of attempt

8.   It is not an offence to attempt to commit an offence against this section.

Meaning of serious offence

9. In this section:

serious offence means an offence that is punishable by imprisonment for life or a period of 5 or more years.

Section 477.2 Unauthorised Modification of Data to Cause Impairment

1. A person is guilty of an offence if:
   a. the person causes any unauthorised modification of data held in a computer; and
   b. the person knows the modification is unauthorised; and
   c. the person is reckless as to whether the modification impairs or will impair:
      i. access to that or any other data held in any computer; or
      ii. the reliability, security or operation, of any such data; and
   d. one or more of the following applies:
      i. the data that is modified is held in a Commonwealth computer;
      ii. the data that is modified is held on behalf of the Commonwealth in a computer;
      iii. the modification of the data is caused by means of a carriage service;
      iv. the modification of the data is caused by means of a Commonwealth computer;
      v. the modification of the data impairs access to, or the reliability, security or operation of, other data held in a Commonwealth computer;
      vi. the modification of the data impairs access to, or the reliability, security or operation of, other data held on behalf of the Commonwealth in a computer;
      vii. the modification of the data impairs access to, or the reliability, security or operation of, other data by means of a carriage service.

   Penalty: 10 years imprisonment.

2. Absolute liability applies to paragraph (1)(d).
3. A person may be guilty of an offence against this section even if there is or will be no actual impairment to:
   a. access to data held in a computer; or
   b. the reliability, security or operation, of any such data.
4. A conviction for an offence against this section is an alternative verdict to a charge for an offence against section 477.3 (unauthorised impairment of electronic communication).

Section 477.3 Unauthorised Impairment of Electronic Communication

1. A person is guilty of an offence if:
   a. the person causes any unauthorised impairment of electronic communication to or from a computer; and
   b. the person knows that the impairment is unauthorised; and
   c. one or both of the following applies:
      i. the electronic communication is sent to or from the computer by means of a carriage service;

ii. the electronic communication is sent to or from a Commonwealth computer.

Penalty: 10 years imprisonment.

2. Absolute liability applies to paragraph (1)(c).
3. A conviction for an offence against this section is an alternative verdict to a charge for an offence against section 477.2 (unauthorised modification of data to cause impairment).

Division 478—Other Computer Offences

Section 478.1 Unauthorised Access to, or Modification of, Restricted Data

1. A person is guilty of an offence if:
   a. the person causes any unauthorised access to, or modification of, restricted data; and
   b. the person intends to cause the access or modification; and
   c. the person knows that the access or modification is unauthorised; and
   d. one or more of the following applies:
      i. the restricted data is held in a Commonwealth computer;
      ii. the restricted data is held on behalf of the Commonwealth;
      iii. the access to, or modification of, the restricted data is caused by means of a carriage service.

Penalty: 2 years imprisonment.

2. Absolute liability applies to paragraph (1)(d).
3. In this section:

   restricted data means data:
   a. held in a computer; and
   b. to which access is restricted by an access control system associated with a function of the computer.

Section 478.2 Unauthorised Impairment of Data Held on a Computer Disk Etc.

1. A person is guilty of an offence if:
   a. the person causes any unauthorised impairment of the reliability, security or operation of data held on:
      i. a computer disk; or
      ii. a credit card; or
      iii. another device used to store data by electronic means; and
   b. the person intends to cause the impairment; and
   c. the person knows that the impairment is unauthorised; and
   d. the computer disk, credit card or other device is owned or leased by a Commonwealth entity.

Penalty: 2 years imprisonment.

2.   Absolute liability applies to paragraph (1)(d).

Section 478.3 Possession or Control of Data with Intent to Commit a Computer Offence

1.   A person is guilty of an offence if:
   a.   the person has possession or control of data; and
   b.   the person has that possession or control with the intention that the data be used, by the person or another person, in:
        i.   committing an offence against Division 477; or
        ii.   facilitating the commission of such an offence.

Penalty: 3 years imprisonment.

2.   A person may be found guilty of an offence against this section even if committing the offence against Division 477 is impossible.

No offence of attempt

3.   It is not an offence to attempt to commit an offence against this section.

Meaning of possession or control of data

4.   In this section, a reference to a person having possession or control of data includes a reference to the person:
   a.   having possession of a computer or data storage device that holds or contains the data; or
   b.   having possession of a document in which the data is recorded; or
   c.   having control of data held in a computer that is in the possession of another person (whether inside or outside Australia).

Section 478.4 Producing, Supplying or Obtaining Data with Intent to Commit a Computer Offence

1.   A person is guilty of an offence if:
   a.   the person produces, supplies or obtains data; and
   b.   the person does so with the intention that the data be used, by the person or another person, in:
        i.   committing an offence against Division 477; or
        ii.   facilitating the commission of such an offence.

Penalty: 3 years imprisonment.

2. A person may be found guilty of an offence against this section even if committing the offence against Division 477 is impossible.

No offence of attempt

3. It is not an offence to attempt to commit an offence against this section.

Meaning of producing, supplying or obtaining data

4. In this section, a reference to a person producing, supplying or obtaining data includes a reference to the person:
   a. producing, supplying or obtaining data held or contained in a computer or data storage device; or
   b. producing, supplying or obtaining a document in which the data is recorded.

Relevant Provisions of Cyber Crime Act, 2001, of Australia

Division 477—Serious Computer Offences

477.1 Unauthorised Access, Modification or Impairment with Intent to Commit a Serious Offence

Intention to commit a serious Commonwealth, State or Territory offence

1. A person is guilty of an offence if:
   a. the person causes:
      i. any unauthorised access to data held in a computer; or
      ii. any unauthorised modification of data held in a computer; or
      iii. any unauthorised impairment of electronic communication to or from a computer; and
   b. the unauthorised access, modification or impairment is caused by means of a telecommunications service; and
   c. the person knows the access, modification or impairment is unauthorised; and
   d. the person intends to commit, or facilitate the commission of, a serious offence against a law of the Commonwealth, a State or a Territory (whether by that person or another person) by the access, modification or impairment.
2. Absolute liability applies to paragraph (1)(b).
3. In a prosecution for an offence against subsection (1), it is not necessary to prove that the defendant knew that the offence was:
   a. an offence against a law of the Commonwealth, a State or a Territory; or
   b. a serious offence.

Intention to commit a serious Commonwealth offence

4. A person is guilty of an offence if:
    a. the person causes:
        i. any unauthorised access to data held in a computer; or
        ii. any unauthorised modification of data held in a computer; or
        iii. any unauthorised impairment of electronic communication to or from a computer; and
    b. the person knows the access, modification or impairment is unauthorised; and
    c. the person intends to commit, or facilitate the commission of, a serious offence against a law of the Commonwealth (whether by that person or another person) by the access, modification or impairment.

5. In a prosecution for an offence against subsection (3), it is not necessary to prove that the defendant knew that the offence was:
    a. an offence against a law of the Commonwealth; or
    b. a serious offence.

Penalty

6. A person who is guilty of an offence against this section is punishable, on conviction, by a penalty not exceeding the penalty applicable to the serious offence.

Impossibility

7. A person may be found guilty of an offence against this section even if committing the serious offence is impossible.

No offence of attempt

8. It is not an offence to attempt to commit an offence against this section.

Meaning of serious offence

9. In this section:

serious offence means an offence that is punishable by imprisonment for life or a period of 5 or more years.

477.2 Unauthorised Modification of Data to Cause Impairment

1. A person is guilty of an offence if:
    a. the person causes any unauthorised modification of data held in a computer; and
    b. the person knows the modification is unauthorised; and
    c. the person is reckless as to whether the modification impairs or will impair:
        i. access to that or any other data held in any computer; or
        ii. the reliability, security or operation, of any such data; and
    d. one or more of the following applies:

    i.   the data that is modified is held in a Commonwealth computer;

    ii.   the data that is modified is held on behalf of the Commonwealth in a computer;

    iii. the modification of the data is caused by means of a telecommunications service;

    iv. the modification of the data is caused by means of a Commonwealth computer;

    v.   the modification of the data impairs access to, or the reliability, security or operation of, other data held in a Commonwealth computer;

    vi. the modification of the data impairs access to, or the reliability, security or operation of, other data held on behalf of the Commonwealth in a computer;

    vii. the modification of the data impairs access to, or the reliability, security or operation of, other data by means of a telecommunications service.

Penalty: 10 years imprisonment.

2.   Absolute liability applies to paragraph (1)(d).

3.   A person may be guilty of an offence against this section even if there is or will be no actual impairment to:

    a.   access to data held in a computer; or

    b.   the reliability, security or operation, of any such data.

4.   A conviction for an offence against this section is an alternative verdict to a charge for an offence against section 477.3 (unauthorised impairment of electronic communication).

477.3 Unauthorised Impairment of Electronic Communication

1.   A person is guilty of an offence if:

    a.   the person causes any unauthorised impairment of electronic communication to or from a computer; and

    b.   the person knows that the impairment is unauthorised; and

    c.   one or both of the following applies:

       i.   the electronic communication is sent to or from the computer by means of a telecommunications service;

       ii. the electronic communication is sent to or from a Commonwealth computer.

Penalty: 10 years imprisonment.

2.   Absolute liability applies to paragraph (1)(c).

3.   A conviction for an offence against this section is an alternative verdict to a charge for an offence against section 477.2 (unauthorised modification of data to cause impairment).

Division 478—Other Computer Offences

478.1 Unauthorised Access to, or Modification of, Restricted Data

1.   A person is guilty of an offence if:

    a.   the person causes any unauthorised access to, or modification of, restricted data; and

b. the person intends to cause the access or modification; and
c. the person knows that the access or modification is unauthorised; and
d. one or more of the following applies:
    i. the restricted data is held in a Commonwealth computer;
    ii. the restricted data is held on behalf of the Commonwealth;
    iii. the access to, or modification of, the restricted data is caused by means of a telecommunications service.

Penalty: 2 years imprisonment.

2. Absolute liability applies to paragraph (1)(d).
3. In this section:

restricted data means data:
    a. held in a computer; and
    b. to which access is restricted by an access control system associated with a function of the computer.

478.2 Unauthorised Impairment of Data Held on a Computer Disk Etc.

1. A person is guilty of an offence if:
    a. the person causes any unauthorised impairment of the reliability, security or operation of data held on:
        i. a computer disk; or
        ii. a credit card; or
        iii. another device used to store data by electronic means; and
    b. the person intends to cause the impairment; and
    c. the person knows that the impairment is unauthorised; and
    d. the computer disk, credit card or other device is owned or leased by a Commonwealth entity.

Penalty: 2 years imprisonment.

2. Absolute liability applies to paragraph (1)(d).

478.3 Possession or Control of Data with Intent to Commit a Computer Offence

1. A person is guilty of an offence if:
    a. the person has possession or control of data; and
    b. the person has that possession or control with the intention that the data be used, by the person or another person, in:
        i. committing an offence against Division 477; or
        ii. facilitating the commission of such an offence.

Penalty: 3 years imprisonment.

2.   A person may be found guilty of an offence against this section even if committing the offence against Division 477 is impossible.

No offence of attempt

3.   It is not an offence to attempt to commit an offence against this section.

Meaning of possession or control of data

4.   In this section, a reference to a person having possession or control of data includes a reference to the person:
   a.   having possession of a computer or data storage device that holds or contains the data; or
   b.   having possession of a document in which the data is recorded; or
   c.   having control of data held in a computer that is in the possession of another person (whether inside or outside Australia).

478.4 Producing, Supplying or Obtaining Data with Intent to Commit a Computer Offence

1.   A person is guilty of an offence if:
   a.   the person produces, supplies or obtains data; and
   b.   the person does so with the intention that the data be used, by the person or another person, in:
      i.   committing an offence against Division 477; or
      ii.   facilitating the commission of such an offence.

Penalty: 3 years imprisonment.

2.   A person may be found guilty of an offence against this section even if committing the offence against Division 477 is impossible.

No offence of attempt

3.   It is not an offence to attempt to commit an offence against this section.

Meaning of producing, supplying or obtaining data

4.   In this section, a reference to a person producing, supplying or obtaining data includes a reference to the person:
   a.   producing, supplying or obtaining data held or contained in a computer or data storage device; or
   b.   producing, supplying or obtaining a document in which the data is recorded.

data storage device means a thing containing, or designed to contain, data for use by a computer.

APPENDIX 10

Relevant Provisions from Information Technology Act, 2000. [As Amended by Information Technology (Amendment) Act 2008][8]

Chapter IX: Penalties, Compensation and Adjudication

Section 43. Penalty and Compensation for Damage to Computer, Computer System, etc

If any person without permission of the owner or any other person who is in charge of a computer, computer system or computer network -

a.   accesses or secures access to such computer, computer system or computer network or computer resource

b.   downloads, copies or extracts any data, computer data base or information from such computer, computer system or computer network including information or data held or stored in any removable storage medium;

c.   introduces or causes to be introduced any computer contaminant or computer virus into any computer, computer system or computer network;

d.   damages or causes to be damaged any computer, computer system or computer network, data, computer data base or any other programmes residing in such computer, computer system or computer network;

e.   disrupts or causes disruption of any computer, computer system or computer network;

f.   denies or causes the denial of access to any person authorised to access any computer, computer system or computer network by any means;

g.   provides any assistance to any person to facilitate access to a computer, computer system or computer network in contravention of the provisions of this Act, rules or regulations made thereunder,

h.   charges the services availed of by a person to the account of another person by tampering with or manipulating any computer, computer system, or computer network,

i.   destroys, deletes or alters any information residing in a computer resource or diminishes its value or utility or affects it injuriously by any means

j.   Steals, conceals, destroys or alters or causes any person to steal, conceal, destroy or alter any computer source code used for a computer resource with an intention to cause damage, he shall be liable to pay damages by way of compensation not exceeding one crore rupees to the person so affected.

Explanation - for the purposes of this section -

i.   "Computer Contaminant" means any set of computer instructions that are designed -
    a.   to modify, destroy, record, transmit data or programme residing within a computer, computer system or computer network; or
    b.   by any means to usurp the normal operation of the computer, computer system, or computer network;

ii. "Computer Database" means a representation of information, knowledge, facts, concepts or instructions in text, image, audio, video that are being prepared or have been prepared in a formalised manner or have been produced by a computer, computer system or computer network and are intended for use in a computer, computer system or computer network;

iii. "Computer Virus" means any computer instruction, information, data or programme that destroys, damages, degrades or adversely affects the performance of a computer resource or attaches itself to another computer resource and operates when a programme, data or instruction is executed or some other event takes place in that computer resource;

iv. "Damage" means to destroy, alter, delete, add, modify or re-arrange any computer resource by any means.(v) "Computer Source code" means the listing of programmes, computer commands, design and layout and programme analysis of computer resource in any form

Section 43 A. Compensation for Failure to Protect Data

Where a body corporate, possessing, dealing or handling any sensitive personal data or information in a computer resource which it owns, controls or operates, is negligent in implementing and maintaining reasonable security practices and procedures and thereby causes wrongful loss or wrongful gain to any person, such body corporate shall be liable to pay damages by way of compensation, not exceeding five crore rupees, to the person so affected.

Explanation: For the purposes of this section

i. "body corporate" means any company and includes a firm, sole proprietorship or other association of individuals engaged in commercial or professional activities

ii. "reasonable security practices and procedures" means security practices and procedures designed to protect such information from unauthorised access, damage, use, modification, disclosure or impairment, as may be specified in an agreement between the parties or as may be specified in any law for the time being in force and in the absence of such agreement or any law, such reasonable security practices and procedures, as may be prescribed by the Central Government in consultation with such professional bodies or associations as it may deem fit.

iii. "sensitive personal data or information" means such personal information as may be prescribed by the Central Government in consultation with such professional bodies or associations as it may deem fit.

Chapter XI: Offences

Section 65. Tampering with Computer Source Documents

Whoever knowingly or intentionally conceals, destroys or alters or intentionally or knowingly causes another to conceal, destroy or alter any computer source code used for a computer, computer programme, computer system or computer network, when the computer source code is required to be kept or maintained by law for the time being in force, shall be punishable with imprisonment up to three years, or with fine which may extend up to two lakh rupees, or with both.

Explanation -

For the purposes of this section, "Computer Source Code" means the listing of programmes, Computer Commands, Design and layout and programme analysis of computer resource in any form.

Section 66. Computer Related Offences

If any person, dishonestly, or fraudulently, does any act referred to in section 43, he shall be punishable with imprisonment for a term which may extend to three years or with fine which may extend to five lakh rupees or with both.

Explanation: For the purpose of this section,-

a. the word "dishonestly" shall have the meaning assigned to it in section 24 of the Indian Penal Code;
b. the word "fraudulently" shall have the meaning assigned to it in section 25 of the Indian Penal Code.

Section 66 A. Punishment for Sending Offensive Messages through Communication Service, Etc

Any person who sends, by means of a computer resource or a communication device,-

a. any information that is grossly offensive or has menacing character; or
b. any information which he knows to be false, but for the purpose of causing annoyance, inconvenience, danger, obstruction, insult, injury, criminal intimidation, enmity, hatred, or ill will, persistently makes by making use of such computer resource or a communication device,
c. any electronic mail or electronic mail message for the purpose of causing annoyance or inconvenience or to deceive or to mislead the addressee or recipient about the origin of such messages shall be punishable with imprisonment for a term which may extend to three years and with fine.

Explanation: For the purposes of this section, terms "Electronic mail" and "Electronic Mail Message" means a message or information created or transmitted or received on a computer, computer system, computer resource or communication device including attachments in text, image, audio, video and any other electronic record, which may be transmitted with the message.

Section 66 B. Punishment for Dishonestly Receiving Stolen Computer Resource or Communication Device

Whoever dishonestly receives or retains any stolen computer resource or communication device knowing or having reason to believe the same to be stolen computer resource or communication device, shall be punished with imprisonment of either description for a term which may extend to three years or with fine which may extend to rupees one lakh or with both.

Section 66 C. Punishment for Identity Theft

Whoever, fraudulently or dishonestly make use of the electronic signature, password or any other unique identification feature of any other person, shall be punished with imprisonment of either description for a term which may extend to three years and shall also be liable to fine which may extend to rupees one lakh.

Section 66 D. Punishment for Cheating by Personation by Using Computer Resource

Whoever, by means of any communication device or computer resource cheats by personation, shall be punished with imprisonment of either description for a term which may extend to three years and shall also be liable to fine which may extend to one lakh rupees.

Section 66 E. Punishment for Violation of Privacy

Whoever, intentionally or knowingly captures, publishes or transmits the image of a private area of any person without his or her consent, under circumstances violating the privacy of that person, shall be punished with imprisonment which may extend to three years or with fine not exceeding two lakh rupees, or with both Explanation.- For the purposes of this section—

a. "transmit" means to electronically send a visual image with the intent that it be viewed by a person or persons;
b. "capture", with respect to an image, means to videotape, photograph, film or record by any means;
c. "private area" means the naked or undergarment clad genitals, pubic area, buttocks or female breast;
d. "publishes" means reproduction in the printed or electronic form and making it available for public;
e. "under circumstances violating privacy" means circumstances in which a person can have a reasonable expectation that—
    i. he or she could disrobe in privacy, without being concerned that an image of his private area was being captured; or
    ii. any part of his or her private area would not be visible to the public, regardless of whether that person is in a public or private place.

Section 66 F. Punishment for Cyber Terrorism

1. Whoever,-
    A. with intent to threaten the unity, integrity, security or sovereignty of India or to strike terror in the people or any section of the people by –
        i. denying or cause the denial of access to any person authorized to access computer resource; or
        ii. attempting to penetrate or access a computer resource without authorisation or exceeding authorized access; or
        iii. introducing or causing to introduce any Computer Contaminant. and by means of such conduct causes or is likely to cause death or injuries to persons or damage to or destruction of property or disrupts or knowing that it is likely to cause damage or disruption of

supplies or services essential to the life of the community or adversely affect the critical information infrastructure specified under section 70, or

B. knowingly or intentionally penetrates or accesses a computer resource without authorisation or exceeding authorized access, and by means of such conduct obtains access to information, data or computer database that is restricted for reasons of the security of the State or foreign relations; or any restricted information, data or computer database, with reasons to believe that such information, data or computer database so obtained may be used to cause or likely to cause injury to the interests of the sovereignty and integrity of India, the security of the State, friendly relations with foreign States, public order, decency or morality, or in relation to contempt of court, defamation or incitement to an offence, or to the advantage of any foreign nation, group of individuals or otherwise, commits the offence of cyber terrorism.

2. Whoever commits or conspires to commit cyber terrorism shall be punishable with imprisonment which may extend to imprisonment for life'.

Section 67. Punishment for Publishing or Transmitting Obscene Material in Electronic Form

Whoever publishes or transmits or causes to be published in the electronic form, any material which is lascivious or appeals to the prurient interest or if its effect is such as to tend to deprave and corrupt persons who are likely, having regard to all relevant circumstances, to read, see or hear the matter contained or embodied in it, shall be punished on first conviction with imprisonment of either description for a term which may extend to three years and with fine which may extend to five lakh rupees and in the event of a second or subsequent conviction with imprisonment of either description for a term which may extend to five years and also with fine which may extend to ten lakh rupees.

Section 67 A. Punishment for Publishing or Transmitting of Material Containing Sexually Explicit Act, Etc. in Electronic Form

Whoever publishes or transmits or causes to be published or transmitted in the electronic form any material which contains sexually explicit act or conduct shall be punished on first conviction with imprisonment of either description for a term which may extend to five years and with fine which may extend to ten lakh rupees and in the event of second or subsequent conviction with imprisonment of either description for a term which may extend to seven years and also with fine which may extend to ten lakh rupees.

Exception: This section and section 67 does not extend to any book, pamphlet, paper, writing, drawing, painting, representation or figure in electronic form-

i. the publication of which is proved to be justified as being for the public good on the ground that such book, pamphlet, paper, writing, drawing, painting, representation or figure is in the interest of science, literature, art, or learning or other objects of general concern; or

ii. which is kept or used bona fide for religious purposes.

Section 67 B. Punishment for Publishing or Transmitting of Material Depicting Children in Sexually Explicit Act, Etc. in Electronic Form

Whoever,-

a. publishes or transmits or causes to be published or transmitted material in any electronic form which depicts children engaged in sexually explicit act or conduct or
b. creates text or digital images, collects, seeks, browses, downloads, advertises, promotes, exchanges or distributes material in any electronic form depicting children in obscene or indecent or sexually explicit manner or
c. cultivates, entices or induces children to online relationship with one or more children for and on sexually explicit act or in a manner that may offend a reasonable adult on the computer resource or
d. facilitates abusing children online or
e. records in any electronic form own abuse or that of others pertaining to sexually explicit act with children, shall be punished on first conviction with imprisonment of either description for a term which may extend to five years and with a fine which may extend to ten lakh rupees and in the event of second or subsequent conviction with imprisonment of either description for a term which may extend to seven years and also with fine which may extend to ten lakh rupees:

Provided that the provisions of section 67, section 67A and this section does not extend to any book, pamphlet, paper, writing, drawing, painting, representation or figure in electronic form-

i.   The publication of which is proved to be justified as being for the public good on the ground that such book, pamphlet, paper writing, drawing, painting, representation or figure is in the interest of science, literature, art or learning or other objects of general concern; or
ii. which is kept or used for bonafide heritage or religious purposes Explanation: For the purposes of this section, "children" means a person who has not completed the age of 18 years.

Section 67 C. Preservation and Retention of Information by Intermediaries

1. Intermediary shall preserve and retain such information as may be specified for such duration and in such manner and format as the Central Government may prescribe.
2. Any intermediary who intentionally or knowingly contravenes the provisions of sub section (1) shall be punished with an imprisonment for a term which may extend to three years and shall also be liable to fine.

Section 68. Power of Controller to Give Directions

1. The Controller may, by order, direct a Certifying Authority or any employee of such Authority to take such measures or cease carrying on such activities as specified in the order if those are necessary to ensure compliance with the provisions of this Act, rules or any regulations made there under.

2. Any person who intentionally or knowingly fails to comply with any order under sub-section (1) shall be guilty of an offence and shall be liable on conviction to imprisonment for a term not exceeding two years or to a fine not exceeding one lakh rupees or to both.

Section 69. Powers to Issue Directions for Interception or Monitoring or Decryption of Any Information through Any Computer Resource

1. Where the central Government or a State Government or any of its officer specially authorized by the Central Government or the State Government, as the case may be, in this behalf may, if is satisfied that it is necessary or expedient to do in the interest of the sovereignty or integrity of India, defense of India, security of the State, friendly relations with foreign States or public order or for preventing incitement to the commission of any cognizable offence relating to above or for investigation of any offence, it may, subject to the provisions of sub-section (2), for reasons to be recorded in writing, by order, direct any agency of the appropriate Government to intercept, monitor or decrypt or cause to be intercepted or monitored or decrypted any information transmitted received or stored through any computer resource.

2. The Procedure and safeguards subject to which such interception or monitoring or decryption may be carried out, shall be such as may be prescribed

3. The subscriber or intermediary or any person in charge of the computer resource shall, when called upon by any agency which has been directed under sub section (1), extend all facilities and technical assistance to -
    a. provide access to or secure access to the computer resource containing such information; generating, transmitting, receiving or storing such information; or
    b. intercept or monitor or decrypt the information, as the case may be; or © provide information stored in computer resource.

4. The subscriber or intermediary or any person who fails to assist the agency referred to in sub-section (3) shall be punished with an imprisonment for a term which may extend to seven years and shall also be liable to fine.

Section 69 A. Power to Issue Directions for Blocking for Public Access of Any Information through Any Computer Resource

1. Where the Central Government or any of its officer specially authorized by it in this behalf is satisfied that it is necessary or expedient so to do in the interest of sovereignty and integrity of India, defense of India, security of the State, friendly relations with foreign states or public order or for preventing incitement to the commission of any cognizable offence relating to above, it may subject to the provisions of sub-sections (2) for reasons to be recorded in writing, by order direct any agency of the Government or intermediary to block access by the public or cause to be blocked for access by public any information generated, transmitted, received, stored or hosted in any computer resource.

2. The procedure and safeguards subject to which such blocking for access by the public may be carried out shall be such as may be prescribed.

3. The intermediary who fails to comply with the direction issued under subsection (1) shall be punished with an imprisonment for a term which may extend to seven years and also be liable to fine.

Section 69 B. Power to Authorize to Monitor and Collect Traffic Data or Information through Any Computer Resource for Cyber Security

1. The Central Government may, to enhance Cyber Security and for identification, analysis and prevention of any intrusion or spread of computer contaminant in the country, by notification in the official Gazette, authorize any agency of the Government to monitor and collect traffic data or information generated, transmitted, received or stored in any computer resource.
2. The Intermediary or any person in-charge of the Computer resource shall when called upon by the agency which has been authorized under sub-section (1), provide technical assistance and extend all facilities to such agency to enable online access or to secure and provide online access to the computer resource generating, transmitting, receiving or storing such traffic data or information.
3. The procedure and safeguards for monitoring and collecting traffic data or information, shall be such as may be prescribed.
4. Any intermediary who intentionally or knowingly contravenes the provisions of sub-section (2) shall be punished with an imprisonment for a term which may extend to three years and shall also be liable to fine.

    Explanation: For the purposes of this section,
    i.   "Computer Contaminant" shall have the meaning assigned to it in section 43
    ii. "traffic data" means any data identifying or purporting to identify any person, computer system or computer network or location to or from which the communication is or may be transmitted and includes communications origin, destination, route, time, date, size, duration or type of underlying service or any other information.

Section 70. Protected System

1. The appropriate Government may, by notification in the Official Gazette, declare any computer resource which directly or indirectly affects the facility of Critical Information Infrastructure, to be a protected system. Explanation: For the purposes of this section, "Critical Information Infrastructure" means the computer resource, the incapacitation or destruction of which, shall have debilitating impact on national security, economy, public health or safety.
2. The appropriate Government may, by order in writing, authorize the persons who are authorized to access protected systems notified under sub-section (1)
3. Any person who secures access or attempts to secure access to a protected system in contravention of the provisions of this section shall be punished with imprisonment of either description for a term which may extend to ten years and shall also be liable to fine.
4. The Central Government shall prescribe the information security practices and procedures for such protected system.

Section 70 A. National Nodal Agency

1. The Central Government may, by notification published in the official Gazette, designate any organization of the Government as the national nodal agency in respect of Critical Information Infrastructure Protection.

2. The national nodal agency designated under sub-section (1) shall be responsible for all measures including Research and Development relating to protection of Critical Information Infrastructure.
3. The manner of performing functions and duties of the agency referred to in sub-section (1) shall be such as may be prescribed.

Section 70 B. Indian Computer Emergency Response Team to Serve as National Agency for Incident Response

1. The Central Government shall, by notification in the Official Gazette, appoint an agency of the government to be called the Indian Computer Emergency Response Team.
2. The Central Government shall provide the agency referred to in sub-section (1) with a Director General and such other officers and employees as may be prescribed.
3. The salary and allowances and terms and conditions of the Director General and other officers and employees shall be such as may be prescribed.
4. The Indian Computer Emergency Response Team shall serve as the national agency for performing the following functions in the area of Cyber Security,-
   a. collection, analysis and dissemination of information on cyber incidents
   b. forecast and alerts of cyber security incidents © emergency measures for handling cyber security incidents
      d. coordination of cyber incidents response activities
      e. issue guidelines, advisories, vulnerability notes and white papers relating to information security practices, procedures, prevention, response and reporting of cyber incidents
      f. such other functions relating to cyber security as may be prescribed
5. The manner of performing functions and duties of the agency referred to in sub-section (1) shall be such as may be prescribed.
6. For carrying out the provisions of sub-section (4), the agency referred to in sub-section (1) may call for information and give direction to the service providers, intermediaries, data centers, body corporate and any other person
7. Any service provider, intermediaries, data centers, body corporate or person who fails to provide the information called for or comply with the direction under sub-section (6), shall be punishable with imprisonment for a term which may extend to one year or with fine which may extend to one lakh rupees or with both.
8. No Court shall take cognizance of any offence under this section, except on a complaint made by an officer authorized in this behalf by the agency referred to in sub-section (1).

Section 71. Penalty for Misrepresentation

Whoever makes any misrepresentation to, or suppresses any material fact from, the Controller or the Certifying Authority for obtaining any license or Electronic Signature Certificate, as the case may be, shall be punished with imprisonment for a term which may extend to two years, or with fine which may extend to one lakh rupees, or with both.

Section 72. Breach of Confidentiality and Privacy

Save as otherwise provided in this Act or any other law for the time being in force, any person who, in pursuant of any of the powers conferred under this Act, rules or regulations made there under, has secured access to any electronic record, book, register, correspondence, information, document or other material without the consent of the person concerned discloses such electronic record, book, register, correspondence, information, document or other material to any other person shall be punished with imprisonment for a term which may extend to two years, or with fine which may extend to one lakh rupees, or with both.

Section 72 A. Punishment for Disclosure of Information in Breach of Lawful Contract

Save as otherwise provided in this Act or any other law for the time being in force, any person including an intermediary who, while providing services under the terms of lawful contract, has secured access to any material containing personal information about another person, with the intent to cause or knowing that he is likely to cause wrongful loss or wrongful gain discloses, without the consent of the person concerned, or in breach of a lawful contract, such material to any other person shall be punished with imprisonment for a term which may extend to three years, or with a fine which may extend to five lakh rupees, or with both.

Section 73. Penalty for Publishing Electronic Signature Certificate False in Certain Particulars

1. No person shall publish a Electronic Signature Certificate or otherwise make it available to any other person with the knowledge that
   a. the Certifying Authority listed in the certificate has not issued it; or
   b. the subscriber listed in the certificate has not accepted it; or
   c. the certificate has been revoked or suspended, unless such publication is for the purpose of verifying a digital signature created prior to such suspension or revocation.
2. Any person who contravenes the provisions of sub-section (1) shall be punished with imprisonment for a term which may extend to two years, or with fine which may extend to one lakh rupees, or with both.

Section 74. Publication for Fraudulent Purpose

Whoever knowingly creates, publishes or otherwise makes available a Electronic Signature Certificate for any fraudulent or unlawful purpose shall be punished with imprisonment for a term which may extend to two years, or with fine which may extend to one lakh rupees, or with both

Section 75. Act to Apply for Offence or Contraventions Committed Outside India

1. Subject to the provisions of sub-section (2), the provisions of this Act shall apply also to any offence or contravention committed outside India by any person irrespective of his nationality.

2. For the purposes of sub-section (1), this Act shall apply to an offence or contravention committed outside India by any person if the act or conduct constituting the offence or contravention involves a computer, computer system or computer network located in India.

Section 76. Confiscation

Any computer, computer system, floppies, compact disks, tape drives or any other accessories related thereto, in respect of which any provision of this Act, rules, orders or regulations made there under has been or is being contravened, shall be liable to confiscation:

Provided that where it is established to the satisfaction of the court adjudicating the confiscation that the person in whose possession, power or control of any such computer, computer system, floppies, compact disks, tape drives or any other accessories relating thereto is found is not responsible for the contravention of the provisions of this Act, rules, orders or regulations made there under, the court may, instead of making an order for confiscation of such computer, computer system, floppies, compact disks, tape drives or any other accessories related thereto, make such other order authorized by this Act against the person contravening of the provisions of this Act, rules, orders or regulations made there under as it may think fit.

Section 77. Compensation, Penalties or Confiscation not to Interfere with Other Punishment

No compensation awarded, penalty imposed or confiscation made under this Act shall prevent the award of compensation or imposition of any other penalty or punishment under any other law for the time being in force.

Section 77 A. Compounding of Offences

1. A Court of competent jurisdiction may compound offences other than offences for which the punishment for life or imprisonment for a term exceeding three years has been provided under this Act.

Provided that the Court shall not compound such offence where the accused is by reason of his previous conviction, liable to either enhanced punishment or to a punishment of a different kind.

Provided further that the Court shall not compound any offence where such offence affects the socio-economic conditions of the country or has been committed against a child below the age of 18 years or a woman.

2. The person accused of an offence under this act may file an application for compounding in the court in which offence is pending for trial and the provisions of section 265 B and 265 C of Code of Criminal Procedures, 1973 shall apply.

Section 77 B. Offences with Three Years Imprisonment to be Cognizable

1. Notwithstanding anything contained in Criminal Procedure Code 1973, the offence punishable with imprisonment of three years and above shall be cognizable and the offence punishable with imprisonment of three years shall be bailable.

Section 78. Power to Investigate Offences

Notwithstanding anything contained in the Code of Criminal Procedure, 1973, a police officer not below the rank of Inspector shall investigate any offence under this Act.

ENDNOTES

1. Main text of the Criminal Code is available at http://laws.justice.gc.ca/eng/C-46/index.html
2. Main text of this Act is available @ http://www.opsi.gov.uk/acts/acts1997/ukpga_19970040_en_1
3. The main text of the Act is available at http://www.opsi.gov.uk/acts/acts2010/ukpga_20100015_en_1
4. The main text of this Act can be found at http://www.opsi.gov.uk/acts/acts1990/ukpga_19900018_en_1.htm
5. Main text of this Act is available at http://www.opsi.gov.uk/acts/acts2006/ukpga_20060048_en_1
6. The full text of the Criminal Code Act, 1995 is available at http://www.austlii.edu.au/au/legis/cth/consol_act/cca1995115.txt/cgi-bin/download.cgi/download/au/legis/cth/consol_act/cca1995115.txt
7. The full text of the Cyber Crime Act, 2001 is available at http://www.comlaw.gov.au/ComLaw/Legislation/Act1.nsf/0/C08D6D864EC7E09ACA257435000B5595/$file/1612001.pdf\
8. The main text of this Act could be found at http://www.cyberlawtimes.com/itact2008.pdf

About the Authors

Debarati Halder is an advocate and legal scholar. She is the managing director of the Centre for Cyber Victim Counselling (http://www.cybervictims.org), an NGO, which works to help cyber crime victims in India. She is also the Vice President of WHOA, USA (Working for Halting Online Abuse) Kids-Teen Division and Internet Safety Advocate. She is the current Secretary of the South Asian Society of Criminology and Victimology (SASCV). She received her LLB from the University of Calcutta and LLM in international and constitutional law from the University of Madras. She is currently working toward her PhD at the National Law School of India University, Bangalore, India. She has published many articles in peer-reviewed journals and chapters in peer-reviewed books. Her work has appeared in scholarly journals, including the Journal of Law and Religion, Murdoch University Electronic Journal of Law, ERCES Online Quarterly Review, TMC Academic Journal (Singapore), and Indian Journal of Criminology & Criminalistics and edited volumes, Crimes of the Internet (Prentice Hall, 2008, Trends and Issues of Victimology (Cambridge Scholars Publishing, UK, 2008), International Perspectives on Crime and Justice (Cambridge Scholars Publishing, UK, 2009), et cetera. Her research interests include constitutional law, international law, victim rights, and cyber crimes and laws.

K. Jaishankar, PhD, is a senior Assistant Professor in the Department of Criminology and Criminal Justice at Manonmaniam Sundaranar University in Tirunelveli, India. During November 2009 - April 2010, he was a Commonwealth Fellow at the Centre for Criminal Justice Studies, School of Law, University of Leeds, UK. He is the founding editor-in-chief of the International Journal of Cyber Criminology (http://www.cybercrimejournal.com) and editor-in-chief of the International Journal of Criminal Justice Sciences (http://www.ijcjs.co.nr). He is the founding president of the South Asian Society of Criminology and Victimology (http://www.sascv.org) and the founding executive director of the Centre for Cyber Victim Counselling (http://www.cybervictims.org). He was awarded the prestigious Commonwealth Academic Staff Fellowship, 2009–2010 tenable, from the University of Leeds. He was a member of the United Nations Office on Drugs and Crime core group of experts (15-member group) on identity-related crime (2007–2008). He was recently appointed as a fellow of the African Centre for Cyberlaw and Cybercrime Prevention. The recent books he has written and/or edited are: *Cyber Criminology: Exploring Internet Crimes and Criminal Behavior* (CRC Press, Taylor & Francis Group, USA, 2011), *Cyber Bullying: Profile and Policy Guidelines* (DOCCJ, Manonmaniam Sundaranar University, India, 2009) *and International Perspectives on Crime and Justice* (Cambridge Scholars Publishing, UK, 2009). He pioneered the development of the new field of cyber criminology and is the proponent of the space transition theory of cyber crimes. His areas of academic competence include cyber criminology, victimology, crime mapping, Geographic Information Systems, communal violence, theoretical criminology, policing, and crime prevention.

Index